To Kill and Take Possession

Daniel Friedmann

To Kill and
Take Possession

Law, Morality, and Society
in Biblical Stories

Hendrickson Publishers, Inc.
P. O. Box 3473
Peabody, Massachusetts 01961–3473

Printed in the United States of America

First Printing — December 2002

Except where otherwise noted, Scripture quotations are from the New
Revised Standard Version of the Bible copyright © 1989 by the Division
of Christian Education of the National Council of the Churches of Christ
in the United States of America and are used by permission.

Original edition: *To Kill and Inherit* [Hebrew: *Ha-ratsahta ve-gam yarashta*].
© Dvir Publishing House, Tel Aviv, 2000.

Library of Congress Cataloging-in-Publication Data

Friedmann, Daniel, 1936–
    [Ha-ratsahta ve-gam yarashta. English]
    To kill and take possession : law, morality, and society in biblical stories
/ Daniel Friedmann.
        p. cm.
    Includes bibliographical references and index.
    ISBN 1-56563-641-4
    1. Ethics in the Bible. 2. Law (Theology)—Biblical teaching.
    3. Murder—Biblical teaching. 4. Bible stories, Hebrew—O.T. I. Title.
    BS680.E84 F7513 2002
    221.6—dc21

                                                    2002012404

Table of Contents

Part One: Concepts of Legal and Moral Responsibility

Foreword

This book deals with the stories of the Hebrew Bible (or Old Testament), yet it does not discuss the philological aspects of the text or its various literary genres. Nor does it seek to discover the ancient sources on which the Bible rests. Needless to say, it makes no attempt to tackle the immensity of scholarly literature in these fields.

The purpose of this book is to infer from the biblical stories the legal and moral concepts they reflect and the system of laws underlying them, which seems not to conform with many of the laws of the Pentateuch. I discuss such questions as how King Saul could give his daughter Michal to Palti son of Laish, though she was married to David and had not been divorced; what was the legal principle that caused the Israelites to honor the pact they had made with the Gibeonites after they discovered that it had been obtained by fraud; and the possible connection between this case and the idea that Isaac's blessing to Jacob was valid, even though it was obtained when Jacob was disguised as Esau. I also look into some issues of political implication, such as what principles might have guided the royal succession in the kingdoms of Judah and Israel.

Occasionally I draw analogies between biblical stories and later historical events or legal cases, or bring illustrations from mythology and literature. The link between historical developments and the evolution of laws is also noted—for example, the possible connection between the political situation of the Jews in the time of Ezra the scribe and the revolution he carried out in Jewish marriage laws. I then examine the possible connection between the consequences of that revolution and the judicial decision made in the State of Israel on the question known as "Who is a Jew?"

I am grateful to many friends and colleagues for their help and advice. First and foremost I wish to thank Prof. Reuven Yaron, Prof. Meir Sternberg, Prof. Nili Cohen, Prof. Daniel Sinclair, and Prof. Elimelech Westreich, who read the manuscript and enlightened me on many subjects; likewise I thank Prof. Zvi Yavetz and the writer Hanoch Bartov for their advice and assistance. I also owe thanks for comments and advice to Justice Mishael Cheshin, Prof. Nadav Na'aman, Dr. Asaf Lachovsky, Dr. Arieh Edrei, Judge Boaz Okon, Ms. Gabriela Williams, and Ms. Navah Korman.

The book was originally published in Hebrew in 2000 and translated into English by Louis Williams. Certain alterations have been made in the English edition, some of them in consequence of comments made by readers and reviewers, notably the scholarly and generous review by the late Justice Haim H. Cohn, former Vice-President of Israel's Supreme Court. My thanks also to Prof. Aron Dotan, Prof. Yairah Amit for her comments, Guy Rotkopf, Ron Friedmann, and Yael Lotan in particular, and Dr. John Kutsko for their helpful comments and for editing the English version.

Daniel Friedmann

Timeline

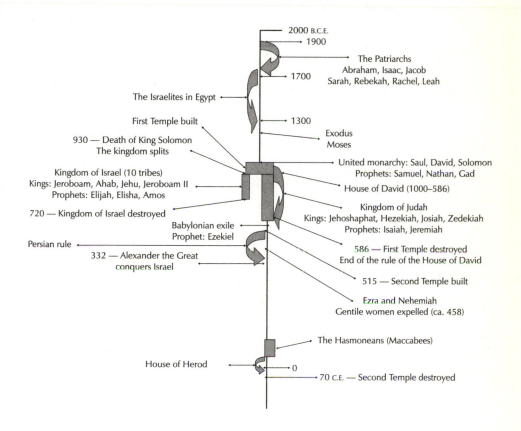

2000 B.C.E.
1900
The Patriarchs
Abraham, Isaac, Jacob
Sarah, Rebekah, Rachel, Leah
1700

The Israelites in Egypt

First Temple built
1300

930 — Death of King Solomon
The kingdom splits

Exodus
Moses

United monarchy: Saul, David, Solomon
Prophets: Samuel, Nathan, Gad

Kingdom of Israel (10 tribes)
Kings: Jeroboam, Ahab, Jehu, Jeroboam II
Prophets: Elijah, Elisha, Amos

House of David (1000–586)

720 — Kingdom of Israel destroyed

Kingdom of Judah
Kings: Jehoshaphat, Hezekiah, Josiah, Zedekiah
Prophets: Isaiah, Jeremiah

Babylonian exile
Prophet: Ezekiel

Persian rule

332 — Alexander the Great
conquers Israel

586 — First Temple destroyed
End of the rule of the House of David

515 — Second Temple built

Ezra and Nehemiah
Gentile women expelled (ca. 458)

The Hasmoneans (Maccabees)

House of Herod
0

70 C.E. — Second Temple destroyed

Comments

Dates for events earlier than 900 B.C.E. are speculative, and there is no external evidence for their historicity. The historiographical narratives in the Bible (Old Testament) end shortly after the fall of the first Temple (586 B.C.E.) (2 Kings, Jeremiah, and 2 Chronicles). A description of subsequent events appears in the books of Haggai, Ezra, and Nehemiah and ends about 430 B.C.E. Data about later events are taken from extrabiblical sources. The list of kings and prophets is not exhaustive.

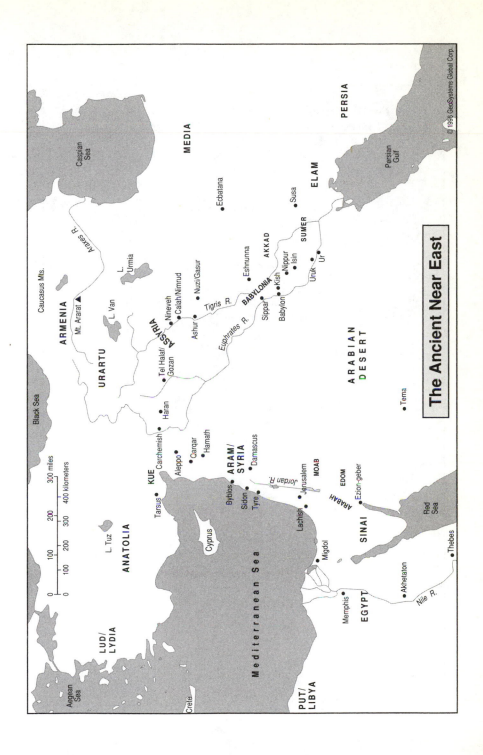

The Ancient Near East

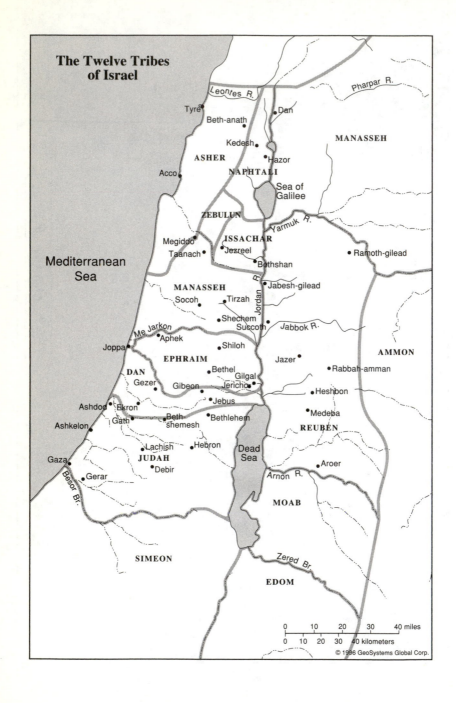

The Twelve Tribes
of Israel

Leontes R.

Pharpar R.

Tyre

Dan

Beth-anath

MANASSEH

Kedesh

ASHER

Hazor

Acco

NAPHTALI

Sea of
Galilee

Mediterranean
Sea

ZEBULUN

Yarmuk R.

ISSACHAR

Megiddo

Jezreel

Ramoth-gilead

Taanach

Bethshan

Jabesh-gilead

MANASSEH

Socoh

Tirzah

Jordan R.

Shechem

Succoth

Jabbok R.

Me Jarkon

Aphek

Shiloh

AMMON

Joppa

Jazer

EPHRAIM

Rabbah-amman

Bethel

DAN

Gilgal

Gezer

Gibeon

Jericho

Heshbon

Ashdod

Ekron

Jebus

Medeba

Ashkelon

Gath

Beth-
shemesh

Bethlehem

REUBEN

Lachish

Hebron

Dead
Sea

Gaza

JUDAH

Aroer

Debir

Besor Br.

Gerar

Arnon R.

MOAB

Zered Br.

SIMEON

EDON

0   10   20   30   40 miles

0 10 20 30   40 kilometers

© 1996 GeoSystems Global Corp.

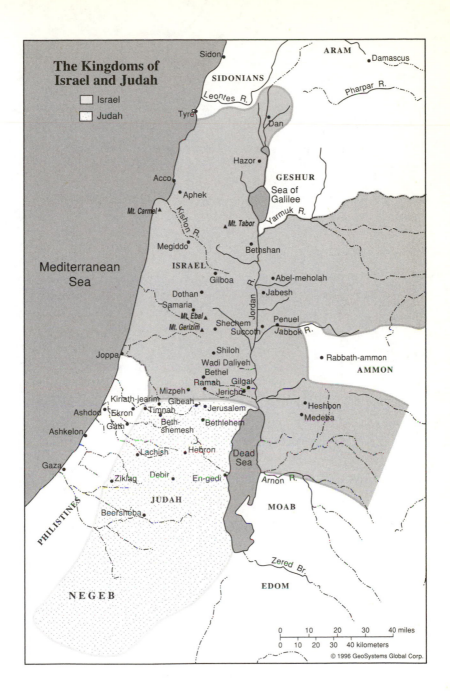

The Kingdoms of Israel and Judah

☐ Israel
☐ Judah

Sidon
SIDONIANS
ARAM
Damascus
Leontes R.
Pharpar R.
Tyre
Dan
Hazor
Acco
GESHUR
Sea of Galilee
Aphek
Mt. Carmel ▲
Kishon R.
Yarmuk R.
Mediterranean Sea
Mt. Tabor ▲
Megiddo
Bethshan
ISRAEL
Gilboa
Abel-meholah
Jordan R.
Jabesh
Dothan
Samaria
Mt. Ebal ▲
Shechem
Penuel
Mt. Gerizim ▲
Succoth
Jabbok R.
Shiloh
Joppa
Wadi Daliyeh
Rabbath-ammon
Bethel
AMMON
Ramah
Gilgal
Mizpeh
Jericho
Kiriath-jearim
Gibeah
Ashdod
Ekron
Timnah
Jerusalem
Heshbon
Gath
Beth-shemesh
Bethlehem
Medeba
Ashkelon
Gaza
Lachish
Hebron
Dead Sea
Ziklag
Debir
En-gedi
Arnon R.
JUDAH
MOAB
Beersheba
PHILISTINES
NEGEB
Zered Br.
EDOM

0   10   20   30   40 miles
0   10   20   30   40 kilometers

© 1996 GeoSystems Global Corp.

Abbreviations and Notes on Abbreviations

Bible Translations

JPS	Jewish Publication Society
KJV	King James Version
NJB	New Jerusalem Bible
NJPS	*Tanakh: The Holy Scriptures: The New JPS Translation according to the Traditional Hebrew Text*
NRSV	New Revised Standard Version

Legal Citations and the Arrangement of Information

E.R.	English Reports
F.	Federal Reporter
N.E.	North Eastern Reporter
P.D.	Decisions of the Supreme Court of Israel *(piskai din)*
U.S.	Unites States Supreme Court Reports

Legal citations follow a consistent format. By way of example, "*Roytman v. Bank Mizrahi* 29(2) P.D. 57, 62 (Hebrew)" identifies the case (in italics), the volume number (and, in this case, the part number), the report title in abbreviated form (see above), and the page number(s).

Introduction: Bible Stories
and the Biblical Code

❧

The Bible describes historic events spanning hundreds of years. The period of the patriarchs—Abraham, Isaac, and Jacob—described in the book of Genesis is estimated as the first quarter of the second millennium B.C.E. (roughly 1900–1700 B.C.E.), concluding with the migration of Jacob and his family to Egypt. The book of Exodus, continuing the story, skips some four hundred years spent in Egypt, with the terse statement that the Israelites[1] "multiplied and grew exceedingly strong, so that the land was filled with them" (Exodus 1:7). The historical narrative resumes with their enslavement by Pharaoh, the exodus from Egypt, and the formation of the Israelites into a nation as they crossed the desert on their way to the promised land.

The exodus is estimated to have taken place in the thirteenth century B.C.E., and, according to Exodus, Leviticus, Numbers, and Deuteronomy, the biblical laws were given not long thereafter, while the Israelites were in the desert. God gave Moses the laws, and Moses passed them on to the people. The nation of Israel was forged in the desert and appeared on the stage of history with a law book in hand. Jewish[2] tradition describes the giving of the law as a singular act at a specific time and place—Mount Sinai. The Mishnah tractate *Avot* opens with the words: "Moses received the Law on Sinai"—all of it there and then—and since then God has neither added

---

[1] *Israel* was the second name given to Jacob after his struggle with the angel (Genesis 32:28), hence the name *Israelites* given to his descendants.

[2] The term *Jew* was used to describe members of the tribe of Judah (one of Jacob's sons) and eventually became synonymous with *Israelite*.

nor detracted from it. According to religious belief, these laws are eternal and valid forever.

The laws are included in the four books that follow Genesis, occasionally interrupting the narrative, which describes the Israelites' desert experiences. The legal principles are integrated into the historical-literary text in all four desert-period books. The books of the Former Prophets (Joshua, Judges, 1–2 Samuel, and 1–2 Kings), Chronicles, Ezra, and Nehemiah continue the historical narrative (alongside other materials) for another eight centuries, from Joshua's conquest of Canaan—apparently at the end of the thirteenth century B.C.E. or early twelfth—until the time of Ezra and Nehemiah in the fifth century B.C.E.

The fact that the law was given to the Israelites after the exodus from Egypt does not mean that there was no prior law. Every society has binding rules of conduct, and the Israelites were no exception. Tradition has it that prior to Sinai, a set of rules known as the seven commandments of the sons of Noah[3] (the Noahide laws) was in force. These Noahide laws, which might be described as a divine-natural code, applied to all human beings since the creation of humanity. According to Jewish tradition, the Noahide laws continue to apply to the Gentiles, while the Israelites became subject instead to the laws of the Torah from the day that they were given. The Noahide commandments include, inter alia, the prohibitions of idolatry, of the spilling of blood, of plunder, and of incest. But, according to the traditional view, those incest prohibitions were more limited than the biblical law and did not ban the marriage of brother to sister from the same father (e.g., the marriage of Abraham and Sarah), only of the same mother. There was also no prohibition of marriage to two sisters (Jacob with Rachel and Leah). Clearly the commandments of the sons of Noah were designed to suit the Bible stories from the period preceding the giving of the law of the Torah and to show that the patriarchs did not violate the commandments that were binding upon them.

According to traditional logic, the legal situation would therefore include the following:

(a) Before the giving of the Torah law, following the exodus from Egypt, the Israelites (like all other nations) were bound by the seven commandments.

(b) From the giving of the law on, including of course the period described in the books of the Prophets and in Chronicles, the Israelites were bound by the law of the Torah.

The difficulty lies in the many stories of the Bible which indicate clearly that, after the giving of the Torah laws, the Israelites did not consider them-

---

[3] Babylonian Talmud, *Sanhedrin* 56a.

selves bound by those laws and in fact followed a completely different set of rules. Traditional commentary made every effort to resolve the contradictions between the stories and the laws. But the results were often forced and contrived, as a few examples may illustrate.

The book of Ruth centers on Ruth the Moabite who joins the people of Israel. She marries Boaz and gives birth to Obed, destined to be the grandfather of King David. Yet the book of Deuteronomy prescribes that "no Ammonite or Moabite shall be admitted to the assembly of the LORD. Even to the tenth generation, none of their descendants shall be admitted to the assembly of the LORD" (Deuteronomy 23:3). How then can the story of Ruth, the ancestress of King David, who joined the congregation of Israel, be compatible with the Torah ruling that excluded Moabites? The answer given by traditional commentary is simple—it limits the Deuteronomist prohibition to Ammonite and Moabite men and argues that it does not apply to women. Accordingly, Ammonite and Moabite women could enter into the congregation of the Lord and marry Israelite men.[4] This interpretation is highly problematic. Normally, in Hebrew the male form in legislation includes the female. The Ten Commandments, for example, are worded in the male form, yet they are clearly intended to apply equally to women. Thus there can be no doubt that the male form of "You shall not murder" is directed at men and women alike.

The alternative, and more reasonable, explanation of Ruth's story is that there was no legal rule that forbade the entry of Ammonites and Moabites into the congregation of Israel and that there was no prohibition against the marriage of Israelite men or women to Ammonites and Moabites. This interpretation is strengthened by other discrepancies between the laws of the Torah and events related in the book of Ruth, which will be examined in a later chapter.

Another example is that of Michal, the daughter of King Saul, who married David but was later given to Palti son of Laish, though she was never divorced (1 Samuel 25:44). Clearly this runs contrary to biblical law. David's marriage to Bathsheba also did not conform to Hebrew law.[5]

The laws and mores of Israel's neighboring nations were also profoundly influential. The book of Numbers has the Lord putting into Balaam's mouth a description of Israel as "a people living alone, and not reckoning itself among the nations" (Numbers 23:9). This did not reflect reality: Israel's culture and its belief in a single god did influence many other nations, but the influence was reciprocal, and Israel was deeply affected by its cultural surroundings

---

[4] Mishnah, *Yevamot* 8:13. This interpretation was adopted by Rashi in his commentary on Ruth 4:6.

[5] See the chapter "To Kill and Take Possession," pp. 83–84.

throughout its long history. The Bible itself contains many descriptions of the adoption of pagan gods and alien practices. The use of amulets for ritual and fortune-telling prevailed for many generations, though the Ten Commandments stipulate, "You shall not make for yourself an idol, whether in the form of anything that is in heaven above, or that is on the earth beneath, or that is in the water under the earth. You shall not bow down to them or worship them" (Exodus 20:4–5).

Rachel stole her father Laban's idols and took them with her when Jacob returned to Canaan. This happened before the giving of the law, but stories of idols occurred afterwards, too. For example, when King Saul sought to kill David, who lived in the court, his wife Michal helped him escape and placed an idol in his bed (1 Samuel 19:13). The story refers to idols without a word of condemnation—on the contrary, the use of the idol proved advantageous to David, destined to become the king of Israel.

It is reasonable to assume that alien influences extended beyond religion and worship—which in the Bible were matters of law—to other areas, including government organization, matrimony, and interpersonal relations. The advent of monarchy in Israel demonstrated the extent of foreign influence. The elders of Israel, relying on the practice in other nations, demanded of Samuel to give them a king: "Appoint for us, then, a king to govern us, like other nations" (1 Samuel 8:5). Samuel vigorously opposed the demand but was eventually forced to concede. The Torah does contain an explicit instruction for installing a king: "You may indeed set over you a king whom the LORD your God will choose. One of your own community you may set as king over you; you are not permitted to put a foreigner over you" (Deuteronomy 17:15). Yet the elders of Israel did not refer to the Torah but rather to the practice of "other nations." Samuel himself ignored the Deuteronomic precept. So it seems that the law of kingship, as it appears in Deuteronomy, was neither implemented nor even known in Israel in those days.

An extraordinary story describes the finding of the Torah in the reign of Josiah, who ascended the throne of Judah in 640 B.C.E. Josiah reigned for thirty years, toward the end of the Davidic dynasty.[6] In the course of his reign Josiah ordered a renovation of the Temple. During the works, a copy of the Torah was discovered. Shaphan the scribe read the book to the king, who realized that his people did not know it, nor did they observe its instructions. Fearing the wrath of God, he decided to mend his ways and those of his people: "The

---

[6] Some twenty years after Josiah's death, in 586 B.C.E., Nebuchadnezzar, king of Babylon, conquered Jerusalem, destroyed the Temple, and deposed Zedekiah, the last king of the house of David. The kingdom of Israel was destroyed some 130 years earlier, i.e., in 720 B.C.E., by Assyria.

king went up to the house of the LORD, and with him went all the people of Judah, all the inhabitants of Jerusalem . . . ; he read in their hearing all the words of the book of the covenant that had been found in the house of the LORD. The king stood by the pillar and made a covenant before the LORD, to follow the LORD, keeping his commandments, his decrees, and his statutes, with all his heart and all his soul. . . . All the people joined in the covenant" (2 Kings 23:2–3).

This remarkable event took place about 622 B.C.E., some thirty-five years before the destruction of the first Temple. Clearly the Torah had been unknown for many years, but the story sheds no light on how or when it disappeared. Was there only one copy? Who had it, and when was it last used before it vanished? To these questions is added the mystery of the book that was found. Was it the entire Torah (all five books), or only Deuteronomy, as some Bible scholars believe, or again was it only an excerpt from the Torah? In any event, the story does confirm that at least part of the Torah was hidden from the people and that for a long time they could not have observed its laws, of which they were totally unaware.

Was Josiah's Torah the book from the time of Moses, or was it a reconstruction of an early document or a book written, in part or in its entirety, during Josiah's reign? It seems clear that it contained rules that had not previously existed, such as the ban on Ammonites and Moabites entering the congregation of the Lord (Deuteronomy 23:3). It is hard to believe that this provision was in force in the time of Ruth the Moabite. In all probability it was first introduced in the times of Josiah, or even later.[7] We do know that it did not affect Ruth's life, centuries before Josiah. Little wonder that the elders of Israel, in demanding a king from Samuel, did not rely on Deuteronomy, which perhaps had not yet been written or was unknown to anybody at the time. We may therefore conclude that, between the exodus from Egypt and the time of Ezra and Nehemiah, the people of Israel lived by a system of law other than that reflected in the five books of the Torah. This system might have included some of the laws of the Torah, but there were clear deviations on important issues.

We know very little about the binding laws during the biblical times. A few details about those laws and customs can be deduced from the biblical stories, but in many cases the conclusions are ambiguous, and we often grope in the dark and make do with suppositions. By and large, the legal question is not central to the story. Consequently, we do not know whether the author, whose

---

[7] It is conceivable that this injunction was only added when Ezra was fighting against mixed marriages. See the chapter "The Expulsion of the Foreign Women: Ezra's Legal Revolution," pp. 98–99.

focus was elsewhere, recorded all the facts that would have helped us to understand the law. In addition, it is not always clear whether the described behavior accorded with prevailing rules or was in breach of them. Yet in spite of all these limitations, we can occasionally deduce the existence of a certain custom or social norm and sometimes understand the moral and legal outlook. The following chapters represent an attempt to analyze the biblical stories from this perspective.

PART ONE

Concepts of Legal and Moral Responsibility

1

From the Trial of Adam and Eve to the Judgments of Solomon and Daniel

This chapter describes how the conduct of trials passed from God to humans and how this process is reflected in the stories of the Bible. The first two trials of the Bible occur in the mythological era. The trials are conducted, from beginning to end, by God, who serves as the investigator, the prosecutor, and the judge. The first crime, the original sin, committed in the garden of Eden, is discovered by God, who asks Adam: "Have you eaten from the tree of which I commanded you not to eat?" (Genesis 3:11). The first transgression of humankind leads to the first interrogation of an accused person, conducted by God personally. Adam blames Eve for the transgression, and Eve deflects the blame to the serpent. After listening to Adam and Eve, God sentences them and the serpent each to a separate fate. Though an omniscient God has no need to interrogate, God nonetheless plays the role of investigator, allowing the accused to state their arguments. God, as the judge, renders the verdicts and imposes the penalties. The second trial of the Bible is concerned with the murder of Abel by his brother Cain: "Where is your brother Abel?" the Almighty asks Cain. Cain denies the murder, stating, "Am I my brother's keeper?" The Almighty, knowing all the facts, informs Cain that "your brother's blood is crying out to me from the ground!" (Genesis 4:10), and God imposes punishment.

There are some differences between the first two trials. The case of Adam and Eve concerns a transgression against God, the nonfulfillment of a divine command; the case of Cain deals with the highest crime among humans: the willful ending of another's life. Adam and Eve confess taking the fruit while assigning the blame to another, Adam by denouncing his wife and Eve by blaming the serpent. Cain, on the other hand, denies outright the murder of

9

his brother. Humans have little role in these trials other than to stand as the accused and give their testimonies. The proceedings of the trials follow an inherent biblical logic; since there was no one around to investigate, prosecute, or judge Adam and Eve—they being the sole inhabitants of the garden of Eden—God must fill all these functions. The case of Cain and Abel is an interfamily crime, which the ancients had difficulties coping with, and it certainly would have been difficult for Adam and Eve to avenge one dead son by punishing the other; therefore God must conduct the trial. After these trials, the roles of investigator, prosecutor, and judge passed into human hands. However, in the beginning, human judicial process still involved divine assistance. Though God is not at the trial in person, humans often approach God for decisive answers. Humanity's function is to submit questions to God and to interpret the answers given.

This stage of judicial process in the Bible is reflected in the story of Achan, son of Carmi, a story related in detail in chapter 7 of the book of Joshua. The chapter opens with a brief statement that the children of Israel had violated the interdiction on taking of the "forfeiture," that is, the spoils of war set aside to be destroyed as an offering to the Lord. The man who stole from the forfeiture is named as Achan, son of Carmi, and as a result of his actions "the anger of the LORD burned against the Israelites" (Joshua 7:1). The violation took place shortly after the conquest of Jericho. The next step in settling the land was to be the capture of the Canaanite town Ai. But the attempt to conquer the city, described as small and weak, ends in disaster. The campaign is thwarted, and the Israelites flee, defeated. Joshua and the elders mourn, and God explains the reason for their defeat: "the Israelites are unable to stand before their enemies; they turn their backs to their enemies, because they have become a thing devoted for destruction themselves. I will be with you no more, unless you destroy the devoted things from among you" (Joshua 7:12). The search for the transgressor takes place the following morning according to God's explicit instructions:

> In the morning therefore you shall come forward tribe by tribe. The tribe that the LORD takes shall come near by clans, the clan that the LORD takes shall come near by households, and the household that the LORD takes shall come near one by one. And the one who is taken as having the devoted things shall be burned with fire, together with all that he has. (Joshua 7:14–15)

Apparently the ceremony consisted of arranging the tribes and families in front of the ark and, by means of a certain signal or perhaps by lot or some other method, pointing out first the tribe of the transgressor, then the clan, and finally the transgressor himself. The process took its course, and the tribe of Judah was pointed out or "taken," followed by the clan and family of Zabdi, and finally Achan himself. Achan confessed that he had taken from the spoils a "beautiful mantle from Shinar, and two hundred shekels of silver, and a bar of gold weighing fifty shekels" and that these items were hidden in his tent. The punishment was severe. Achan, his family, and cattle were stoned to death: "They burned them with fire, cast stones on them, and raised over him a great heap of stones that remains to this day. Then the LORD turned from his burning anger" (Joshua 7:24–26). After God "turned from his burning anger," Israel overcame its enemies, the town of Ai was conquered, its inhabitants put to the sword, and the town's cattle and spoils were plundered.

The story of Achan is thematically similar to many other stories found throughout the Bible and in various mythologies: a disaster occurs, the people approach a deity for assistance, and the deity reveals that the disaster has been inflicted as a punishment for a certain transgression. Once the misdeed is corrected, either by punishing the offender or by some other method, the divine anger is appeased and order is restored to the world. Thus we read in Genesis 12 that when "the famine was severe in the land," Abraham (still called Abram) went to Egypt and chose to present his wife Sarah (Sarai) as his sister, because he felt she was so beautiful the Egyptians would kill him if he was known as her husband, but would treat him well if he were believed to be her brother. Pharaoh indeed took Sarah to his harem when his officials sang of her praises, and "for her sake he dealt well with Abram; and he had sheep, oxen, male donkeys, male and female slaves, female donkeys, and camels" (Genesis 12:16). But God was not appeased by such household arrangements, and the reaction against Pharaoh was swift: "But the LORD afflicted Pharaoh and his house . . . because of Sarai, Abram's wife." At this point in the story Pharaoh summons Abraham to him and asks, "Why did you not tell me that she was your wife? Why did you say, 'She is my sister'?" (12:18). The narrative, however, leaves out the way in which Pharaoh came to know about the sin for which he was "afflicted . . . with great plagues." Presumably, a way was found for Pharaoh to receive God's explanations. Pharaoh restores Sarah to Abraham, expels them from the land, and order returns to Pharaoh's household.

The famous Greek myth of Oedipus demonstrates the same logic as these biblical stories: when Oedipus becomes king of Thebes, having unknowingly killed his father and married his mother, the Theban queen Jocasta, disaster does not come quickly to the city of Thebes. Yet when the children of the incestuous king and queen reach maturity, pestilence and hunger overtake the city. Consultation with the oracle at Delphi reveals the cause: Oedipus's murder of his father and the marriage to his mother. Jocasta commits suicide, Oedipus blinds himself, and their children remain accursed, but the tribulations of Thebes come to an end.

One may ask to what purpose does God punish a whole community because of the sin of a single individual. Why must all Thebes suffer because of the sins of Oedipus, sins he committed unwittingly? Why must Israelite warriors be killed and suffer defeat because of the sin of Achan? The Bible does not lack instances where God reacts directly to acts of which he disapproves. One example is related in Genesis 38. Er, son of Judah, died shortly after his marriage to Tamar. According to the custom of levirate marriage, a childless widow is married to her husband's brother in order to maintain the dead man's name. Onan, Judah's brother, should have impregnated Tamar, but he refused and "spilled his semen on the ground whenever he went in to his brother's wife, so that he would not give offspring to his brother" (Genesis 38:9). In this case God's reaction is swift and direct: God singles out the offender, Onan, and brings about his death.

The function of stories based on the model of Achan and Oedipus may have been to explain the calamities that endanger a community and to suggest a way to cope with such dangers. The stories offer the hope that a community may cleanse itself and escape the wrath of God's punishment, once they understand the reason for God's anger and eliminate the problem—for example, by banishing or executing a certain individual. This literary-mythological model constitutes an attempt to give logical explanations to the harms and dangers to which humans are exposed. The stories interpret reality according to the belief that there is a causal connection between human conduct and the events that happen to people and their surroundings. This worldview validates and strengthens the belief that the individual and the group have the power to control their destiny and if necessary to rectify wrongs. By this logic, if the community takes care that its members behave fittingly, the wrath of God will not be aroused. Furthermore, should a member stray from the standards of acceptable conduct, it is possible, through suitable action, to appease God's wrath and save the community.

Let us now return to the process by which Achan was caught and punished. God revealed to Joshua the cause of the Israelites' defeat but did not tell him who had taken from the forbidden spoils. The first verse of chapter 7 informs the reader that Achan was the one who took of the forfeiture, setting a literary form wherein the identity of the transgressor is known to the audience but not to Joshua or the Israelites, who are required to conduct the appropriate ceremony. The procedure God commands of Joshua and the people constitutes a *divine investigation,* characterized by the fact that at the outset there is no specific suspect. The only fact known to the participants in the ceremony is that a crime has been committed. This feature distinguishes the procedure from that of the *divine ordeal,* to which I refer later in this chapter, the purpose of which is to determine the guilt of a specific suspect. In the case of Achan, the people do not know whom to suspect. They carry out the process that activates divine power, but they do not determine the outcome of the procedure; humans conduct the process, but God determines the result.

The technique of divine investigation is founded on the binary method, similar to the one on which computer language is based. The public is divided into groups, each of which is tested either by casting lots or by coming before the Urim and Thummim, which were probably stones or darts that served to cast lots or elicit some other kind of sign. The divine response evoked in this manner was either "yes" or "no," that is, guilty or innocent. The divine procedure fulfills the function of an investigation by detecting the group containing the delinquent one and finally the specific criminal. Since the procedure is governed by divine guidance, the guilt of the accused is obvious, and no further trial or scrutiny of the evidence is necessary. In this aspect the case of Achan is similar to those of Adam and Eve and of Cain and Abel. Though the Bible goes on to tell us that Achan confessed his guilt and revealed the place where the forbidden loot had been hidden, the evidence was not required to prove guilt but rather to demonstrate to the people the glory and power of the divine investigation and the justice of its result.

Another example of such procedure is related in 1 Samuel 14. Jonathan, the son of King Saul, had fought courageously in the battle against the Philistines, defeating the enemy, who turned and fled. To ensure success in the pursuit of the enemy, Saul had adjured his people to refrain from eating until evening. Jonathan did not hear his father's vow and "extended the staff that was in his hand, and dipped the tip of it in the honeycomb, and put his hand to his mouth; and his eyes brightened" (14:27). The oath having been broken, the story unfolds in the pattern previously described. In need of divine counsel regarding whether or not to continue the battle with the Philistines, Saul appeals to God: "Shall I go down after the Philistines? Will you give them into the hand of Israel? But he did not answer him that day" (14:37). God's refusal to advise Saul constituted an ill turn of fate that demanded clarification. This time, in contrast to the case of Achan, there were witnesses who had seen Jonathan taste of the honeycomb, and one of whom actually accused him of doing so. Jonathan was not put on trial; instead, the process of divine investigation was launched to find the culprit. Perhaps because Jonathan was already suspect, the procedure of divine investigation was carried out in a summary manner: the people gathered together and stood to one side, the king and his son on the other. In the first stage Saul and Jonathan were taken. In the second stage the two were separated and Jonathan was taken. He confessed to having "tasted a little honey" and added, "here I am, I will die" (14:43). However, the people refused to have him executed and presumably made a sacrifice in his place. This step was later justified by traditional commentators on the grounds that Jonathan had not heard his father's interdiction, and under Jewish law as subsequently developed expiation is possible, if a person does not consciously break the law but unwittingly commits a transgression.

The technique of divine investigation to detect a culprit is also described in the familiar tale of Jonah and the large fish. When Jonah flees from God by boarding a ship to Tarshish, God reacts to his flight by calling a mighty storm upon the sea, and when the ship is in danger of sinking, the sailors cast lots to find the man responsible for the catastrophe about to overtake them (Jonah 1:7). When Jonah is discovered, he confesses and by his own wish is thrown into the water. After this is done "the sea ceased from its raging." We are not told by which method the lots are cast, although the casting of lots would not have taken place by the Urim and Thummim since these were used exclusively in Israel.

This biblical detection procedure was used not only to discover criminals but also to reveal God's choice of ruler over Israel. When God advised the prophet Samuel that Saul was the divine choice for king, Samuel anointed Saul, but, perhaps because the people demanded further evidence of Saul's divine entitlement to the throne, the selection was repeated through the binary method. The tribes presented themselves for the divine test, and the tribe of Benjamin was taken. The tribe was divided into clans, the family of Matri was taken, and at the end of the process, Saul was selected to become king (1 Samuel 10:20–23). Here the binary method was not used to discover the perpetrator of a crime, so there was no risk that a factual mistake could occur. The selection of a wrong or unfit ruler might be unfortunate but would not represent a factual mistake, as in the case of a person wrongly accused and convicted.

The binary method of eliciting responses from the deity also assisted in military and political decisions. Questions to God were formulated that enabled only one of two possible answers. In 1 Samuel 23:11–13, David, through the priest Abiathar, consults the ephod—which apparently contained the Urim and Thummim—to ask: "Will Saul come down as your servant has heard? . . . Will the men of Keilah surrender me and my men into the hand of Saul? . . . The LORD said, 'he will come down. . . . They will surrender you.'" The same method was used when making the decision to pursue the Amalekites (1 Samuel 30:8): "David inquired of the LORD, 'Shall I pursue this band? Shall I overtake them?' He answered him, 'Pursue; for you shall surely overtake and shall surely rescue.'"

Anthropological studies indicate that primitive tribes often employ sorcery and witchcraft in order to discover the perpetrator of a crime. Various methods are used, often in impressive ceremonies during which a tribal witch doctor enlists lots or other techniques in order to finger the culprit. Hugh Goitein describes one method used by an African tribe to discover a thief: several young men were given sticks, and after a ceremony in which they lost self-control (perhaps through hypnotism), they walked through the village holding the sticks until the sticks pointed to the hut of one of the chief's wives.[1]

Goitein links these methods of detecting a criminal to the belief that the body of a murdered person can single out the murderer. In this context Goitein also mentions the tale of the murder of Siegfried, legendary hero of *The Nibelungen,* the famous Germanic and Scandinavian legend that Richard Wagner used for his operas. Siegfried, like the Greek hero Achilles, was impervious to injury. Both, however, had a vulnerable spot where they could be hurt—for Achilles it was his heel, for Siegfried it was between the shoulder blades. As Siegfried knelt to drink from a spring, his archenemy Hagen thrust a spear through his vulnerable point and killed him. During the burial ceremony, Siegfried's widow asked all the mourners to touch the body of her husband. As soon as Hagen did so, the wounds of the corpse began to bleed, revealing the identity of the murderer.[2]

There are other fables that employ the notion of using the body for detection, in various contexts. The great Hebrew poet H. N. Bialik wrote about a legendary trial held before the young King Solomon.[3] A rich merchant sent his son to Africa. During his absence, the merchant died and his slave, the

---

[1] In this specific case the suspect vigorously denied the charge, and a second ordeal proved her innocence. H. Goitein, *Primitive Ordeal and Modern Law* (1923; repr., Littleton, Colo.: F. B. Rothman, 1980), 69–70. The cited pages refer to the 1980 reprint.

[2] Goitein also refers to Shakespeare's play *Richard III,* act 1, scene 2, where it is mentioned that upon the approach of Richard blood flows afresh from the wounds of the dead Henry VI. Goitein also discusses an English case of 1688 in which a certain Philip Standsfield was accused of murdering his father. Standsfield's conviction and death sentence were based mainly on the fact that when he lifted the corpse, blood welled from the wound onto his hand (Goitein, *Primitive Ordeal and Modern Law,* 68–69). The charge against Standsfield mentions that God usually employs this method to uncover murderers. The case was published in two other works: Thomas Bayly Howell, ed., *Cobbett's Complete Collection of State Trials and Proceedings for High Treason and Other Crimes and Misdemeanors from the Earliest Period to the Present Time* (33 vols.; London: R. Bagshaw, 1809–1826), 11:1371; and included in Thomas Bayly Howell, ed., *A Complete Collection of State Trials and Proceedings for High Treason and Other Crimes and Misdemeanors from the Earliest Period to the Year 1783* (5 vols.; London: Longman, Hurst, Rees, Orme & Browne, 1816). A closer study of the case indicates that there was circumstantial evidence against the defendant, although Goitein believes that it was not decisive.

[3] "The Inheritance Case," in Hayyim Nahman Bialik, *And It Came to Pass* (Hebrew) (Tel-Aviv: Dvir, 1965), 54.

majordomo, seized the inheritance. When the son returned, the slave continued to claim that he was the rightful son and heir. Solomon commanded the slave to bring the dead man's arm; he then told each disputant to shed some of his blood into a bowl, and the dead man's arm was then dipped into each. The arm emerged clean from the slave's bowl—the blood of the slave did not stick to it. But when the arm was placed in the second bowl it reddened and absorbed the blood. The son was recognized as the true heir, and the slave was punished.

Inevitably, these methods of discovering criminals began to lose their credibility. It is hard to believe that in reality they were ever useful; in many cases it must have been obvious that the method of divine investigation did not produce reliable results. One of the best known incidents discussed in the literature concerns the scholar Anselm, who, in 1100, proposed to employ the biblical method used to uncover Achan in order to find the thief of the sacred vessels from the church in Laon. Anselm proposed to select one child from each city parish and subject the children to the cold-water ordeal. In this ordeal, subjects are submerged in water: those who float are considered guilty, while those who sink are deemed innocent. Having discovered the suspected parish, the ordeal was to be applied to a child from each of that parish's households, following which all the members of that household would undergo the cold-water ordeal, and so the thief would be discovered. The town people agreed in principle to Anselm's proposal but demanded that before involving the whole town, the ordeal should first be administered to persons who had easy access to the church vessels—including Anselm himself. Anselm was one of six people arrested and incarcerated to await trial, during which time he was terrified and asked to undergo a test ordeal while still in prison. He was immersed in a tank of water and happily sank to the bottom. Anselm was relieved, but at the real ordeal before the whole assembly, the results were different: three suspects sank and were declared innocent, but Anselm and two others floated and were found guilty. Anselm's protestation of innocence was to no avail.[4]

---

[4] The story of Anselm appears in John Henry Wigmore, *A Kaleidoscope of Justice* (Washington, D.C.: Washington Law Books, 1941), 15–16. Wigmore relies on Henry C. Lea, *Superstition and Force: Essays on the Wager of Law, the Wager of Battle, the Ordeal, Torture* (1870; 2d ed.; repr., New York: Haskell House, 1971). This story also impressed Goitein, who relies on Lea's work. Lea mentions the story in two additional contexts. One, in the context of judicial combat, relates how Anselm stole the vessels and sold them to a merchant, swearing him to silence (Lea, *Superstition and Force*, 159). The latter did not keep his promise and accused Anselm, who then challenged the merchant to trial by combat. Anselm won the duel and was thereby acquitted. Anselm's victory was explained by the fact that the merchant, who had received the

The divine ordeal, unlike the divine investigation, does not single out a guilty party from a group or tribe. Before the divine ordeal can take place, there must be suspects. The case of Anselm has elements of the divine investigation as well as the divine ordeal—Anselm proposed to pick random children and subject them to the cold-water ordeal, for the purpose of pinpointing the specific parish and household of the guilty party. This is comparable to the casting of lots in the process of divine investigation of Achan. In general, however, the divine ordeal is employed after a suspect has been apprehended through a preliminary investigation, an accusation of some sort, or other suspicious circumstances. Thus there are two distinct and separate stages of the divine ordeal: the pretrial investigation, in which it is decided whether the accused should stand trial, and the trial itself by means of the ordeal. The pretrial investigation is wholly in human hands and is governed by human decision; the investigator enjoys no divine counsel. Only if the findings of the pretrial investigation justify a trial can the investigation proceed and divine assistance be called upon. The fact that human beings must compile incriminating evidence against an individual before delivering him or her as a suspect to be judged by God represents the cardinal stage between the divine investigation and the divine ordeal.

The element of physical risk also distinguishes the divine ordeal from the divine investigation. Divine investigation, or posing a question to a deity, involves techniques of lot casting or interpreting signs from a holy artifact. Since there is no particular suspect at the outset of the investigation, the application of anything entailing risk of corporal injury or death is out of the question at this stage. Divine ordeal that involves such risk can only be allowed if there is sufficient evidence against a specific suspect to justify the process. The position regarding torture is in this respect similar. Torture in the pretrial stage is only possible when the number of suspects is limited, and usually when there already is some sort of evidence against them. In the Christian world, examination under torture was prevalent for many centuries. Yet it was not allowed on the basis of mere suspicion. There even existed sets of judicial regulations that specified the type of evidence required in order to allow the examination under torture for the purpose of extracting a confession.[5] Clearly, these rules were not always kept.

---

stolen goods, broke his oath of silence. The second context in which Lea cites the story of Anselm concerns torture (366). After Anselm was acquitted of stealing the vessels, he stole again, was convicted by the cold-water ordeal, and subsequently tortured until he revealed the hiding place of the stolen goods.

[5] John H. Langbein, *Torture and the Law of Proof* (Chicago: University of Chicago Press, 1977), 4–5, 12–16.

A case involving the divine ordeal is described in the Bible in the book of Numbers, chapter 5. The issue concerns a married woman who lies with another man where there are no witnesses to the act. The text does not specify whether some kind of evidence of adultery is required in order to administer the ordeal, or whether a jealous husband can demand the ordeal on mere suspicion. Some verses in this chapter state that the ordeal ought to take place if the husband is overcome by a "spirit of jealousy . . . and he is jealous of his wife" (5:14, 30). In these verses it appears as though the husband's jealousy suffices in order for the bitter-water ritual to be applied to the wife. However, the description of the whole case begins in verses 12–13 with the words: "If any man's wife goes astray and is unfaithful to him, if a man has had intercourse with her. . . ." This statement makes it seem as though one were dealing with a known and proven fact. Jewish scholars have rejected a broad interpretation of the husband's right to demand that his wife undergo divine ordeal, considering that it was dangerous and humiliating for the accused. Consequently, Jewish law interprets the term "jealousy" as a warning of the husband to his wife, made in front of witnesses, not to be confined alone with a particular man.[6] If the wife then disobeys the warning, the husband is entitled to demand the ordeal.

Numbers 5 provides a detailed description of the bitter-water ordeal. The ritual begins with the husband bringing his wife and an offering of barley to the tabernacle. The priest offers up the sacrificial barley, then takes holy water and mixes it with dust from the floor of the tabernacle. He uncovers the woman's hair and charges her with an "imprecatory oath" (5:21), effectively cursing her if she committed the sin. The woman must then drink the "bitter water." If her belly swells, it is a sign she is guilty and "shall be cursed," whereas if the water has no effect, she is considered pure. The law prescribes no sanction against the husband if the wife withstands the ordeal so that the suspicion proves to be unfounded—another aspect of how the bitter-water ordeal was bitter for the woman in more ways than one.

The bitter-water ordeal belongs to the relatively rare category of tests by poisonous concoctions and potions. Goitein mentions several examples of tribes that employ certain potions to ensure the truth of an oath.[7] Our interest here lies in the use of the ordeal in cases of insufficient evidence. In the biblical system, as elsewhere, a suspect must undergo an ordeal after swearing her innocence. The Bible is not satisfied with a suspect's word alone and requires the ordeal in order to confirm the veracity of an oath. In the case of adultery,

---

[6] Mishnah, *Sotah* 1:1–2.

[7] Goitein, *Primitive Ordeal and Modern Law*, 50. Lea also mentions tests with poisonous drinks (*Superstition and Force*, 286–87).

the Bible stipulates that there must be two witnesses in order for a suspect to be found guilty. The assumption in the case of the ordeal described in Numbers 5 is that two witnesses are not available. There is an intermediary situation between complete lack of evidence, in which no judicial steps are taken, and sufficient proof for human judgment to settle the case. The matter is therefore submitted for divine adjudication.

A major distinction between the biblical "bitter-water ordeal" and the divine ordeals elsewhere concerns the results of the ordeal. Exoneration of the accused was the standard result in a verdict of innocence. The ways of dealing with a verdict of guilty, however, varied widely. The general rule was that if the divine ordeal indicated guilt, the finding was tantamount to conviction. If the crime entailed a death penalty, the accused was sentenced accordingly. Yet this approach was not adopted in the "bitter-water ordeal." According to biblical law, the penalty for adultery was death, but if a woman was found guilty by ordeal, she was not sentenced to die. The usual formula was to say that her punishment was in the hands of God and that the mortal judges would not command her execution. According to Jewish law, the woman was liable to civil sanctions: divorce or loss of property rights.

The use of the bitter-water ordeal ended at the order of Rabbi Yohanan Ben Zakkai, who lived in the first century C.E., at the time of the destruction of the second Temple. The step was explained by the fact that "adulterers multiplied," and the ordeal was ineffective if the husband was an adulterer himself and thus not above reproach.[8] The belief in the power of the ordeal to discover the truth had probably waned. Theoretically the ordeal remained valid, and Maimonides, who lived more than a thousand years after Rabbi Yohanan Ben Zakkai, dealt with it in his massive oeuvre *Mishneh Torah* ("Repetition of the Law," Book on Women, The Suspected Adulteress). Nevertheless, the rule was no longer applied. Thus ordeals were abolished in Jewish law rather early. In Christian Europe they continued to flourish for over a thousand years.

A more commonly used ordeal than that of the "bitter water" was the submersion in cold water ordeal, already mentioned in various contexts in the Code of Hammurabi (ca. 1750 B.C.E.). According to section 2 of the Code, if a person accuses another of practicing sorcery, but has no proof, the accused is "tested" in the holy river. The accused is plunged into the river; if the river overcomes him, it is a sign of his guilt and the accuser gets all his property. But if the river clears the accused and he survives, then the accuser is executed and his property given to the accused. Here we see a feature built into the Code serving to discourage false accusations, unlike the husband in Numbers 5, who

---

[8] Mishnah, *Sotah* 9:9; Babylonian Talmud, *Sotah* 47b.

was to remain blameless regardless of the outcome of his wife's ordeal. The submersion in cold water or the "divine river ordeal" was also used when a married woman was accused of adultery. If a member of the general public accused the woman, the husband had the right to demand application of the holy-water ordeal (§132). On the other hand, if it is the husband who initially accuses his wife, without evidence that she committed adultery, the woman is not put to the test. Rather, she must swear by the god that she is pure. If she does so, she has the right to return to her husband (§131).

The laws of Hammurabi thus ascribe different consequences to adultery, depending on the evidence brought against the accused. If there is definite proof of adultery, such as witnesses to the act, the woman and her partner in crime are sentenced to death. There is, however, an exemption: the husband is free to forgive his wife, in which case both she and her partner are spared execution (§129). If there are no witnesses to a woman's adultery, yet a member of the public accuses her of betraying her husband, she must submit to the divine river ordeal. If the woman floats in the holy-water ordeal and survives, it means she is innocent and is saved. If she is guilty and sinks, she dies in the ordeal itself. Because the Hammurabi Code places less trust in the accusation of a member of the public than in the testimony of witnesses to the event, the divine ordeal is administered and offers a chance for the suspect's acquittal. Public accusation, however, does command greater weight than the accusation of a husband, in the Code of Hammurabi.[9] In the latter case, the accused wife is merely forced to swear her innocence, a less dangerous method and one that provides a better chance of survival than the divine river ordeal.

Though the form of the ordeal changed from time to time, the basic worldview underlying the ordeal system endured for thousands of years. To reiterate, the divine ordeal, both in the Hammurabi Code and the biblical "bitter water," served for cases of uncertainty in which a suspicion was considered reasonably founded yet there was no conclusive evidence to produce a conviction. The ordeal was supposedly not administered when suspicions were considered to be unfounded. The story of Anselm reveals his mistake: Anselm suggested that innocent children, against whom there was no evidence of wrongdoing, undergo an ordeal. The tables were turned, and Anselm himself became a victim of this procedure.

Ordeal by submersion in water was widely used in various locations throughout Europe. Its acceptance was based on the belief that water is a holy element; the Christian ritual of baptism served to strengthen this belief. Being

---

[9] G. R. Driver and John C. Miles, *The Babylonian Laws* (2 vols.; London: Oxford University Press, 1952; repr., 1968), 1:284.

holy, water, it was believed, would refuse to "accept" criminals who had per-jured themselves and sworn falsely to their innocence. It was therefore be-lieved that innocent persons would sink in water because the water would accept them, while guilty ones would float. The catch, of course, is that if you are innocent and sink, you may drown. On the other hand, if you float, you will be considered guilty and executed. To get around this problem, the ordeal was conducted as follows: after a suitable ceremony, the accused was bound and immersed in a receptacle of water or a lake, held by a rope that served to pull him or her out. If lucky, the suspect sank, was considered innocent, and pulled out in time. In the other case, the suspect floated and was convicted. This water ordeal is thus the exact opposite of Hammurabi's divine river or-deal, in which the guilty sank and the innocent floated.

Other ordeals widely accepted in medieval Europe included combat (de-scribed in the next chapter), fire, boiling water, and hot iron. In the fire ordeal, the accused walked through flames, placed according to certain rules and in-structions; one who passed through without injury was considered inno-cent.[10] The boiling-water ordeal entailed immersing one's hands in boiling water; in the hot-iron ordeal the accused had to carry a hot iron for a certain distance. After the boiling-water and hot-iron ordeals, the hands of the ac-cused were bound and examined three days later. If the wounds had healed, the accused was deemed innocent, but if the wounds were larger than a pre-scribed size, the accused was deemed guilty.

Trust in the power of ordeals to reveal the truth dwindled in the Middle Ages, and in 1215 the Lateran Church Council decided to abolish ordeals al-together, after which they declined, though were not eradicated from the Eu-ropean continent. The need to find an alternative system of justice became the principal incentive for the development of the jury system. The English adopted the jury system in preference to the ordeal but continued to employ trial by combat for several centuries more.

There is no need to elaborate on the shortcomings of trial by ordeal, and the question arises how this method could survive for so many years. The an-swer is, presumably, that the very belief in the power of the ordeal to attain just results had social significance that sufficed to sustain it. Social stability

---

[10] A description of this ordeal is given in Wigmore, *Kaleidoscope of Justice,* 12–14. Goitein describes these ordeals as well (*Primitive Ordeal and Modern Law,* 58–60). An allusion to the hot iron and fire ordeals appears in Sophocles' play *Antigone,* written in the fifth century B.C.E. In the play, a guard swears his and all the other guards' inno-cence, declaring their willingness to undergo the ordeal of fire and hot iron in order to prove it (lines 260–265). The ordeal was not employed in the time of Sophocles, but its mention indicates that it was used in the past. See John Walter Jones, *The Law and Legal Theory of the Greeks* (London: Oxford University Press, 1956), 136–37.

and order are affected by the trust in the reliability of the judicial system and the faith in its ability to punish the culprit and acquit the innocent. Such trust may prevail for some time despite the fact that it fails to measure up to reality. The belief in the effectiveness of the system is also important in individual cases—if criminals believe that their guilt will be exposed by the judicial process, there is a greater likelihood they will confess to their crimes and avoid going through the process itself. Herein also lies the importance of the precise and detailed ceremonies that accompanied the various ordeals—these strengthened the belief in the power of the ordeal and could lead, indirectly, to the revelation of the truth. When faith in the ordeal system declined, however, so necessarily did the power of the system itself, and its demise became inevitable. Several scholars maintain that in the period leading up to the church's decision to abolish the ordeal, relatively little danger existed of an innocent person being convicted, while at the same time a guilty person stood a fairly good chance of escaping condemnation. The reason is that people were generally not put to ordeal unless there was some concrete evidence against them, and the accused could frequently succeed in manipulating the result of the ordeal in their favor.[11]

Another interesting question is whether the ordeal system contained psychological factors that improved the chances of obtaining a correct judgment. It may well be that in certain cases this was so. We know there is a link between a person's mental and physical condition; thus the dread of the ordeal coupled with a feeling of guilt or a fear of lying could cause physical reactions over which the accused had no control. The psychologist H. J. Eysenck tells the following story, based on anthropological sources: a tribal chief is murdered, and suspicion falls on five people who had been injured by the victim. The witch doctor gathers the suspects and, in front of the whole tribe, conducts an awe-inspiring ceremony during which the suspects are told repeatedly that they will have to eat a portion of rice; the innocent will be able to eat the rice easily, but the guilty will be unable to swallow. When the rice is offered, the witch doctor's prophecy comes true, and the guilty party, unable to swallow, confesses his guilt and is thrown to the crocodiles.[12] The guilty party cannot swallow the rice because his fear of the ordeal causes his mouth to dry and prevents him from swallowing normally. The involuntary nervous system, which governs heartbeat, perspiration, digestion, and the like, reacts to feel-

---

[11] See Wigmore, *Kaleidoscope of Justice,* 6.

[12] Hans Jurgen Eysenck, *Sense and Nonsense in Psychology* (Harmondsworth, Eng.: Penguin, 1957), 74. In the report of the Cahn Committee (1981) concerning the polygraph, the rice-swallowing ordeal is mentioned as a Chinese custom. Also mentioned is the ordeal of licking a hot iron employed by bedouin tribes.

ings of fear in a manner that cannot be consciously controlled. The modern polygraph, or "lie detector," is based on similar processes.

It should be reiterated that the efficacy of certain ordeals, such as the rice-swallowing one just described, varies, in part, according to the suspect's belief that it really works. The stronger the suspect's faith in the process, the more the body will react, involuntarily, to fear or other related emotions. The psychological aspect of the ordeal, as it influences the involuntary nervous system, is, of course, of little consequence in determining whether or not a suspect will float when immersed in a cold-water ordeal or whether a suspect's wounds will heal for better or worse after the fire or boiling-water ordeals.

Let us return to the biblical ordeal of the bitter water. Jewish sources vividly describe the method of warning a woman about to undergo the ordeal. She is told the water will not injure her if she is innocent. She is cautioned not to drink if she is guilty and encouraged to drink it if she is pure.[13] There is also a legend of two identical sisters: the husband of one of them sought to make his wife drink the bitter water. Being impure, she asked her sister to submit to the ordeal in her place. The sister agreed and was found innocent. On her way home from the ordeal, she met her sinful twin and the two kissed. The adulteress smelled the bitter water on the lips of her sister and fell dead on the spot.[14] The legend has a clear purpose: to implant faith in the power of the bitter water, since the stronger the faith, the greater the probability that a guilty woman would not risk submitting to the ordeal and would rather confess. Another interesting aspect of this story is the use of disguise in order to manipulate the divine ordeal.[15] Although the impersonation of one sister by the other succeeded initially, in the end the power of the bitter water reached beyond the confines of the actual trial, when the two sisters met and the guilty party was smitten by the slightest taste of the bitter water. The description of this meeting between the two sisters emphasizes the power of God and the fact that eventually the ordeal did serve, albeit indirectly, to discover the truth and thus fulfilled its function as a deterrent to future offenses of similar nature.

Let us look now at one of the most famous judicial cases, in which a wholly different method from the above ordeals was employed to decide a case in which there was no evidence other than the testimonies of the parties involved. The judgment of Solomon, described in 1 Kings 3, was rendered in the

---

[13] Mishnah, *Sotah* 1:4; Tosefta, *Sotah* 1:6; *Midrash Tanhuma*, parashat *Naso* 1; *Sifre*, parashat *Naso*. For a detailed description of this ordeal, see also Philo, *On the Special Laws* 3.52–62.

[14] *Midrash Tanhuma*, parashat *Naso* 6.

[15] See also the chapter "Stories of Disguise" and the discussion of the trial of Isolde on pp. 56–57.

case of two mothers, both prostitutes, involved in a stormy dispute. One, the plaintiff, declared that the other woman's son had died and that in the middle of the night this woman had arisen and exchanged the dead baby for her own. The other woman denied this, claiming that the living baby in her arms was her own and that the dead infant belonged to the plaintiff. In response to these arguments, King Solomon ordered a sword to be brought and then commanded, "Divide the living boy in two; then give half to the one, and half to the other" (1 Kings 3:25–26). Then one of the women spoke, "because compassion for her son burned within her":

> "Please, my lord, give her the living boy; certainly do not kill him!" The other said, "It shall be neither mine nor yours; divide it." Then the king responded: "Give the first woman the living boy; do not kill him. She is his mother." All Israel heard of the judgment that the king had rendered; and they stood in awe of the king, because they perceived that the wisdom of God was in him, to execute justice. (1 Kings 3:26–28)

This story is one of a group of tales intended to exalt Solomon's exceptional wisdom. It opens with two conflicting testimonies, neither of which is supported by any external evidence, nor are there any circumstances to indicate that one version is more plausible than the other. The babies were born days apart. The women were alone in the house when the alleged crime occurred. Both women were prostitutes, so we may surmise that the fathers were unknown or that they felt no connection to the babies and had not seen them. Hence no one could state to whom the living child belonged, while each woman declared the child to be hers. How then to decide between these conflicting testimonies? Present-day justice also has difficulties in coping with such problems, though modern science can now assist in determining the maternity of a child. In ancient times this was a classic case for divine judgment.

The taking of an oath was another method developed by ancient justice to deal with such problems. In certain respects, oath taking resembles the divine ordeal, since the underlying assumption of a sacred oath is that God will punish the perjurer. Some scholars regard the oath as an ordeal by tongue.[16] Like an ordeal, the efficacy of an oath depends, in part, on the suspect's belief that God knows the truth and will punish the culprit and exonerate the innocent. Such a popular belief served as a deterrent to crime, and the ancients took great pains to encourage such belief by surrounding ordeals and oaths with impressive ceremonies. For example, Abraham adjured his eldest servant who managed his property not to bring a Canaanite wife for his son Isaac but to go to Abraham's

---

[16] Goitein also refers to the oath as a bridge between the ordeal and legal claim (*Primitive Ordeal and Modern Law*, 49).

native land and to bring from there a wife to Isaac. To reinforce the oath, Abraham asked his servant to put his hand under Abraham's thigh and then swear by the Lord, "the God of heaven and earth," to do as requested (Genesis 24:2–4). Another story relates how Jacob escaped from Laban's house and how Laban pursued Jacob and overtook him. Eventually their reconciliation took the form of an oath that they swore to each other in a ceremony that included the erection of a memorial stone. Such ceremonies were elaborated and improved upon throughout the ages and included swearing on the Bible or holy relics. Oaths were often accompanied by the threat of a curse that would fall upon a perjurer.

The technique that developed in Jewish law and various other legal systems[17] involved selecting one of the disputants and imposing the oath on him or her. For example, in the judgment of Solomon, one might say that the burden of proof lay on the woman who held the dead child, since it was she who sought to take the living baby from the arms of the other woman. The oath would therefore be imposed on the defendant—the woman holding the living child. Taking into account the prevailing belief of the time that God would punish a perjurer, it is conceivable that if the woman holding the living child was not its mother, she would abstain from swearing that the child was hers and the plaintiff would win her claim. However, if the defendant was prepared to swear that she was the true mother, the child would have remained with her.

The distinguishing feature in Solomon's judgment is that, despite the difficulty deriving from the absence of any evidence to support the two conflicting testimonies, the king did not take recourse to divine ordeal, not even in the moderate form of an oath. Instead, the king chose a psychological test. This is the singular greatness of the story, set against the background of the prevailing worldview of the time. Though some divine ordeals contained certain psychological elements, their general ideological foundation was different, being based on the belief that the deity would intervene and assist in solving or clarifying the issue. Solomon's judgment employed only human device in order to reach a decision. The trial of Solomon signifies the passing of judgment into human hands—it is no longer God, but judges, who are to decide cases through their human wisdom.

---

[17] The oath was recognized by the Mejelle, the Ottoman civil law legislation, which was based on Islamic law and was in force throughout the Ottoman Empire. According to the Mejelle, "When a claimant is unable to prove his claim the defendant is sworn at the request of the plaintiff" (§1742 of the Mejelle). If, following this request, the defendant swore to the truth of his own version, the claim was dismissed. However, if the defendant refused to take the oath, the claim was allowed, even in the absence of other evidence. This oath was named the "decisive oath" because it led to the conclusion of the case. The Mejelle was in force in Israel during the British Mandate. It remained in force in the State of Israel until 1984.

The story of Solomon's judgment raises the question regarding the efficiency of the king's stratagem. Though the king's method may seem preferable, or more sensible, than a divine ordeal, Solomon's psychological experiment constituted something of a gamble that could easily have failed and that could not be easily repeated. For instance, it is conceivable that both women would object to the king's proposal, or that both would be willing to give up the child, or that both would agree to have the child cut in half and his subsequent death. We presume that the chances the true mother would object to the gruesome cutting of the child were higher than those of the false mother, yet this is far from certain. Indeed, how do we know that the king reached the correct conclusion and that the true mother received the child? Though the Bible assumes that Solomon's judgment revealed the truth, there is no independent evidence indicating this was the case. The tale of Solomon's judgment even lacks the usual idealistic ending of ordeal stories, in which the villain confesses to his or her evil deeds. The narrator probably assumed this to be obvious. Meir Sternberg notes another paradoxical point. The Bible does not tell us which of the two women obtained the child: the one who held the live baby in her arms, or the one who held the dead one and claimed that her live baby had been stolen. We get the impression that the plaintiff won, but careful examination of the text shows that nothing is said about the matter.[18]

Another legend concerning a psychological test of King Solomon is entitled "Who Is the Thief?" It is told by the poet H. N. Bialik:[19] Three merchants set out on their travels with money in their bags. During the night one of them robbed his two colleagues. Their case was brought before King Solomon. The king told them a tale about several imaginary characters: a wealthy girl; a poor youth whom the wealthy girl had sworn to marry; a wealthy young man, chosen by the girl's father to be her bridegroom; and an old robber chief who captures the girl and her bridegroom. As the story unfolds, all the characters behave very nobly and the old robber chief is persuaded to release the girl and the groom and to give back all their property. At the end of the story the king asked the merchants who, in their opinion, had behaved in the most admirable and worthy fashion. One chose the girl, the second the groom, and the third the old robber chief who gave up the girl and the booty. King Solomon pointed to the third merchant and pronounced "That one is the thief." The man confessed his crime, revealed where he had hidden the stolen money, and was duly punished.

---

[18] Meir Sternberg, *The Poetics of Biblical Narrative: Ideological Literature and the Drama of Reading* (Indiana Studies in Biblical Literature; Bloomington: Indiana University Press, 1985), 167–69.

[19] Bialik, *And It Came to Pass*, 104.

In this case, it is crucial to add that the culprit confessed to his crime. It is the confession that proves the power of the psychological test, which otherwise appears far from convincing.

The inherent uncertainties of these two psychological tests ascribed to King Solomon reveal the difficulty of the method. Trials operate according to fixed patterns designed to deal with a variety of situations. The divine ordeal, whether it be the bitter water, the immersion in cold water, or the hot iron, can be used an infinite number of times under a variety of conditions and circumstances. This is not the case with a psychological test such as the one employed by King Solomon in the trial of the two mothers. It can be used only once and cannot be applied to other disputes, or even repeated in similar circumstances. A new test must be tailored for every case and adapted to its specific facts. The legendary ability of King Solomon to do so every time lies beyond the capacity of a normal legal system.

After the responsibility for judgment passed from God to human hands—or perhaps seized by the human hands of Solomon—the next development in the history of Hebrew trials is reflected in the story of "Susanna and the Elders" told in the addition to the book of Daniel.[20] The tale gained great popularity in the Christian world and was a popular subject in Christian art. The tale also drifted into Islamic sources and appears in *A Thousand and One Nights* under the title "Story of the Virtuous Israelite Woman and the Two Old Villains." The outline of the story is as follows: virtuous and beautiful Susanna was married to a wealthy man who had an orchard beside his house. As Susanna walked in the orchard she was watched by two old men; according to one version, the old men observed her while she was bathing in the orchard's pool. The men lusted after her and demanded that she grant them her favors. When she refused, they threatened her with terrible vengeance. Susanna remained steadfast in her virtue, and the two men then falsely accused her of betraying her husband with a man who had fled from the orchard. The two men satisfied the two-witness rule, required for conviction, and Susanna was sentenced to death for adultery. However, before her execution, God heard her supplication and sent an angel to grant wisdom to Daniel, who at the time was still a youth. Just before Susanna's execution, Daniel rose and bade the crowd that had gathered to release the accused and permit him to question each of the witnesses separately. In the interrogation, which became a kind of trial, Daniel asked each witness where the adulterous act had taken place, under which tree, and so forth. The testimonies conflicted, and Daniel decreed Susanna to be innocent. The two villains were

---

[20] Susanna appears in the Apocrypha and is not included in the canonized Jewish Bible.

sentenced to death. According to one version the men were arrested and the angel of God sent fire and killed them. In another version Daniel himself sentenced the men to death, in accordance with the biblical law that decrees that false witnesses should suffer the same punishment that would have been imposed on the person whom they had falsely accused (Deuteronomy 19:18–19).

Daniel employed a method of investigation that derived from Jewish law developed during the period of the second Temple (sixth century B.C.E.–first century C.E.). The tractate *Sanhedrin* in the Mishnah gives clear instructions how witnesses are to be cautioned and interrogated, not only on the main issue of the litigation, but also on the circumstances surrounding the event. The book indicates that the more one questions, the better. When a witness declared that a certain act had taken place under a fig tree, Rabbi Yohanan Ben Zakkai is said to have examined the witnesses' recollection of the "thorns of figs" (5:2). He questioned the witnesses as to whether the thorns of the fig tree branch were thick or thin. Of course, it is highly probable that true witnesses would not remember such minor details, and the fact that their testimonies conflict on several points as to the description of the crime scene does not necessarily indicate that their testimonies regarding the cardinal issue of the trial are false. Most significantly, Daniel's demand to examine and interrogate witnesses marks a turning point, where Jewish law shook off the bonds of the formal "two-witnesses rule." Under this rule the court was bound to accept the testimonies of two witnesses and give judgment accordingly: "On the evidence of two or three witnesses the death sentence shall be executed; a person must not be put to death on the evidence of only one witness" (Deuteronomy 17:6). Thereafter, the testimonies of two witnesses had to be examined and tested; contradictions in the testimonies could lead to their rejection.

There are certain common features between the judgments of Daniel and King Solomon. In both cases, the verdict derives from a human judge rather than a divine ruling. In both cases, the human judges are endowed by God with superior wisdom. But in each case the judicial process is conducted without divine intervention. Not even the oath, a central part of ancient law, plays a role in these trials. Yet the two trials differ in the nature of the human method employed by the judges. Solomon uses a psychological test in order to arrive at a verdict, while Daniel reaches his judgment through logic. Solomon tests the emotional reaction of the disputants to a drastic, dramatic proposal. Daniel examines the plausibility of the two witness statements; he interrogates each of them separately and compares their answers. The story of Daniel reflects a major landmark in the development of the law. Daniel's technique corresponds to the modern procedure of reviewing the content and plausibility of evidence and checking for possible inconsistencies.

From the stories of Daniel and Solomon the function of the judge expands and grows in importance. From being a technician in charge of the quantitative examination of evidence the judge becomes responsible for the qualitative appraisal of that evidence. From the literary and dramatic point of view, Solomon's judgment may be more interesting and exciting than that of Daniel, but Daniel's method of arriving at the truth can be applied to a variety of cases and is more in line with modern techniques of judicial proceedings. The psychological elements uncovered by Solomon in the judicial process still play a role, as judges and juries take into account the demeanor and reactions of a witness, and not only the reasonableness and consistency of his or her answers. The witness is not, however, normally subjected to psychological tests but only to questions relating to the case.

Postscript: The Polygraph (The Lie Detector)

The ancients believed that God was ready to assist humankind to distinguish between truth and falsity. This belief waned, and responsibility for judgment passed into human hands. The difficulty of ascertaining the truth, however, remains—mortal judges and juries are often incapable of reaching unequivocal conclusions. Jewish tradition holds that "only with the coming of the Messiah will a judge never be confounded by false testimony."[21] Courts often rely on scientific evidence for assistance; fingerprints are used for the identification of a person, ballistics for gun identity, and the question of parental identity, for which Solomon drew upon a psychological test for his answer, can now be solved by means of DNA testing. Science has its limitations, however, and difficult questions concerning credibility, similar in some respects to those faced by Solomon, continue to arise in a great variety of situations. The difficulty often arises in cases where conflicting testimonies are submitted by opposite parties, and no other reliable evidence is available to support either version.

The polygraph, dubbed "the lie detector," reflects a human attempt to offer a modern scientific solution to the problem of telling truth from lies. The instrument itself cannot, of course, reveal truth or lie. The polygraph measures a person's physical reactions to certain external stimuli. The measurements record the results of some of the involuntary reactions of the human nervous system, such as those reflected in blood pressure, heartbeat, and perspiration. It is thought that the nervous system evolved in response to

---

[21] Judge Kister in the Israeli case of *Roytman v. Bank Mizrahi* 29(2) P.D. 57, 62 (Hebrew).

the dangers with which primordial humans had to cope by either "fight or flight." Both fighting and fleeing required increased supply of blood and oxygen, the lowering of the pain threshold, and a temporary suspension of the digestive system. It may be that these reactions, so useful to prehistoric humans, are of little use in the modern world, where the economic, social, and legal struggles of life require an unperturbed, cool state of mind.[22] The polygraph measures the physiological changes in breathing, pulse, blood pressure, and the skin's electrical conductivity, which occur in response to questions put to the person being tested. The various reactions are recorded on graphs, hence the name polygraph. The underlying assumptions of the test are that false answers cause tension and excitement, which are manifested in the activities of the autonomous nervous system, and the differences in the graphs that record the answers can indicate whether the person is speaking the truth or is lying. Just as a suspect's belief in the power of the swallowing-rice ordeal to determine innocence and guilt could affect the outcome of this ordeal, so the greater a person's belief in the efficacy of the polygraph, the greater the prospect of the examiner's reaching correct results. Since the suspect's belief in the polygraph will increase his or her agitation when lying and calm one when speaking the truth, the examiner will make every effort to persuade the examinee that the instrument is reliable and can tell truth from nontruth.[23] The tactics underlying such persuasion are not far removed from those of the priests and witch doctors who cautioned the suspects of divine ordeals regarding the efficacy of their tests.

During a polygraph test the person under examination is asked a number of questions on topics that have nothing to do with the critical issue for which the test is conducted. Such questions are emotionally neutral, for example, "Where do you live?" The person is also questioned on matters that are emotionally charged but are not directly connected to the investigation, as well as direct questions such as "Did you steal the money?" The purpose is to compare the different reactions to the various types of questions and to find out whether the reactions to incriminating questions differ from the reactions to other questions, indicating that a suspect may be lying. The polygraph does not analyze these reactions to determine truth or falsity—that is left to the examiner, who reports his or her conclusions based on the deciphering of the results.

The polygraph is being used widely in police and other investigations. The central questions regarding this machine concern the degree of its reliability

---

[22] Eysenck, *Sense and Nonsense in Psychology*, 79.

[23] One of the methods of persuasion is the "card test." The person under examination (connected to the polygraph) is asked to choose a card out of a pack. The examiner then identifies the chosen card through the person's responses to questions.

and whether the results are admissible in court. The decision rendered in the United States as early as 1923, in *Frye v. U.S.*,[24] had significant impact on the matter. It was stated that the courts would allow the introduction of expert testimony based on a scientific principle or on an invention that was generally recognized to be reliable and accurate. However, it was stated that the "deception test has not yet gained such standing and scientific recognition . . . as would justify the courts in admitting expert testimony deduced from the discovery, development, and experiments thus far made." Israeli courts adopted a similar approach. A committee chaired by the former president of the Supreme Court, Justice Itzhak Cahn, stated that, as far as it knew, polygraph tests were admitted as evidence in Japanese courts, but otherwise "there is almost no country in the world where polygraph results are admitted as evidence in court."[25] The committee recommended that the situation should remain unchanged, that the polygraph results remain inadmissible in criminal cases, even if both the prosecution and the defense agree to have them introduced. Furthermore, the court should not be informed if the accused had or had not agreed to undergo a polygraph test. The results of the test are also inadmissible in civil cases, except when both parties agree to their introduction.[26]

The recommendations of the Cahn Committee reflect the present state of law in Israel. The reservation about using polygraph results in court may in part be explained by the fear that too much weight will be attached to them. The court has no control over the evidence; such control is exercised by the investigator operating the machine and interpreting its results. There is a fear that the findings of the investigator will prove decisive, an idea too reminiscent of the ordeals of ancient times.

---

[24] 293 F. 1013 (Court of Appeals of the District of Columbia Circuit). In this case it was the accused who asked to introduce the expert testimony of the "lie detector" test, which, according to his assertion, indicated he was telling the truth. His request was denied.

[25] The report was published in *Itzhak Cahn Book* (Hebrew) (ed. Menahem Elon et al.; Tel-Aviv, Papyrus Publishing House, 1989), 29–85.

[26] The general rule adopted by most American courts is that polygraph test results are inadmissible in either criminal or civil cases. However, a substantial number of courts accept the results of such tests, both in criminal and in civil actions, if the parties stipulated to their admission prior to the testing and if certain conditions are satisfied. In addition, very few jurisdictions grant the trial judge discretion to admit polygraph evidence in special circumstances even in the absence of such stipulation. See Charles T. McCormick, *McCormick on Evidence* (ed. J. W. Strong; 2 vols.; 4th ed.; St. Paul, Minn.: West Publishing, 1992), 1:907–17; Jack B. Weinstein et al., *Evidence: Cases and Materials* (9th ed.; Westbury, N.Y.: Foundation Press, 1997), 467–71; Charles F. Torcia, *Wharton's Criminal Evidence* (4 vols.; 14th ed.; Rochester, N.Y.: Lawyers Co-operative Publishing, 1985–1987), vol. 3, §535.

2

David and Goliath: Trial by Combat

❦

The duel of David and Goliath is perhaps the most fascinating of biblical tales, one that has left a mark in history, literature, and art. The story opens with Israel's army, led by King Saul, massed on a mountain above the Elah Valley and the Philistines camped on another mountain, "with a valley between them" (1 Samuel 17:3). Then a Philistine champion "named Goliath, of Gath, whose height was six cubits and a span," stepped forward (1 Samuel 17:4). The chapter goes on to describe this giant's terrible weapons and his challenge: "Choose a man for yourselves, and let him come down to me. If he is able to fight with me and kill me, then we will be your servants; but if I prevail against him and kill him, then you shall be our servants" (1 Samuel 17:8–9). The Israelites balked at this contest: "When Saul and all Israel heard these words of the Philistine, they were dismayed and greatly afraid" (1 Samuel 17:11).

At this dramatic point the story moves to Bethlehem, where Jesse and his son David lived. According to prevailing practice, men called to war had to bring their own supplies and equipment. Jesse dispatched David with food for his mobilized brothers and instructed the lad to give ten cheeses to the captain of his sons' unit—a gift that presumably conferred some advantages.

David arrived at King Saul's camp in time to witness Goliath's arrogant performance, which went on for forty days. King Saul was offering great wealth and the hand of his daughter in marriage to any champion, but not one of the Israelite heroes stepped forward, only the young David remained undeterred. He asked: "Who is this uncircumcised Philistine that he should defy the armies of the living God?" (1 Samuel 17:26). David persuaded Saul to let him meet the challenger. Saul offered him his own armor and sword, but the untrained youth could not move in them. Taking five smooth stones, he went to face the Philistine. Goliath mocked him, but David responded that he came "in the name of the LORD of hosts, the God of the armies of Israel, whom you have defied" (1 Samuel 17:45). In the battle that ensued David slung a stone at Goliath's forehead, and the giant dropped to the ground. Drawing Goliath's own sword, David hacked his head off. The story ends with the Philistines seeing "their champion was dead" and fleeing, chased by the Israelites. Thereafter David remained at Saul's court.

The story presents considerable difficulties. In the previous chapter (1 Samuel 16), Saul had called for "someone who can play well." A servant recommended David as "skillful in playing, a man of valor, a warrior . . . and the LORD is with him" (1 Samuel 16:17–18). Clearly the versions are inconsistent. According to chapter 16, David was not a youth incapable of moving with armor and sword but an experienced warrior who had come to Saul's court before his duel with Goliath.

Furthermore, 2 Samuel 21:19 records that an Israelite named Elhanan killed Goliath. To resolve the contradiction, Rashi suggested that Elhanan was David,[1] while Rabbi David Kimchi (Radak) considered that Elhanan was not David, nor was his protagonist Goliath, but rather the giant's brother. This latter version is supported by 1 Chronicles 20:5, which says that Elhanan "killed Lahmi the brother of Goliath the Gittite," though it is possible that 1 Chronicles was using this version to solve the problem.

The attribution of personal heroism to David is also exceptional. He was a leader with sharp political instincts; he charmed his men, who were willing to sacrifice everything for him. On one occasion, when he was thirsty, three of his warriors stole into the Philistine camp, drew water, and brought it back to him. But he won their hearts by refusing to drink water obtained with "the blood of the men who went at the risk of their lives" (2 Samuel 23:17). There were better warriors than David, and he eventually withdrew from martial matters, entrusting them to his officers and soldiers. Indeed, in one battle with the Philistines, David was almost slain by a giant, and only saved by Abishai. As a result, he was told by his men, "You shall not go out with us to battle any longer, so that you do not quench the lamp of Israel" (2 Samuel 21:17).

The idea that David's life was too precious to risk in war recurs during Absalom's rebellion, when the king wanted to join his soldiers. The idea was rejected by "the men" (2 Samuel 18:3). David had already abstained from leading the army during the war against the Ammonites, which was led by Joab while David remained in Jerusalem. Then came the Bathsheba interlude, which resulted in the murder of Uriah. In this David differed from many other kings, who led their armies and who sometimes fell in battle (Saul, Ahab, and Josiah).

---

[1] This interpretation is based on *Targum Pseudo-Jonathan*.

By itself this does not suggest a personal failing in David. The talents required to lead a nation are not necessarily those of a warrior and general. David's ability to appoint superior generals, and his pool of first-rate warriors willing to risk all for him, indicate his greatness as a leader. The story of his clash with Goliath is, therefore, an exception in David's record, but whether or not it is correctly described, it does present a message: not only can the weaker prevail over the stronger by virtue of faith, but, more importantly, Goliath had provoked more than Saul and the Israelites. David, in confronting the giant, was representing "the LORD of hosts, the God of the armies of Israel," implying that God intervenes on the side of the righteous. In passing, we may note that this battle was not presented as fought between warring gods, as, for example, is the Trojan War described in the *Iliad,* where some gods support the Greeks while others act on the Trojan side. There gods descend to the battlefield to give assistance each to his favorite side. In David versus Goliath, only one god is found in the background. Goliath certainly had his own gods (elsewhere, the Bible tells of Philistines worshiping Dagon), but they are not relevant. David, with the help of the Almighty in whose name he comes, overcomes only Goliath—not his gods. The one God is the only power that controls the battlefield and determines the outcome.

This conception that God intervenes in struggle and resolves it in favor of the righteous is akin to another idea that the Bible emphasizes: rewards for keeping God's commandment, and punishment for failing to do so. The injunction to honor one's father and mother is supplemented with the promise "so that your days may be long in the land" (Exodus 20:12). More generalized language promises prolongation of life to whoever observes God's "statutes and commandments" (Deuteronomy 4:40), and what applies to the individual also applies to the community. If the people followed alien gods, the Almighty would impose strong sanctions, but if they remained loyal to their own God, they could "go in and occupy the good land" and repel all their enemies (Deuteronomy 6:18–19). In common with all the instructions regarding reward and punishment, the focus is on one side, whether an individual among the Israelites or the entire nation. The one who acts appropriately will benefit. The sinner will be punished. There are occasional references to other parties—for example, in the promise that enemies would be overcome—but this is a side effect. Conversely, God's intervention in conflict does focus on both sides and their dispute that needs resolution. The narrative does not then refer to one side only, but deals with both.

The belief that the Almighty decides the outcome of battles or conflicts according to the degree of righteousness of each side is very close to the concept of "divine ordeal," which determines innocence or guilt. The ordeal differs from combat in that it is directed at one side (though the results may have implications for others). Combat is a dual test, involving two sides. Another possible difference is that the ordeal, usually, determines only the question of guilt, whereas the punishment is likely to be set by humans. If, on the other hand, God resolves the outcome of battle, the decision will both identify the righteous side and determine the results for the loser. However, this distinction has no bearing on the legal battle, if combat is waged not by the parties themselves but by their representatives. Moreover, the outcome of such a battle could resolve a civil conflict, in which case the civil result would be added to the damage inflicted by the combat.

Combat by champions is exceptional in the Bible.[2] It was known among other nations, though it is not clear whether there was always agreement that the results would resolve the conflict. The Trojan War, in Homer's *Iliad*, contains a few descriptions of duels between individuals from each camp. One such duel was fought by Paris, whose elopement with Helen had caused the war, and Menelaus, her wronged husband. The contest ended to Menelaus's advantage, but Paris was saved by the intervention of the goddess Aphrodite. Agamemnon, leader of the Greeks, relied on the results to demand the return of Helen, thereby ending the affair. The Trojans might have agreed, but for the intervention of the goddesses Athena and Hera, and the war went on.[3] Another famous duel from the same war took place between the Greek hero Achilles and Hector, the son of the king of Troy. Achilles won and Hector died, but this did not end the war.

Roman legend also provides a well-known story of combat between champions. In the war between Rome and the nearby town of Alba Longa, during the reign of Tullus Hostilius, a duel took place between the three Horatii brothers, representing Rome, and the three Curiatii brothers. Two of the Roman Horatii were killed, but the surviving brother slew all three adversaries.

There are other examples of a champion stepping forward from one army and challenging an adversary to sole combat. But it was mostly an introduction to the main act rather than an agreement to let the duel decide the larger encounter.[4]

---

[2] In 2 Samuel 2 we read of a battle between the men of David's general, Joab, and of Saul's commander, Abner. It began with a clash of twelve representatives from each side, all of whom were killed. It seems that the contest was not designed to resolve the conflict but as a prelude to the main battle that immediately ensued.

[3] Edith Hamilton, *Mythology* (New York: Grosset & Dunlop, 1940), 265–66.

[4] George Neilson, *Trial by Combat* (New York: MacMillan, 1891), 211, brings an example of a duel between a Scot and an Englishman that preceded a battle in 1333 C.E.

No biblical examples can be found of representative contests between nations other than David and Goliath, nor is there support for a legal resolution of conflict by a duel between individuals. It seems that this way of resolving judicial arguments was not part of the ancient Near East. It is not mentioned in the Hammurabi legal texts, nor in any other regional laws that have come down to us—and certainly not in the laws of the Torah. Conversely, trial by ordeal was customary in certain cases, both in Hammurabi and Torah laws.

Postbiblical Jewish law did selectively adopt resolution of conflict by a physical struggle between the parties. *Bava Batra* 34b of the Babylonian Talmud records a dispute between two men over the ownership of a riverboat. One of them petitioned the Beth Din (religious court), which ordered seizure of the craft until he produced witnesses to his ownership. There were no witnesses. So the court began to debate whether to impound the boat or release it and allow decision by physical contest. Rabbi Papa was in favor of this solution, while Rabbi Judah saw no cause either to seize or to release the craft. The issue was analogous to that which arose in a dispute over property in which Rabbi Nahman ruled in favor of contest so that the one who was stronger would take possession. That was the solution adopted by Maimonides, who discussed two persons contesting the ownership of a field, "the one says it is mine and the other says it is mine." If neither has witnesses, or both have witnesses to support their versions, the field should be left to them and "the one who overpowers the other takes possession of the field."[5] This seems to be a situation in which neither party is in possession and neither can produce evidence supporting his case.[6] The court is therefore unable to reach a decision, and for want of another solution, the choice fell on private contest. It is in fact a case in which the law eludes the issue. The court recognizes that it does not have the means to resolve the conflict, and in view of the helplessness of the law and the absence of a judicial avenue, the parties are free to resolve the problem through a physical contest.[7] Many questions remain unanswered: How is the struggle to be waged? Must the protagonists themselves wrestle, or

---

[5] Maimonides, *The Code of Maimonides (Mishneh Torah): Book 13, The Book of Civil Laws* (trans. Jacob J. Rabinowitz; New Haven, Conn.: Yale University Press, 1949), part 4: Laws concerning Pleading 15:4.

[6] If one party is in possession, then the other party must produce evidence of entitlement. If both parties hold the property (as in the case of two holding a prayer shawl), then it seems that in the absence of other evidence, the two must share it.

[7] Samuel Atlas, *Individual Contest: Pathways in Hebrew Jurisprudence* (Hebrew) (New York: American Academy for Jewish Research, 1978), 76, offers an alternative explanation, that the parties are given the opportunity to resolve the matter in accordance with natural law, under which ownership can be acquired by conquest in war. But he notes that the idea of contest is based on the inability of the court to decide.

may they be helped by others? Are they free to use weapons? If the case is beyond the law, then everything may be open.[8] I could not find any material concerning the scope of the method or to how it was applied in practice. Nor did I find any hint at the faith that a just result was achieved or that God took the side of the righteous party. Clearly the approach was entirely different from that of the European trial by combat, which is discussed below. Jewish law speaks of combat away from the supervisory eyes of the judges, an apparently "extralegal" process. The European trial by combat was itself a judicial process, conducted according to rules, and the outcome was for all intents and purposes a legal resolution.

This method of judicial decision by combat was adopted by Scandinavian and German tribes in early times[9] and remained in use for many centuries. The duel between David and Goliath was occasionally cited to justify this means of judicial resolution. This reasoning was considered very seriously by Pope Nicholas I in 867 C.E., though he finally decided that it was not convincing.[10] In any event, it seems that the source for trial by combat, as applied in Europe, was not the Bible, but rather the traditions of Scandinavian and German tribes.

The method was adopted in medieval Europe and was used for a long time not only in personal disputes but also in matters of state. In the course of time it found its way into the literature of romance and chivalry. Both in literature and reality, judicial duels were used for many purposes, including proof of a queen's faithfulness to her husband the king, criminal accusations, inheritance, and other ownership matters. It is not always easy to differentiate between fact and legend. Legend has it that King Arthur won his kingdom in a duel, but since the king himself is a legendary figure, the historicity of the story is doubtful.[11] However, it is clear that the use of this method was not

---

[8] Another question relates to the time frame in which the contest must be concluded and whether the loser may return yet again in the hope of succeeding the second time. Jewish law is divided on this point, but it seems that preference is given to nonrenewal of the contest. The loser can only gain the asset if he can produce witnesses to his claim (ibid.).

[9] A discussion of sources indicating use of the method in early times can be found in Lea, *Superstition and Force*, 91–99.

[10] William Blackstone, *Commentaries on the Laws of England* (1765–1769; repr., 4 vols.; Chicago: University of Chicago Press, 1979), 3:338, notes that this was a strange reason. See also Neilson, *Trial by Combat*, 2.

[11] Neilson mentions other stories of decision by combat in gaining control of a kingdom (*Trial by Combat*, 25–30). The romantic side of this legal process is reflected in coronation ceremonies where a knight appears on horseback and declares that he is ready to prove with his own body that the king currently being crowned is the true monarch (193–96).

confined to personal matters. According to one source, even in diplomatic negotiations over a conflict between nations, each side was ready to produce a champion as a means of reaching resolution.[12]

The Catholic Church took a clear stand against the practice, though there were exceptional cases where individual Catholics sided with resolution by combat. Eventually the opposition of the Church caused the practice to fade away, though some cases of duels to resolve legal conflicts can be found in the fifteenth and sixteenth centuries.[13]

This legal institution arrived in England with the Norman invaders in 1066 C.E. The literature contains legends of judicial duels in England before the eleventh century, due to the presence of Scandinavian and German tribes, but there does not seem to be any convincing proof prior to the Norman conquest.[14] However, the method known as "wager of battle" did take hold thereafter with some strange consequences. The accepted usage of the institution was in "appeal of felony," which was a criminal accusation brought by a private individual. Sometimes the accuser was the actual victim or a relative, but in many cases he was a criminal who could obtain clemency in return for his help in removing from this world some of his partners in crime (these accusers were known as "approvers"). In this process, the accused had the option of judicial duel. The method was also applied in military courts and in certain civil actions. The initial principle in criminal cases was that the parties themselves must fight. In civil cases they were entitled to hire champions to fight for them, and it seems that hiring professionals eventually found its way into criminal cases. Some people maintained a fighter, or fighters, whom they were prepared to hire out to others in need.[15]

Trial by ordeal was prohibited in England following a decision of the Church in 1215. But, surprisingly, there was no ban on judicial duel, which continued for many years. The Church was not sympathetic to the idea, and there were judges who tried to prevent it, with the result that the practice was rarely used in the ensuing centuries—but it did remain part of English law.

The English jurist William Blackstone, in his famous book on the *Laws of England,* written in the mid-eighteenth century, described the practice in

---

[12] William Holdsworth, *A History of English Law* (ed. A. L. Goodhart and H. G. Hanbury; 7th ed.; London: Methuen, 1956–), 1:308–9. Material relating to the use of this method to resolve international disputes is presented in Lea, *Superstition and Force,* 153–56.

[13] Neilson, *Trial by Combat,* 16–17.

[14] Ibid., 19–30.

[15] Frederick Pollock and Frederick William Maitland, *History of English Law before the Time of Edward I* (2d ed.; 2 vols.; 1898; repr., London: Cambridge University Press, 1923), 2:633.

considerable detail.[16] Referring to a plea regarding the land rights of a tenant, he noted that the battleground was a fenced-in area of sixty square feet. The judges, "in their scarlet robes," sat on one side of the enclosure "and also a bar is prepared for the learned serjeants at law." Action began at dawn as the parties' champions took their places, equipped with batons (in military courts these would be replaced by swords). Each would make an oath that the right in issue belonged to the party he represented and would also swear that he did not use "any inchantment, sorcery or witchcraft by which the law of God may be abased, or the law of the devil exalted." Battle would then commence, and it could continue till the stars came out.

This legal institution continued to exist in England, at least in theory, until it was put to practical use in 1818, in the case of *Ashford v. Thornton.*[17] Thornton was accused of murdering a young woman named Mary Ashford. He was acquitted in a trial by jury, but the suspicion of guilt remained and the victim's brother submitted an "appeal of murder" against Thornton (a process that was possible at the time). Asked how he pleaded, Thornton replied, "Not guilty, and I am prepared to defend that with my body," whereupon he threw down a gauntlet on the floor of the court. By doing so he was fulfilling the ceremonial requirement of asking for decision by duel. The court ruled that there was no avoiding the conclusion that he was entitled to such a process. The accuser was not prepared to take up the challenge, and Thornton was released.[18] Following this case a law was enacted in 1819 ending the method of judicial duel.

In legal writings on this subject, it is generally assumed that judicial duel was not based solely on faith in the physical prowess of the protagonists but also on the belief that Divine Providence would give victory to the righteous side.[19] At first this was a belief in the gods, but Christianity replaced that with the intervention of the Supreme Divinity. But there are literary examples of an attitude that did not pin hopes on justice and suggest that God sides with the stronger.

The Icelandic *Njal's Saga*[20] contains a good deal of legal material, including stories of judicial duels. This saga, perhaps the finest in Icelandic literature,

---

[16] Blackstone, *Commentaries on the Laws of England,* 3:339–41.

[17] 106 E.R. 149. In this case the exceptions to the right of the accused to trial by combat were discussed, and found that none of them applied. Accordingly, the senior judge, Lord Ellenborough, noted that the procedure should be decision by combat, unless the accuser refused to fight (p. 168).

[18] Neilson, *Trial by Combat,* 330, mentions an Irish precedent from 1815 with a similar outcome.

[19] Holdsworth, *History of English Law,* 1:308–9.

[20] Translated to English by Magnus Magnusson and Hermann Pálsson (Baltimore: Penguin, 1960).

was written by an anonymous author in the late thirteenth century. It narrates events beginning in the tenth century, not long after the exile of Norwegians to Iceland. The plot is complex with many characters, among them a man named Hrut who was betrothed to Unn. He then went to Norway, was accepted at the royal court, and had a romantic relationship with the king's mother. When he wanted to return to Iceland, his royal lover put a spell on him to prevent him from making love to his betrothed. He married Unn, but the spell worked and she divorced him. Mord Fiddle, Unn's father, demanded the return of his daughter's dowry, warning Hrut that if he did not comply he would have to pay a heavy fine. Hrut responded that Mord was acting aggressively out of greed and demanded trial by combat. Mord, an old man, stood no chance in an encounter in which he would lose both the dowry and his life. He preferred not to fight, and the claim was dismissed. Sometime later Mord died, and Unn turned to a relative, Gunnar Hamundarson, one of Iceland's most accomplished warriors, to help her recover her dowry. Gunnar agreed, and Unn assigned to him the dowry claim. Gunnar consulted his friend Njal about the way to renew the action. Following Njal's advice, Gunnar disguised himself as a man named Hedin and presented himself at Hrut's house, accompanied by two friends. Gunnar guided the conversation to the question of divorce and the dowry claim. When Hrut bragged about the way the claim had been dismissed, the disguised Gunnar asked casually if the claim could be reinstated. Suspecting nothing, Hrut said that it could be done by someone addressing him in a particular form of summons at his residence. What, then, would be the form, Gunnar asked. Hrut told him, and Gunnar repeated it word for word, and whispered to his two companions that he was making this summons in the dowry claim assigned to him by Unn, daughter of Mord. That night Gunnar and his friends sneaked out of Hrut's house. Their next meeting, after Gunnar had taken off his disguise, was at the Althing, which the Icelanders consider to be the oldest parliament in the world. Gunnar summoned Hrut to court, where he announced that he was offering the same option that Hrut had offered Mord. He was inviting him to a duel, the winner of which would be victorious in the case—and if Hrut refused, he had to repay the dowry. Hrut understood that it was a lost cause. He gave in and paid. Gunnar returned the dowry to Unn.

Here are two elements worthy of note: first, Gunnar used a disguise and deception, but these did not detract from the validity of the legal process. The use of the appropriate formality was decisive, and it acted to the advantage of the man behind the mask, even though the other party was mistaken as to his identity. This point is further examined in the following chapter on "Stories of Disguise." The second element relates to the challenge to a duel that occurred twice. Evidently, the winner in both cases was the stronger and better fighter. Nowhere in the story is there any suggestion of divine intervention on behalf of the righteous side, though paradoxically the two episodes cancelled each other and the final result could be seen as fair and just. Yet from the story itself it is clear that the protagonist stood alone. He could make use of any means acquired in this world but could not expect divine intervention to support a just cause.

This is also the obvious explanation for the end of trial by ordeal and judicial combat. The belief of earlier generations that God was available to solve day-to-day problems, and it was only necessary to know how to address God, had passed from this world. Humans have to confront their difficulties and doubts by themselves with the tools that they have created.

3

Stories of Disguise

❧

World literature throughout the ages is full of stories of disguise. They are found in mythologies, folk stories, and classical and modern literature. The Bible in particular contains a large number of disguise stories, all characterized by the intent to deceive, driven by diverse motives. Let us open with a story in which disguise is employed in an attempt to elude fate.

First Kings 22 tells of the last war of Ahab, king of Israel, against Aram (Syria). For three years there had been no wars, but in the third year the king said to his servants: "Do you know that Ramoth-gilead belongs to us, yet we are doing nothing to take it out of the hand of the king of Aram?" (1 Kings 22:3). The rhetoric was accompanied by action. Ahab enlisted the aid of King Jehoshaphat of Judah, who promptly confirmed the alliance between them: "I am as you are; my people are your people, my horses are your horses." In accordance with the practice of those days, the next move was to consult the Almighty. The Greeks were in the habit of going to their famed oracle at Delphi, while the kings of Israel went to the prophets. In Ahab's day the kingdom of Israel had been accused of observing pagan rites, primarily because of the inclinations of Jezebel, Ahab's wife. However, Jehoshaphat requested that the entreaty should be made to the prophets of the God of Israel. Complying with Jehoshaphat's wishes, Ahab turned to the prophets of the true God. He convened four hundred prophets and posed the question: " 'Shall I go to battle against Ramoth-gilead, or shall I refrain?' They answered: 'Go up; for the LORD will give it into the hand of the king' " (1 Kings 22:6). The traditional interpretation is that the prophets were, in fact, prophets of Baal who, to satisfy Jehoshaphat, had disguised themselves as prophets of God. However, this interpretation is not supported by the text.

Jehoshaphat was not satisfied with this prophecy, perhaps because of the prophets' uniform response, or maybe because they seemed to be doing Ahab's will rather than their own. So Jehoshaphat asked for yet another prophet of the Lord. Ahab was not enthusiastic. He conceded that there was indeed another prophet—Micaiah the son of Imlah—but expressed reservations: "I hate him, for he never prophesies anything favorable about me, but only disaster" (1 Kings 22:8). Yet, in view of Jehoshaphat's resolve, Micaiah was summoned and indeed prophesied as Ahab had predicted. Micaiah did not predict the outcome of the war but rather focused on Ahab, foreseeing that his fate would be decided in this battle and that he would fall in Ramoth-gilead. This was not an easy prophecy for Micaiah. He was beaten by one of the false prophets, and Ahab ruled: "Put this fellow in prison, and feed him on reduced rations of bread and water until I come in peace" (1 Kings 22:27).

Ahab now faced a fateful dilemma: whom to believe? It was not easy to distinguish between true and false prophets. It could only be resolved in hindsight, based on results. If a prophecy came to pass, then it was true. However, this was of little use in real time, when a person actually had to decide. Ahab, a brave warrior, chose the advice of the prophets who were to his liking and who prophesied only good—though perhaps he had little alternative: he was surrounded by his servants and hundreds of loyal prophets. Jehoshaphat had joined him, and the army was ready. How could he retreat from such a situation without losing face? Nevertheless, the fear aroused by Micaiah's prophecy continued to trouble him, so Ahab decided to go to war in disguise.

The trick was of no avail. A Syrian soldier "drew his bow and unknowingly struck the king of Israel between the scale armor and the breastplate" (22:34). The wounded Ahab remained standing valiantly in his chariot so that his men would not be disheartened by his injury. It is not clear whether one side or the other won the battle. In any event, Ahab died at the end of that day.

The story of Ahab's disguise expresses the human desire to evade one's fate. In biblical terms this was not random fate, but rather God's decision about future happenings—a decision reflected in the divine prophecy. Ahab's disguise was an attempt to prevent the outcome of the divine decision, and it had to fail. From this standpoint, the act parallels other legendary stories of desperate, though hopeless, efforts to evade the decree of fate, though not necessarily by disguise.

Greek mythology supplies many examples, such as the story of Oedipus. Laius, king of Thebes, received word of a prophecy that Oedipus, his son, would kill him. He tried to cause the child's death, but Oedipus was saved and adopted by a stranger. As an adult, he heard a prophecy that he would kill his father and marry his mother. Believing his adopters to be his true parents,

Oedipus chose to go to Thebes to avoid this doom. On the way he met Laius and, unaware that this was his father, killed him and married the widow, his mother. The irony of the story lies in Oedipus's attempt to escape fate by leaving his adoptive parents' home, thereby actually fulfilling the prophecy.[1] Parenthetically, I would note that the biblical view does not always hold the divine decision as rigid and unchangeable as Greek fate. God could relent and could sometimes be persuaded by means of prayer, entreaty, or repentance. An extreme example is that of Abraham's negotiation with God in an attempt to save Sodom (Genesis 18). Ahab's fate in the battle of Ramoth-gilead was unchangeable, yet it was a conditional verdict, since he was free to decide against going to war, in which case, presumably, he would have been saved.

Disguise was occasionally designed to obtain information. This was a common tactic often employed by a ruler seeking temporary respite from the fear he inspired in the people around him: the disguise would enable his interlocutor to speak freely without fear of punishment. This was the technique of Haroun el-Rashid, a central figure in *A Thousand and One Nights,* who used to roam the streets of Baghdad in disguise.

The tragic story of Saul, the first king of Israel, who turned in desperation to a witch, falls into the same category of seeking information. The incident began with King Saul's army facing the Philistines on Mount Gilboa. According to the practices of the day, Saul asked the Almighty about the outcome of the impending battle, but "the LORD did not answer him, not by dreams, or by Urim, or by prophets" (1 Samuel 28:6). In despair Saul decided to consult a witch. Saul himself had destroyed witches, but he was told that one still remained at Endor. He understood that she would never help him knowing that he could have her put to death, so he decided to disguise himself. The witch did not recognize him. The two began a dialogue in which she expressed her fear of the death penalty imposed by Saul if she was to do as the stranger asked. Saul swore that she would come to no harm. She invoked the spirit of the dead prophet Samuel, whereupon she realized who her visitor really was. "When the woman saw Samuel, she cried out with a loud voice; and the woman said to Saul, 'Why have you deceived me? You are Saul!'" (1 Samuel 28:12). Saul's disguise, which had misled the witch, was worthless as soon as the spirit of the prophet Samuel appeared. The disguise could fool humans,

---

[1] Another legend from Greek mythology that illustrates the inability to escape fate is that of Perseus. King Argos received a prophecy that his daughter would bear a son who would kill him. To prevent this, he imprisoned his daughter. But the god Zeus entered her prison in the form of a shower of gold. She became pregnant by him, and she and the baby Perseus were thrown into the sea in a box. They were saved, and eventually Perseus (by mistake) killed his grandfather (Hamilton, *Mythology,* 197–99).

but not God or God's representative. Samuel's spirit recognized King Saul despite the disguise and exposed him to the witch.

This leads to two distinctions: the use of disguise to mislead the Lord cannot succeed, while the attempt to deceive humans, as related in biblical stories, usually works. Another important distinction that will continue to engage our attention is between disguise with intent to deceive, the results of which are on the purely physical-factual plane, and that used with the intention of eliciting the promise of legal rights.

The first category is manifest in Ahab's disguise. The physical impact of the weapon was on Ahab, king of Israel. Who the injured party was is not a legal question, but rather a purely factual matter. The biblical story of Tamar (Genesis 38) is in this respect similar. Tamar was married to Judah's son. After her husband's death she married his brother, who also died, leaving no offspring. She then disguised herself as a prostitute, managed to seduce Judah, her father-in-law, and thus obtained his seed—a physio-factual outcome by which she conceived and bore sons. These are physical facts that existed in reality and were not dependent on any legal determination. The law could attribute legal consequences to these facts. For example, Tamar giving birth to children could raise questions about their legal rights to inherit. In parallel, there could be a question of obligation, as, for example, the obligation to provide the children's maintenance. Nevertheless, Tamar's conception and delivery, achieved by means of disguise, were on a purely physical plane.

I shall illustrate the second category of disguise, the results of which are on the normative-legal plane, by starting with a hypothetical case. Let us assume that a man named Jacob seeks to offer payment to a young woman called Rachel. But at the rendezvous agreed between them, her sister Leah appears disguised as Rachel. Jacob, believing that the woman before him is Rachel, undertakes to make the payment to her. Here comes the question: Must Jacob pay the money to Rachel, to whom he had intended the obligation, or should he pay Leah, to whom he said the words—or is he exempt from making the payment extracted by subterfuge? There is no answer on the factual plane. The question relates to the way in which Jacob must behave, and this can only be done on the moral or legal level. Factually, nothing has occurred to change the physical reality apart from the few words spoken by Jacob. The significance of the event is entirely sociolegal.

Jacob's disguise as Esau to get his father's blessing and the Gibeonites' disguise in order to forge a pact with the children of Israel, which will be discussed shortly, both fall into this category of deception as a tactic in a legal action. Leah's disguise on her wedding night, which is discussed below, falls between the two categories: on the one hand, it was a legal act, a marriage contract (and, in principle, one could question the validity of the wedding). On the other hand, the marriage did involve a physical act—the consummation by Jacob and Leah.

The distinction between the two can be illustrated as follows: when the issue is disguise that leads to purely physical results, the law is at a loss to change reality. If the arrow that was shot indeed hit Ahab, the law could not restore him to life, and whether the arrow was aimed at Ahab or at what seemed to be a simple soldier becomes irrelevant. The arrow hit the man behind the disguise and killed him. The law can respond to physical results, whether deriving from the disguise or from some other cause, by imposing suitable punishment on those involved or by awarding damages. However, the physical reality of what happened is beyond the power of the law to change.

This is not the case in the second category, where a person aspires to acquire rights for himself or herself and to this end uses a disguise to mislead others. The validity of the rights derives from the law, and the law will not necessarily recognize rights acquired in this fashion. In this respect there is indeed a dramatic difference between the approach of modern legal systems and the worldview of the Bible, which will be discussed below. For the moment, I shall deal with the Bible stories that emphasize this second category.

The story of the Gibeonites is, in many respects, the most amazing tale of disguise in the Bible. It took place during the conquest of the country and the process of settlement of the people of Israel under the leadership of Joshua. The Israelites had been successful, and the nations standing in their way had been overcome by catastrophe. Their lands were conquered, and, in accordance with the command attributed to God, they were destroyed. Terror engulfed the peoples of the promised land. Some of them decided to unite against the common enemy. The Gibeonites looked for another way out. They had heard what Joshua had done to the towns of Jericho and Ai:

> They on their part acted with cunning: they went and prepared provisions, and took worn-out sacks for their donkeys, and wineskins, worn-out and torn and mended, with worn-out, patched sandals on their feet, and worn-out clothes; and all their provisions were dry and moldy. They went to Joshua in the camp at Gilgal, and said to him and to the Israelites, "We have come from a far country; so now make a treaty with us." (Joshua 9:4–6)

The children of Israel were suspicious and asked: "Perhaps you live among us; then how can we make a treaty with you?" (Joshua 9:7)—for, in such a case, God's command would have obliged them to destroy them and to settle on their lands. The men of Gibeon insisted that they were not inhabitants of Canaan but had come from a remote land. In support, they pointed to their clothes, their equipment, and their shoes worn out from the road. The argument was convincing, and the two nations made a pact between them, sealed by the oath of the princes of the congregation of Israel. Within three days the deception was uncovered, but the act could not be repudiated:

> But the Israelites did not attack them, *because the leaders of the congregation had sworn to them by the LORD, the God of Israel*. Then all the congregation murmured against the leaders. But all the leaders said to all the congregation, "*We have sworn to them by the LORD, the God of Israel*, and now we must not touch them." (Joshua 9:18–19, italics added)

Thus the Gibeonites were saved, though they were enslaved and became hewers of wood and drawers of water for the children of Israel. The oath sworn by the princes was valid and binding, despite the disguise and deception perpetrated by the Gibeonites. The issue of the legal validity of a contractual oath obtained by deceit clearly emerges from the story: the contract was binding. The same holds true with regard to the parties bound by the promise: Did the children of Israel's promise obligate them to the Gibeonites, or only to some people in a foreign land that the Gibeonites had chosen as their disguise? According to the Bible, the promise given to the Gibeonites was binding toward those who had participated physically in the ceremony, even if they did so in disguise. Neither the deception nor the disguise detracted from its validity.

The Gibeonite story is in a way more startling than the sale of Esau's birthright to Jacob and Isaac's blessing to his son disguised as his brother. The reason is that the birthright sale and the blessing conform to the general trend of the Bible, which attributes to God the intention of bestowing the birthright on Jacob. By contrast, the contract with the Gibeonites stands in stark conflict with God's commandment to destroy them. However, the agreement, though obtained through the Gibeonites' deception, remained in force—and even took precedence over the divine commandment.

A similar result appears in the story of Jacob's marriage to Leah. Jacob had worked for Laban seven years in return for Laban's promise to give him Rachel, his youngest daughter, to be his wife. At the end of the period, Jacob said, "Give me my wife . . . for my time is completed" (Genesis 29:21). Laban behaved as though acquiescing to the request. He gathered the local people and threw a party to celebrate the wedding. But that evening, at the end of the party, Laban took his daughter Leah, who had disguised herself as Rachel, and gave her to Jacob for his wife. It was only the following day that Jacob realized that a switch had been made:

> When morning came, it was Leah! And Jacob said to Laban, "What is this you have done to me? Did I not serve with you for Rachel? Why then have you deceived me?" Laban said, "This is not done in our country—giving the younger before the firstborn." (Genesis 29:25–26)

Jacob took part in the wedding ceremony. He was convinced that he was marrying Rachel. That was the agreement he had made with Laban. But it was Leah who was given to him, and it was she who slept with him. To the author of the story, there was no doubt as to the validity of Jacob's marriage to Leah, despite the mistake, for the physical contact had been with her, and that apparently was part of the wedding ceremony. It was also clear to the writer that there had been no marriage to Rachel, though she was the person supposedly presented to Jacob and whom he believed to be his bride. The bond was with Leah, precisely as in the pact in Joshua's time between the children of Israel and the Gibeonites who had shared in the ceremony, rather than the unknown people from afar. Yet there are two major differences. Firstly, Jacob had before his eyes the image of another woman, Rachel, whom he thought he was marrying. The children of Israel, in their pact with the Gibeonites, did not know the foreign people with whom they were entering into contract. The other difference lies in the physical contact—the consummation—of Jacob with Leah, while the agreement with the Gibeonites was only a formal ceremony, even though it involved an oath.

Esau was the older of the twins: "The first came out red, all his body like a hairy mantle; so they named him Esau. Afterward his brother came out, with his hand gripping Esau's heel; so he was named Jacob" (Genesis 25:25–26). Of the two, Rebekah, their mother, preferred Jacob, who was "a quiet man, living in tents," while Isaac loved Esau, the hunter, because "he was fond of game." The conflict between the two over the birthright began, according to the legend, in their mother's womb. The first stage came when Esau returned from the field exhausted and faint from hunger. Seeing Jacob cooking a lentil stew, he begged, "Let me eat some of that red stuff, for I am famished!" In exchange Jacob asked for Esau's birthright. His brother, at the end of his flagging strength, answered: "I am about to die; of what use is a birthright to me?" There ensued a ceremony of sale of the birthright for the stew—a transaction sealed by Esau's oath. Jacob, displaying largesse, gave Esau bread to go with the pottage. Esau ate and drank and went on his way, "having despised his birthright."

The second stage occurred when Isaac, now blind in his old age, sensed that his end was near. He called Esau and asked him to bring venison and prepare a meal, whereupon Isaac would give him his blessing before dying. Rebekah, hearing these words, decided to foil Isaac's intent. She called Jacob, dressed him in Esau's garments, put goatskins on his hands and neck, and sent him with dishes of savory meat to his father. Jacob presented himself as Esau. Isaac wondered that "the voice is Jacob's voice, but the hands are the hands of Esau," yet he was persuaded and gave his blessing: "Be lord over your brothers, and may your mother's sons bow down to you." Esau then appeared and Isaac realized that he had been tricked. He told Esau that Jacob had obtained the blessing through deception and that what had been done could not be reversed.

While Isaac, the initial target of the trick, apparently accepted the result, the indirect (and true) victim wanted his revenge. According to the story, Esau intended to kill Jacob: "The days of mourning for my father are approaching; then I will kill my brother Jacob" (Genesis 27:41). Beside the desire for revenge, Esau was showing his positive side. In order not to upset his father, he kept his temper and postponed the act until after Isaac's demise and the period of mourning. Isaac actually died many years later, and in the period that elapsed the brothers were reconciled. Rebekah, meanwhile, heard about Esau's plan, though it is not clear how she found out, since Esau had kept it to himself. Rashi explains that she had been told by the holy spirit. In any event, Jacob, the hero of the piece, was saved. Rebekah decided to send him to her family in Aram. To arrange that, she used diversionary tactics. She said nothing to Isaac about her fear that Jacob would be killed. Instead she told him that she was weary of "the Hittite women" whom Esau had married. Isaac commanded Jacob not to marry a Canaanite woman; he was to go to Rebekah's family in Aram to choose a wife. Jacob arrived at the home of Rebekah's brother, Laban, married his two daughters, Rachel and Leah, and, many years later, having fathered all his children (except for Benjamin, who was born in Canaan), he returned home. Esau met him, and they made their peace.

The English anthropologist James Frazer attempted, in *Folk-Lore in the Old Testament,* to explain the struggle for the inheritance between the two brothers in a possible context of reversed birthright: in other words, a custom based on the rights of the younger sons (ultimogeniture). He assumed that in certain periods inheritance was in fact dealt with in this way and took as his basis the Bible itself: Abraham's bequest fell not on his eldest, Ishmael, but on his youngest, Isaac. Thus it follows that Isaac, in giving his blessing to the younger Jacob, was only repeating his father's treatment of himself. Jacob also for a long time preferred Joseph, who, until the birth of Benjamin, was his youngest. Later, when Jacob was in Egypt, Joseph asked the old man to bless his sons. While blessing his grandsons, Jacob put his right hand on the younger Ephraim, not on the elder Manasseh. There are many more such cases. When Adam's sons, Cain and Abel, brought offerings to God, the Almighty preferred that of Abel, the youngest. David, king of Israel, was Jesse's youngest, and even Solomon, though not the youngest son, was given preference over his elder brother.

Additional support for Frazer's argument of inheritance by the younger son may be found in practices that exist in various places in Europe, Asia, and

Africa, of which Frazer brings many and varied examples. The explanation offered, and supported by the law historian Maitland,[2] was that the older sons would usually leave the parents' home to set up their own families. Thus it was the younger son who usually remained with his aging parents and accordingly would inherit upon their death.

This is an interesting explanation that conforms to a certain extent with the story of Ishmael's banishment. Nevertheless, I doubt that it fits the story of the conflict between Jacob and Esau, since Isaac wanted to respect Esau's birthright and never intended to grant precedence to his younger son. Moreover, it was Jacob who later had to flee from home, while Esau was the son who stayed with his parents.

In my view, at least, the preference of the younger brother in the Bible is based on a different concept. It is similar to the concept reflected in many biblical stories of barrenness and the miracle when a barren woman gives birth to offspring destined to be a hero or leader. In childhood, the youngest son is smaller and weaker than his brothers. By virtue of God's grace, the hero is able to overcome obstacles and the inferiority that marks his beginnings. This element is noticeable in the story of David and Goliath. David is the youngest son of Jesse and still a youth, yet he is destined to be king, and, despite his natural weakness, he succeeds in his mission—he overcomes the Philistine giant Goliath, who had bested the bravest of the warriors of Israel. Similar themes are found in many folk tales. The youngest son starts out from a position of inferiority and in the legendary miracle rises to greatness. Such is the thrust of "Puss in Boots," the story of three brothers, the elder of whom inherits a windmill, while the second gets a donkey. Nothing is left for the youngest except a cat. As the story evolves, the youngest, thanks to the cat, wins a fortune and the hand of the king's daughter in marriage. Here, of course, the younger son has no precedence in inheritance. Quite the contrary, it is his inferiority that underlines the miracle. Folk stories supply parallel tales of the younger sister eventually winning over her elder siblings.[3] Cinderella is one such variation, where the stepmother discriminates against her in favor of her own daughters. Cinderella's inferiority serves to emphasize the miracle when she wins the prince's hand. Andersen's "Ugly Duckling" turns the victim of his brothers' mockery into a full-fledged, beautiful swan.

---

[2] James George Frazer, *Folk-Lore in the Old Testament: Studies in Comparative Religion, Legend and Law* (abridged ed.; New York: Tudor, 1923), 176.

[3] Stith Thompson, *Motif-Index of Folk-Literature: A Classification of Narrative Elements in Folktales, Ballads, Myths, Fables, Mediaeval Romances, Exempla, Fabliaux, Jest-Books, and Local Legends* (rev. and enlarged ed.; 6 vols.; Bloomington: Indiana University Press, 1955–1958), 5:L50–L71.

To return to the legal aspects of the birthright conflict, the first stage was the lentil-stew transaction. In modern terms it could be argued that Esau's desperate hunger did not overpower his free will and that he valued the readily available stew over his elder son's birthright, the advantage of which could only come much later. Indeed, the story of the deal concludes with the words, "Thus Esau despised his birthright" (Genesis 25:34).

Nevertheless, it is likely that in modern law this transaction, if it was intended to give Jacob real economic advantage in the division of inheritance, could be avoided. In modern terminology it was an "unconscionable bargain," containing an element of exploitation, as defined in section 18 in the Israeli Law of Contracts. This section provides that a person is entitled to rescind a contract made as a result of the other party taking advantage of one's distress, weakness, or inexperience, and the terms of the contract are to an unreasonable degree worse than is customary. It is not clear whether Esau's hunger had reached the point of distress that would justify the application of this provision. Yet his words in asking for the stew—that he was dying and therefore the birthright was of no relevance—do indicate the severity of his condition.

In this context, the decisions of the English courts of equity are of special interest. There have been quite a few sons of aristocratic families who have led spendthrift lives in anticipation of future inheritance. While waiting, they got into financial difficulties that made them easy prey for moneylenders and other sharp figures who sought to acquire their inheritance rights or to "enslave" them. The equity courts, beginning in the second half of the seventeenth century, laid down rules for agreements about anticipated inheritance. Such agreements, which were in effect traps, known in English parlance as "catching bargains," could be avoided if the consideration given for the inheritance rights was inappropriate. This rule, which is still in force, holds for all cases of exploitation of someone who has an expectancy of receiving property in the future (not necessarily by inheritance) and who needs cash urgently, where one's interest has been purchased for a price below its value.[4]

To the biblical author, the deal was valid, and the author apparently saw nothing improper in it, even though the biblical term for that lentil stew—"mess of pottage"—still stands for a worthless return for a valuable asset (the phrase was used in the heading to Genesis 25 in the 1560 Geneva Bible). Moreover, the transaction was sealed with an oath, which in the biblical world made it valid even if extracted by deception, as we have seen in the case of the Gibeonites, and it was certainly not invalidated by exploitation or worthless

---

[4] Guenter H. Treitel, *The Law of Contract* (10th ed.; London: Sweet & Maxwell, 1999), 383.

consideration. This does not exhaust the problematics of the mess of pottage, as noted by Nili Cohen:

> An additional problem raised by the internal contractual deal struck between Jacob and Esau is its very legality or propriety. Did it relate to a deal that could be made or implemented? In our terms, we would ask: does primogeniture constitute an assignable right—a right that is tradable—or is it a personal right that is not transferable? . . . In the *Merchant of Venice* Shakespeare does not cast doubt on the legal validity of the pound of flesh transaction. Here the birthright is clearly not regarded as purely personal, but as an interest that could be traded—something in the nature of property, that could be exchanged or become the subject of a deal.[5]

Another question that the Bible does not clarify touches on the significance of that bargain, the sale of a birthright for a lentil stew. What in fact did Esau sell? Was it his right to inherit his father or to receive a bigger portion of the inheritance? According to the text, Esau attached no importance to his birthright. Was it because the anticipated bequest had little value, or was it so far in the future that Esau considered it irrelevant? According to the biblical law, the firstborn was entitled to a share twice that of his brothers (Deuteronomy 21:17). But this law was enacted only after the exodus from Egypt, namely, hundreds of years later than the patriarchs, and it is not clear how inheritance was divided in their time. It is conceivable that there was a similar law in the days of the patriarchs. It is also possible that the firstborn had a right to choose the kind of property (for example, real estate as opposed to livestock), with the remainder going to his brother. In any event, the biblical text does not say what happened to Isaac's estate after his death and how it was divided.

All we know is that, after Jacob received his father's blessing by deception, he fled to Mesopotamia and stayed for twenty years in Laban's home (Genesis 31:38). Upon his return, Jacob met his father, a meeting that is mentioned without any details (35:27). Immediately after it is stated that Isaac died at the age of one hundred and eighty and that his two sons, Esau and Jacob, buried him. Nothing is said about his property and whether it was divided between the sons, and if so, how. The book of *Jubilees*[6] describes how Isaac divided up his estate close to his death, giving the greater part to Esau and the lesser to Jacob (chapter 36). But Esau generously declared that he had sold his birthright and accordingly would take the smaller part and leave the larger for Jacob. The logic of the biblical account points to a different conclusion. The

---

[5] Nili Cohen, "Law and Book" (Hebrew), *Tel-Aviv University Law Review* 16 (1991): 435.

[6] A pseudepigraphical book from the second century B.C.E. that was not included in the Hebrew Bible.

families of the patriarchs were shepherds who moved with their herds. Most of the property was in movables, mainly sheep, cattle, and perhaps money. When Jacob fled to Mesopotamia, Isaac was old and blind. He therefore placed the management of his property in the hands of Esau, his favorite son. It can be assumed that the property remained Esau's after Isaac's death, though he might have given a part of it to Jacob. According to the story, Esau moved to the hill country of Seir with his flocks and herds, was living there when Jacob returned from Mesopotamia, and continued to do so afterwards. Jacob settled in Canaan and retained possession of the cave of Machpelah, the family burial place, because he lived nearby and possibly because of an agreement with Esau. It may be that in the division of Isaac's estate he received it to make up for the fact that the flocks and herds stayed with Esau.

So far we have considered the possibility that Esau's sale of the birthright to Jacob was an economic transaction relating to the firstborn's priority and advantage in the division of the father's estate. It is also conceivable that other advantages, such as status in the family, were at stake, rather than precedence in the inheritance. One legend about Jacob and Esau has it that Jacob wanted the precedence since, in those days, it was the firstborn who made sacrifices to the Lord, and he wanted that role in place of Esau, who, according to the same legend, was evil.[7] Jewish tradition stresses those aspects of the agreement. From this standpoint, Jacob's priority was intended to indicate that he, not Esau, would be the next in the chain of the family dynasty, which had begun with Abraham and continued through Isaac and which had been blessed with God's choice. It would then follow that Jacob and his sons would be granted God's promise of the land of Israel.[8]

Finally, it is possible that the sale of the birthright by Esau had to do with the right to receive the father's blessing. According to this interpretation, when Jacob dressed up as Esau he did so to obtain what had already been promised by the lentil-stew transaction,[9] even though the method was not fitting. The difficulty of this interpretation is that it is not clear if the agreement between Esau and Jacob was binding on their father, Isaac. An additional problem lies in the fact that Jacob and Rebekah had not gone to Isaac with the contention that Jacob was entitled to the blessing by virtue of the agreement. Instead, they resorted to subterfuge. Moreover, another biblical story implies that the giver

---

[7] *Genesis Rabbah* 63:13 and Rashi's interpretation of Genesis 25:31.

[8] For a discussion of the legends that attempt to explain the exclusive right of Jacob to the Holy Land, see Louis Ginzberg, *The Legends of the Jews* (trans. Henrietta Szold; 7 vols.; 1925; repr., Philadelphia: Jewish Publication Society of America, 1942), 5:320–21 n. 316.

[9] Cohen, "Law and Book," note 5 above.

of the blessing had the right to choose who would receive it. When Jacob himself was dying, he was asked to bless his grandsons, Manasseh and Ephraim. Jacob insisted on giving the more generous blessing to the younger son, Ephraim, by placing his right hand on his head. Although this was the blessing of a grandfather, not that of a father, it could suggest that there is no basis for the assumption that the eldest son was entitled to receive the more generous blessing. Perhaps Isaac had chosen to give his blessing to Esau not because he was the eldest (or not only for that reason) but because he loved Esau more than Jacob.

Now to the story of the blessing itself. It appears that, from a biblical viewpoint, the blessing was of a legal character. In the first part of this chapter a distinction was made between disguise and deception whose results are plainly on the physical-factual level and disguise designed to achieve results on the purely normative-legal level. Isaac's blessing to his son belongs to the second category. The issue is the binding force of the spoken words, given in the form of a blessing, which in the context of the story assume the quality of a promise or obligation. Clearly this was not Isaac's obligation, but his words seem to have been binding on the Creator, the guardian of history, so that God was required to ensure that Isaac's blessing to his son would indeed come to pass. Isaac intended the blessing to be for Esau, but Jacob participated in the ceremony disguised as Esau. Again the question, raised in other contexts, of whether a promise given in such circumstances is valid, and if so, whom does it benefit: Jacob, who took part in the ceremony, or Esau, who was the intended beneficiary? The biblical text is clear. It takes for granted that the validity of the blessing was not impaired by the deception and that the blessing inured to the benefit of Jacob. The explanation offered is as follows:

> The fact that the blessing was made and given to Jacob personally (even though he was disguised as Esau) is of central importance. . . . The fact that the blessing was made between those present overcomes the stratagem and the question of identity. The Bible assumes that the bond was created with Jacob. It was he who was standing before Isaac, which implies that he physically received the blessing. Once it was given, there could be no retraction. This was an expression of the rule of ascendancy of form over content, a characteristic of ancient legal systems. The physical form overcomes the spiritual-abstract intention. The blessing was obtained deviously, but it was given personally, not to Esau, but to Jacob who stood before Isaac. An analogy would be an arrow shot on the same occasion piercing Jacob's heart—not Esau's. The same goes for the blessing.[10]

This explanation, according to which the blessing (like the legal promise) parallels the arrow that struck Ahab, seems to me to reflect the biblical

---

[10] Ibid.

thinking. The distinction, discussed earlier, between a physical blow and a blessing or a legal obligation, does not exist in this thinking. We may assume that the blessing was given in a formal ceremony, in which Isaac placed his hands on Jacob's body (dressed as it was in Esau's garments) or on his head. Isaac felt Jacob, was convinced that he was Esau, and blessed him. Thus the blessing passed into Jacob's body. The fact that Jacob was disguised did not disrupt the flow.

Another way to explain the biblical conception is based on the assumption that the law was God's domain. Humans could use the rules of law in appropriate ceremonies of swearing an oath or giving a blessing, but the law was under God's supervision, and God knew the truth. God was not distracted by disguise or masks. Accordingly, if Isaac blessed the son who stood before him, God knew that it was Jacob, and therefore Jacob was the beneficiary of the blessing. The fact that Isaac was mistaken neither added to nor detracted from the blessing.

The modern conception of the validity of a legal action procured by trickery is completely different. It attributes the legal action not only to human act but also to human will. Accordingly it attaches a decisive importance to intention. If a person makes a legal transaction under a fundamental mistake, it may be invalidated, or its effects may be modified to conform to its author's intention. Hence, if a person gives an impostor a gift intended for someone else, modern legal systems would allow the donor to recover it back. If we regard Isaac's blessing as akin to a gift, there is no doubt that under modern law he could have revoked it. Furthermore, if we regard the blessing as a form of a will or testament, it is obvious that Isaac could have modified it once he discovered the fraud. The clear conclusion is, therefore, that modern law would reach a result contrary to that reflected in the biblical story.

Descriptions of a legal process reflecting a similar attitude to that of the biblical story are found in medieval literature. One example is the well-known story of Tristan and his love for Isolde.[11] Tristan grew up at the court of his uncle, King Mark, and excelled in many feats of valor. One day he was asked by his uncle to get for him the beautiful Isolde, daughter of the king of Ireland. Tristan's bravery and feats enabled him to ask the king for his daughter's hand, yet he did not ask for himself but for his monarch. To guarantee the success of the marriage, the queen of Ireland, Isolde's mother, gave her daughter's servant a love potion that Isolde and Mark were to drink on their wedding night. Tristan carried Isolde in his ship. On the way home to King Mark,

---

[11] Another example from Icelandic sagas is presented in the earlier chapter "David and Goliath: Trial by Combat," p. 40.

Tristan and Isolde drank the potion and spent a night of love on the ship. Henceforward their love for each other dominated the rest of their lives. According to the widely accepted version, the potion was taken by mistake. According to another dramatic reading, which is psychologically more impressive, Isolde was enraged that Tristan had requested her hand not for himself but for his king. She, therefore, gave Tristan the potion knowingly, intending to enslave him to her.[12] Whatever the case, Isolde married the king though her love link to Tristan continued. After many adventures, their enemies revealed the truth to King Mark, and Isolde was put on trial. Before the trial, Tristan disguised himself as a pauper (according to one version, as a leper). As Queen Isolde approached the place where the trial was to take place, she had to be carried across a stream. The disguised Tristan jumped forward, took her in his arms, and brought her to the shore. At Isolde's command, Tristan slipped and the two fell to the ground in an embrace. Isolde was taken to the scene of the trial, which was held in the presence of the legendary King Arthur. Called upon to take an oath, Isolde proposed to swear that she had never been in the arms of any man other than King Mark and the pauper who had just carried her before the eyes of a multitude. Her form of oath was approved by Mark and Arthur, and she so swore. Her words were put to the test of the divine ordeal and were found to be the truth.[13] The method of trial by ordeal was discussed earlier in the chapter about Solomon and Daniel, and the story of Isolde's trial is a literary example of its application.

It is clear that the story regards trial by ordeal as providing absolute proof of the truth of Isolde's oath. But her words contained mere "formal truth," which was actually a calculated deception based on Tristan's disguise. Isolde swore that she had been in no arms other than those of King Mark and the pauper. But the pauper was only a disguise, creating the impression that this could not be Tristan. In similar fashion, the children of Israel concluded from the words and disguise of the Gibeonites that they were not inhabitants of Canaan, and Isaac concluded that the figure in front of him was not Jacob but

---

[12] This version is presented by the French author, René Louis, in *Tristan et Iseult* (Paris: Librairie Général Française, 1972). This theme by which the hero acquires a beloved for another king repeats itself in the epic *The Nibelungen,* the great Germano-Scandinavian poem on which Richard Wagner based his famous opera series. In this poem, Siegfried acquires Brunhilde for King Guenther. The complications lead to the ensuing tragedy.

[13] The modern and most popular version of the Tristan and Isolde legend was published at the beginning of the twentieth century by Joseph Bedier. According to this version, Isolde underwent the hot-iron ordeal. This is also the version that appears in the earlier *Tristan,* written in the thirteenth century by Gottfried von Strassburg. But according to René Louis (*Tristan et Iseult*) the oath was on a sacred relic of bones.

Esau. For the purposes of the sacred oath sworn by Isolde, these circumstances made no difference. The disguise and the distraction had achieved their purpose. Paradoxically, it seems that the governing viewpoint is that of the cheat—when Isolde swore that no one had held her in his arms other than King Mark and the poor wretch, she saw the pauper as Tristan. From her standpoint it was the truth, though based on a lie presented to the public as though Tristan was not her lover, while the pauper was a stranger unknown to anyone. But the real explanation is that the test was trial by divine ordeal. God knew the truth: the wretch was Tristan. Therefore, Isolde's oath conformed to the reality obvious to God, who was not deceived by disguises.

When Jacob receives Isaac's blessing, he understands that the benediction is being given to him, while to Isaac he presents the lie. When the children of Israel make a compact with the Gibeonites, the latter know that the treaty is made with them, though the victims of the deception believe that they have made a pact with the people of a far-off country. What counts is the formal pattern—the oath ceremony. The intention of the participants—who have been taken in by the trick (Isaac in blessing his son, the children of Israel making a treaty with the people of an unknown nation, the organizers of Isolde's trial by ordeal)—is of no consequence. The ceremony is binding, and its results are decisive, ignoring the lost link between the meaning imparted to it and the intention of the naive side participating in it.

Isolde's oath can be compared to the case of the hollow cane *(kanya deraba)* presented in the Babylonian Talmud *(Nedarim* 25a). This is the case of a man who sued his friend for a sum of money that he had lent him. The borrower claimed that he had paid off the loan, so the two presented themselves for trial before Raba, who ruled that the judgment had to be resolved by a sworn oath by the borrower. The borrower went home, took a hollow cane, placed the money inside it, and returned to the court, where he leaned on the cane. When called upon to swear, the borrower asked the lender to hold the cane so that he could swear on the Bible. Taking the Bible in his hand, he swore that he had returned the money to the lender. The angry plaintiff slammed the cane, which broke, spilling the coins on the ground.

The most amazing point in the story of the hollow cane, as described in the Talmud, is in its conclusion, that the coins falling out of the broken cane proved that the oath was true. To us, of course, this was a false oath—the borrower had not repaid the creditor. He only handed him the cane for a moment, meaning to get it back. This did not constitute repayment of the loan or the return of the coins, which the borrower was supposed to give to the lender permanently. But in those days that oath was considered to be true. The formal setting, in which the defendant gave the plaintiff the cane in which the coins were concealed, was enough to validate the oath. An earlier version of this tale is found in a Hellenistic essay from the first century B.C.E. From there it found its way into German literature and church literature, where it was enhanced by a miracle performed by Saint Nicholas, upon whose altar the oath was sworn. The view that the trick may effectively ensure the truth of the oath is common to all the versions of the story. Indeed, it is their essence.[14]

The explanation of this point is similar to that of Isolde's oath. However, there is a basic distinction between the two. While Isolde was acquitted in her trial, the borrower in the final resort failed. Though his oath was considered to be the truth, it seems reasonable to assume that once the cane was broken and the coins fell out, the lender was entitled to have them. There is a double explanation: first, though both cases were covered by the formal conception of the oath, the moral view in the talmudic story did not allow the perpetrator to emerge victorious. Second, Tristan and Isolde were the heroes of a love story, and their transgressions were forgiven because of their love. The author and the audience could easily sympathize with the trick played by the lovers. In the talmudic version there is not one positive attribute about the borrower seeking to avoid repayment of his debt.[15]

It is interesting to note that even in much later periods we find expression of this approach. English law recognizes the form of promise in a document under seal. Today there is little doubt that such a promise could be avoided on the ground of fraud, trickery, or undue influence, and in this context it would be judged like an ordinary contract. But in the past it was covered by a rule similar to the biblical concept, according to which whoever signed such a document would not be able to plead fraud or even duress (except in very extreme cases).[16]

Acts of disguise in the Bible include Jacob's dressing as Esau to gain his father's blessing; the Gibeonites disguising themselves as inhabitants of a remote land in order to make a pact with the children of Israel, thereby preventing their extermination; Tamar's disguise as a prostitute to obtain Judah's seed; and Leah's appearance as Rachel at her marriage to Jacob. All these stories have common elements. First, in all of them the disguise serves to deceive.

---

[14] The subject is discussed in detail in Itzhak England, "Kanya Deraba, Nicholas' Altar and the Chain of David: The Problem of Deception in an Oath" (Hebrew), *Tarbiz* 52 (1983): 591, which examines many versions of the story and the halakic debate over the fitting form of oaths.

[15] An outcome in which the borrower finally fails is common to all the versions of the story discussed by England (ibid.). In some of them the borrower receives an additional punishment.

[16] Alfred W. Brian Simpson, *The Rise of the Action of Assumpsit* (vol. 1 of *A History of the Common Law of Contract*; Oxford: Clarendon, 1975), 99.

There is nothing remarkable about that—disguise, if not used as a game or a joke or as a theatrical device, is intended to mislead. But it is characteristic of all these stories that the act of trickery, achieved by means of disguise, succeeds, and the perpetrator achieves his or her purpose. The second common denominator is that the biblical author shows understanding for the deceptive act. It is not depicted as a sin or crime, and in none of the cases is there any moral condemnation of the stratagem of disguise and deception in the story. The perpetrator is not only exempt from punishment by humans or God (nowhere does the Lord threaten or harm the perpetrator), but also gains the full benefit aimed for.[17]

This aspect of the act of disguise is common to many other deceptions described in the Bible, to which I devote the next chapter. In the present context I will refer only to the course of events that relate to Isaac's blessing given to Jacob. After receiving the benediction, Jacob's life was full of hardships and tragedies. He fled to Mesopotamia, where he was indentured to his uncle who cheated and exploited him for twenty years. After fleeing from Laban, Jacob's beloved wife Rachel died giving birth to Benjamin. His much-loved son, Joseph, was sold into slavery and taken to Egypt, and Jacob was convinced that a wild beast had devoured him. His daughter, Dinah, was raped, and his eldest son, Reuben, slept with Bilhah, Rachel's maidservant. It is no wonder that Jacob, standing before Pharaoh, complained that "few and hard have been the years of my life" (Genesis 47:9). Jacob's hardships and torments could be seen as punishment for the way he obtained his father's blessing, thereby implying the Bible's reservations about the act. But this interpretation does not fit well with the traditional approach, according to which Jacob was entitled to the precedence. Nor does it fit the fact that Jacob became the father of the tribes of Israel, and the entire people of Israel were named after him (the name Israel was bestowed on Jacob after his struggle with the angel). Moreover, the Bible itself does not relate Jacob's tribulations to the deception of the blessing, and it is impossible to find any reservations about the act in the text.

---

[17] See also Sternberg, *Poetics of Biblical Narrative*, 458 and 537–38 n. 12, for a discussion of deception in the Bible. Sternberg alludes to the fact that the Bible makes frequent use of the term "fraud" (and synonyms such as "guile" and "subterfuge"), without attaching a negative value judgment to them. Thus, for example, in the case of the rape of Dinah, it is said that the sons of Jacob responded deceptively to Shechem's proposal to give Dinah to his son for a wife, demanding that all the sons of Shechem be circumcised. Shechem accepted this demand and when the sons of Shechem were in pain, two brothers of Dinah killed them and released Dinah from captivity. This trick carried no negative implication since it is justified by the circumstance. The classic Aramaic translation of the Bible, known as *Targum Onqelos*, gives the term "deception" as "wisdom." In Sternberg's view, this is farfetched, since the use of the term in the Bible is flexible, and there are contexts in which the connotation is negative.

Tradition has sought to deal with the issue of the blessing through a large number of legendary stories, which offer two principal contentions. The first is that Jacob was entitled to the birthright from the beginning but was unjustly deprived of it. The second is that Jacob was the symbol of innocence, while Esau was the symbol of evil. Accordingly, Jacob was entitled to the blessing, while the evil Esau was undeserving. The first argument appears in a legend in which Esau was already fighting with Jacob in their mother's womb over who would emerge first and gain the right of primogeniture. Esau then threatened Jacob that if he did not let him come out first, he would kill their mother. Jacob, upon hearing this terrible threat, gave way, thereby allowing Esau to gain the precedence.[18] The second argument is found in such statements as that Esau had committed five crimes on the day that Abraham (their grandfather) died: "he ravished a betrothed maiden, committed murder, doubted the resurrection of the dead, scorned the birthright, and denied God."[19] The dubious transaction of the birthright for a lentil stew is explained by stating that Jacob was seeking the right then reserved to the eldest to make sacrifices to the Lord and to prevent this being done by the evil Esau, who reviled the faith.[20] It was said of the blind Isaac that he was not only stricken by physical blindness but also by spiritual blindness, that the Divine Spirit deserted him so that he could not discern the nature of the evil Esau.[21] Rebekah did what she did not from love of Jacob but to save the righteous Isaac from stumbling by giving the blessing to Esau.[22]

There is no hint of any of this in the biblical text itself. To a certain degree the contrary can be seen. It can be assumed that Esau loved his father and cared for him and that Isaac's love for Esau was not unfounded. Esau also forgave Jacob for all his tricks and allowed him to return safely to Canaan. But this does not detract from the importance of these legends. It is a literature that portrays a development of major significance—in effect, a revolution in moral understanding. While the period in which the biblical stories were shaped took no particular exception to disguise and trickery (and perhaps even saw cause to admire the perpetrators), later periods adopted a moral stance that could not reconcile itself to acts of this kind. The new conception gave birth to the legends that endeavored to put a different coloring on the story of the conflict over the birthright.

---

[18] Ginzberg, *Legends of the Jews,* 1:313–14.

[19] Ibid., 1:318, based on Babylonian Talmud, *Bava Batra* 16b.

[20] See note 7 above, p. 53.

[21] *Genesis Rabbah* 65:4, cited in Ginzberg, *Legends of the Jews,* 1:329.

[22] Ginzberg, *Legends of the Jews,* 1:331.

Postscript: Isaac's Benediction and the Issue of Its Manifestation

The story of Isaac's blessing ends in a touching scene describing Esau's agony and distress. Having learned that Jacob had fraudulently received the blessing intended for him, he cried to his father: " 'Have you only one blessing, father? Bless me, me also, father.' And Esau lifted up his voice and wept" (Genesis 27:38). But the deed could not be undone. Esau received a modest blessing, which stated expressly that he would remain subordinate to Jacob. At the core of Isaac's blessing to Jacob are the following words: "Let peoples serve you, and nations bow down to you. Be lord over your brothers, and may your mother's sons bow down to you" (Genesis 27:29). Isaac was unable to give the same blessing to Esau. If the blessing determined that Jacob would be lord over Esau (though Isaac had not intended this), it was no longer possible, after the deception was discovered, to make Esau lord over Jacob. But did the blessing indeed manifest itself? In the conflict between the children of Israel and the Edomites—who according to tradition were the offspring of Esau—the answer is at least in part affirmative. Edom was conquered in the days of King David, and it is even related that Joab, the general of David's armies, "killed every male in Edom" (1 Kings 11:16). But the Edomites recovered. In the Hasmonean (the Maccabees) period, they were conquered by John (Johanan) Hyrcanus (second century B.C.E.), who forced them to convert. The result was that, shortly thereafter, the kingdom of Israel fell to Herod, an Edomite and the product of this conversion. Herod wiped out the Hasmonean dynasty and ruled the country, under Roman patronage, with an iron hand.

The principal difficulty with Isaac's blessing lies in the words: "Let peoples serve you, and nations bow down to you." That did not happen. Throughout its long history, the nation of Israel enjoyed periods of independence, in which it even ruled other nations. But these were relatively short episodes, and most of the time Israel was enslaved by other peoples. One of the legends suggests that Jacob and Esau divided the inheritance between them and that Esau (perhaps as representative of the nations of the world) inherited this world while Jacob inherited the next. This legend enjoys the advantage that no one has ever complained about breach of promise regarding the world to come.

4

The Fruits of Deceit

※

The Torah has several prohibitions of deceit (Leviticus 25:13–17), even when used to defraud strangers (Leviticus 19:33), but there are many tales that point to a very different system of law and moral values. Like many other biblical laws, the prohibition of fraud is not evident in the stories of the Torah and the books of the Prophets.

The previous chapter on "Stories of Disguise" describes many acts designed to fool others, among them Jacob's disguise as Esau to get his father's blessing, the Gibeonites' pretense to come from a distant land so as to get a treaty with the Israelites and avoid extermination, Tamar's act as a prostitute to get Judah to lie with her, and Leah's disguise as Rachel to marry Jacob. All these tricks succeeded, and the text does not evince any moral condemnation or reservation about these uses of disguise and deceit.

Disguise is a subgroup in the wider category of fraud that abounds in the Bible. The common denominator is forgiveness—the deceiver is not punished but usually achieves his or her aim. Meanwhile, the victim often suffers serious harm without compensation. Occasionally the victim voices strong criticism, but the perpetrator wins the prize. Genesis offers its share of successful deceit. Abraham, fearing that the Egyptians would kill him in order to take his wife, decided to present her as his sister. The result is predictable. Pharaoh took Sarah, "and for her sake he dealt well with Abram; and he gave him sheep, oxen, male donkeys, male and female slaves, female donkeys, and camels" (Genesis 12:16). Abraham was rewarded for his deceit, but God, angry at the deed, chose to punish Pharaoh: "But the LORD afflicted Pharaoh and his house with great plagues because of Sarai, Abram's wife" (Genesis 12:17). According to biblical concepts, Pharaoh committed adultery. That he did so in all innocence, as a result of Abraham's deceit, did not detract from his responsibility. No wonder that Pharaoh complained, "What is this you have done to me? Why did you not tell me that she was your wife? Why did you say, 'She is my sister,' so that I took her for my wife? Now then, here is your wife, take her, and be gone" (Genesis 12:18–19). The text reveals nothing of Abraham's response to this. Pharaoh expelled Abraham but there were no other sanctions, and Abraham departed from Egypt with his wife and all that Pharaoh had paid for her.

A similar affair, with Abraham and Sarah on one side, and King Abimelech of Gerar on the other, is described in Genesis 20. Abraham, having returned from his successful venture with Pharaoh, presented Sarah to the king of Gerar as his sister. Abimelech also complained that Abraham had deceived him. This time Abraham chose to explain: "Besides, she is indeed my sister, the daughter of my father but not the daughter of my mother; and she became my wife" (Genesis 20:12).[1] This is a poor excuse—even if Sarah was his sister, presenting her as such was deceitful, for it suggested that she was no more than that. In modern jurisprudence such a description would be called a "half-truth," being technically or formally correct, offering a partial picture that is highly misleading.[2] In any event, Abraham emerged again safely from this affair.

Genesis 26 describes a similar incident in the next generation. This time the parties are Isaac and Rebekah, and the ruler is once again Abimelech. Isaac introduces his wife Rebekah as his sister. When the fraud is revealed, Abimelech complains: "So she is your wife! Why then did you say, 'She is my sister'?" In contrast to Abraham's evasive answer, Isaac responds honestly: "Because I thought I might die because of her" (Genesis 26:9). His fear of death justified the deceit.

The deceits described above tell us little about the Bible's attitude to fraud. Both Abraham and Isaac acted with the threat of death hanging over them, and it could be argued that a lie essential to preserving life cannot be criticized. Neither Pharaoh nor Abimelech deserved much sympathy. They were rulers who took women from the families of shepherds who crossed their lands and did not hesitate to use force to obtain them. Pharaoh indeed paid Abraham for Sarah, showing some generosity. Yet Abraham saw no alternative but to make the deal, and, in the circumstances, he derived maximum benefit.

---

[1] The issue of marriage between brother and sister is discussed later in the chapter "Levirate Marriage and Incest," pp. 248–49, 251–52.

[2] Traditional commentators have also described Abraham's excuse as hollow. Nahmanides, in his commentary on Genesis 20:12, says: "I know no justification for the apology, for if she truly was his sister and wife, and in their desire for a woman they told them she was his sister, to mislead them, he wronged them by bringing upon them a great sin."

Another act of deceit described in Genesis relates to Rachel's theft of idols when Jacob, after consulting both Rachel and Leah, decided to leave Laban's house with all his property. The departure was surreptitious for fear of Laban's opposition. Jacob exploited the opportunity of Laban's absence from home, as did Rachel, his wife: "Now Laban had gone to shear his sheep, and Rachel stole her father's household gods" (Genesis 31:19). Laban and his brothers set off in hot pursuit, catching up with Jacob at Mount Gilead. He did not dare harm Jacob, for God had warned him in a dream: "Take heed that you say not a word to Jacob, either good or bad" (Genesis 31:24). But Laban challenged him, "Why did you steal my gods?" Jacob, not knowing of the theft, denied the accusation and offered to let Laban search his tents: "But anyone with whom you find your gods shall not live. . . . Point out what I have that is yours, and take it" (Genesis 31:32). Unaware that the culprit was his beloved wife, Jacob pronounced a sentence of death. Laban started his search and reached Rachel's tent: "Now Rachel had taken the household gods and put them in the camel's saddle, and sat on them. Laban felt all about in the tent, but did not find them. And she said to her father, 'Let not my lord be angry that I cannot rise before you, for the way of women is upon me.' So he searched, but did not find the household gods" (Genesis 31:34–35).

Rachel's deception succeeded, and Laban failed to find his stolen property. Rachel's distress is understandable with the threat of death hovering over her. It could also be argued that Laban was himself a sinner and therefore deserved what he got. But the fact remains that the regular biblical formula, by which the deceiver comes out on top, recurs in this story. Later commentaries, accepted by Rashi and Ibn Ezra, viewed Jacob's promise that the thief would not live as a curse, since Rachel died on the way to Canaan, giving birth to Benjamin. This interpretation derives from a moralistic view that developed much later and has no foundation in the story itself. In my view, Jacob's words were not a curse but rather the sentence that he (or Laban) would pronounce on the thief.

Another example of deceit in distress appears in 1 Samuel 21 in the account of David's flight from Saul. David reached Nob, the city of priests, where he lied to Ahimelech that he was on a mission for the king. He received food and weapons and moved on. Again, the one who is punished is the victim of the lie—when Saul discovered that David, whom he regarded as a rebel, had received aid from Nob, he ordered the execution of Ahimelech and the priests of Nob and the destruction of their city. David escaped unscathed.

Deceitful acts to escape the threat of death are understandable, but the pattern that rewards the deceiver and punishes the victim occurs also where there is no such danger. Isaac blessing Jacob, who was disguised as Esau, is a prime example. In Jacob's subsequent flight he encountered his uncle Laban, who surpassed him at deception. The two made an agreement that Jacob would receive in marriage Rachel, Laban's youngest daughter, in return for seven years' labor. At the end of his term of service, Laban delivered Leah disguised as her younger sister. Jacob protested that he had been cheated, but Laban dismissed the charge with the argument that the younger daughter may not be married when the elder is still unwed. This feeble excuse apparently justified the deception. Jacob accepted the result, having little alternative. Laban held the upper hand, for he was head of the family. So Jacob labored another seven years to win his beloved Rachel. Again the deceiver is rewarded, and the victim concedes. God does not intervene. There are some acts that bring down the wrath of the Almighty. In the book of Genesis, God killed Onan, the son of Judah, for the grave sin of disobeying the commandment to marry and impregnate Tamar, his deceased brother's widow. But deception does not fall in this category: Laban was not punished. On the contrary, the marriage between Jacob and Leah, founded in deceit, became a central element in the tradition of the people of Israel and a reason for their existence to the present day.

Two famous fraudulent acts described in Judges relate to the wars fought by Israel with its neighbors. Both involve women, and in both the trick succeeds and the victim comes to a bitter end. The first is during the war of Deborah and Barak son of Abinoam against King Jabin of Hazor and Sisera, the captain of the king's armies. Sisera was defeated in a battle at the foot of Mount Tabor. He fled on foot, reaching the tent of Jael, wife of Heber the Kenite. Jael invited him in: "Turn aside, my lord, turn aside to me; have no fear" (Judges 4:18). The exhausted Sisera accepted the invitation, entered the tent, and lay down to sleep. Jael took a hammer and drove a tent peg into Sisera's temple. Deborah's song praised this act. This is understandable, given that a bitter enemy of Israel has been eliminated. In the second case, the situation is reversed. This time the woman, Delilah, belongs to the enemy nation and her victim is the legendary hero of the tribe of Dan. The motive is not nationalistic but pure greed. The Philistines offered Delilah a bribe to hand Samson over to them. She tempted him to reveal the source of his strength. Learning that the answer lay in his hair, she sedated him, shaved his head, then summoned the Philistines. They took him prisoner and put out his eyes. Delilah received the promised reward, with no hint of punishment for her treachery. We do not even know if she was in the temple of Dagon when Samson, in his last act of heroism, brought down the edifice on its occupants, crying, "Let me die with the Philistines" (Judges 16:30).

Another deceit, to which I devote a separate chapter, has to do with a man of God, who prophesied to Jeroboam and was misled by an aging prophet at Bethel. Here it suffices to note the recurring pattern of success to the deceiver and severe punishment to the victim.

How to explain this approach? It seems to be based on ancient concepts. Morality, and following it early jurisprudence, focused on the prohibition of physical harm, primarily of murder. Thereafter it related to damage to property (theft) and, of course, to ritual offenses. Other transgressions were permissible and even respected as legitimate stratagems in the struggle for existence, for honor or prestige. This is the reason the Bible contains so many stories of deceit in which the perpetrators are rewarded. Fraud and deceit, which in our day would be considered wrong, are for the ancients acceptable and not deserving of judicial action.

Guile was regarded as a praiseworthy talent, legitimate in the attainment of just ends. This, to my mind, is the explanation for many of the stories and the manner in which they are told. Jacob is the younger son, but his shrewdness enables him to win the birthright for the mess of pottage agreement that he makes with his naive brother. The transaction leaves no stain on his character but rather highlights the shrewdness with which he manages his affairs. The disguise used to win the blessing from his equally naive father is not illegitimate but rather proof of his mother Rebekah's intelligence as well as his luck and talent. The tactic used by Tamar to acquire Judah's seed shows initiative, dedication of purpose, and worthiness of the status of matriarch to the tribe of Judah. Rachel's deceit in stealing her father's household gods and hiding them displays similar initiative that exempts her from punishment.

A similar attitude of the ancient world is found in the *Iliad* and *Odyssey*. The artful Odysseus is the hero of the Greek epic named after him. Slyness and deceit mark his power and talent and the secret of his greatness and enable him to overcome every obstacle.

Though the slyness of the serpent in the story of creation is condemned, it is in relation to the violation of God's commandment. In all other contexts, deceit is treated with tolerance and even admiration. Subterfuge was always considered legitimate in struggles between nations, and it is perhaps so still today. Odysseus used his craftiness mainly against enemies; Joshua employed cunning in the conquest of Canaan. The incidences of deceitful behavior to parents and relatives, as in the families of Isaac, Jacob, and Laban, belong to a different category, yet all fall in a value system that permitted and even admired slyness and subterfuge in the attainment of one's ends.

Postscript: Speech, Vows, and Oaths

A society in which deceit and breach of promise are tolerated and even encouraged must inevitably face functional difficulties and be prone to disintegration. When people cannot rely on the word of their associates, they must behave in similar fashion. They will avoid paying today for future goods and will not assist their allies for fear that they will not be repaid in a similar way. It therefore becomes necessary to find a mechanism that negates the usual exemption from truth telling and breach of promise, one in which a promise given can be relied upon.

Such a mechanism did exist in the biblical world and in the ancient world. This was the system of oath and vow.[3] Words in themselves are not binding. To ensure their validity and honesty it is necessary to involve divine intervention and the threat of divine sanctions. The oath, with its implied fear of divine punishment if it is not kept, greatly increases its reliability.

The other side of the tolerance of deceit in the Bible is the extensive use of oaths. When Abraham wished to make sure that his servant Eliezer would find for his son Isaac a wife from his homeland, he made him swear a ceremonial oath: "Abraham said to his servant, the oldest of his house, who had charge of all that he had, 'Put your hand under my thigh and I will make you swear by the LORD, the God of heaven and earth, that you will not get a wife for my son from the daughters of the Canaanites, among whom I live, but will go to my country and to my kindred and get a wife for my son Isaac' " (Genesis 24:2–4).

An oath-swearing ceremony also took place between Laban and Jacob after Laban's pursuit of Jacob and his wives. When the search for the images hidden by Rachel proved fruitless, the two men made an alliance. Both were very experienced in sly acts, both had reaped benefits, and both had learned the sorrow and pain of being the victim. This time they wanted an honest deal. In those days, the oath ceremony was the instrument that required even the greatest of tricksters to make a promise with reasonable expectation that it would be kept. The ceremony is described in detail, and the two men erected a monument of stones as evidence of their oath and alliance.[4]

---

[3] In the ancient world, an oath suggested that God would punish its giver for telling a lie or for failing to keep a promise. A vow was usually an obligation made not to another person but directly to God. Thus while the oath sworn to another is supported by God's power, the vow is given to God and others need not know of it. The vow might relate to other people, as it did in the case of Jephthah, who sacrificed his daughter, but it was not made to her, was not known to her, and was not designed to affect her behavior. The oath, therefore, is intended to influence others, while the vow only influences its maker and God. It could be said that in the case of an oath, God's function is "indirect," while in the case of a vow God is "a direct party."

[4] Frazer (*Folk-Lore in the Old Testament*, 243–50) describes the custom of oaths over stone monuments that was practiced in various tribes and nations. It is based on the belief that the solidity of the stone would ensure the solidity of the words, of the speaker, and of the one to whom they were directed. Sometimes it is believed that the stone possesses the power to harm the giver of lying oaths. Tamar Alexander compares

Another aspect of oaths and vows touches on their formal foundations. The formal-ceremonial basis of the oath having been observed, there was an absolute obligation to keep the promise. An argument that the oath was given in error or with lack of true understanding of its implications was not a viable option. The formal side was conclusive, no matter what the outcome. Thus the Israelites were required to keep their oath to the Gibeonites, though it had been extracted by deceit. Thus Jephthah was obliged to sacrifice his daughter, and Jonathan, the son of Saul, was almost put to death for breaking the oath to fast until evening to which his father had sworn the Israelites.

The formal aspect of an oath also determined its limitations, for it could be manipulated, and tricks could be used to circumvent it. The Gibeonites manipulated the Israelites into swearing an oath, the implications of which were not understood at the time. The previous chapter on "Stories of Disguise" showed how Queen Isolde succeeded in manipulating her oath to survive the divine test, even though she had been unfaithful to her husband. The *kanya deraba* story that appears in the same chapter illustrates the many ways in which an oath can be misused.

---

the role of the stone monument with that of the inhuman witnesses in the story of "The Rat and the Pit" ("The Broken Oath," in *Readings from Genesis* [Hebrew] [ed. Ruti Ravitsky; Tel-Aviv: Yediot Aharonot, 1999], 234).

5

Samson Loses a Bet

Samson's escapades, as described in the book of Judges, are written in a different style from other biblical stories.[1] They have an aura of childish adventures and mischievousness, with a flash of humor not found in other chapters of the Bible. Only the book of Esther, which takes place in a completely different setting from the somber context of Judges, contains a few similar elements. The main difference between the two is that Samson's tale is a tragedy interspersed with moments of comedy, while that of Esther is a farce from beginning to end.

Samson's revenge against the Philistines, provoked by his wife's father giving her to one of Samson's Philistine colleagues, is portrayed as an impish child's prank. Samson traps three hundred foxes, ties them in pairs by their tails, inserts a fiery torch in the knot, and sends them forth to burn Philistine cornfields.

In response, the Philistines burn his wife and father-in-law, whereupon he responds by thrashing them. This time they decide to catch him. They threaten the Israelites, who turn their hero over, bound hand and foot. Samson exerts his immense strength, breaks the bonds, and in the battle that ensues he beats a thousand men with the jawbone of a donkey, crying out: "With the jawbone of a donkey, heaps upon heaps, with the jawbone of a donkey I have slain a thousand men" (Judges 15:16). Even here it is difficult to avoid the

---

[1] Robert Graves offers the explanation that Samson, whose name in Hebrew evidences a link to the sun (*shemesh* in Hebrew means sun), was originally a Philistine sun god whose exploits were incorporated into the Bible (*The White Goddess* [New York: Vintage, 1958], 344). Graves brings other examples from mythology in which heroes paid with their lives for revealing their vulnerabilities to their lovers.

conclusion that Samson's choice of weapon was intended not only to kill but also to mock the Philistines—again part of the somewhat coarse humor that typifies the Samson story cycle. This is particularly marked in Samson repeating the word "donkey," in the Hebrew original version, no less than four times.

The same holds true for the riddle posed to the Philistines by Samson, as described in Judges 14. Samson, who is planning to marry a Philistine woman, stays with his parents in Timnah. There, in the vineyards, a young lion attacks him. Barehanded, he tears the lion apart "as one might tear apart a kid." Some days later he returns to the spot and "there was a swarm of bees in the body of the lion, and honey. He scraped it out into his hands, and went on, eating as he went" (Judges 14:8–9). The wedding feast took place immediately thereafter, with the participation of thirty young Philistine men. This is where he poses his famous riddle:

> "Let me now put a riddle to you. If you can explain it to me within the seven days of the feast, and find it out, then I will give you thirty linen garments and thirty festal garments. But if you cannot explain it to me, then you shall give me thirty linen garments and thirty festal garments." So they said to him, "Ask your riddle; let us hear it." He said to them, "Out of the eater came something to eat. Out of the strong came something sweet." (Judges 14:12–14)

Unable to solve the riddle, the Philistines decide to take by force what they cannot get by wit. They threaten Samson's wife: "Coax your husband to explain the riddle to us, or we will burn you and your father's house with fire. Have you invited us here to impoverish us?" (Judges 14:15). The threat pays off. She needles Samson through the seven days of the feast, and he, with his strong body but soft heart—especially for his ladies—reveals the answer. She promptly tells her compatriots, who proudly reply to Samson: "What is sweeter than honey? What is stronger than a lion?" (Judges 14:18). Samson understands the source of their answer: "If you had not plowed with my heifer, you would not have found out my riddle."

His response is characteristic. Recognizing that he has lost the bet, Samson decides to repay the Philistines—he pays his debt, but with property looted from other Philistines: "And he went down to Ashkelon. He killed thirty men of the town, took their spoil, and gave the festal garments to those who had explained the riddle" (Judges 14:19). Thus the Philistines' win becomes punishment for their countrymen. As the plot develops, Samson abandons the wife who revealed the solution. Her father assumes that he has divorced her and gives her to another. Samson responds with the foxes. The Philistines retaliate by burning his wife and her father. The irony of it all is that Samson's wife, who revealed the secret and betrayed her husband's trust to escape burning, ends up with exactly the fate she tried to avoid.

The Philistines burn her without remembering that her betrayal had won them the bet.

Here it is worth noting a point that seems obvious. Samson, like the narrator, had no doubt that he had lost the bet. The conclusion was so clear that there could not be any dispute. He had posed a riddle and gambled on the Philistines' inability to solve it. The gift of making riddles and solving them was a sign of wisdom in the ancient world. Even God, when revealed to humans in a dream, often expressed meanings in riddle form.[2] One who could solve a dream riddle had a divine spark. Joseph won a high position in Egypt and the name Zaphenath-paneah for interpreting the dreams of Pharaoh and his chief butler and baker. It was also to Daniel's great credit that he interpreted Nebuchadnezzar's dream.

Respect for the ability to pose and solve riddles appears in many folk tales, to some extent to the present day. The Queen of Sheba came to try King Solomon with riddles, and he knew how to answer all of them (1 Kings 10:3). But each nation has its own stories, and Solomon did not win such an elevated status among other peoples. Flavius Josephus quoted an author named Dius who described a riddle contest between Solomon and King Hiram of Tyre. Hiram was unable to solve Solomon's riddles and had to pay a sizeable forfeit. But a resident of Tyre named Abedhemon did succeed in resolving all of Solomon's puzzles while Solomon was unable to solve his. This time Solomon had to pay Hiram.[3]

Greek mythology tells of Oedipus, who, on his way to Thebes, had to pass a terrible sphinx. Anyone who couldn't solve a riddle posed by the sphinx was condemned to death at the hands of the monster. The riddle put to Oedipus was as follows: Who walks in the morning on four, at noon on two, and in the evening on three? Oedipus responded that humans crawl on all four as babies,

---

[2] The Almighty does, however, sometimes speak in plain terms in dreams, such as in the nocturnal instruction (apparently in a dream) to the prophet Nathan to tell David that it would not be he who would build the Temple, but rather his son (2 Samuel 7:4). It seems that divine instructions were in plain language, while predictions about the future, if given in a dream, were enigmatic.

[3] Flavius Josephus, *Antiquities of the Jews* 8.5.3. A riddle contest between rulers of kingdoms, assisted by their advisors, appears in the ancient Assyrian work, History and Proverbs of Ahiqar, probably from the seventh century B.C.E. Ahiqar was an advisor to King Sennacharib of Assyria. Nadan, Ahiqar's protégé, accused him falsely, and the king ordered that Ahiqar be put to death. But the hangman took pity on him and hanged a slave instead, hiding Ahiqar. When the news of the wise man's death spread around, Pharaoh, the king of Egypt, proposed a "battle of riddles," in which the loser kingdom would pay tax to the winner. When it was realized that Ahiqar still lived, he was dispatched to Egypt, where he solved all Pharaoh's riddles. Returning to Assyria, he was restored to his former status, and the treacherous protégé was punished.

walk on two legs as adults, and support themselves with a stick in old age.[4] Puccini's opera *Turandot* also has a gamble of life or death based on the solution of riddles. The cruel Princess Turandot poses riddles to her suitors. The successful suitor would gain her hand in marriage, while the failures would be executed.

The point about Samson's riddle was not the bet or its intrinsic worth, but the illegitimate way in which it was solved. The riddle was designed to test the sharpness of the contestants. The inventiveness and imagination of the author was pitted against the intelligence of the audience. The discovery of the answer, by deceit or threat, surely invalidated the whole contest. It could also be argued that the riddle itself was not exactly perfect. A fair riddle is one in which both sides have equal access to the data needed for the solution. When the contest refers to facts within the personal knowledge of the author, the balance between the sides is upset. Samson's riddle related to an event in which he alone was involved, to facts of which only he knew. However, this did not seem to bother the two sides.

If the issue of the winning of the wager between Samson and his Philistine adversaries were placed in a modern courtroom, the judge would certainly rule that the Philistines lost and have to pay.[5] It could be said that a wager of this kind contains a condition of fair play and that this condition was violated by the Philistines, who failed to solve the riddle. Legal systems that pose a requirement of good faith would clearly conclude that obtaining the answer by threatening Samson's wife constitutes a breach of that principle.

---

[4] Another riddle showing the divine wisdom of its author is described by Graves in *White Goddess*, 16–17. It is taken from Welsh mythology and is attributed to the legendary wise young Taliesin. What is "[t]he strong creature from before the Flood, Without flesh without bone . . . without head, without feet, in field in forest . . . it is as wide as the surface of earth, and it was not born nor was it seen"? The answer: the wind. Another famous riddle appears in the German folktale "Rumpelstiltskin," in which the miller's daughter was required to discover the name of the dwarf who helped her spin gold from straw. The number of tales that contain riddles is endless. Some stress the prize given for the solution, others the danger inherent in failure, some are pure guesswork, others demand some mission based on contrary conditions—for example, to appear both clothed and naked, the answer to which is long hair, such as Lady Godiva. Stith Thompson has a whole chapter dealing with tests in folk tales, with an extensive subsection devoted to riddles (*Motif-Index of Folk-Literature*, 3:H530–H899).

[5] In many legal systems wager agreements are void or unenforceable. Such obligations are therefore called "debts of honor," since they are unenforceable in a court of law. The result of the riddle competition in Samson's case did not depend on fate, guesswork, or coincidence but rather on the Philistines' understanding and ability. In modern jurisprudence there are two options: either there is no legal obligation from this kind of competition, or Samson won. In no event would he be required to pay up, for the Philistines had been unable to solve the riddle honestly.

Nevertheless, though present-day concepts would declare Samson the winner and exempt him from liability, the biblical text shows that in the mindset of those days the judgment would have been the reverse. In the story, Samson did not doubt for a moment that he had lost and had to pay the forfeit. He knew, of course, how the solution had been obtained, for he had said to them: "If you had not plowed with my heifer, you would not have found out my riddle." Yet no one suggested that this exempted him from liability to pay. It could perhaps be claimed that Samson was interested in this outcome, since he used it to go down to Ashkelon and kill thirty Philistines. But that was not the case. He wanted to win the bet and was furious when he found out that his wife had betrayed his trust. In fact, he abandoned her and returned to his parents' house.

What then is the foundation for the view that the Philistines won the bet? The question parallels those posed in previous chapters on deception and disguise. As we have seen, deception did not detract from the validity of the judicial act and was perhaps considered a permissible tactic. Other stratagems that would today be ruled illegitimate were similarly viewed. Jacob won his birthright for a mess of pottage in circumstances that we would describe as "exploitation" of Esau's fatigue, hunger, and naivete in order to strike a dishonest bargain. Yet in the concepts of those days the validity of the deal was not questioned.

In Greek mythology the Trojan War originated from a competition between gods. At a banquet of the gods, Eris threw a golden apple inscribed "to the most beautiful of all." The candidates to win the apple were Hera, the wife of Zeus; Athena, his daughter; and Aphrodite, goddess of love. Paris, the son of the king of Troy, was nominated to choose between them. Each of the goddesses promised Paris a substantial prize if he awarded her the apple. Hera promised Paris power, Athena promised victory in war, while Aphrodite promised him the love of the most beautiful of women. Paris chose love, gave the apple to Aphrodite, and won the love of Helen, wife of King Menelaus of Sparta. Paris fled with Helen to Troy, and Menelaus's brother Agamemnon led the Greek fleet to war on Troy. In the legend, the contest between the goddesses took the shape of a trial, though without any reference to the central issue of the beauty of the ladies, which became irrelevant. In its place the question became which of the goddesses would offer the judge the most impressive and appealing bribe. Though this was mythology, it hints at the prevailing view of stratagems permissible in such contests. These were goddesses, but they were created in the mind of the people who endowed them with their characteristics, and their behavior patterns were borrowed from the human realm.

If a beauty contest could be won in this fashion, then the tactic that the Philistines used to win their bet with Samson is understandable. However, there was a mitigating circumstance in the contest of the goddesses in that all three employed the same stratagem of trying to bribe the judge. Thus they were competing on equal footing. The result was that the competition changed its nature from a beauty contest to a bribery race. In Samson's case, the threat to his wife's life completely undermined the rules of the game, though it did not prevent the win.

The turning point in the view of deceit and extortion occurred during the period of the great prophets, beginning with Amos in the eighth century B.C.E. Amos cried out against extortion, deceit, and greed:

> Hear this, you that trample on the needy, and bring to ruin the poor of the land, saying, . . . "We will . . . practice deceit with false balances, buying the poor for silver and the needy for a pair of sandals. . . ." Shall not the land tremble on this account, and everyone mourn who lives in it . . . ? (Amos 8:4–6, 8)

A similar cry for social justice appears in Isaiah and Jeremiah, the great moral prophets who followed Amos. This changed viewpoint demanded a reinterpretation of the Bible narratives, such as the stories relating to Jacob and Esau referred to in the chapter on "Stories of Disguise." These legends and commentaries sought to explain Jacob's behavior in the light of the progressive moral codes adopted by later generations. But there was no need to seek justification for the stratagem employed by the Philistines to solve Samson's riddle. The Philistines, Israel's enemies, were considered evildoers by definition, and there was no need to search for justification for their sins.

6

To Kill and Take Possession

Two of the most amazing and gripping stories in the Bible deal with murder and the murderer's inheritance. In both cases the offenders are powerful kings, unsatisfied with what they have, coveting that which belongs to a subject and convinced that they can do no wrong. They want to get their desires without wrongdoing, but it does not work. They are distressed, and, as often happens, when a king is distraught the subject pays with his life. Murder is committed, and the inheritor inherits. In both cases a prophet turns up to denounce the crime, but here the cases differ. In the one, there is an opening for hope. In the other, the judgment is clear-cut and decisive. In both cases the king is remorseful, but the deed is irreversible. The biblical attitude to the kings remains basically unchanged. One king is beloved by God, and he remains so. His remorse is accepted. An innocent baby pays the price, but the outcome will add to the nation's glory. The other is hated to begin with. His remorse is of secondary importance, and he remains in disgrace.

The first incident is that of David and Bathsheba; the second, Ahab and Naboth's vineyard. During David's reign, war broke out between Israel and Ammon. The army was commanded by Joab, and, as in many other wars, David did not lead his forces but stayed in his Jerusalem palace awaiting news of the outcome. While the Israelite army marched on Rabbah, capital of Ammon, David was taking an evening stroll on the palace roof, and "he saw from the roof a woman bathing; the woman was very beautiful" (2 Samuel 11:2). David evidently did not know her, but that was easily corrected. He found out that she was the wife of one of his officers, Uriah the Hittite, who was with the army fighting against the Ammonites. David sent for the woman, Bathsheba, and slept with her. There is no suggestion that she objected. David, the king who had charmed many women before her, captured her heart. He was no longer a youngster, though his exact age is unknown; it was probably about fifty. She was much younger, but age is not necessarily an obstacle between a powerful man and a young woman. For David it was the latest of many amorous adventures. Among others, the Bible mentions Saul's daughter Michal, Abigail the wife of Nabal, Ahinoam (the mother of Amnon), Maacah (the mother of Absalom), Haggith (the mother of Adonijah), Abital, and Eglah. Moreover, when David fled from his rebellious son, Absalom, he left ten concubines to "look after the house" (2 Samuel 15:16).

This encounter between David and Bathsheba did not, in David's eyes, necessitate another meeting. Bathsheba went home, and there is no suggestion that she was again invited to the palace. But a few weeks later she discovered that she was pregnant. This was a dramatic development. Bathsheba had not contacted David until then, but now she did approach him, though it is not clear how.

Her approach to David is given in the usual Bible brevity. She just said: "I'm pregnant." The consequences could be horrifying. A married woman impregnated by another man was considered an adulteress, punishable by death. The prohibition on adultery was one of the Ten Commandments, and the punishment was specified: "If a man commits adultery with the wife of his neighbor, both the adulterer and the adulteress shall be put to death" (Leviticus 20:10). There is ample evidence from additional sources that this was the punishment that an adulteress could face.[1]

Bathsheba therefore faced a danger of death, which Uriah could demand and even perhaps carry out himself. Though the same would also apply to David, it is unlikely that he was in any immediate danger. Uriah the Hittite could hardly demand that the king should be put to death or punished in any other way. But David was endowed with sharp political instincts, which had already helped him to seize power from Saul's dynasty. Bathsheba was apparently of respectable family, supposedly the granddaughter of Ahitophel, the king's counselor. The proximity of their house to the palace, which had enabled David to watch her in the first place, indicates Bathsheba and Uriah's wealth and status. Her execution by Uriah could cause a scandal that would damage David.

David sought a solution to prevent the dire consequences and to close the episode quietly. He told Joab to send Uriah to him, pretending when that officer arrived that he wanted a briefing on the battle. David asked after Joab and how "the people fared, and how the war was going" (2 Samuel 11:7). Uriah's answers were clearly unimportant, and perhaps he understood as much. David

---

[1] See also the chapter "The Prohibition of Another Man's Wife," pp. 211–15.

then sent him home to "wash [his] feet." Uriah did not respond, nor did he go home. In what was to become the most dramatic part of the story, he lay down to sleep at the door of David's house, avoiding a meeting with his wife.

Among the many interpretations that seek to justify David's crime, there is one that suggests that Uriah was "a rebel against the crown," because he disobeyed the king's direct order to go home, thereby incurring his own death sentence.[2] This is, of course, fanciful. Telling Uriah to go home was hardly an order and certainly not in the class of matters on which the king would issue commands. Moreover, had the words indeed been understood as a direct order, David could have issued a public death sentence instead of resorting to base trickery.

In any event, David did not accuse Uriah of disobedience but merely summoned him again and asked him to explain his behavior. Uriah gave a patriotic response: "The ark and Israel and Judah remain in booths; and my lord Joab and the servants of my lord are camping in the open field; shall I then go to my house, to eat and to drink, and to lie with my wife?" (2 Samuel 11:11). David plied him with food and drink, but Uriah persisted in his refusal to go home. Was he being patriotic, or had he perhaps heard a rumor about the king's assignation with Bathsheba? The battlefield was only a day or two away from Jerusalem, and messengers were going back and forth frequently. Even though David and Bathsheba had met only once, it must have been fairly common knowledge. The Bible even mentions that David had sent messengers to bring her. Perhaps Uriah had heard of it, in which case his behavior was clear. He had been summoned to the king in peculiar circumstances and must have asked himself why he was called in the middle of the battle. Why had the king chosen him to report, and why was he so insistent that he should go home? If Uriah harbored any suspicions about his wife's behavior in his absence, he was now getting ample signals that should impel him homeward to see what had happened. Yet he stretched out demonstratively before the king's door, as if to declare: "You are all witnesses that I did not go home and did not see my wife." His explanation must have seemed strange to David and all who were present. David had told him to go home and bathe his feet, but in declining to do so Uriah specifically said "and to lie with my wife," even though David had not mentioned the wife.[3]

---

[2] Babylonian Talmud, *Shabbat* 56a.

[3] According to the interpretation of David Altschuler, *Metzudat David (Fortress of David)* to 2 Samuel 11:8, the term "wash your feet," which David used when he asked Uriah to go home, was a euphemism for sexual relations. That is extremely doubtful. It was not the customary interpretation of the expression, and David probably did not feel comfortable talking about the subject. As for what Uriah knew or did not

When Uriah refused the offered way out, David faced the cruel choice between the death of Bathsheba, which would expose his role, and the death of Uriah. Without going into the dilemma of having to choose the candidate for death, there was clearly no justification for David to make that choice, since he was responsible for the whole mess, nor was it just to sacrifice Uriah, who was totally innocent.[4]

In making the choice between Bathsheba and Uriah, David chose to sacrifice the husband, though there is no evidence that he was madly in love with her. He did not murder Uriah to win Bathsheba; on the contrary, he was prepared to let her go. As we have seen, he did not meet her again after the first episode. Had Uriah complied with the king's repeated requests that he go home, David's link with Bathsheba would have been over. After Uriah's death, David "inherited" her. But this was the unavoidable outcome, not the motive for murder. The story in fact clearly indicates that David was prepared to give up Bathsheba and let Uriah live. But Uriah refused the opportunity to hush the affair and stuck to his own principles. For this he paid with his life.

Uriah was sent back to the battlefield, carrying a dispatch to Joab that contained instructions for the murder. Thus he became an unwitting accessory in his own execution. David ordered Joab: "Set Uriah in the forefront of the hardest fighting, and then draw back from him, so that he may be struck down and die" (2 Samuel 11:15). The motif of a messenger carrying his own sealed death warrant recurs in history. It occurs in the tale of Rosencrantz and Guildenstern in Shakespeare's *Hamlet* and in a modern play by Tom Stoppard. From the murderer's viewpoint, the cynicism is twofold: not only has he imposed on his victim to deliver his own death warrant, but the more loyal the man is, the more certain it is that he will fulfill his macabre role. In David's case, the explanation lies in anger and frustration because Uriah failed to provide an easy way out.

Both Uriah's obstinacy and the king's helplessness reflect the sexual morality of the Bible and biblical society, which focused on the stringent prohibition

---

know, the various suppositions are presented in Moshe Garciel, "Introduction to 2 Samuel 11," in *The World of the Bible* [Hebrew] (24 vols.; Tel-Aviv: Davidson-Atai, 1993–1997). An interesting literary analysis appears in Sternberg, *Poetics of Biblical Narrative,* 193–222. In Sternberg's view, the power of the text lies in it leaving the question of Uriah's knowledge open.

[4] A famous case of a choice between two men sentenced to death appears in the New Testament (Matthew 27:15–25; Mark 15:6–15; Luke 23:17–25; John 18:39–40). The Roman governor customarily released one convict, at the request of the people, at Passover. Two candidates awaited execution—Jesus and Barabbas, who was accused of rebellion and murder. The priests persuaded the people to choose Barabbas. Jesus' execution followed immediately.

of the taking of another man's wife and the sanctity of property. Adultery was an assault on the husband's property and the "purity of his dynasty." Respect of property rights and a wife's loyalty to her husband could even impinge on the power of a king.

In other societies, with different customs, family law, and sexual mores, the result could have been much less tragic. When Emperor Augustus lusted after Livia, he was able to demand that her husband divorce her. But in Israel in David's time, such a possibility was inconceivable.

Joab carried out David's instruction, but with a sharp deviation. Though David had ordered that he send Uriah to a vulnerable position on the battle-field and then abandon him to face the enemy alone, Joab must have feared that the murder would be too transparent. So he sent Uriah with a handful of men, to a place where all were in danger of getting killed. That was not the end of it. David, having barely recovered from the vision of Uriah sprawled at his door, now had to face another humiliation. Joab sent him word of the battle, instructing the messenger to tell the king, first, how Joab had positioned his men so that they were sure to die in battle, without mentioning Uriah. Joab continued: "When you have finished telling the king all the news about the fighting, then, if the king's anger rises, and if he says to you, 'Why did you go so near the city to fight? Did you not know that they would shoot from the wall? . . . Why did you go so near the wall?' then you shall say, 'Your servant Uriah the Hittite is dead too'" (2 Samuel 11:19–21). So Joab was telling his messenger to wait for David's angry response to the faulty management of the battle and only then to complete his message: "Your servant Uriah the Hittite is dead too." The intent was to mock David and make him look foolish. This was a serious psychological mistake: criticism of a superior is possible, but mockery of failure instead of constructive comment is a sure recipe for hatred. But it would seem that the messenger did not obey Joab's instruction precisely and tried to soften the impact. He did not wait for David's rebuke but told the whole story in one breath, including the death of Uriah. David responded: "Thus you shall say to Joab, 'Do not let this matter trouble you, for the sword devours now one and now another; press your attack on the city, and over-throw it'" (2 Samuel 11:25).

This development shows that the David-Bathsheba affair was already common knowledge. Joab seems to have understood the reasoning behind the terrible order that he had received. The messenger sent to deliver Joab's mock-ing communiqué also grasped what it was all about.[5]

---

[5] Sternberg (*Poetics of Biblical Narrative*, 215–19) assumes that the messenger did not realize that Uriah's death was murder.

Finally, what of Joab's behavior? His loyalty to David impelled him to carry out the order, though he was known for occasional independence. For example, at the climax of Absalom's rebellion, Joab killed him despite David's instructions to spare him. This time, he understood David's dilemma and perhaps concluded that this was the only solution. In any event, the Bible does not hold him responsible for the murder. After David's death, Solomon had Joab killed for supporting the rival heir to the throne, Adonijah son of Haggith. Solomon claimed he was obeying David's last will and testament, though it is doubtful that such a will was made. Be that as it may, Solomon's instruction to his general Benaiah stated that Joab was being punished for the killing of Abner the son of Ner and Amasa the son of Jether (1 Kings 2). Neither David nor Solomon dared to attribute Uriah's murder to Joab. In modern jurisprudence, the king's order would be considered manifestly illegal, and the carrying out of such a command would not negate Joab's responsibility. Indeed, it seems that even according to the basic biblical view, Joab did share the responsibility for the murder done at the king's behest.[6]

After Uriah's death Bathsheba mourned as a widow was supposed to, then David married her. It was the second time that David took a widow to wife. The first was Abigail, but he had been only indirectly responsible for the death of her husband, Nabal.[7]

The next stage involved the prophet Nathan. David was lucky in that his reign fell between great powers—Egypt had gone into decline, and Assyria and Babylon had not yet arisen, which facilitated his conquests. Samuel, who had made Saul's life a misery, was dead. The opposition prophets, Amos, Jeremiah, or Elijah and Elisha, had not yet been born. The seers of David's day were "court prophets," and Nathan was the king's counselor. David consulted him when he wanted to build the Temple. At first Nathan approved the project, but

---

[6] It is interesting to compare Joab's responsibility with David's blaming the Amalekite boy who claimed to have killed Saul at the latter's request after his defeat by the Philistines at Gilboa. Though that was regicide, the fact remains that the king had asked to be killed, making the act one of assisted suicide. Nevertheless, as far as David was concerned, this did not diminish the boy's responsibility (according to the biblical narrative, that did not happen; Saul committed suicide by falling on his sword).

[7] In Nabal's case the responsibility was not legal. Though David had planned to kill him, he did not do so. According to the narrative, while David and his men were being pursued by Saul, David sent messengers to Nabal to ask for contributions (in fact, "protection money"). Nabal refused, and David was about to attack his house, meaning to kill all its inhabitants. Abigail heard about it, rushed to bring David a suitable gift, and persuaded him to relent. She returned home and told Nabal what she had done. He promptly had a stroke and died. After his death, Abigail married David (1 Samuel 25:39). Meir Shalev suggests that Abigail did play an active part in her husband's death, in agreement with David (*Bible Now* [Hebrew] [Tel-Aviv: Schocken, 1985], 19–23). In such a case David would have been legally responsible.

God told him in a dream that the Temple was to be built by David's son (2 Samuel 7). At the same time, Nathan heaped blessings and affection on the king, which not unnaturally strengthened his own status. Nathan informed David that God had promised, not only that his mercy would not be withdrawn, but that "your throne shall be established forever" (2 Samuel 7:16). Nathan's deep court involvement was further expressed in his naming the newborn Solomon, Jedidiah (in Hebrew, God's friend), as a sign that God loved him (2 Samuel 12:25). Nathan's influence peaked with the role that he played in enthroning Solomon. As a part of the court, and probably on David's payroll, it is no wonder that he made no public criticism of the Bathsheba affair. David was given an opportunity to express remorse and receive forgiveness, and the punishment was eventually imposed on his family.

Nathan began with a parable:

> There were two men in a certain city, the one rich and the other poor. The rich man had very many flocks and herds; but the poor man had nothing but one little ewe lamb, which he had bought. He brought it up, and it grew up with him and with his children; it used to eat of his meager fare, and drink from his cup, and lie in his bosom, and it was like a daughter to him. Now there came a traveler to the rich man, and he was loath to take one of his own flock or herd to prepare for the wayfarer who had come to him, but he took the poor man's lamb, and prepared that for the guest who had come to him. (2 Samuel 12:1–4)

The king responded in fury: "The man who has done this deserves to die; he shall restore the lamb fourfold, because he did this thing, and because he had no pity" (2 Samuel 12:5–6). To which Nathan responded, dramatically, "You are the man!" David had fallen into the prophet's trap. The same thing happened to him again with the woman from Tekoa.[8] Joab employed the same tactic of sending a messenger to report on the war casualties then to wait for the king's angry response before adding that Uriah the Hittite was also dead.

The parable of the lamb had little to do with David's case, but for the reference to a poor man unjustly treated by someone better off than he. The somewhat contrived traditional interpretation points out the analogy in that David had many wives, while Uriah had but one. There the similarity ended. Bathsheba (the lamb) was, of course, not slaughtered, but became queen and mother of the next king, Solomon. David's cry that "the man who has done

---

[8] In 2 Samuel 14, we are told how Absalom, who had found shelter with the king of Geshur after ordering the murder of his brother Amnon, was brought back. Joab sent David a woman from Tekoa who told the king that she had had two sons, one of whom had killed the other and now faced death for it. David took pity on her and wanted to pardon the son. Immediately afterward he realized that the woman's story related to his son Absalom.

this deserves to die" could be written off as a thoughtless response, but his reference to a fourfold restoration was in keeping with biblical law. Exodus 22:1 establishes the thief's penalty at five oxen for one, four sheep for one. The mode of punishment enforced in those days was to set a fixed sanction for defined offenses, which could not be modified because of circumstances not taken into account by the law relating to the offense.

Some commentators sought to close the gap between the parable and the affair by developing the human imagery attributed to the lamb—it grew up and ate with the family and slept with the poor man.[9] But this explanation does not resolve the incompatibility in that the "ewe lamb," far from being slaughtered, actually rose to greatness.

Another possible explanation for the doubtful similarity, and the moderation of the parable by comparison with the seriousness of David's deed, lies in Nathan's status as court prophet and the caution that this necessitated.[10] Following the parable, and Nathan's dramatic "You are the man," David was seized with remorse, and then the prophet could pronounce three punishments: first, that David's house would never be free of the sword; second, for taking Uriah's wife, "I will raise up trouble against you from within your own house; and I will take your wives before your eyes, and give them to your neighbor, and he shall lie with your wives in the sight of this very sun. For you did it secretly; but I will do this thing before all Israel, and before the sun" (2 Samuel 12:11–12); and third, that the child of the union would die.

By present concepts, this is an exceptionally strange punitive system. David's main crimes were murder and adultery, and the punishments ought to fit the crimes. Under "an eye for an eye" reasoning, since David committed adultery with Uriah's wife, his "neighbor" would do so with his wives. The prophecy came true, after a fashion. Absalom, David's rebellious son, lay with his father's concubines before the eyes of the people. Moreover, "I will raise up trouble against you from within your own house," could be said to relate to Absalom's deeds. But the prophecy spoke of David's wives, and it is not entirely

---

[9] The erotic element in the relations of the poor man and the lamb is discussed in Daniel Boyarin, "The Married Monk: Babylonian Aggada As Evidence of Changes in Babylonian Halacha," in *A View into the Lives of Women in Jewish Societies* (Hebrew) (ed. Yael Azmon; Jerusalem: Zalman Shazar Center for Jewish Studies, 1995), 77, 87–88.

[10] Meir Sternberg (*Poetics of Biblical Narrative*, 429–30) suggests that, to achieve an objective ruling on David, he had to be told a parable that would not allow him to recognize himself. The parable is discussed in detail in Uriel Simon, *Reading Prophetic Narratives* (Hebrew) (Jerusalem: Bialik Institute; Ramat Gan: Bar-Ilan University, 1997), 132–55, which offers another explanation for the incompatibility: the parable tends to present a more moderate act than the reality, so that when David "passed sentence" on the rich man, the conclusion regarding himself was self-evident.

clear whether the reported incident included wives or only concubines. Additionally, Absalom's rebellion took place more than a decade later, and there is no explanation as to the length of the punishment's postponement.

The prophecy of the son's death was also fulfilled. That first child born to Bathsheba was the fruit of adultery. By our standards, it is incomprehensible that the innocent child should be punished for his parents' sins. To which offense did this punishment relate? One possibility is the adultery—the father should not gain a son by a prohibited act. The second possibility is the murder of Uriah, but here the "eye for an eye" thesis does not apply. That would call for David to be killed, which of course did not happen. We do find examples in ancient laws of killing a family member in punishment for the father's deeds; such punishment may be inflicted for the killing of a member of equivalent rank in another family. Thus, for example, the Hammurabi Code provides that if a builder constructs a faulty house and the house collapses and causes the death of the householder, the builder is to be executed. But if the householder's son is killed, then it is the builder's son who will suffer the penalty (§§ 229–230 of the Code). According to this logic, had David killed Uriah's son, there would have been cause to kill David's son. Since this was not the case, the death of David's son had to be punishment, not for the murder, but for the adultery.

David emerged completely clean from the most serious aspect of the affair, namely, the murder of Uriah (assuming that the death of his son was punishment for adultery). The element of the prophecy that his house would never be free of the sword was meaningless. It was tantamount to saying that David would one day join his ancestors. History is full of wars. No nation or royal dynasty is exempt. This prophecy, therefore, was self-evident, and the punishment was meaningless. The prophecy spoke of evil from within David's house, and, indeed, there were many internal disputes and tragedies. David's son Amnon raped his sister, Tamar. Another son, Absalom, then murdered Amnon and rebelled against his father. He was killed in the course of the revolt. But these could hardly be regarded as punishment for Uriah's murder, particularly not since the words "trouble . . . from within your own house" referred to the neighbor lying with David's wives, rather than to other internal disputes.

The main difficulty with the punishment story lies in the great success of the foul deed. David and Bathsheba were married, though such a union would be prohibited under later Jewish law, which determined that an adulterous woman is forbidden alike to her husband and lover. Solomon, the couple's second child, won the kingdom and greatness, though, according to the rules of succession, he was not entitled to the throne, since David had other sons before him. Moreover, amazingly, Nathan came to the parents of the newborn Solomon and named the child "Jedidiah" as a sign that God loved him. Again, the sin was rewarded.

The severity of the crime of adultery committed by David and Bathsheba caused legend to try and soften the seriousness of the act with a theory that in the reign of the house of David everyone who went to war wrote his wife a conditional *get* ("instrument of divorce"), under which if he was killed in war, she would be retroactively divorced, as from when he left.[11] The inference clearly was that, since Uriah died in the war, Bathsheba was retroactively divorced and was no man's wife; therefore she was not an adulteress. This legend also brushes off the difficulty, which arises from later Jewish law, according to which a married woman who had an affair was not allowed to marry her lover after she divorced her husband. If Bathsheba was regarded as having divorced Uriah when she had the affair with David, there was no obstacle to their marriage. This is, undoubtedly, a wondrous way to justify the affair—by murdering Uriah, King David absolved himself of the sin of adultery. It is difficult to enthuse over logic that grants such a prize for murder.

It is interesting to contrast this affair with the population census that David ordered, though it did constitute a transgression in those days. On that occasion, Gad, another court prophet described as "David's seer" (2 Samuel 24:11), presented himself. Their relationship dated back to Saul's pursuit of David, when Gad advised the future king to go to the land of Judah (1 Samuel 22:5). Gad now informed David, in God's name, that he had a choice: "Shall three years of famine come to you on your land? Or will you flee three months before your foes while they pursue you? Or shall there be three days' pestilence in your land?" (2 Samuel 24:13). Gad and David seem to be negotiating the punishment. This is the only occasion in the Bible where the transgressor is offered a choice of penalties. Not surprisingly, David opted for a punishment exacted from others rather than from himself. His response was, "Let me not fall into human hands," with the result that the punishment was pestilence that caused the deaths of seventy thousand Israelites. David was untouched, unless the death of his subjects can count as damaging a king. The Bible does say that David, toward the end of the incident, expressed willingness to bear punishment personally, even adding "But these sheep, what have they done?" Gad demanded that he build an altar to the Almighty on the threshing floor of Araunah the Jebusite. David bought the threshing floor, built the altar, made sacrifices—and the pestilence stopped. The turn of events suggests atonement

---

[11] Rashi, in his commentary on 2 Samuel 11:15, based on Babylonian Talmud, *Shabbat* 56a. See also Ginzberg, *Legends of the Jews*, 4:103.

and perhaps holds the key to understanding the punishment exacted after the murder of Uriah. Both emissaries of God were court prophets whose moral message was delivered in private and in moderation.

Here we may draw the distinction between punishment and atonement. Punishment is decreed by an external force, over which the offender has no control. It is intended to hurt the transgressor. Atonement focuses on purifying the offender. In practice, its purpose is to prevent punishment. To this end the offender has to carry out an "act of purification," such as a sacrifice or some other ceremony. Usually one is not compelled to do this, though one's willingness is not completely free of pressure, since it is done to avoid penalty. Sometimes the atonement requires some forfeit, but that typically harms someone else rather than the offender: for example, the animal offered as sacrifice.[12] Though the distinction between punishment and atonement is fundamentally clear, there are borderline cases. Thus, for example, if the offender is required to make an expensive sacrifice in order to avoid punishment, the incident may be seen as atonement, but the heavy cost could be viewed as penalty.

The price paid by David, in both cases, was on that borderline and perhaps closer to atonement. The choice offered in the case of the census was certainly in that direction. In the Bathsheba and Uriah affair, David's son was sacrificed, without choice. It did hurt David, for he lost a son, but this was a child whom David had been prepared to give up. Had Uriah gone home to his wife, as David requested, the child would have been considered his. Moreover, this incident clearly has a purification base that is typical of atonement. After the sacrifice of the innocent baby, the relationship between David and Bathsheba was "purified." The terrible crime was forgiven. Solomon, the second child of this marriage, went on to become king, while Bathsheba became the dowager queen of his reign.

Years after the event, the house of David was beset by tragedies, including rape, murder, and rebellion. But the attempt to relate these disasters to crimes committed many years before is unconvincing. It becomes an effort to seek justice where there is none, to see our world in an unrealistically positive light. These catastrophes could be attributed to other acts of David; for example, Absalom's revolt could be viewed as retribution for David's seizure of Saul's throne. Indeed, when David and his men fled from Absalom, they were met by a kinsman of Saul's, Shimei the son of Gera, who cursed David: "Out! Out! Murderer! Scoundrel! The LORD has avenged on all of you the blood of the

---

[12] Some societies hold that atonement requires a form of mortification, including self-harm that can be severe (for example, the amputation of a finger in Japan). In Judaism, fasting is used as the means of atonement, but this is merely discomfort.

house of Saul, in whose place you have reigned; and the LORD has given the kingdom into the hand of your son Absalom. . . . For you are a man of blood" (2 Samuel 16:7–8). In other words, while Nathan's prophecy may be connected, if not to Absalom's revolt, then at least to his taking of David's concubines, the remnants of Saul's family were free to view the son's rebellion as divine retribution for David's treatment of their ancestor.

Another instance of murder and inheritance is that of Ahab and Naboth's vineyard.[13] Ahab, the son of Omri, was king of Israel a century after David, after the latter's united kingdom had split into Israel and Judah. The story begins much like that of Uriah. The king desired a vineyard belonging to one of his subjects, Naboth the Jezreelite. Ahab had no evil intentions. He approached Naboth and asked: "Give me your vineyard, so that I may have it for a vegetable garden, because it is near my house; I will give you a better vineyard for it; or, if it seems good to you, I will give you its value in money" (1 Kings 21:2). From Ahab's standpoint, it was an eminently fair offer, and its acceptance would have prevented the ensuing tragedy. So far, it could be compared with David's suggestion to Uriah to go home to his wife, the difference of course being that Ahab—at least at this stage—was innocent of any wrongdoing, while David's behavior was already less than perfect. But Naboth, like Uriah, rejected the proposal: "The LORD forbid that I should give you my ancestral inheritance."

That answer, like that of Uriah, illustrates the limit of the king's power. Ahab could not take the vineyard against Naboth's will, just as David was not at liberty to take Uriah's wife. Neither the law nor public opinion would countenance a ruler treating a subject in this way. But the imposition of such limitations on a ruler's power is not always effective. A ruthless king could find a way to satisfy his desires. In parentheses, we may note that in the modern age, a government would have no difficulty in expropriating Naboth's vineyard against suitable compensation, if there was an appropriate public purpose. Here we note that the traditional commentators, who searched every avenue to justify David, were not so gracious to Ahab. Nobody has suggested that Naboth was violating some injunction by refusing to sell the vineyard to the king—the Bible's plain position is that Ahab was not authorized to order the sale. Naboth was legally entitled to refuse, but the consequences were not long in coming.

---

[13] The link between Uriah the Hittite and Naboth the Jezreelite is discussed in Reuven Yaron, "Social Problems and Politics in the Ancient Near East," in *Law, Politics and Society in the Ancient Mediterranean World* (ed. Baruch Halpern and Deborah W. Hobson; Sheffield: Sheffield Academic Press, 1993), 21. The Naboth affair is discussed in Benjamin Uffenheimer, *Ancient Prophecy in Israel* (Hebrew) (Jerusalem: Magnes, 1973), 206–28.

Ahab was one of the great warrior kings of Israel. The Naboth affair happened after a major war in which Ahab inflicted heavy casualties on Syria. It is easy to understand his rage, humiliation, and helplessness at Naboth's refusal, at his inability, despite all his greatness and power, to persuade a subject to sell him a vineyard at a fair price. He returned home sick with fury and took to his bed, "turned away his face, and would not eat" (1 Kings 21:4). Jezebel, his wife and the daughter of the king of Sidon, was summoned to the unhappy monarch, who told her that Naboth had refused to sell despite the fair price offered to him,[14] and Jezebel calmed him: "Do you now govern Israel? Get up, eat some food, and be cheerful; I will give you the vineyard of Naboth the Jezreelite" (1 Kings 21:7). The method she chose, like David's instruction to Joab, was to send letters with orders to kill Naboth. This was to be a judicial murder:

> So she wrote letters in Ahab's name and sealed them with his seal, and sent the letters to the elders and the nobles who lived in the same town with Naboth. In the letters she wrote as follows: "Proclaim a fast and seat Naboth at the front of the assembly. And seat two scoundrels opposite him, and let them testify against him: 'You have reviled God and king!' Then take him out and stone him to death." (1 Kings 21:8–10 NJPS)

The orders were carried out to the letter. When Jezebel heard that Naboth was dead, she informed Ahab and invited him to inherit the vineyard: "Ahab set out for the vineyard of Naboth the Jezreelite to take possession of it" (1 Kings 21:16 NJPS).

That merited an immediate response. God sent Elijah to Ahab in Naboth's vineyard to tell him, "Have you killed, and also taken possession? . . . In the place where dogs licked up the blood of Naboth, dogs will also lick up your blood." Elijah did as he was bid, prophesied the destruction of Ahab's house, and added that Jezebel was also condemned to be eaten by dogs. When Ahab heard this, "he tore his clothes and put sackcloth over his bare flesh; he fasted, lay in the sackcloth, and went about dejectedly." God expressed his satisfaction to Elijah that Ahab had humbled himself and postponed the sentence to Ahab's son. It is doubtful whether that was amelioration of punishment. Ahab died a warrior's death in battle against Syria. The story of his death ends with the washing of the chariot in which he died in the pool of Samaria: "the dogs licked up his blood, and the prostitutes washed themselves in it, according to the word of the LORD that he had spoken" (1 Kings 22:38). Jehu's revolt against

---

[14] According to the Bible, Ahab did not explain that Naboth had justified his refusal by saying, "The LORD forbid that I should give you my ancestral inheritance." Ahab merely told Jezebel that the man had said, "I will not give you my vineyard," a phrasing that was likely to infuriate her.

the house of Ahab took place in the reign of Jehoram, Ahab's son. Jehu killed Jehoram (also called Joram) and Jezebel and exterminated all the house of Ahab with great cruelty. The lack of respect for Ahab as compared with David is plain to see. Elijah, who was no court prophet, needed no parables, and his prophecies were blunt and outspoken. Ahab's punishment was far more severe—Ahab himself was condemned to death, and his dynasty was destroyed. His remorse had only marginal effect on his fate and that of his house.

David's legal responsibility for Uriah's murder was clear, even though the order was carried out by Joab, with the help of the Ammonite enemy. But the incident of Naboth's vineyard raises difficult legal questions. First, what was Ahab's responsibility for his wife's actions? Second, what was the responsibility of the false witnesses? If an innocent person is imprisoned or executed because of false testimony, does the witness share blame? Is the witness responsible only for the false testimony or also for the verdict, as though one carried it out oneself? Third, how did Ahab inherit the vineyard after Naboth's death?

The Legal Responsibility for the Murder

The answer to the first question depends on Ahab's share in Jezebel's exploits. The narrative attributes the entire incident to Jezebel: she told Ahab that she would solve the problem, without saying how. She wrote letters, used Ahab's seal, and sent them to people who would obey her wishes. If Ahab had no idea that she intended to behave unlawfully, then he was not responsible for the deed, though he was shortly to reap its fruits. The second extreme possibility, which is not mentioned specifically, is that he cooperated by giving his consent and lending her the royal seal. In that case, and in modern law, he was fully responsible as an accessory, and his liability would be as though he had sent the letters himself. Bible commentators were aware of the difficulty regarding Ahab's responsibility, and the *Metzudat David* commentary on 1 Kings 21:19 explains his guilt as based on his having consented to Jezebel's deed. Yet the same commentary holds that Ahab denied his guilt in saying to Elijah, "Have you found me, O my enemy?" (1 Samuel 21:20). *Metzudat David* believed the meaning to be: "So you have found me guilty of this thing, though Jezebel did it and not I." But the commentator considered the denial unfounded.

Between the two extremes (no part in the murder or full complicity) are middle-of-the-road possibilities that fit the text but raise tough legal questions. The central option is that Ahab knew of Jezebel's plan and knew that she was using his seal. These facts are not given in the story, but there is circumstantial evidence: the marriage relationship; the fact that Jezebel told Ahab she would get the vineyard for him, and he had to realize that the implication was an improper act; the probability that he asked how she intended to obtain possession; and the assumption that the royal seal was under his control. The evidence is not decisive, and if we do not deduce the guilt from the fact that God, represented by Elijah, treated Ahab as an accomplice to murder, then the problem with the evidence remains.

Let us assume that Ahab was aware of Jezebel's plan and did not prevent her from taking and using the seal—what then would be his responsibility? This highly probable possibility raises complex questions. In that case, Ahab's unacceptable behavior was an omission, namely, his failure to act: he did not prevent Jezebel from carrying out her plan, though he could have done so.

Normally, legal liability is based on the commitment of a wrongful act. The law generally does not impose liability for a mere failure to act. But there are some exceptions to this rule, in which a person is under a duty to prevent a wrongful act, or is in control of the wrongdoer, or is in possession of the property in which, or by which, the act is done. If the person in control is aware of the intention to commit a wrongful act and does nothing to prevent it, he or she may be held as an accomplice—for example, a driving instructor who could prevent a pupil from committing a driving violation but fails to do so, or a property owner who knows that his or her property is being used as a venue for the illegal sale of drugs but does nothing to stop it.[15]

We may therefore assert that Ahab, as king of Israel, had to ensure that his monarchy and its symbols should not be used to the detriment of his subjects.[16] Therefore, if he was aware of Jezebel's intentions, he could be regarded as her accomplice, since he did not stop her from carrying them out and did not prevent her from using the royal seal.

Another issue relating to the liability for failure to act has to do with the duty to come to another person's rescue. Imagine someone standing on the water's edge with a life buoy near at hand and who sees a person in danger of drowning, yet does nothing to save that person. The moral duty to try to rescue the individual in the water is clear, but what of the legal responsibility? Such a case illustrates the difference between the stricter demands of morality and those of the law and the higher level of conduct that moral values

---

[15] Andrew Ashworth, *Principles of Criminal Law* (3d ed.; Oxford: Clarendon, 1999), 433–34; Joshua Dressler, *Understanding Criminal Law* (2d ed.; New York: M. Brender, 1995), 436; George P. Fletcher, *Rethinking Criminal Law* (Boston: Little, Brown & Co., 1978), 611–34.

[16] Cf. also Jeremiah's admonition to the king and his servants to protect the oppressed from their oppressors (Jeremiah 22:3).

demand. While the law normally confines itself to forbidding the causing of harm to another, morality goes further and demands active help to others, at any rate when they are in dire need. Different legal systems deal with this issue in different ways. The continental European systems impose such duty so long as it does not jeopardize the rescuer or others.[17] Some even contain specific injunctions to prevent a crime that might hurt another person, as well as general ones that impose a duty to rescue. Israeli law also imposes an obligation upon a person who knows that someone is planning to commit a felony to take reasonable steps to prevent it.[18] Furthermore, a law passed in 1998 makes it obligatory to come to the aid of a person whose life or health is in sudden danger, if it is possible to do so without jeopardizing oneself or others. The penalty for this misdemeanor is a fine. The law is derived from the biblical injunction, "you shall not stand against the blood of your neighbor" (Leviticus 19:16; so KJV and JPS 1917; cf. NJB). The phrasing is obscure, but Jewish law interpreted it to impose an obligation to rescue.[19]

Anglo-American law differs in this regard and maintains that in the absence of a prior connection or special relations between the parties there is no duty to come to the rescue. Thus, a person who avoids saving another, though able to do so without great effort, would not be criminally liable nor be liable to pay damages in a civil suit. This is a typically individualistic approach, and

---

[17] Ashworth, *Principles of Criminal Law,* 49–50; Andrew Ashworth and Eve Steiner, "Criminal Omissions and Public Duties: The French Experience," *Legal Studies* 10 (1990): 153.

[18] Section 262 of the Penal Code. The penalty for such an offense is two years' imprisonment. The best-known case in Israel where this law was imposed is that of Margalit Har-Shefi, who was charged with failure to act to prevent the assassination of Prime Minister Yitzhak Rabin by Yigal Amir. Har-Shefi was a student at Bar-Ilan University, where she met Amir, who told her on several occasions that the Prime Minister should be regarded as an enemy of the Jewish people *(din rodef),* that he was dangerous, and that he, Amir, intended to kill him. On November 4, 1995, he did assassinate Rabin. Har-Shefi claimed that she did not believe that Amir was in fact intending to kill the prime minister and regarded him as a "fantasist" who was trying to impress her. Her argument was rejected by the Magistrates Court, which convicted her and sentenced her to two years' imprisonment, fifteen months of which was suspended. The District Court upheld the conviction by majority. In February 2001 the Supreme Court unanimously upheld the conviction, but Justice Tyrkel's minority opinion favored a more lenient sentence. Justice M. Cheshin referred to the murder of Gedaliah son of Ahikam, who had been appointed by the Babylonians as governor of Judah after the fall of the first Temple in 586 B.C.E. The murderer was Ishmael of the house of David, and the consequences for the Judean population were very severe (2 Kings 25:25–26; Jeremiah 41:43). The day of the assassination, which took place over two and half millennia ago, remains a day of mourning and abstinence.

[19] On the position of Jewish law, see Aaron Kirschenbaum, " 'The Good Samaritan' and Jewish Law," *Diné Israel: An Annual of Jewish Law Past and Present* 7 (1976): 7.

there have been calls to alter it.[20] Indeed, in some of the American states such legislation has been passed.[21] But even when a legal duty to rescue does exist, it is obvious that to convict a person for failing to carry it out, it is necessary to show that he or she was aware that the victim was in danger.

All this leads to the conclusion that, if Ahab did not know what Jezebel was planning, he was exempted from responsibility, though he benefited after the fact. Conversely, if he knew of the plan and did not prevent the deed, which depended on his name and seal—as does appear, though indirectly, in the story—then he must be regarded as an accomplice to the act, but not as the principal who actually committed the crime. However, Jezebel has to be considered as responsible for the crime, though it was not done by her hand. It suffices that she gave the order.

This, of course, is also the position of King David in the affair of Uriah the Hittite. Though David did not kill Uriah with his own hands, he initiated the murder and ordered it done. This, therefore, was a murder committed by David, to which end he used people who were under his command.

Comparing the two incidents, it can be said that David decided on the terrible murder when he was in distress of his own doing, at a juncture where the only choice was to let Bathsheba die or to eliminate Uriah. Ahab did not face such a situation—he wanted the vineyard, and the way to get it was by murdering the owner. There were women involved in both cases: in the Naboth affair, Jezebel initiated the plan and carried it out. Ahab came through it looking passive at best. In the case of David, it was his own decision and he implemented it. Bathsheba did not ask for it nor, according to the narrative, was she a party to the act. Nevertheless, Bathsheba's notice to David that she was pregnant set off the chain of events that led to Uriah's murder. Did Bathsheba understand what the king would be forced to do to save her? There is no indication in the biblical story. Some fifteen years later, Bathsheba was involved in stratagems to bring about the crowning of her son, Solomon, in circumstances that show that she was far from naive. She was the prime beneficiary from the murder of her husband Uriah. But we do not know what exactly she had in mind when she accepted David's invitation to lie with him

---

[20] There is much material on the subject. To cite very few: Ernest J. Weinrib, "The Case for a Duty to Rescue," *Yale Law Journal* 90 (1980): 247; Steven J. Heyman, "Foundations of the Duty to Rescue," *Vanderbilt Law Review* 47 (1994): 673.

[21] Among them Rhode Island, Vermont, and Wisconsin. Moreover, in many states there are laws imposing a duty to help others in specific situations. The question arises whether a person who breached the duty to help is only liable for this breach or is also responsible for the consequences (e.g., for the death of a victim who might have been saved). For a discussion, see Paul H. Robinson, *Criminal Law* (New York: Aspen Law & Business, 1997), 198–99.

and what she expected when she told him of the pregnancy. We can only speculate that she expected the king to release her from her husband and take her for himself. The decision on how it was to be done, she left to David.

Between these two incidents was a role reversal between man and woman. In Uriah's case, the man, David, was the active partner and the initiator of the murder. Bathsheba was passive and merely supplied the motive. In Naboth's case, the woman, Jezebel, was the active initiator, and Ahab was passive. The factor common to both was that the passive participant was the main beneficiary from the deed.

Responsibility for False Evidence

Another legal question touches on Jezebel's crime, in which Ahab is regarded as an accomplice or as responsible for failing to prevent the deed. At Jezebel's request, two false witnesses testified that Naboth had cursed God and the king. The testimony was given at Naboth's trial, following which he was taken outside the city walls and stoned to death. Doubtless Jezebel was responsible for the false testimony, as much as the false witnesses who acted on her instructions. The question is whether the false witnesses, and Queen Jezebel, were responsible for the outcome of their testimony—the execution of an innocent man.

There is a yawning abyss between ancient and modern law on this issue. Ancient jurisprudence moved gradually from the stage in which the parties resolved disputes between themselves to one in which they had to resort to a judicial tribunal. Blood revenge is the outstanding example of sanctions imposed at source, without need for legal procedure. Numbers 35:19 states specifically that "the avenger of blood is the one who shall put the murderer to death." Later on, however, this injunction was subjected to the rule that an offender could not be killed without trial, and it follows that the avenger could not act on his own. Indeed, this development is already reflected in the book of Numbers, which distinguishes between intentional murder and accidental killing. The intentional murderer was liable to be killed by the blood avenger, while the one who killed accidentally was entitled to escape to a city of refuge. The blood avenger was not entitled to decide if the killing was intentional— the decision was to be reached in a legal process: "the congregation shall judge between the slayer and the avenger of blood" (Numbers 35:24). Hence, the transgressor had to be brought to trial, and only if the court passed a sentence of death could the avenger carry it out.[22] A further stage in the legal evolution

---

[22] Mishnah, *Sanhedrin* 1:6.

was needed to transfer the implementation of the sentence to an official body and remove it from the interested parties.

In modern criminal procedure the prosecution is represented by the state. In ancient law the victim was the party primarily involved. Thus, for example, "When someone steals an ox or a sheep, and slaughters it or sells it, the thief shall pay five oxen for an ox, and four sheep for a sheep" (Exodus 22:1). The text does not say to whom the fine should be paid. While in modern law it is self-evident that a fine is paid to the state (or other appropriate governing authority), the clear implication in the text is that it should be paid to the aggrieved party, the owner of the stolen animal. Equally clear is the assumption that it was up to the victim to arrange the trial.

Trial was seen as a struggle between the accuser and the accused, the fate of both being in the balance. Thus the first clause of the Hammurabi Code states that, if a man accuses his fellow of homicide and is unable to provide proof, then he (the accuser) is put to death. The second clause goes even further and provides that if a man accuses his fellow of witchcraft, the accused will be submitted to the divine river ordeal. If his guilt is established and he drowns, his property goes to the accuser. If, however, the ordeal clears the accused and he emerges alive, then the accuser is put to death and his property is given to the accused.

The Hammurabi Code has an additional provision regarding the accuser's right to receive the property of the accused. Article 26 states that if a soldier or a fisherman who has been ordered to go on a royal campaign does not go or hires a substitute, he shall be put to death, and the one who informs against him shall take possession of his estate. Here there is no suggestion of equal fate for the accuser if the accusation is proved false, probably because it is not practical to assume false accusation in such a case.

The fundamental concept of trial by combat, practiced in medieval times, is similar. The risk was imposed on both parties, each of whom could be killed, though the risk was not exactly equal.[23] There is some literature, though possibly legendary, about a system wherein the winner acquired all the loser's property.[24]

A notable example of "mutual risk" to accuser and accused (albeit without reference to property) is the biblical law relating to a "scheming witness,"

---

[23] If the accuser won and the accused was not killed but only wounded, he could expect to be executed as an offender whose guilt was proven. If, on the other hand, the accuser was beaten but not killed, remaining alive but injured, it may be assumed that he was not exposed to possible punishment merely for having lost. Moreover, when the system of using mercenary replacements was adopted, the physical risk was lifted from the accuser.

[24] Neilson, *Trial by Combat*, 21–24.

one who by false testimony seeks to incriminate another. Deuteronomy 19:19 declares: "Then you shall do to the false witness just as the false witness had meant to do to the other. So you shall purge the evil from your midst." Thus the scheming witness would suffer the same punishment that would have been imposed on the victim. Later commentary sought to confine that ruling in capital punishment cases to instances where the accused was found innocent, as distinguished from cases in which the accused was found guilty and executed. In any event, the punishment of a scheming perjurer matched that facing the accused. The principle holds true both for the type of punishment and the mode of its execution.

In the popular view, the above provisions of the Hammurabi Code and Deuteronomy conform to the concept of "measure for measure" or "an eye for an eye." Deuteronomy follows the ruling on a false witness with: "Show no pity: life for life, eye for eye, tooth for tooth, hand for hand, foot for foot" (19:21). But the scheming witness was punished for the mere attempt to harm another by perjury. According to Jewish law, the perjurer faced execution if his testimony was given in a capital case, even though the accused was found innocent. Whatever an accuser sought to do, even though unsuccessfully, would be done to the accuser. This, therefore, was more than "measure for measure." It was the kind of justice applied in the book of Esther, where Haman and his household were subjected to the same fate that he had sought for the Jews.

Beyond "an eye for an eye," this law expresses the principle of "equal risk" inherent in a trial that is a struggle between accuser and accused. If the accused faced possible death, then so did the accuser. Today, the witness would be considered a neutral third party whose sole function is to provide information. Ancient law often regarded witnesses as partners to the struggle. They were identified with the party whose cause they supported, and their fate might be similar. The judgment of scheming witnesses in Deuteronomy was the same as that of the accuser in the Hammurabi Code. They were parties to the matter, while the judicial system was merely the mechanism that helps to guide the battle between rival parties. A similar idea is found elsewhere in Deuteronomy, in the text that mandates the death penalty for idolatry and rules that two or three witnesses are required in order to convict. The sequence is enlightening: "The hands of the witnesses shall be the first raised against the person to execute the death penalty, and afterward the hands of all the people" (17:7).

This special role, which accorded the witnesses as the first to carry out the death sentence, indicates their status. They are not onlookers who merely relate whatever they know. They have a responsibility in the process, and a primary role in the execution. Modern law rejects this approach. Even in civil cases, in which the main interest is that of the private parties involved, it is inconceivable that a person who sued for a sum of money and lost would be obligated by a "measure for measure" principle to pay the same amount to the defendant.

The basic approach of modern criminal jurisprudence is totally different from that of the ancient world. Usually the state prosecutes, and the government's legal machinery plays a key role. Involved parties, such as the victims of the offense or the witnesses, are required to assist in enforcing the law. But the role of prosecuting belongs to a public official. This is not, then, a struggle between injured parties (or witnesses) and the accused, but rather a clash between government and the accused. The consequence of placing the legal system at the center of law enforcement and removing the burden from other interested parties is that the responsibility for the process, its failures and mistakes, has been transferred from the aggrieved parties and witnesses to the legal machinery. At the same time the exalted status of the legal system and those participating in the judicial process has led to a reluctance to impose responsibility for failures of the prosecution or for mistaken and unsuccessful decisions.

The "equality of risks" between accuser (and sometimes witnesses) and the opposing party, which had prevailed in ancient law, has thus been replaced by a completely different attitude, which encourages resorting to the courts, while granting wide immunity to those involved in the legal process. The immunity was given first to the judges, then partially to lawyers and witnesses. The aggrieved party, the prosecutor or the witnesses, ceased to be held responsible for the trial or its results. The responsibility is placed upon the legal system, from which it follows that no special liability can be imposed on anyone involved if the accused is pronounced innocent. The tendency to encourage resort to the legal machine and to testify in court has led to rules under which judges, witnesses, parties, and their representatives are exempt from libel and slander actions for anything said during court proceedings, and the judicial authority enjoys wide immunity from damage claims. Similarly, submission of criminal charges or complaints does not place responsibility on whoever does so, at least if one acts in good faith, and the fact that an indictment is rejected or held to be unfounded does not expose the prosecutor or the witnesses to sanctions.

English law also developed a rule under which a court judgment breaks the causal link between the actions of the parties and the witnesses. Accordingly, if a testimony leads to conviction and imprisonment, the judgment is deemed "responsible" for the result, not the witness whose testimony formed the basis for conviction. It is as if the judgment constitutes an independent element, standing on its own, and this fiction severs the link between it and the testimonies on which it is based. Even in an extreme case, where it becomes clear that false testimony caused the execution or the imprisonment of an innocent person, the perjurer is not responsible for murder or false imprisonment (though one could be found guilty of perjury).[25] However, there are states in the U.S. that have adopted a different approach: if deliberate perjury, or conspiracy to bring about conviction through such testimony, results in execution, then those responsible may be held guilty of murder.[26]

According to English law the giving of false testimony in court does not in itself expose the perjurer to civil claims for the resulting damage to one of the parties. The sanctions are limited to a process that may be initiated against the perjurer for the false testimony. A qualification of the approach is found in the civil damages claim for the tort known as "malicious prosecution." It is mainly concerned with the initiation or conduct of criminal or bankruptcy proceedings against a person. The precondition for a claim based on malicious prosecution is that the defendant acted "maliciously and without justifiable reason." In addition, the claim must have failed: in other words, if the original proceeding was criminal, the accused must have been acquitted or the trial must have been stayed. Giving information to the police that leads to prosecution by a public authority against the accused is not sufficient to expose the giver of information to a claim for malicious prosecution. The defendant must have been involved in the proceeding. Such involvement may occur in the rather rare cases in which a private person is authorized to undertake criminal proceedings.[27] In general, modern law seeks to encourage resort to legal proceedings, and this philosophy brings with it wide immunity to those involved. The possibility of a civil claim for

---

[25] R. v. MacDaniel (1754) 168 E.R. 124.

[26] Codes adopted by a number of states include in the first-degree-murder category the case of procuring execution by perjury: Wayne R. LaFave and Austin W. Scott Jr., Criminal Law (2d ed.; St. Paul, Minn.: West Publishing, 1986), 615, supporting this approach. Section 28-303 of the Statutes of Nebraska provides an example of such legislation. It states: "A person commits murder in the first degree if he kills another person . . . by willful and corrupt perjury or subornation of the same he purposely procures the conviction and execution of any innocent person."

[27] It was also held in a few American cases that a person may be considered as involved in criminal proceedings instituted by the authorities if he or she pressed the prosecution to file an indictment or influenced to initiate criminal process. This approach was sometimes extended to include a person who knowingly gave false information, understanding that it would lead to criminal proceedings (William L. Prosser and W. Page Keeton, On the Law of Torts [5th ed.; St. Paul, Minn.: West Publishing, 1984], 873). In addition, American law extended the ambit of the tort claim for damages to other instances of abuse of legal process, including wrongful initiation of civil suits (ibid., 889–900).

damages is a narrow exception to this basic approach; this exception has been somewhat expanded in the United States, where liability has been imposed for abuse of legal process.

Postbiblical Jewish law retreated from the death penalty for witnesses and held that if the scheming witnesses succeeded and the accused was executed, they would not be killed—because the Torah speaks of witnesses who plotted to achieve a certain end but not when their desired result was actually achieved.[28] The implication is that for capital offenses, the witnesses faced a similar judgment only if they were found out before the accused was condemned (in which case the accused would presumably be exonerated) or if the sentence had not yet been carried out. If execution took place before the lie was exposed, the witnesses would not be executed, and it is not at all clear whether there would be any punishment.

Obviously the suggested interpretation is problematic: if, in the easier situation, where the plot had failed and the accused was not executed, the witnesses were sentenced to death—then logic dictates that in the more serious event, where the false testimony led to an innocent person being executed, the witnesses should certainly face the death penalty. Moreover, why should this interpretation apply only to the death penalty? According to Maimonides, if in consequences of the false testimony the accused was sentenced to punishment other than death—such as flogging—the witnesses should face the same punishment, though the sentence had been carried out.

It seems that the explanation for the Jewish law approach lies in its desire to restrict the scope of capital punishment and its tendency—similar to modern law—to encourage the giving of evidence and to limit the risks that this entails (the conclusion that witnesses are scheming is based on other evidence; there is always a risk of mistake or even false evidence seeking to prove the witnesses' plot).

According to the original biblical law, Jezebel and the false witnesses deserved the death penalty. That result would seem more just than the modern view that fears, perhaps too much so, to scare off witnesses and to subject them to the most severe liability. Paradoxically, according to the later, softened Jewish law, the false witnesses in Naboth's trial were exempted from execution because their plot had succeeded and they had caused the death of the innocent accused.

It is not clear whether today, in English or Israeli law, Jezebel and the perjurers could be charged with murder (though they could clearly be charged

---

[28] Babylonian Talmud, *Makkot* 5b; Maimonides, *The Code of Maimonides (Mishneh Torah)*, Book 14, *The Book of Judges* (trans. Abraham M. Hirsh; New Haven, Conn.: Yale University Press), part 2: Laws concerning Evidence 20:2.

with perjury).[29] It is arguable that in the extreme circumstances of Naboth's case, the rules that apply in ordinary trials ought not to apply and that the false witnesses and plotters should be held responsible not only for false testimony or obstruction of justice but also for murder. The Naboth affair involved not only false testimony—there was a conspiracy to hold a fictitious trial for the purpose of legal murder. Jezebel wrote letters to the elders and notables of Naboth's city. They agreed to participate in the plot, recruited false witnesses, and very possibly those same elders and notables took part in the trial, either as judges or by appointing judges to their liking, or perhaps as partners in collusion. If that was the case, this was not a genuine trial but a staged drama in which Naboth's fate had been decided in advance. The special system of rulings that in modern law limits the liability of false witnesses (and exempts them from responsibility for the results of the judgment) does not hold for a fictitious trial, and the organizers and participants must be held directly responsible for the terrible outcome.

The Inheritance of the Vineyard

After the murder of Naboth, Jezebel informed Ahab that the way was clear for him to inherit the vineyard. Ahab made haste to go down to the vineyard and take possession. The question arises: How did Ahab acquire the dead man's property? Possibly there was a law that the property of a person executed for offenses against the kingdom reverted to the king. Another possibility, mentioned by Rashi and Rabbi David Kimchi (Radak), is that Naboth was Ahab's nephew and the king inherited by virtue of kinship. A third possibility was that Naboth had no heirs, in which case the king inherited just as today the state inherits the property of people who die intestate and have no relatives as defined by law.

The difficulties regarding the inheritance of Naboth's vineyard are augmented by another story that derives from the chain of events. Some time later Ahab went again to war against Syria and was killed in battle. His successor, King Ahaziah, died of an illness and was followed by yet another son of Ahab—Jehoram. During Jehoram's reign, Jehu led a revolt against the house of Ahab. At the start of the rebellion, Jehu himself shot an arrow at Jehoram and killed him. He then ordered his adjutant to dump Jehoram's body on the land that had belonged to Naboth, justifying his action by saying: "For the

---

[29] Some states of the U.S. adopt a different approach (see above note 26 and accompanying text and note 27).

blood of Naboth and for the blood of his children that I saw yesterday, says the LORD" (2 Kings 9:26).[30] This "blood of his children" raises a serious problem. Radak offers a number of interpretations: first, Naboth's sons died with him; second, the reference was to unborn sons, whose birth was prevented by Naboth's death; finally, "the blood of his sons" was a literary device referring to the cry of the sons whose inheritance had been stolen by the king.

The suggestion that Naboth's sons died with him does not seem reasonable. There are in the Bible cases of sons killed for their father's sins: for example, when Achan was caught taking banned war spoils during the conquest of Jericho, his sons and daughters (and even his livestock) were stoned to death, then burned. But it is doubtful that such an extreme penalty would have been imposed for the transgression of which Naboth was accused (blasphemy against God and king). Moreover, the main account of the Naboth incident, in 1 Kings 21, makes no mention of sons or their execution. Such an important fact would hardly have been left out, so it must be assumed that Ahab and Jezebel's crime, bad as it was, did not include such a killing. The addition of Naboth's sons is first mentioned by Jehu, who slayed his king, Ahab's son. Seeking to justify his own actions, he saw fit to recall and embroider on the Naboth affair.

The means by which Ahab seized Naboth's vineyard after his death have not been clarified, but the version of the confiscation of an offender's property is the most reasonable. What is the source of that ruling? The Bible makes no mention of it. Deuteronomy 17 says that when the nation comes to its land, it may take to itself a king and adds a few rules relating to the king, but nothing about confiscation of transgressors' property. Samuel, in response to the people's demand for a king, lists the disadvantages of monarchy (1 Samuel 8) but does not mention such a practice. Nevertheless, the possibility cannot be discounted that such a law did evolve, and if it did, the question arises: What was its origin? Here we may point, first and foremost, to the law of "forfeiture," that is, spoils of war set aside to be destroyed as an offering to the Lord. This law was rooted in the nation from the moment of exodus from Egypt.

---

30 Based, inter alia, on these words, it has been suggested that the story of Naboth's trial is a later insertion and that he and his sons were murdered without trial (Alexander Rofé, "Research of Biblical Law in Light of the Historical-Philological Method" (Hebrew), *Mishpatim: The Student Law Review, Faculty of Law, The Hebrew University of Jerusalem* 13 [1984]: 477). According to this opinion, the law in Ahab's time did not require conviction to be based on two witnesses. The trial story was added later, and the reference to two witnesses was an adjustment to meet the requirements of a later law. This view was criticized in Itzhak Englard, "The Story of Naboth the Jezreelite" (Hebrew), *Mishpatim: The Student Law Review, Faculty of Law, The Hebrew University of Jerusalem* 14 (1984): 521.

Forfeiture is religious in origin and primarily requires the destruction of property and life in dedication to God. The reason for forfeiture, or ban, could be an oath sworn to the Almighty, in other words, a kind of "deal" by which God would give an enemy into Israel's hands, in return for which the enemy and their property would be banned. Numbers 21 reports that the Canaanite king of Arad fought Israel and took prisoners. The Israelites swore an oath to God that, if God delivered the enemy into their hands, they would "forfeit" the king's people and cities, namely, destroy them as an offering to the Lord. God heard the plea and delivered the initial part of the bargain, so the Israelites followed suit and kept their part as well. In this case, the ban was clearly a dedication to God and was, therefore, tantamount to offering a sacrifice, but with some differences.

The first difference was ceremonial. The Bible contains detailed instructions on the manner of offering sacrifices. It would seem that the ceremonial aspect had no bearing on forfeiture, the destruction of the victim as a result of an oath. Secondly, sacrifices usually included animals and food stuffs, perhaps because of earlier assumptions that these were needed to feed the god. Forfeiture, on the other hand, was total. It included people, livestock, and all property. In addition, sacrifice entailed the division of the part dedicated to God from other parts of meat, which were permissible as food, some of which were given to the priests, and others to the owner of the animal who was making the offering. There could be no benefit from a forfeiture.

Forfeiture originating in an oath to God was less severe than the other variety named in the Bible—a ban necessitating extermination because of a sin (of defined type) or an act that aroused God's wrath. Deuteronomy 7 lists such a ban on the seven nations that lived in the land of Israel: Hittites, Girgashites, Amorites, Canaanites, Perizzites, Hivites, and Jebusites. A most severe ban was imposed on a city in Israel where "sons of Belial" (i.e., wicked persons) had induced the residents to worship other gods: "You shall put the inhabitants of that town to the sword, . . . and everything in it—even putting its livestock to the sword. All of its spoil you shall gather into its public square; then burn the town and all its spoil with fire, as a whole burnt offering to the LORD your God. It shall remain a perpetual ruin, never to be rebuilt" (Deuteronomy 13:15–16).

That was the extremist ideology of forfeiture, but pressures evolved to soften the law that disregarded practical considerations. The concept of forfeiture obviously entailed immense waste, and even those who were prepared to turn a blind eye to human victims tended to regret the loss of valuable property. Accordingly, various texts in the Bible illustrate a spectrum of banning, in which the extreme version was not applied.

Deuteronomy 2–3 tell of Israel's wars with King Sihon of Heshbon and King Og of Bashan. In both cases Israel was victorious, and a ban was imposed on the defeated cities, including women and children. Apparently the cattle and other property were not destroyed but taken as loot (3:7).

Joshua 6 contains a strict warning to observe the ban: the punishment of Achan, who infringed the ban, and all his household, has been noted earlier. Jericho was banned, yet at the same time, the text notes an exception: "But all silver and gold, and vessels of bronze and iron, are sacred to the LORD; they shall go into the treasury of the LORD" (6:19). The easing of the ban is also reflected in the etymological development of the Hebrew word *herem*, which originally meant complete destruction. It would take on another meaning—namely, "confiscation," which means a transfer of ownership, mostly to the authorities. This second meaning is the one that has come down to modern day.

The easing of the ban described in Joshua was done to the benefit of the tabernacle treasury. In those days, religious and secular authority were concentrated in the hands of one leader. Possibly, when religious leadership and secular kingdom were separated, a dispute arose over who was to supervise the ban and who was authorized to moderate it so that seized property (and possibly captives) could be confiscated rather than destroyed. Such an argument underlay the friction between Samuel and Saul after the latter's victory over Amalek.[31] Probably, with consolidation of the monarchy, the king's power gradually dominated, so that confiscated but not destroyed property was transferred to the royal coffer rather than to the priests. In Ahab's day, property came to him rather than to the temple treasury.

We have seen that the Hammurabi Code occasionally provided that an offender's property be transferred to his accuser. Other nations probably had a similar law for confiscation to the benefit of the crown, at least for certain offenses, particularly those committed against the king or the state,[32] and the kings of Israel, having learned of the law, adopted it.

Another hint at such a law in other lands is to be found in the book of Esther, where the queen threw a banquet for King Ahasuerus and Haman, at which she accused the latter of being an enemy seeking to destroy her people. Haman, pleading for his life, fell on the queen's couch. The king, thinking that Haman was assaulting Esther in her own home, ordered that Haman be hanged. The story continues: "On that day King Ahasuerus gave to Queen

---

[31] See the later chapter "The Rise of the House of David: The Problem of Legitimacy," p. 147.

[32] Uffenheimer (*Ancient Prophecy in Israel*, 225) mentions an Akkadian tablet from the fifteenth century B.C.E. that indicates that the property of an offender who had been executed went to the king.

Esther the house of Haman, the enemy of the Jews" (Esther 8:1). How did Ahasuerus take Haman's house? Did he have a general authority to confiscate his subjects' property? Or was there a law that the property of an offender was forfeit to the throne? The book of Esther is not a strong authority for the existence of such a law, for it is more a farce than an attempt at serious history. Haman himself, for all his evil, was executed for a crime that he had not committed. The enemies of the Jews, including all Haman's sons, were also killed. It is doubtful, therefore, whether a conclusion can be drawn from the giving of Haman's house to Esther.

The book of Ezra relates that, in the days of King Darius of Persia, a document was found dating from the reign of Cyrus that contained instructions for the building of the Temple. Darius sent the document to the governor of the province Beyond the River, with the instruction that anyone who deviated from the command should be impaled on a beam from his or her house, after which the house was to be destroyed (Ezra 6:11).[33] The Persian Empire, where Esther was written and where Ezra acted, was founded centuries after Ahab, but the above injunction may support the assumption of the existence of a law confiscating, to the king's benefit, the property of people condemned to death or authorizing the king to take it for himself.

The scope of the law, if indeed it existed in Ahab's day, is far from clear. To this end, offenses entailing a death sentence can be divided into three groups:

(1) Offenses against religion, such as violation of the Sabbath, idolatry, and perhaps witchcraft.

(2) Offenses against the king and state—for example, rebellion.

(3) Offenses between humans, such as manslaughter, selling someone into slavery, and even striking a father and mother (Exodus 21:15).

It is certainly possible to imagine a law ordering the confiscation of an offender's property in the first two categories, but not in the third. The confiscation might also benefit various bodies, depending on the offense. As for offenses between humans, it can be assumed that a fine or compensation would benefit the aggrieved party, not the treasuries of the king or temple. But there is no mention in the Bible of a law that would give the aggrieved party an offender's entire property.

The story of Naboth's vineyard could indicate the development of a law of confiscation to the king's benefit, but its scope is unclear. Did it cover all capital

---

[33] According to Haim H. Cohn, the punishment was not for disobeying the command but for altering it ("Studies in the Book of Ezra," in *Selected Essays* [Hebrew] [ed. Aharon Barak and Ruth Gavison; 2 vols.; Tel-Aviv: Bursi, 1991], 1:57, 65).

crimes, or only those against the king (group 2 above), or maybe also crimes against religion (group 1 above)? Naboth was charged with blasphemy against God and the king. The offense therefore was against both. The transgression against the king may have been enough for his property to be seized by the crown. Indeed, R. David Kimchi (Radak), in his commentary, notes that when death is imposed for a crime against monarchy, the property goes to the king; in other cases in which the court orders execution, the heirs inherit. This was presumably the reason why Jezebel insisted that the witnesses testify to blasphemy against God and king. Had Naboth only blasphemed God, his judgment would have been strictly a court ruling, and his property would have passed to his heirs. This interpretation raises the question as to why the witnesses could not accuse Naboth merely of "cursing the king." Radak explains that "cursing God" was added to heighten the anger at Naboth. Whatever the case, the addition did not detract from the king's right to confiscate the property.

With the continuing evolution of Jewish law came an assumption that the property of a condemned person, who had committed a crime against the monarchy, belonged to the king. Maimonides said: "All who are killed by the king, their wealth goes to the king" (*Hilkhot Melakhim* 3:9). This rule was apparently based on the Naboth affair. The alternative interpretation, that Ahab inherited through kinship, was thereby rejected.

Still, the story of Naboth is a weak authority for the existence of such a rule and its acceptance in Jewish law. The biblical and traditional opinion of Ahab is negative, and if he enforced such a rule of confiscation, he could have learned it from one of the neighboring peoples with whom he had contact (his wife Jezebel, it will be remembered, was the daughter of the king of Sidon). But the Jewish commentators of the Mishnah and Talmud times, and the Middle Ages, did know other legal systems, and the ruling about confiscation of an offender's property was not unknown to them.

The rule that a condemned person's property went to the state was customary in early Roman law. It originally related to offenses against the state (*crimen maiestatis* and *perduellio*). That category covered a long list of crimes, among them relations with enemy states, violation of civil or religious obligations, and even harm to public functionaries. But there is a belief that the law of confiscation was also enforced in a few other cases. The death penalty was sometimes commuted to exile, called by the Romans "negation of the right to fire and water," but such a commutation left the confiscation in force. Nevertheless, considerable flexibility was applied. Sometimes part of the property was exempted, and usually the children were allowed as much as half the estate.

Because property confiscation was conditional on conviction of the offender, some chose to prevent that result by committing suicide. Tacitus states emphatically that suicide was a way of avoiding confiscation.[34] A well-known example is that of Gnaius Piso,[35] who had been appointed governor of Syria by Tiberius. Sometime later Germanicus, Tiberius's nephew whom he had adopted as a son, was sent there. There was some friction between the two, and Germanicus died in mysterious circumstances amid rumors that Piso had poisoned him. Other rumors pointed to the emperor himself, claiming that he envied Germanicus for his popularity. Some people suspected that Tiberius wanted to get rid of Germanicus in order to ensure the succession for his son Drusus and that Piso had acted on instructions. Piso's trial was held in the Senate. There was no evidence of poisoning, but the atmosphere was hostile and the charge augmented by contentions that he had behaved badly to his troops in Syria. The likelihood of conviction was, therefore, substantial. Before the culmination of the trial, Piso was found dead, his throat slit and a sword lying by him. The accepted assumption was suicide, though it could have been murder. The Senate debate continued, and eventually Tiberius approved the transfer of half of Piso's estate to his son—on condition that he change his name.[36]

Another incident involves Sejanus,[37] who rose to power in the reign of Tiberius. Sejanus was appointed commander of the Praetorian Guard. During Tiberius's prolonged residence in Capri, Sejanus was the main channel of information from Rome to the emperor. Though he acquired immense power, in 31 C.E. his fortunes abruptly declined, perhaps because he was suspected of plotting a coup d'état, or perhaps for other reasons. Tiberius craftily summoned Sejanus to attend a Senate debate, where the emperor's bill of accusations against him was read out. Sejanus was sentenced to death and executed. Tiberius then put on trial a long series of people connected one way or another to Sejanus, who were accused of treason. Again some opted for suicide before trial in order to avoid confiscation.

However, during the period of the emperors, resistance developed to the "evasion" of confiscation by suicide, at least in serious cases, and property was sometimes nevertheless confiscated.[38] Suicide ceased to provide a safe way to protect property for the family, though the door was not completely shut.

---

[34] Tacitus, *Annals* 6.29.

[35] Zvi Yavetz, *Tiberius and Caligula: From Make-Believe to Insanity* (Hebrew) (Tel-Aviv: Dvir, 1995), 33–39.

[36] Richard Bauman, *Crime and Punishment in Ancient Rome* (London and New York: Routledge, 1996), 58.

[37] Yavetz, *Tiberius and Caligula*, 78–102.

[38] Theodor Mommsen, *Römisches Strafrecht* (1899; repr. Gratz, Austria: Akademische Druck-U. Verlagsanstalt, 1955), 1007; Bauman, *Crime and Punishment in Ancient Rome*, 59–60.

There remained a way to make an early accommodation with the emperor, whereby the latter gave approval to the accused to take his own life and the confiscation law would not be enforced. This happened to the eminent philosopher and playwright Seneca, who was the tutor and counselor to Nero (emperor of Rome in 54–68 C.E.). In 65 C.E. Seneca was accused of involvement in a plot by Gaius Piso. It is unlikely that he was involved, but he might have known about it and kept silent. Nero reacted harshly. Seneca was condemned to death in absentia but was given permission to commit suicide.[39] It seems that the suicide prevented confiscation, even though it took place after conviction.

Punishment with confiscation of property opened the way to miscarriages of justice. The Naboth affair was an outstanding example. The false accusation was made solely for the purpose of acquiring his property. Once the law allowed the confiscation of the convicted offender's property, Naboth's case ceased to be an exception. There is no shortage of parallels in Roman law. Suetonius, in his book *Twelve Caesars,* writes about the emperor Domitian (81–96 C.E.), son of Vespasian and brother of Titus, the conqueror of Jerusalem, that he was in sore financial straits because of his profligacy. The solution was plunder, inter alia, by confiscating the properties of the living and the dead. "Any charge, however slight—to have spoken or acted in prejudice of the Emperor's welfare was enough—might result in confiscation of man's property, even if he were already dead."[40] Domitian was not the only one to make cynical use of the law. Caligula, so it is said, also needed a regular source of wealth to cover his excesses. Once in a single session, he sentenced more than forty men, then boasted to his wife about how much he had acquired while she slept.

The viewpoint that supported the confiscation of the offender's property was adopted by medieval European law and the feudal system. The idea came to England following the Norman conquest of 1066 and was enforced for "felony"—a word adopted from the French that originally referred to offenses of a vassal in his obligations to his lord, to whom he owed loyalty and service. Since the feudal system was based on the granting of land by a lord to a vassal, any offense against feudal obligations was punishable by the retraction of the

---

[39] Tacitus, *Annals* 15.61–63. Bauman (*Crime and Punishment in Ancient Rome,* 87–88) mentions also the case of Antistius Vetus, who killed himself when he heard that he was to be tried by the Senate. Nevertheless, he was tried after death and sentenced to execution. The sentence would incur confiscation, but Nero intervened and permitted the suicide (which had already taken place). The property was thereby saved.

[40] Suetonius, *Domitian* 12, in *The Twelve Caesars* (trans. Robert Graves; New York: Penguin, 1979).

land rights. While the continental concept of felony was limited to feudal offenses against the lord, in England the concept spread to cover any serious crime, the penalty for which was death or amputation—irrespective of feudal connections. One contention was that the extended scope of felony resulted from greed for the felon's property.[41]

The rule regarding confiscation rested on powerful but conflicting interests, in which the loot was divided between king and nobles. The Magna Carta, the great English bill of rights given by King John to the barons, included a specific provision that, in the case of a felony, the criminal's land would be given to the lord.[42] But this rule did not apply in cases of treason, which was seen as directly affecting the crown. Then the confiscation would be to the king's benefit. The broad definition of treason led to a dispute between the king and the nobles. The two sides reached a compromise reflected in a 1352 legislation, which distinguished between high treason and petty treason. High treason included an attack on the monarch, his family, and certain functionaries; participation in war against the monarchy; and the forging of coin of the realm. All these resulted in confiscation for the crown. Conversely, in cases of petty treason, as for example the killing of a lord by a servant, the confiscation would be to the lord's benefit, subject to the king's right to the land for "a year and a day."[43]

This division of rights between monarch and nobility, which related to land, did not cover other assets of the offender. Movables and money in any event went to the king. The lust after such property was so great that, in the case of thieves or bandits, their stolen loot was deemed fit for confiscation, rather than returnable to the rightful owners.[44] Similarly to what happened in ancient Rome, there were English "felons" who opted for suicide in order to preserve the family property and prevent the destructive results of conviction. But England had an interesting variation, a product of the amazing English criminal procedure. A person accused of a crime was expected to plead guilty or not guilty. But what happened if one refused to plead? Today such a refusal is taken as a plea of innocence, and the prosecution has to prove its case. In the past, such silence posed considerable difficulty. The historical background to this lay in the transition from the trial by ordeal to the use of jurors.

---

[41] Pollock and Maitland, *History of English Law*, 1:303–5, 2:464–66.

[42] William Holdsworth, *A History of English Law*, vol. 3 (5th ed.; 1942; repr., London: Methuen, 1966), 69–70.

[43] Theodore F. T. Plucknett, *A Concise History of the Common Law* (5th ed.; London: Butterworth; Boston: Little, Brown & Co., 1956), 443; Pollock and Maitland, *History of English Law*, 2:50.

[44] An exception was the case of private criminal action, the scope of which was limited (Holdsworth, *History of English Law* [5th ed.], 3:328–31).

Trial by ordeal, in which the question of guilt was resolved by immersion in water or the use of white hot irons, though used in many societies, was declining, and in 1215 the Fourth Lateran Council of the Church resolved to abandon it. England exchanged the ordeal for a trial by jury. The transition to the new method was, apparently, conditional on the accused agreeing to be tried by a jury. Any response to the charge, whether guilty or not guilty, was construed as consent to trial. If one refused to plead, the court had no authority to hold a trial. To overcome the problem of an intransigent defendant, the court could resort to torture—a method known as *peine forte et dure*. The tortures included the placing of heavy weights on one's body, to the point of endurance and beyond. It seems that a determined investigator could obtain, in almost every case, a plea from the accused, if the torture was slow and prolonged enough. But occasionally there was willingness to modify the procedure and place on the accused such a heavy load that would cause death within a fairly short time. The accused, in this event, had not been sentenced and thus could not be considered a felon, so the property remained in the family. It was, so to speak, assisted suicide, and some saw in it a form of death penalty imposed without confiscation of property.[45]

The option of preserving property by willingness to endure death by torture was not open to those accused of treason. In such cases, refusal to plead was deemed a confession, and the accused was condemned accordingly.[46] The principle that the court's authority depended on the accused answering the charge is an example, though not the only one, of a legal rule that has historical roots and explanations, yet lacks all logic. Consequently, to overcome or circumvent this rule, another equally illogical rule is adopted, in this case a particularly brutal one.

The law requiring confiscation of a felon's property was abolished in England in 1879, but in fact it had not been enforced for many years from the moment the king gave up his right to confiscation of property.

Postscript: The Diaries of Eichmann and the Modern Principle against Profiting from Wrong

We began the discussion of the confiscation of an offender's property with the Naboth affair and will close with an Israeli episode. Confiscation of that sort has never been customary in the State of Israel. When the state was

---

[45] Langbein, *Torture and the Law of Proof*, 74–77.

[46] Earl Jowitt and Clifford Walsh, "*Peine forte et dure*," in *Jowitt's Dictionary of English Law* (2d ed. by John Burke; London: Sweet & Maxwell, 1977).

established in 1948, that legal institution was already dead and gone. Nevertheless, there was a rumor that the rule had been applied in the case of Eichmann's diaries. The death penalty for murder has been abolished in Israel but remains as a possible sentence for a number of offenses under the Emergency Security Regulations and the Law for Prosecution of Nazis and their Assistants. In fact, there have only been two cases of death penalty since 1948: one, imposed illegally in the Tobiansky affair,[47] and the other, Adolf Eichmann, one of the main figures responsible for the extermination of European Jewry in World War II.

At the end of the war, Eichmann fled to Argentina. In 1960 he was captured by Israeli agents and brought to Israel for trial. He was convicted and sentenced to death. I am told that after his death his heirs asked for the diaries that he had written in prison. But a legal opinion, delivered by the Ministry of Justice, based on the Jewish law on the confiscation of the property of convicts executed for crimes against the "kingdom," rejected the request. I have been unable to verify the facts or obtain a copy of the opinion. Personally, I do not think that this archaic law applies in Israel. But, if indeed it was used, then this is an ironic twist that a rule originating in the miscarriage of justice in the case of Naboth the Jezreelite should have won a singular modern resurrection following the trial of Adolf Eichmann. As for the diaries themselves, it seems that the government of Israel has no reason to withhold them from the public, as has recently been decided by the Attorney General. There remains the question of copyright and of the income that might accrue from publication. One possibility, the validity of which I doubt, is that the State of Israel is entitled to confiscate the diaries and the copyright. It is to be hoped that in such an event the diaries would be available to the public without charge. But if that is not the case,[48] then the question arises whether the rights belong to Eichmann's heirs, and whether it is possible to deny a criminal (or his heirs) the right to benefit from the fruits of his writing in which he describes his misdeeds. I will return to this point briefly at the end of the chapter.

The shocking phenomenon of murder in order to inherit did not pass from the world after the days of David and Ahab, and after the abolition of the law by which Ahab won Naboth's vineyard.

---

[47] Tobiansky was wrongly convicted of treason by an improperly constituted court-martial during the War of Independence. He was innocent.

[48] Moreover, even if the government made them available free of charge and someone published them, the question could arise whether the heirs can demand compensation on the grounds that this constituted breach of the copyright that they claim to own.

When, in modern times, the system of life insurance developed, it brought with it murder for the sake of the insurance proceeds. Some countries have specific laws to deal with that possibility. In Israel, section 5(a)(1) of the Succession Law provides that a person convicted of intentionally causing or attempting to cause the death of another is disqualified from inheriting from the victim (in the case of attempted murder, the victim who survived can forgive the offender, who is thereby reinstated as an heir). As far as insurance is concerned, the Israeli Insurance Contract Law provides that the insurer is relieved of liability if "the event insured against is brought about intentionally by the insured or the beneficiary."[49]

But even in the absence of explicit legislation, courts have concluded that a murderer may not inherit his or her victim. A well-known decision was rendered by the New York Court of Appeals in 1889, in the case of *Riggs v. Palmer*.[50] It concerned the case of a grandfather who wrote a will in favor of his grandson and thereby sealed his own fate. The grandson murdered his grandfather, while the statute relating to wills and devolution of property as it was formulated did not expressly deny the right of the murderer to inherit. According to the strict wording of the statute, the grandson could inherit, but the court held by majority that "[n]o one shall be permitted to profit from his own fraud, or to take advantage of his own wrong . . . or to acquire property by his own crime."[51] The court therefore decided to qualify the language of the law and so denied the murderer's right to inherit.

The principle underlying the rhetorical question "Have you killed, and also taken possession?" was extended into a general principle that seeks to deny criminals and wrongdoers the fruits of their wrongs. The precise contents of this principle and the range of its application pose complex questions. In the present context, I shall merely refer to one judgment of the Supreme Court of Israel that shows the wide variety of circumstances in which the issue might arise. A childless couple had despaired of having offspring, so the husband (the appellant) decided to seduce the fifteen-year-old daughter of his neighbors, whose mother had died of cancer, so that she would bear a child for him and his wife. The girl, who was younger than he by twenty years, became pregnant. He did not tell her that it was possible to discontinue the pregnancy, and when the fact became known to her family, it was too late. The girl wanted

---

[49] In some legal systems the insurance company is required to pay out, in the case of the insured being murdered by the beneficiary, to the insured's other heirs.

[50] 22 N.E. 188.

[51] Ibid., 190. Additional American decisions are discussed in George E. Palmer, *The Law of Restitution* (4 vols.; Boston: Little, Brown & Co., 1978), 4:233–55, in which relevant legislation adopted by a number of American states is also referred to.

to give the child for adoption. The appellant objected, asking that the child be given to him, while the girl adamantly refused to pass the baby to him and his wife. The behavior of the husband was described by Justice Shlomo Levin in the following words: "It is difficult to describe in words the behavior of the appellant who made such uninhibited use of this young girl's body to exploit her as an instrument of satisfying his desire for a child, with contempt for her sensitivities, her innocence, her dignity and the dignity of her family. The case is exceptional even in the wider world, and the parties have not succeeded in finding a similar deed in all the voluminous literature on the subject, and my research on the matter has also come up empty."[52]

The Israeli law on adoption provides that a child shall not be given for adoption unless both parents agree. There are a number of exceptions to this rule, one of which applies when a parent is incapable of caring properly for the child because of his or her behavior or situation. The question that arose in court, therefore, was: Is it possible to give the child for adoption, as the mother wanted, or was that impossible since the appellant, the biological father, objected and wished to receive the child? All five judges decided that the adoption could be carried out. However, their approaches differed: the majority concluded that the exception applied, and the child could be given for adoption despite the objection of the father, since he was not capable of caring for the child properly. Justice Dalia Dorner stated that "the rearing of the child by the father, who had created him by the forbidden sexual possession of the mother, and had done so by a preconceived plan, in order to acquire a child for himself and his barren wife, is likely to severely harm the child."[53]

I would, however, side with the minority opinion of Justices Cheshin and Levin, who reached the same conclusion by a different route. In their opinion, it could not be said that it was proven that the father was unable to care properly for the child, and according to the language of the law, simply put, the child could not be given for adoption without the father's consent. However, despite the fact that this was the language of the law, it should be qualified by the universal principle that forbids a person to benefit from one's own wrong. Justice Michael Cheshin, who specifically mentioned the cases of Uriah the Hittite and Naboth the Jezreelite, named the principle "to kill and inherit," saying: "It cannot be here in our country, that a man may murder and inherit his victim, and we shall not accept—in principle—that a man may do wrong and profit from his wrongdoing."[54] He added that the principle "to kill and

---

[52] *Anon. v. Anon.* 50(3) P.D. 133, 146 (Hebrew).
[53] Ibid., 145.
[54] Ibid., 169.

inherit—in its wider context—remains valid in Israeli law." This principle, based on public policy, exists alongside the laws enacted by the Knesset (Parliament), and in the present case it denied the father the right to obtain his son by preventing his adoption.

To return to Eichmann's diaries, a question arising in modern jurisprudence is whether it is possible, under the principle against profiting from wrong, to take away the profits of offenders who by virtue of the publicity accorded their crimes receive fees or royalties for media appearances or the publication of their memoirs. The issue raises profound and controversial questions. In various states of the United States, legislation has been passed denying royalties to a criminal or freezing them to provide compensation to the victims. But in one case the Supreme Court of the United States struck down such a statute on the ground that its language was too broad, and it did not distinguish between a situation where the offense was central to the writing or where it was entirely secondary. The U.S. Supreme Court pointed out that the law as drafted could affect the writings of personalities such as Martin Luther King, Bertrand Russell, and Walter Raleigh. The law was thus held to conflict with the principle of free speech embodied in the First Amendment of the U.S. Constitution. However, the Court did acknowledge that the state had an interest "in ensuring that criminals do not profit from their crime" and that "victims of crimes are compensated by those who harm them."[55] It seems, therefore, that the validity of such a law will be recognized in the United States, if it is properly drafted and is not overly inclusive.[56] In any event, the victims of a crime can sue the offender in damages and attach the royalties paid to the criminal in order to collect them.

----

[55] *Simon & Schuster v. Members of the New York State Crime Victims Board*, 502 U.S. 105 (1991). For discussion, see Lord Goff of Chieveley and Gareth Jones, *The Law of Restitution* (5th ed.; London: Sweet & Maxwell, 1998), 810–14; Gareth Jones, "Stripping a Criminal of the Profits of Crime," *Theoretical Inquiries in Law* 1 (2000): 59, 74–78.

[56] Indeed, following the decision of the U.S. Supreme Court, the New York legislature enacted a more narrowly drafted statute on the subject: Executive Law, Art. 22, §632a.

7

A Godly Man Killed by a Lion

✳

After King Solomon's death (ca. 930 B.C.E.), the kingdom split in two. The house of David continued to rule in Judah, while ten tribes led by Ephraim set up a separate kingdom of Israel, ruled by Jeroboam son of Nebat, who had led the rebellion. At first his capital was in Shechem, and later in Penuel. Jeroboam built temples in his kingdom so that his people would not be dependent on Jerusalem. In so doing he made two golden calves, placing one in Bethel and the other in Dan (1 Kings 12:28–29). One feast day as Jeroboam ascended the altar in Bethel, a man of God appeared before him. The story, as told in 1 Kings 13, is in three parts. The first describes the visitor's prophecy to the king, that a son named Josiah would be born to the house of David and that he would smash the altar and defile it by burning on it human bones. As proof of the messenger's credentials, the altar split and ashes poured out of it. In his anger the king reached out to seize the man of God, but his arm withered and he begged the man to pray for him. The visitor did so, and the arm returned to normal. Jeroboam then invited the man to dine and receive a reward, but the invitation was rejected: "If you give me half your kingdom, I will not go in with you; nor will I eat food or drink water in this place. For thus I was commanded by the word of the LORD: You shall not eat food, or drink water, or return by the way that you came" (1 Kings 13:8–9).

Thus far the story has a clearly political motive with the prophecy at its center. Josiah was king of Judah some three centuries after Jeroboam. In his time, a scroll of the Torah was discovered in the Temple and read out to the king, who regained his faith and renewed the covenant with the Almighty. He destroyed the idols and altars dedicated to Baal and Asherah and the temple at Bethel. Jeroboam's altar was split and human bones were burned on it. In

112

telling of Josiah, 2 Kings 23 links his deeds to the earlier prophecy and attributes Josiah's action to the words of the man of God.

It seems that the story of the man of God originated in the times of Josiah, or even later, the intention being to justify the king's actions and to strengthen Jerusalem as the sole place for ritual and sacrifice. The Jerusalem priests were seeking a monopolistic status for their Temple—an interest that coincided with the desire of the house of David to restore the city as the capital of all Israel.

The motive of part one of the story is, therefore, transparent. Other than the politics, it has no particular interest. As for the miracles recounted, the Bible is full of miracles, many of them greater. But the other parts of the story are breathtaking in their forcefulness and do not seem to strengthen the status of the house of David or of Jerusalem. They do contain psychological foundations and a legal aspect to which I will refer.

The man of God, doing as he was told, refused Jeroboam's invitation to partake of bread and water. He began his return home by a route other than the one by which he came.[1] Now the story takes a totally different turn, with a new central figure. An old prophet living at Bethel, hearing of the man of God's prophecy and of the miracle he had performed, set out after him on a donkey. There followed a dialogue between the two (1 Kings 13:14–24):

"Are you the man of God who came from Judah?"
He answered, "I am."
Then he said to him, "Come home with me and eat some food."
But he said, "I cannot return with you, or go in with you; nor will I eat food or drink water with you in this place; for it was said to me by the word of the LORD: You shall not eat food or drink water there, or return by the way that you came."
Then the other said to him, "I also am a prophet as you are, and an angel spoke to me by the word of the LORD: Bring him back with you into your house so that he may eat food and drink water."
But he was deceiving him.
Then the man of God went back with him, and ate food and drank water in his house.
As they were sitting at the table, the word of the LORD came to the prophet who had brought him back; and he proclaimed to the man of God who came from Judah, "Thus says the LORD: Because you have disobeyed the word of the LORD, and have not kept the commandment that the LORD your God commanded you, but have come back and have eaten food and drunk water in the place of which he said to you, 'Eat no food, and drink no water,' your body shall not come to your ancestral tomb."

---

[1] Uriel Simon suggested that the prohibition of returning by the same route is rooted in the superstition that the retracing of steps implies retreat or a failure of the mission (*Reading Prophetic Narratives*, 169–70).

> After the man of God had eaten food and had drunk, they saddled for him a donkey belonging to the prophet who had brought him back. Then as he went away, a lion met him on the road and killed him.

This is not the end of the story. Word of the man of God's death reached the aged prophet, who picked up the body, took it to his own town, and arranged a decent burial. Then he told his sons that when his time came, they were to bury him in the grave of the man of God, for his prophecy would come to pass. In the chapter in 2 Kings that deals with Josiah breaking up the altar and desecrating the graves, the king discovers the burial place of the man of God, hears of his prophecy, and decides to extend his protection to the tomb: " 'Let him rest; let no one move his bones.' So they let his bones alone, with the bones of the prophet who came out of Samaria" (2 Kings 23:18).

The second part of the story, therefore, deals with the aged prophet's trickery and the punishment of the man of God who was deceived. The third part refers to the prophet's reaction to the death of the man of God. The old man was probably absent when Jeroboam offered the sacrifice on the altar but did hear about the man of God's miracles. Introducing himself as a prophet, he added the lie that an angel of the Lord had ordered him to bring the man of God home to eat and drink. The story offers no reason why the prophet brought about the downfall of his guest.[2] Was he angry that the word of the Lord and the miracles came from the man of God rather than from himself? Maybe he sought reinstatement as a prophet by hosting a man with a proven link to the Almighty? Does his behavior indicate a belief that proximity to the man of God causes something to rub off on him? The sequel seems to hint at that. Alongside the ancient superstition that impurity is contagious, there was a similar belief that the touch of a holy man, or even passing through his shadow, radiated protection and benefit. Similar beliefs persist to this day. Maybe this was his reason, or he was simply seeking contact with someone from Judah to hear what was happening there. Whatever the answer, the old man succeeded and the man of God came to his house, ate his bread, and drank his water.

Here the story takes yet another turn. God told the prophet that his visitor, having eaten and drunk where he had been told not to, would be killed and that his body would not be interred with his ancestors. This is indeed a surprising turn. The Almighty chose to speak to the prophet who had just committed a

---

[2] Simon (ibid., 170–71) offers the supposition that the old man wanted to invalidate the prophecy and protect Bethel. A contrary theory, referred to by Simon, is offered by Don Isaac Abarbanel, who suggests that the man was not a false prophet but really wanted to help the man of God. A third thesis presented by Josephus, *Antiquities of the Jews* 8.9, suggests that the prophet wanted to increase his own prestige by hosting the holy man.

shocking act in deceiving the man of God and to pass through him a message of the bitter fate that awaited his messenger. The traditional commentators dealt with this difficulty. Rashi and R. David Kimchi (Radak) offered the following explanation: the old man was a false prophet, and the man of God was a true prophet, but he was punished for disobeying the Lord. The first level of punishment was God's refusal to speak directly to him. What did the false prophet gain? Rashi explained that the holiness of the man of God did indeed permeate his surroundings. The resulting inspiration persisted even though the true prophet was being punished and his power of prophecy was being taken from him. The holiness of his prophetic ability only did him harm and brought down strict judgment upon him. The paradox is that the same holiness that could not help the holy man himself could still benefit the old prophet. He was forgiven his deceit and even received some little holiness from the man who had had his taken from him. The trick achieved its objective.

The next surprise is silence. The old prophet delivered the message of impending fate, the meal was over, and the prophet provided a donkey for the man of God, who departed without a word. He had nothing to say to the man who had tricked him and caused the sentence of death to be pronounced, with its denial of burial in his ancestral tomb. He was not angry; he did not shout nor did he complain. He went in silence, accepting his fate—and the lion killed him.

But the chronicler of this world of special morality is not finished. The old prophet collected the body, buried it, and requested his sons to bury him, when his time came, alongside the man of God. The request presumably reflects the belief that, though the Almighty had abandoned the holy man, there still remained in his body a residual holiness that could benefit his bones. The old man got the benefit he sought. Three hundred years later, when Josiah desecrated the graves and burned human bones on the broken altar, he did not touch the tomb of the man of God, with the bones of the old prophet.

The next focal point is the legal aspect of the viewpoint that would punish the man of God while rewarding the old prophet for his deception. The main difficulty lies in placing responsibility on a man who has performed a forbidden act unwittingly. According to the story, the man of God had every intention of obeying the Lord's command: he abstained from food and drink, prophesied as required, and departed by the route he was supposed to take. He only agreed to eat in the aged prophet's home after being persuaded that an angel of the Lord had so ordered. How then could he be punished so severely for an act performed in all innocence, in the belief that he was obeying God's commandment?

In modern law criminal guilt or intent *(mens rea)* is a central component of responsibility. The absence of intent to cause a forbidden result usually negates criminal responsibility. Similarly, a person is likely to be exonerated if one acts in error or self-defense. But the issue was viewed differently by the ancients. The essence of responsibility in ancient law has engaged the attention of many scholars. The primary question is whether guilt was a condition of responsibility or whether responsibility was absolute in ancient jurisprudence, in which case it was enough to commit a forbidden act, even without moral guilt (as we see it) or in all innocence, for punishment to ensue.

Justice Holmes, perhaps the greatest of American jurists, held that the form of ancient responsibility that was based on revenge (in many cases blood vengeance) was founded on guilt and limited to intentional acts, for "even a dog distinguishes between being stumbled over and being kicked."[3] But this view is mistaken. Other scholars are of the opinion that responsibility in ancient society was absolute. It was imposed for prohibited acts regardless of whether the offender was acting knowingly and with malice or innocently. In this view, gradations of this responsibility only developed in time. This is clearly reflected in mythology, literature, and even in law.

Another noted scholar, John Wigmore, presents the following example from Norse mythology.[4] The handsome and beloved god Baldur, son of Odin, was bothered by dreams that augured evil. His mother, the goddess Frigg, adjured fire and water and everything else that they would do no harm to Baldur. One solitary plant, the mistletoe, was considered too weak to do harm. All the gods threw things at Baldur to prove that he was indeed immune. But the jealous Loki found out that the mistletoe had not been sworn. Turning to the blind god Hodor, Loki suggested that he try his strength. Loki handed Hodor an arrow made of mistletoe and guided his hand. The arrow struck and killed Baldur. The gods tried to catch Hodor, but he got away, provoking Odin, father of Baldur and king of the gods, to declare: "Who will avenge the death of Baldur and send the murderer to hell?" Baldur's younger brother, Vale, took up the challenge and neither washed his hands nor combed his hair until he had slain Baldur's killer.[5]

---

[3] Oliver Wendell Holmes, *The Common Law* (Boston: Little, Brown & Co., 1881), 3.

[4] John H. Wigmore, "Responsibility for Tortious Acts: Its History," *Harvard Legal Review* 6 (1894): 315, 319–20. Richard A. Posner, *Law and Literature* (rev. ed.; Cambridge, Mass.: Harvard University Press, 1998) 49 et seq. devotes an extensive chapter to the motif of revenge in literature and its implications for the development of jurisprudence. He rightly indicates that the method of retaliation or punishment based on vengeance is not dependent on differentiating between damage originating in guilty intent or that which is justified, and there is no tool or mechanism to make that differentiation.

[5] Thomas Bulfinch, *Bulfinch's Mythology* (New York: Random House, 1934), 274–76, presents a different version in which Loki is punished.

Wigmore notes that a more obvious example of innocence, by our standards, would be difficult to find. Greek mythology also provides quite a few examples of the responsibility and the punishment of anyone who commits a forbidden act, regardless of innocent intent, mistake, or any other reason that we would deem exonerating. The well-known story of Oedipus fits this category. He grew up in the home of foster parents, never knowing who his real father and mother were. As a grown man Oedipus set out for Thebes, killing a man in a fight while on the way, not knowing that the man was his father. Reaching Thebes he married the king's widow, Jocasta, not thinking for one moment that this was his mother. Terrible catastrophes struck Thebes, and the oracle placed the blame on Oedipus's unwitting crimes. Jocasta committed suicide, while Oedipus went mad and put out his own eyes. The curse continued to haunt his children, as described in Sophocles's *Antigone*. This story too is based on the assumption that Oedipus's innocence could not detract from the severity of his deeds.

Biblical law contains a few references to a softening of the rules of absolute responsibility. In Numbers 35 and Deuteronomy 19 Israel is required to name cities of sanctuary, to which a person who killed unintentionally could flee. There such a one could be protected from blood vengeance, but if the act was intentional, then the sentence was death and the killer had to be handed over to the avenger.

If in a city a man lay with a virgin betrothed to another, both were to be stoned: "The young woman because she did not cry for help in the town and the man because he violated his neighbor's wife" (Deuteronomy 22:24). But if the act took place in the field, then only the man would be stoned to death, and the woman would go free, for there would be no one to hear her cries (Deuteronomy 22:26–27).

But this relaxation of strict responsibility is partial. The unintentional killer could be killed by the avenger if caught outside the city of sanctuary or before reaching it (Numbers 35:27). Enjoying protection only within the city of sanctuary, the killer had to stay there until the death of the high priest, for according to Ibn Ezra, that death "forgives Israel" for any act committed in his lifetime.

Responsibility without guilty intent also appears prominently in the stories of the Bible and perhaps teaches more about the thinking of the ancients. In a battle between Israel and the Philistines at Michmash, Jonathan, son of Saul, attacked and killed a few of the enemy. There was immediate uproar in the Philistine camp, and they began to flee. Saul ordered his men to give chase, making them swear not to stop to eat before evening. Jonathan, ahead of the army, did not hear the oath and, on his way, dipped his rod in a honeycomb and ate from it. That night Saul asked God if he should continue the pursuit of the Philistines, but the Lord did not answer. Saul understood that there had been a transgression. The men cast lots, and Jonathan, who was caught, admitted that he had tasted honey, adding, "Here I am, I will die." Saul replied, "God do so to me and more also; you shall surely die, Jonathan" (1 Samuel 14:43–44). The people of Israel protested against the sacrifice of Jonathan, who had brought them a great victory. A compromise was found, and the people redeemed Jonathan, though it is not clear at what price. Perhaps something else was sacrificed in his place.

For our purposes the concept of strict responsibility at the root of matters is important. Jonathan knew nothing of the oath and acted in error, so by our standards was guilty of no sin. But this breach of the oath, though innocent, caused God to withhold his answer from Saul, who presumably posed his question in the usual manner through the Urim and Thummim, the holy artifacts of the priests. Why did God punish Saul when Jonathan had acted in error? The traditional commentators have already delved into this question, and Radak, relying on R. Saadia Gaon, explains that it was done to show that a sin had been committed in error and to emphasize that there was no discrimination in favor of the king's son, in particular because the people were not aware that Jonathan was not present when the oath was sworn.

This is a neat explanation, but the story itself reveals an extreme conception of absolute responsibility, as shown by the sequel. Jonathan did not deny his guilt, he understood that he had sinned and that his ignorance of the vow was not an excuse. He expressed readiness to die, and Saul was willing to carry out the sentence, though his son bore no guilt. If we accept even the later traditional interpretation given above, the inadvertent sin is still a sin, and the transgressor is still guilty, even though his or her sin is less than that of a knowing perpetrator, and therefore the sinner can be redeemed.

This later commentary therefore reflects a stage of judicial development in which the inadvertent and innocent commission of a prohibited act is still considered a transgression, but the transgressors are now categorized by degree. The innocent offender (who today would not be an offender at all) can expect punishment, but it will be less than that meted out to a perpetrator who acted with malice. This attitude meshes with the ruling for mistaken manslaughter. The perpetrator is not entirely exempt, but the punishment is reduced.

In the case of the murder of Abner by Joab, the facts were as follows: after the death of Saul, David was anointed in Hebron as king of the tribe of Judah, while Ishbaal, Saul's remaining son, became king of the tribes of Israel. The two kingdoms were at war with each other. Second Samuel 2 relates that one day Joab, commander of David's army, encountered Abner, commander of Ishbaal's men, at the pool of Gibeon. Abner said to Joab, "Let the young men come forward and have a contest before us." Joab responded, "Let them come forward." The "contest" was for life or death. Joab's men won the field. Abner and his men took flight, with Joab in hot pursuit. Among the pursuers was Joab's brother, Asahel, who was known to be as fleet of foot as a deer. Asahel caught up with Abner, who pleaded for his life, but Asahel persisted. Abner struck Asahel with a spear, killing him on the spot. Some time later Abner wanted to defect to David's camp and in fact arrived in Hebron with some of his men. David received them courteously, laid on a feast for them, and sent them away peacefully. Along the way Joab met Abner and, with his brother Abishai, killed him, "because he had killed their brother Asahel in the battle at Gibeon" (2 Samuel 3:30). Joab may have had other scores to settle and probably feared that Abner would take his place as David's general. But it is important to note that the text suggests that the reason for the killing was blood revenge. The fact that Abner was not guilty of killing Asahel, for it happened in battle and in self-defense, while he was attempting to avoid the encounter, made no difference. For the purposes of blood vengeance, responsibility was absolute. The only defense for an unpremeditated killing recognized in the Bible was flight to a city of sanctuary, and even that was limited to mistaken or accidental killing. Other cases of killing without guilt, such as self-defense, are not mentioned.

The man of God belongs to the same category. He was ordered by the Lord not to eat bread or drink water in the place where he was to prophecy, and he disobeyed. According to ancient concepts, in their most extreme and rigid form, his responsibility was absolute, and he was punished accordingly. The fact that he acted innocently and was misled by the old prophet was no defense. Later commentary sought to soften that harsh conclusion by suggesting that the man of God's guilt was in being tempted to eat at the old prophet's house, without checking whether the old man was indeed God's messenger bringing changed instructions. Radak explains that the prophet was false, and the man of God should have "investigated and asked if he is a true prophet, and he transgressed in this and therefore his death was in the hands of heaven" (Radak's interpretation of 1 Kings 13:18).[6]

Radak (Rabbi David Kimchi), who lived from 1160–1235 C.E., more than a thousand years after the completion of the Bible, was unwilling to settle for the man of God's responsibility for unintentional violation of the Lord's

---

[6] Alexander Rofé, in *The Prophetical Stories* (Hebrew) (2d ed.; Jerusalem: Magnes, 1986), 153, also argues that the man of God could tell that the old prophet was lying. The biblical text contains no hint of that.

119

commandment. A more progressive conceptual world required some moral flaw in his behavior as a condition for punishment. The explanation offered, therefore, is that the man of God was negligent in not checking whether the old prophet spoke the truth—an explanation not supported by the text. Nowhere does it say that the old man was a false prophet. The story implies that he prophesied in the name of the God of Israel, not a pagan god such as Baal, for otherwise the man of God would clearly have rejected his invitation as he had done with Jeroboam. In those circumstances it is doubtful whether he could ascertain if the prophet usually spoke truth (as emanating from the Lord or his angels). Logic also suggests that prophets of the Almighty differed in appearance and garb from the prophets of other gods. If indeed it was so, then it must be assumed that the old prophet looked the part. Accordingly, it is doubtful that the man of God could check. Even if we accept Radak's thesis, the inference would be that the man of God was negligent in failing to check the prophet and his words. That does not detract from his innocence and belief that he was carrying out God's command. Modern criminal jurisprudence recognizes offenses of mere negligence, namely, actions lacking in criminal intent but defined as offenses in order to deter dangerous conduct. However, these are usually not very severe. In present-day conceptions, they would not lead to punishment of the kind described in the tale of the man of God and the old prophet. The story is founded on a totally different concept of responsibility—one in which the act, or prohibition, is the important factor while the accompanying intent and other circumstances are of little significance.

Another surprising aspect of the story is that the aged prophet, who played what seems to be a despicable trick, not only escaped punishment but was actually highly rewarded. God delivered him the prophecy of the fate to befall the man of God, and he died of old age, to be buried, at his request, alongside the man of God—in what was to become a protected grave.

This result seems in conflict with one of the most famous stories of the Bible: the snake in the garden of Eden. The serpent offered Eve a taste of the fruit from the tree of knowledge of good and evil. God had warned Adam and his wife that on the day they ate of its fruit they would die. But the serpent allayed her fears by saying: "You will not die; for God knows that when you eat of it your eyes will be opened, and you will be like God, knowing good and evil" (Genesis 3:4–5). Following these words, and struck by the beauty of the tree and its fruit, the woman was tempted to eat and to feed her husband. Their eyes were opened, they were ashamed of their nakedness, and they made themselves clothes. The divine investigation begins. Adam stated that his wife had tempted him, while she related that the serpent had persuaded her to disregard God's command. God turned to the snake and pronounced his sentence: "Because you have done this, cursed are you among all animals and among all wild creatures; upon your belly you shall go, and dust you shall eat all the days of your life" (Genesis 3:9–14).

This story has been the subject of many interpretations and has become interwoven with many motifs. For our purposes it points to the responsibility of an inciter and his punishment. The snake, who in the story is endowed with the human ability to speak, was not required to abstain from eating the fruit of the tree of knowledge of good and evil, nor apparently did he eat it. This did not detract from his cunning. Apparently the serpent had no need for the fruit,[7] and it seems that God had endowed more cunning to it than to humans. However, the fact that the prohibition did not apply to the serpent did not detract from its responsibility for inducing Eve and her husband to commit an act that was forbidden only to them. In Jewish law this story serves as the foundation on which guilt for incitement and seduction is based.

Some question the serpent's interest or motive. To my mind, no special motivation is needed, for the serpent symbolizes evil incarnate. It is the destructive force that comes to upset the good world that the Almighty created. Satan needs no motive for evil, for it is inherent in its nature, as it is in that of the serpent.[8] Legendary literature has offered the proposition that the snake lusted after the woman and wanted to cause Adam's death,[9] but there is no indication as to how Adam would die while Eve would survive. James Frazer suggests that the snake planned to trick the humans and achieve eternal life and did indeed succeed.[10] The theory is based on the ancient belief that snakes are immortal, based on the snake's "rebirth" when it sheds its skin. Frazer finds support for this view in the Sumerian Epic of Gilgamesh, in which the hero strives for immortality. After many ordeals he acquires a plant that can restore youth, but the snake grabs the plant out of his hand.[11]

---

[7] Christian literature contends that the fruit was an apple. Jewish tradition favors a vine with grapes and wine. See Haim H. Cohn, "Wines Tracta," in *Festschrift in Honor of Justice Itzhak Shilo* (Hebrew) (ed. Aharon Barak and Menashe Shava; Tel-Aviv: Israel Bar Publishing House, 1999), 93.

[8] The supposition that the serpent was Satan was rejected by Ibn Ezra (his interpretation of Genesis 3:1), since the snake was punished at the end of the story and compelled to crawl on its belly and eat dust. Clearly this could not be transferred to Satan. To my mind, the snake can be seen as the embodiment of evil without identifying it with Satan, as is done in later tradition.

[9] *Genesis Rabbah* 19:19, cited in Ginzberg, *Legends of the Jews*, 1:72.

[10] Frazer, *Folk-Lore in the Old Testament*, 18.

[11] For a comparison of the garden of Eden with the Epic of Gilgamesh, see Shin Shifra, "Eve the Rebellious Woman," in *Readings from Genesis* (Hebrew) (ed. Ruti Ravitsky; Tel-Aviv: Yediot Aharonot, 1999), 55, which also indicates that the snake spoke the truth.

The serpent did not lie; it spoke words of seduction and persuasion and allayed Eve's fear, but it spoke the truth. God had warned Adam and Eve that if they ate of the fruit of the tree, they would die. The serpent said that they would not die, for "God knows that . . . you will be like God, knowing good and evil." The pair did not die, but their eyes were opened. It is doubtful that they became as gods, but tradition attributes to the eating of the fruit the acquisition of knowledge, or at least the ability to distinguish between good and evil. Adam and Eve, the main transgressors, who violated the commandment, made no mistake and were not misled—they acted in the full knowledge that they were breaking the commandment and committing a forbidden act. From this viewpoint, the serpent's provocation does not detract from their responsibility. The snake did not tell them that the prohibition had been cancelled or that the act was permissible. All he said to Eve was that it was worthwhile to transgress. Before eating the fruit, Adam and Eve apparently could not distinguish between good and evil, so there is something shaky about their responsibility (at least morally), but the biblical author may have assumed that even the naive and unwitting had to understand that God's commands must be obeyed, and the story does contain an explicit instruction.

In any event, the story of the snake's seduction and punishment teaches that, although the transgressors' responsibility for the act remains, it is joined by the responsibility of the seducer and inciter.

Moreover, the traditional commentators found in the story a hint that the seducer's responsibility was the more severe. Under God's interrogation, Adam and Eve were required to give their version. The opportunity offered to the pair served in the early eighteenth century as the basis for Judge Fortescue's reasoning that anyone likely to be adversely affected by a judicial decision must have the right to present his or her case. At issue was the case of one Dr. Bentley, whose academic titles had been taken from him. Judge Fortescue noted: "Even God himself did not pass sentence upon Adam, before he was called upon to make his defence. 'Adam, says God, where art thou? Hast thou not eaten of the tree, whereof I commanded thee that thou shouldst not eat?' And the same question is put to Eve also."[12]

But in the affair of the original sin, the right to present a defense, or explain one's act, is not extended to the serpent. Adam and Eve are asked to explain their behavior. God hears their (inadequate) explanations and only then

---

12 *The King v. The Chancellor, Masters and Scholars of the University of Cambridge* (1723) 93 E.R. 698, 704. There are earlier Jewish sources that refer to God's questioning of Adam and of Cain as the basis to a right to a hearing to which the interested party is entitled. See R. Moses Isserles, *The Responsa of the Rema* (Hebrew) (1525?–1572), §108. The book was published posthumously in Krakow in 1640.

imposes punishment. But the first to be punished is the serpent, who is not asked for an explanation nor granted any hearing. Rashi explains it thus: "From this we learn that we do not give one who seduces people (to do evil) the opportunity to justify his actions" (commentary on Genesis 3:14). There is no point to hearing the snake, for it is clear that he will have a striking argument, presented as a question: "the words of the rabbi (God) or the words of the student (the snake)—whose words are heard?" The contention is based on the snake not lying. It tempted, or persuaded, but it was up to Adam and Eve to keep the commandment of God (the rabbi), and to ignore the seductive tongue of God's own handiwork (the snake). The rule in Jewish law is that the instigator is not responsible for the offense committed by whoever is persuaded, for the instigated person is forbidden to listen to provocation. In modern language it may be said that the independent judgment that the incited person is expected to have severs the causal link between incitement and action. Therefore, the instigator is not responsible for the crime committed by the incited but is responsible solely for the separate offense of incitement. On the other hand, in modern Israeli and Anglo-American jurisprudence, the inciter is considered to be a partner to the offense itself.

We should note the distinction between seduction or incitement and an actual order to commit an illegal act. Incitement implies solicitation to commit an improper act, where the persuader has no authority over the other person, who is perfectly free to ignore the persuasion and behave properly. That was the situation of Adam and Eve vis-à-vis the serpent. An order to commit an offense differs from seduction or incitement, in that the recipient may be punished if he or she does not conform. The question thus arises whether the recipient of the order has the independent judgment that enables one to behave properly and to ignore the illegal order (in the words of Jewish law: to obey the rabbi). Modern jurisprudence resolves this question by distinguishing between a possibly illegal command and a manifestly illegal one. The giver of the order is responsible in both cases, while the recipient is exempt in the first instance, but not in the second. While later Jewish jurisprudence exempts the instigator from responsibility for the offense, biblical law—at least in the case of an order—holds the giver of the order responsible for the outcome. Thus, David is considered responsible for the murder of Uriah, carried out at his command, and Ahab and Jezebel are held responsible for the murder of Naboth, on Jezebel's orders in the name of Ahab.

Returning to the man of God and the aged prophet, there clearly was no order, and the old man was lying when he said that God had given one. The man of God was not subservient to the prophet and was not obliged to obey his instructions. The seduction by the aged prophet is fundamentally different from that of the snake in the garden of Eden. The prophet did not persuade the man of God to perform an act that he knew was forbidden to him. The seduction was founded in trickery. There are midway situations in which the instigator tricks a victim in a manner that detracts from the severity of the offense but does not eliminate it completely. An example would be Iago's influence on Othello in Shakespeare's play, which falls between the cases of the serpent and the aged prophet. Othello is a black general commanding the armies of Venice. Iago, one of his subordinates, suggests that Othello's wife, Desdemona, is betraying her husband with another soldier named Cassio. By a series of tricks, culminating in the planting of Desdemona's handkerchief on Cassio, Iago succeeds in convincing Othello. In the grip of jealousy, Othello strangles his wife. Learning that his suspicion was unfounded and that Desdemona was innocent, Othello commits suicide and Iago is punished.

In this case, Iago the instigator had planted in his victim's mind a false belief in his wife's treachery. Had he spoken the truth, Othello's crime would not have happened. Nevertheless, Iago's trickery was not enough to justify the murder. Perhaps in the mores of the period, there were mitigating circumstances, but there is no doubt that Othello knew he was committing a terrible crime. The serpent's deed in the garden of Eden is less evil than the action of Iago, the "snake" in Shakespeare's play. As we have seen, the serpent did not lie. His seduction and persuasion left the full responsibility upon the shoulders of Adam and Eve. Another distinction is that Iago did not actually incite Othello to commit murder, only provided a false motive, while the serpent did persuade Eve to transgress. For our purposes, it is sufficient to note that Iago's action was founded on ugly trickery, while the serpent told the truth. Iago's deed resulted in the murder of a beloved wife—an offense between humans—while the serpent urged Eve to violate God's command, the moral purpose of which was far from clear (an offense between humans and God).

The trickery in the case of the prophet and the man of God is in some respects more serious than that of Iago, which led Othello to believe that he had "reason" to murder Desdemona. The reason was not sufficient to justify the act. Indeed, Othello's suicide derived not only from guilt at killing an innocent loved one, and the sense of loss that he had brought upon himself, but also from the fact that he had murdered without moral cause (whether or not there was "reason"). This is not the case of the aged prophet. The lying imagery that the old prophet conjured up for the man of God caused the latter to believe that the Lord had ordered him to eat and drink. In that respect there was no moral blame in his behavior. As for the snake in the garden of Eden, Adam and Eve could have obeyed the command and abstained from eating the forbidden fruit. They were free to reject the snake's proposition, and their sin lay in their yielding to him, though they knew that it was forbidden. The same is true for Shakespeare's play. Despite Iago's web of lies and trickery, Othello could have resisted the urge to commit such a terrible crime. The act of the man of God is radically different from the other two cases.

In essence, incitement is irrelevant in the affair of the man of God. Incitement implies persuasion or temptation by another person to carry out some forbidden deed. In modern legal conceptions, the instigator and the perpetrator are parties to the offense. This distinguishes incitement from the case of a murderer who sends a bomb to a victim by means of an innocent carrier who does not know what the package contains. Then the criminal act is entirely committed by the sender of the package. The messenger serves only as a tool used by the killer and is not a partner in the offense. In the reality created for the man of God by the old prophet's trickery, he had to go to the prophet's house to eat and drink. By our standards, the sole transgressor is the aged prophet. (On the surface, there is a problem inherent in the fact that the prohibition against eating and drinking was imposed only on the man of God, so how could the aged prophet, who was not subject to the command, be at fault?) In modern jurisprudence there is nothing to prevent the placing of responsibility on a person who causes the violation of a prohibition, even if the ban does not relate to the instigator, and even if the person affected by the restriction is exonerated on the ground of mistake or innocence. But the story of the man of God is based on a different conception, according to which the very breach of God's command imposes full responsibility, while innocence is not a defense. Meanwhile the aged prophet, the true villain of the piece, gets away unscathed because the prohibition did not apply to him. The text does not deal severely with the trickster, just as it glosses over trickery in other contexts.[13]

The tale of the man of God belongs to a group of stories that stress the importance of full and exact compliance with God's commands. The most famous of these is the sacrifice of Isaac. The fact that Abraham was ready to carry out God's awful command and sacrifice his son is evidence that he is the greatest of the righteous.[14] While Abraham was willing to comply, other stories in this category are characterized by noncompliance, which is severely punished. The common denominator in these stories is the absence of mitigating circumstances and indifference to the question whether the sinner

---

[13] See the earlier chapter "The Fruits of Deceit," pp. 62–66.

[14] Postbiblical literature tries by various means to confront the harsh dilemma raised by this affair. See the legends collected in Ginzberg, *Legends of the Jews*, 1:274–86. But the text is clear: humans must observe the commandment, no matter what its content.

acted knowingly or unwittingly, or what was the reason that caused the sinner to act. The violation of God's command is the only relevant factor in deciding the sinner's fate.

The stories of the blasphemer and the gatherer of sticks fall into this category. The blasphemer was the son of an Egyptian father and an Israelite mother who scuffled with another man and "blasphemed the Name in a curse" (Leviticus 24:11). The stick gatherer was caught on the Sabbath day (Numbers 15). In both cases the offenders are sentenced to death by stoning. The stories differ from that of the man of God in that both offenders act knowingly. However, it is clear that the blasphemer could claim mitigating circumstances, for the words came out in the heat of argument and struggle. We do not know what caused the stick gatherer to commit his offense, but from the biblical viewpoint it makes no difference. Both men violated a prohibition, and the reason was irrelevant.

Another story in this category describes a prophet who prophesied to Ahab after his return from victory over Syria. Ahab had released King Ben-hadad of Syria and made a treaty with him. The reaction was not long in coming and compares with Samuel's response to Saul, who had shown mercy to the king of Amalek. God sent a prophet to prophesy to Ahab about the punishment he and his people should expect. To do so the prophet told Ahab a parable while he was disguised (1 Kings 20:35–42). In order to produce a convincing disguise he needed to be beaten and bruised, so he asked a neighbor to strike him, saying that it was the wish of the Lord. The friend refused, and the refusal, which was tantamount to violation of God's command, resulted in an appropriate sanction. The prophet informed him: "as soon as you have left me, a lion will kill you." And so it came to pass. No reason is given for the neighbor's refusal. Perhaps he did not believe that God had given the command. But for the purpose of the story and its moral lesson, the reason is of no importance—what matters is the failure to obey the command. The content of the order, the questions whether the recipient understood the logic of it and whether he was acting innocently, are of no importance. The responsibility is absolute, and noncompliance determines the sentence.

Returning to the question of the aged prophet's motivation in bringing about the downfall of the man of God, the biblical text tells us nothing. This intriguing question was irrelevant for the author. A characteristic of biblical tales is their brevity. The story of the man of God is designed to emphasize that the prophecy of the destruction of Jeroboam's altar was a true prophecy, spoken by a true prophet—a fact worthy of note and reflected in the aura of holiness that extended even to the aged prophet—and that the violation of God's command, no matter why, resulted in death. The role of the aged prophet is to underline those points and to show that whoever does not comply will be punished severely, with no allowance for mitigating circumstances. The old man is a tool, and it matters not why he does what he does. Only from this standpoint is his status similar to that of the serpent, whose motives were of no interest to the chronicler. Any speculations about motives are outside the stories themselves and are simply the fruit of legends or of later theory.

8

Saul Kills the Priests of Nob

❦

When David fled from Saul, he came to the priestly city of Nob, destitute and hungry. Ahimelech, not knowing that Saul suspected David of treason, gave him food and weapons. Saul, hearing of it, summoned the priest for interrogation. Ahimelech said he had not known that David was fleeing from the king. David, after all, had a position in the king's court and was married to his daughter, Michal. Saul, not believing the priest, sentenced him to death, though Ahimelech contended that he had acted in innocence. This did not satisfy the king, who ordered the town of Nob put to the sword: "Men and women, children and infants, oxen, donkeys, and sheep" (1 Samuel 22:19).

In his *Antiquities of the Jews* 6, Flavius Josephus, writing a thousand years later, lists this killing as one of the sins that brought about Saul's downfall. But the strange fact is that Samuel, when listing the reasons for deposing Saul, did not include this brutal act or even mention it as justifying the taking of the throne from him. The explanation lies in the concept of responsibility and contagious guilt that existed when the book of Samuel was written.

Certain animals are unclean, and impurity is contagious:[1] "But all other winged insects that have four feet are detestable to you. By these you shall become unclean; whoever touches the carcass of any of them shall be unclean until the evening, and whoever carries any part of the carcass of any of them shall wash his clothes and be unclean until the evening" (Leviticus 11:23–25).

---

[1] Compare the idea in classic literature that misfortune is contagious, as is explained in Robert Graves's introduction to his translation of Apuleius, *The Golden Ass* (New York: Pocket Books, 1954). By this logic, sanctity is also catching. See the previous chapter "A Godly Man Killed by a Lion," pp. 114–15.

A menstruating woman is unclean and may not be touched, for the impurity is contagious (Leviticus 15:19). Similarly: "Every bed on which she lies during all the days of her discharge shall be treated as the bed of her impurity; and everything on which she sits shall be unclean. . . . Whoever touches these things shall be unclean, and shall wash his clothes, and bathe in water, and be unclean until the evening" (Leviticus 15:26–27).

The extent to which impurity radiates into the environment depends upon the severity of the deed and of the uncleanliness. The more extreme the act, the wider the area affected by transgression.

Shechem, the son of Hamor, "defiled" Dinah by raping her (Genesis 34:13). Shechem was the transgressor who was guilty of rape, but Dinah, his victim, was "unclean." Tamar, the daughter of King David, raped by her brother Amnon, had been damaged and perhaps lost any chance of marriage. It is no wonder, therefore, that after the rape Tamar put ashes on her head and mourned alone in the house of her other brother, Absalom (2 Samuel 13:19–20). Samuel Butler's *Erewhon,* a satire about Victorian society, describes—not unlike Swift's *Gulliver's Travels*—a voyage to an imaginary country with unique laws and customs. In *Erewhon,* misfortune and catastrophe are crimes. For example, a young man whose guardian cheated him and stole his property was put on trial and appropriately punished.

In the ancient worldview, sin and impurity spread beyond physical reach. Since uncleanliness infects its surroundings, "those born of an illicit union shall not be admitted to the assembly of the LORD" (Deuteronomy 23:2). The aura may be more than environmental: it may be familial and extend to offspring. Such was the case of Dinah. After the residents of Shechem were tricked into circumcising all the men, Dinah's brothers Simeon and Levi killed all the males in the city.[2] And "the other sons of Jacob came upon the slain, and plundered the city, because their sister had been defiled" (Genesis 34:27). The uncleanliness of the rape committed by Shechem, the son of the city's leader, had infected all the men. This was, of course, collective punishment, including men who were innocent, whose responsibility stemmed from their belonging to the same group as the offender, the group over which the uncleanliness spread.

Amalek attacked Israel during the wanderings in the desert, a grave crime that infected the Amalekites forever: "The LORD will have war with Amalek from generation to generation" (Exodus 17:16). Accordingly, the memory of

---

[2] An alternative explanation is that the killing was necessary to liberate Dinah, who was being held captive in the house of Shechem. See Sternberg, *Poetics of Biblical Narrative,* 445–75.

Amalek was to be erased, irrespective of whether the offsprings to be destroyed were guilty or not. The sin of their fathers and the curse passed from generation to generation to the end of time. The children of Israel were the ones required to impose the collective punishment, and it was said of Saul that he lost his kingdom because he had not carried out the punishment of Amalek.

Examples of uncleanliness that pass down the generations are also to be found among the Israelites. A bastard is one born of adultery or incest.[3] Such a child is infected with the impurity of the act, and the uncleanliness is hereditary—"Even to the tenth generation, none of their descendants shall be admitted to the assembly of the LORD" (Deuteronomy 23:3).

Sin and impurity can encompass family members and property. Such was the case with Korah, who with his flock challenged Moses' leadership. This was blasphemy, for Moses was the messenger of God, the chosen one. The punishment was meted out not only to Korah but to all his household and possessions: "The earth opened its mouth and swallowed them up, along with their households—everyone who belonged to Korah and all their goods" (Numbers 16:32).

After the conquest of Jericho, Achan defied the ban placed on the city and took a coat, two hundred silver shekels, and a gold bar. The terrible punishment included all the members of his household, their property, and, of course, the loot that he had taken.[4] All were stoned, then burned to death. This story shows, first, that according to the biblical concept of sin, Achan's violation of a ban infected the entire community. As a result, Israel was defeated in battle with the people of Ai, and warriors with no connection to the sin were killed. Second, after the transgressor was discovered, punishment was meted out to all his people, oxen, donkeys, and sheep. The sin stained the surroundings, the household, the animals, and even inanimate possessions. All were destroyed.

Collective punishment appears in the Bible where the authority of God's messengers is undermined, as is the case with Korah, or following a violation of a divine command—ritual rather than interpersonal. The case of Achan is a good example. Punishment is in many cases a ban or forfeiture, that is, destruction dedicated to God.[5] In dealing with other nations, such destruction could follow if they placed an obstacle in the way of the children of Israel

---

[3] See the later chapter "Death of a Bastard," pp. 293–95.

[4] For discussion, see the earlier chapter "From the Trial of Adam and Eve to the Judgments of Solomon and Daniel," pp. 10–11.

[5] The concept of ban or forfeiture is discussed in the earlier chapter "To Kill and Take Possession," pp. 99–100.

or stood in the way of some divine plan connected with them. Such a ban encompassed the seven nations living in the land of Israel, as described in Deuteronomy 7. The Israelites were ordered to destroy them, and no questions were raised as to their guilt, though it could be argued that their practices "defiled" the land and made it "unclean."

A ban could also be imposed among the people of Israel as the outcome of a serious transgression. As punishment, the ban would mean destruction dedicated to God, and it would preserve its collective nature. An outstanding example is the total ban imposed on a city where evil people of Israel had persuaded the inhabitants to worship other gods. Such a city would arouse God's wrath.[6] Accordingly, the city had to be put to the sword and destroyed, with all its population and flocks. The properties of the town were to be placed in the street and burned with the city itself: "It shall remain a perpetual ruin, never to be rebuilt" (Deuteronomy 13:16).

This concept of collective responsibility is associated with the ancient view of absolute responsibility, which we discussed in the previous chapter, "A Godly Man Killed by a Lion." The fact that the sons of Achan and Korah were in no way guilty of their fathers' sins did not exempt them from retribution. The accountability was absolute, evolving from the severity of the committed crime. But collective responsibility was an earlier and more extensive form of responsibility than personal absolute responsibility. In the case of personal absolute responsibility, people were punished for committing a forbidden act, even if they acted innocently. In collective responsibility, they may be punished not only in innocence but even without committing the act. Punishment is meted out because the prohibited deed was done by someone connected to them by family, tribe, or environment.

The story of David handing over Saul's seven sons to the Gibeonites, who put them to death in retaliation for the harm done to them by Saul in his time (2 Samuel 21), belongs in this context. The act was done in times of hunger, supposedly resulting from the injustice done to the Gibeonites. Perhaps it served David as a means of ridding himself of the last of Saul's house. But the explanation that in order to remove the threat of famine, the Gibeonites had to be allowed to kill the sons for a sin committed by their late father, fits the worldview of those days.

The destruction of the priestly city of Nob, with which this chapter opened, has to be understood against the same background. Ahimelech had sinned (albeit innocently) by giving aid to a rebel against the kingdom. The

---

[6] Regarding the wrath of God, see Haim H. Cohn, "The Wrath of the God of Israel (Ira Dei Iuadaeorum)" (Hebrew), *Tel-Aviv University Law Review* 1 (1971): 13.

sin infected his household and property, so the entire city was put to the sword—including infants and animals. To complete the picture, we note that the narrative itself is not without reservations. It is said that Saul's men were unwilling to carry out his instruction to harm the priests of God (1 Samuel 22:17), and only Doeg the Edomite had no qualms. In any event, the deed was not the cause of Saul's loss of his throne. It seems that the book of Samuel omitted this act from the list of sins for which the king was deposed because, in the concepts of the times, it was permissible for a king to behave in this way with a city whose leader had helped a rebel against the kingdom.

Two hundred years later, in approximately 780 B.C.E., King Joash of Judah was murdered by two of his servants (2 Kings 12:21–22) and was succeeded by his son Amaziah. The murderers must have been men of some status, since Amaziah executed them only when the kingdom was confirmed in his hand (2 Kings 14:5). The Bible stresses Amaziah's righteousness, in that he did not kill the sons of the murderers: "Parents shall not be put to death for their children, nor shall children be put to death for their parents; only for their own crimes may persons be put to death" (Deuteronomy 24:16).[7] It is possible to find contrary instructions in the Bible: God orders visiting the sins of the parents on the children (Exodus 34:7), and it is on this basis that the book of Kings interprets the history of sons punished for their parents' sins, as were the sons and grandsons of Saul. Various attempts have been made to resolve the inconsistency,[8] but it seems that the contexts show different trends. At first, the dominant view placed the individual in the collective, which was infected throughout by the transgression of one of its members. Then came a gradual change leading to the concept of personal responsibility.

To return to King Amaziah, who executed his father's murderers, today no one would comment on the obvious, that the sons of the murderers were not punished. That the Bible makes a point of it as proof of Amaziah's righteousness shows that in those days it was not a matter of course, and it was perhaps expected that the entire family would be executed. Amaziah's moderation was an important step toward abolition of collective responsibility and in the direction of personal accountability.

---

[7] Reuven Yaron, "The Evolution of Biblical Law," in *La formazione del diritto nel Vicino Oriente antico,* by Aristide Theodorides et al. (Naples: Edizioni Scientifiche Italiane, 1988), 77, 82–83, mentions additional legislation of the ancient world, in which emphasis is put on personal responsibility and negates collective responsibility.

[8] For detailed discussion, see Moshe Halbertal, *Interpretive Revolutions in the Making: Values As Interpretive Consideration in Midrashei Halkhah* (Hebrew) (Jerusalem: Magnes, 1997), 122–44, who examines the turnaround in midrashim that negates collective punishment and seeks to interpret the Bible in that spirit.

The idea that there is no room for collective, hereditary, or familial responsibility finds clear expression in the prophecies of Ezekiel, who was one of those exiled to Babylon a few years before the destruction of the Temple. A contemporary of Jeremiah, he prophesied in Babylon from 593 B.C.E. Ezekiel sharply disposed of the verse "The parents have eaten sour grapes, and the children's teeth are set on edge" (Ezekiel 18:2) by declaring, "The person who sins shall die. A child shall not suffer for the iniquity of a parent, nor a parent suffer for the iniquity of a child" (Ezekiel 18:20).[9]

---

[9] See also Jeremiah 31:28–29.

9

Jephthah Sacrifices His Daughter

Jephthah's story unfolds against the background of a war with the Ammonites. Its literary structure is unique. Judges 10–11 describes the Israelites' despair as the kingdom of Ammon prepares to fight, then breaks off to tell the story of Jephthah and his daughter. No less than forty verses are devoted to the subject, though the war is mentioned in only a few words.

First we are told that Jephthah was the son of Gilead and a harlot. Gilead's wife had also borne sons, and they drove Jephthah out to prevent him sharing in their father's estate. However, when the people of Gilead were threatened by the Ammonites, the elders went to Jephthah, who became famous as a warrior and commander, to ask for his help. He rebuked them for hating him and driving him out of his father's house and asked why they had come to him now. Finally he agreed to help, after they confirmed him as their leader in a ceremony at Mizpah.

What can be learned here about inheritance and the rights of an illegitimate son when the father had offspring by his legal wife? Some commentators believe that Jephthah's half-brothers were within their rights in driving him out. One scholar draws an analogy from section 27 of the Lipit Ishtar Laws,[1] which grants inheritance to the son of a harlot when the legal wife has no children. Gilead, the father of Jephthah, did have sons by his legal wife, so local custom would deny the claim of the harlot's son.[2] Another scholar maintains

---

[1] The Lipit Ishtar Laws are a Sumerian codex enacted ca. 1930 B.C.E. in Mesopotamia (now Iraq). These laws preceded the Code of Hammurabi by about two hundred years, and Jephthah's time by eight hundred years.

[2] I. Mendelsohn, "The Disinheritance of Jephthah in the Light of Paragraph 27 of the Lipit Ishtar Laws," *Israel Exploration Journal* 4 (1954): 116.

the reverse: the prevailing law was biblical, and it did not deny the rights of the harlot's son but recognized all the sons, legitimate or not. His conclusion is, therefore, that driving Jephthah out was in violation of the law.[3] The trouble is that the text throws no light on whether biblical law was in force or whether Gilead followed another code, and if so what that was.[4] The author is concerned with Jephthah's expulsion, not with its legality or illegality. From the sequel it is clear that Jephthah was angry with the elders of Gilead because of his expulsion and perhaps demanded the righting of what he considered to be an injustice. Even if they supported Jephthah's brothers at the time, there is no suggestion that they acted illegally. The fact that at a later stage, when they depended on Jephthah, they were forced to concede to his demands does not indicate that the expulsion was illegal. Moreover, the text does not say that Jephthah was given any rights in his father's estate even at this stage, or whether he was merely appointed leader.

At first Jephthah tried to avoid war by repeated messages to the king of Ammon. The words of his emissaries expressed historical knowledge, reason, and wisdom but were to no avail. War became unavoidable. Before going to war, Jephthah made a vow that, if God gave the Ammonites into his hands, he would sacrifice the first person to emerge from his house to meet him upon his return. After the victory, the first to come out of his door to meet him with timbrels and with dances was his only daughter. Jephthah believed that he could not go back on his oath. His daughter understood and encouraged him to obey the dreadful vow. In fact, the language of the vow already indicated readiness to commit human sacrifice. Jephthah faced a fateful mission, and his vow had to contain a significant price. Since the oath specified the sacrifice of the first to emerge from his door to meet him, he clearly knew he would have to sacrifice someone close and dear to him. Perhaps he left the choice to God or to fate, or maybe he knew who was likely to greet him but did not have the courage to name her.

It is also clear that Jephthah, in sacrificing his daughter to God, was convinced that he was acting correctly. Here there is an obvious difference between the brothers' expulsion of Jephthah and the swearing of the oath. The brothers were acting according to their interest in removing Jephthah from the inheritance. The assumption that they acted against the law, because of

---

[3] Joseph Fleishman, "The Legality of the Expulsion of Jephtah," *Diné Israel: An Annual of Jewish Law Past and Present* 18 (1997): 61.

[4] Jephthah's expulsion can be compared with that of Ishmael by Abraham at Sarah's request—an act done with the declared intent of disinheriting Ishmael, though there are differences. See also the later chapter "Infertility, Surrogacy, and Sperm Donation," p. 241.

their self-interest, is possible but not necessarily borne out. On the other hand, Jephthah was acting completely against his self-interest. The inevitable conclusion is that he did so because he believed he had to honor his vow. His daughter said so: "My father, if you have opened your mouth to the LORD, do to me according to what has gone out of your mouth, now that the LORD has given you vengeance against your enemies, the Ammonites" (Judges 11:36). Jephthah had made a contract with God, who had kept the initial part of the deal; Jephthah had to keep his word, in particular as it was believed that nonfulfillment of an oath could bring down heavy divine punishment. And there was no prophet or legal figure among the Gileadites who could tell him that the law prohibited the sacrifice of his daughter or that there was a loophole to release him from the oath.

The sacrifice was performed after the victory over the Ammonites—in other words, after the external pressure had abated and the distress had passed. In this, the story differs from other examples of sacrifice of a leader's son or daughter, which was usually performed in times of great despair, when the father faced actual danger. This was the case of King Mesha of Moab in 2 Kings 3, to which I will return later in the chapter. In Greek mythology, Agamemnon behaved similarly when he set out to the war with Troy and his fleet was becalmed at anchor. Agamemnon chose to sacrifice his daughter, Iphigenia, to the goddess Artemis for favorable winds.[5]

Postbiblical Hebrew literature is very critical of Jephthah and contends that he acted illegally. According to Flavius Josephus, the sacrifice of his daughter was neither according to the law nor according to the wish of God.[6] There are even stronger expressions in the aggadah (legend): "Jephthah was an ignoramus, and that is why he lost his daughter." The description of Jephthah as an ignorant boor is meant to suggest that he did not know the Jewish law and therefore believed that he had no choice. This type of traditional commentary seeks to explain biblical stories that do not conform to the Jewish law as laid down in the Torah or its later interpretation. According to this approach, the prevailing and binding law is the Jewish law, but the concerned parties either misunderstood it or did not know it. The technique is highly problematic, particularly in Jephthah's case: he was a leader and governor, and he would surely have received all the necessary advice from authoritative persons.

---

[5] This is one version. In another version Iphigenia was saved, and a gazelle was sacrificed instead (cf. the saving of Isaac in Genesis 22:13), while she became a priestess in the temple of the goddess. This latter version was adopted by Euripides, who wrote two plays that bear her name.

[6] *Antiquities of the Jews* 5.7.10.

Moreover, Jephthah's daughter asked for a two-month reprieve in which she went with her friends to the mountains to bewail her virginity. That was sufficient time in which to clarify the law and seek a loophole. The aggadah (legend) tries to solve this difficulty with the following version: the high priest Phinehas was there and could have released Jephthah from the oath, but would not do so out of pride, saying "I am a high priest the son of a high priest. Why should I humiliate myself before an ignoramus?" Jephthah was also too proud to approach Phinehas: "I am head of the tribes of Israel. Why should I humiliate myself before this common priest?" So Jephthah's daughter fell victim to the vain pride of her father and the high priest.[7] So much for legends. But the inescapable conclusion remains that the prevailing law of those days mandated carrying out the vow in every detail, with no possibility to redeem it with a substitute. The attempt to describe Jephthah as an uncultured ignoramus does not correspond to his approach to the king of Ammon to prevent the war, an attempt that showed learned historical understanding, reason, and intelligence. It is very hard to believe that such a man would put his daughter to death out of sheer ignorance.

The story of Jephthah and his daughter has a parallel in Greek mythology. Idomeneus[8] was the grandson of King Minos of Crete, who in turn was the son of Zeus, while Minos's wife Pasiphae was the daughter of Helios, the Greek sun god before Apollo.[9] Idomeneus was king of Crete, famous for his good looks and a suitor of Helen. In the Trojan War, he led a Cretan fleet of eighty ships and was noted for his bravery. After the victory over Troy, he headed for home, but his ship was caught in a storm. Idomeneus swore to Poseidon that if he returned safely to Crete, he would sacrifice the first person he met. Upon his return Idomeneus met his son and sacrificed him. From a moral standpoint, the legend of Idomeneus is more progressive, because he was punished for his act—Crete was struck by a plague and its residents drove Idomeneus out. Jephthah's story contains neither remorse nor punishment for a deed described as unavoidable, and perhaps even worthy of merit.

The story of Mesha of Moab also tells us much about the thinking of those days. The setting was the war between him and Jehoram, son of Ahab and king of Israel, and Jehoshaphat, king of Judah. Moab sustained heavy

---

[7] *Midrash Tanhuma*, parashat *Behuqqotay* 5 (*Midrash Tanhuma* has been translated into English by John T. Townsend [2 vols.; Hoboken, N.J., Ktav, 1989, 1997]); *Genesis Rabbah* 60:3.

[8] William Smith, ed., *Dictionary of Greek and Roman Biography and Mythology* (3 vols.; London: Taylor & Walton, 1844–1849), 2:562.

[9] Pasiphae was noted for mating with a bull and giving birth to the Minotaur, a monster held in a labyrinth. The Greek hero Theseus killed the Minotaur and, using a spool of thread given to him by Minos's daughter Ariadne, found his way out of the labyrinth.

blows at various stages of the war. When Mesha grasped the seriousness of his situation, "then he took his firstborn son who was to succeed him, and offered him as a burnt offering on the wall. And great wrath came upon Israel, so they withdrew from him and returned to their own land" (2 Kings 3:27). Mesha's desperate act saved his nation from defeat. The account of the war between Moab and Israel is supported by the well-known inscription on Mesha's stela, discovered in 1868 and later transferred to the Louvre in Paris.[10] The inscription is almost a mirror image of the Bible, given of course that Moab appears in place of Israel and the Moabite gods in place of the God of Israel. The Moabite god Chemosh was angry with Moab and delivered his country to Omri, king of Israel. Moab broke free of the yoke of Israel and won a series of victories. Mesha proclaimed a ban, as a result of which seven thousand Israelite men, women, and children were sacrificed to Ashtar-Chemosh.

The stela makes no mention of the sacrifice of Mesha's son, an event at the center of the biblical version, which is of special significance because it strays from the model that attributes the course of history solely to the determination of the God of Israel. Here Mesha's son is sacrificed to Chemosh, and this determines the outcome of the war. Chemosh is not named specifically, nor is it said that the son was sacrificed to him, but the point is clear. Neither is it stated that Chemosh determined the outcome against the children of Israel, though the unavoidable conclusion is that they believed it to be the case. The biblical story thus implies a clear belief that such a sacrifice could be effective and could save people in distress. It is no wonder, therefore, that Jephthah and the Gileadites shared this belief; convinced that Jephthah had sworn an oath and that God had delivered the Ammonites into his hands, he had to keep it.

These four stories of human sacrifice, two from the Bible and two from Greek mythology, have a common denominator. In every case the sacrifice was a son or daughter of a leader, and all achieved their purpose. Traditional commentary claims that biblical law forbade the sacrifice of sons and daughters. In Deuteronomy 12 the children of Israel are warned not to follow the Gentiles or worship their gods: "You must not do the same for the LORD your God, because every abhorrent thing that the LORD hates they have done for their gods. They would even burn their sons and their daughters in the fire to their gods" (Deuteronomy 12:31). The verse does not say explicitly that sacrifice of sons and daughters is forbidden to the Israelites, but the implication is clear.

---

[10] An English translation of the inscription, by W. F. Albright, entitled "The Moabite Stone," appears in James B. Pritchard, ed., *Ancient Near Eastern Texts Relating to the Old Testament* (3d ed. with supplement; Princeton, N.J.: Princeton University Press, 1969), 320–21. In Albright's opinion, the inscription was written toward the end of Mesha's reign, roughly in 830 B.C.E.

Instructions of a different nature can be found in biblical law. Human sacrifice is approved in the context of forfeiture, namely, the destruction of life and property that is dedicated (or confiscated) to God. The instructions are especially strict. The ban usually concerns a defeated enemy or an Israelite who has violated the boycott of an enemy. The Mesha Stela also speaks of forfeiture, namely, destroying the king's enemies—the children of Israel. Reference to bans on Israelites may also be found in the Bible in other contexts. The laws contain difficult injunctions: "Nothing that a person owns that has been devoted to destruction for the LORD, be it human or animal, or inherited landholding, may be sold or redeemed; every devoted thing is most holy to the LORD. No human beings who have been devoted to destruction can be ransomed; they shall be put to death" (Leviticus 27:28–29). Later interpretation sought to limit the injunctions, but the words are harsh and do present the possibility of ban on any person, not especially an enemy.

Biblical law recognizes the validity of vows made to the Lord and requires that they be kept. The subject is discussed throughout the Bible: Leviticus 27 refers to personal vows translatable into money equivalent, in other words, an obligation to pay sums estimated as the "price" of the person to whom the vow relates. But Numbers 30, which also speaks of vows, makes no mention of such release or redemption. Traditional interpretation considers it allowable to promise to avoid carrying out a permissible act, but not to vow a forbidden one. Accordingly, a vow to sacrifice a son or daughter is invalid, since it is assumed that such sacrifice is prohibited.

Biblical stories also mention the possibility of integrating a vow with a ban. In Numbers 21, the Canaanite king of Arad fought against Israel and took captives. Now the Israelites promised God that, if God delivered the enemy into their hands, they would destroy his cities. God agreed to the transaction, and both sides kept their word: God by delivering the Canaanites and the Israelites by destroying the cities. It may be assumed that, in the course of the destruction, men, women, and children of the vanquished were also killed. There is considerable similarity between a ban leading to destruction of booty and the offering of sacrifice, but it is unlikely that the killing and destruction were in the frame of a religious ceremony.[11] The obvious difference between this event and Jephthah's deed is that he was not sacrificing a vanquished enemy but his own flesh and blood.

The Bible mentions other cases of human sacrifice by the children of Israel. The story of Isaac, in Genesis 22, speaks of God "testing" Abraham and of

---

[11] Other distinctions are discussed in the earlier chapter "To Kill and Take Possession," p. 100.

the alternative sacrifice of the ram. This may be seen as an interim stage, permitting redemption by substitution of an animal, yet the story does indicate an ancient tradition involving human sacrifice.

The historical narratives and the books of the prophets provide clear evidence of the custom, though its scope and circumstances remain shrouded in mist. Human sacrifices were made to Molech at Topheth in the valley of the son of Hinnom in Jerusalem—a place that in time came to stand for the punishment of evildoers in the next world, in other words, "Gehenna" or hell. Of King Ahaz, who ruled in Judah during the rise of the Assyrian Empire (ca. 715–730 B.C.E.), it was written: "And he made offerings in the valley of the son of Hinnom, and made his sons pass through fire, according to the abominable practices of the nations" (2 Chronicles 28:3; cf. 2 Kings 16:3). A century later the righteous king Josiah "defiled Topheth, which is in the valley of Ben-hinnom, so that no one would make a son or a daughter pass through fire as an offering to Molech" (2 Kings 23:10). Later commentary suggested that "passing children through the fire" meant they were to jump over the flames, but it seems that the reference is to human victims burned to death. It is not clear in what circumstances human sacrifices were offered, whether as part of a vow, in desperate situations, or where the sacrificer was seeking to atone some sin or to win God's favor. Other unanswered questions deal with the identity of Molech to whom these sacrifices were made and whether the sacrifices were always to alien gods or also to the God of Israel. The word "Molech" is clearly related to the Hebrew *melek* or "king," and it was used for various gods, including the Almighty. The sacrifice of Isaac, which was not completed, was to the God of Israel. The sacrifice of Jephthah's daughter was clearly to the God of Israel. The later prophets, notably Jeremiah and Ezekiel, came out strongly against human sacrifice, in language that is sometimes horrifying. For example, Jeremiah spoke of the people of Judah who did evil in the eyes of the Lord by building furnaces in the valley of the son of Hinnom: "To burn their sons and their daughters in the fire—which I did not command, nor did it come into my mind" (Jeremiah 7:31). The reference to sacrifices that God did not command, or even consider, indicates that the crime was not rooted in worship of an alien god but was the offering of human beings to the God of Israel, which displeased the Almighty.[12] The English scholar James Frazer considers that there was an ancient tradition of human sacrifice in Jerusalem and points out that in order to sacrifice Isaac, Abraham had to take

---

[12] On this subject, see Jacob Liver's entries on "Moloch" and "Passing of Sons to Moloch" and Shmuel Safrai's "Sacrifice" and "Human Sacrifice" (Hebrew), in *Encyclopaedia Biblica* (Jerusalem: Bialik Institute, 1972–1982); and Jeremiah 19:5; 32:35 and Ezekiel 23:39.

the boy to a mountain in the land of Moriah. Widespread opinion locates Mount Moriah on Mount Zion in Jerusalem.[13]

Postscript: Faust

The phenomenon of human sacrifice has vanished, but the desire to reach agreement with supernatural forces, to acquire powers and goals in this world, continues to fire the imagination. Its best-known personification is Dr. Faustus, the hero of Christopher Marlowe's play (1604) and Goethe's famous work, and various musical compositions, among them operas by Gounod and Boito, and Berlioz's *Damnation of Faust*. The idea has undergone some metamorphosis.

The God of monotheistic religions has become a source of benevolence, with whom such deals are no longer imaginable. But beside God there grew a belief in an evil supernatural being, Satan, with whom it is possible to strike a bargain. This idea has been joined by a belief in the separation of body and soul, where the soul is the important partner, and between this and the next world, of which the one to come is the more important. The belief extends to the payment to be made to the supernatural power for the attainment of ambitions in this world. It is no longer the sacrifice of the human body but the sale of the soul—no longer the giving up of life but the handing over of the soul after death. There is one positive aspect to this development: humans no longer sacrifice sons or daughters to their ambitions. For this one must now give one's own soul.

---

[13] James George Frazer, "Adonis, Attis and Osiris," in *The Golden Bough: A Study in Magic and Religion* (3d ed.; 12 vols. in 13; New York: Macmillan, 1951), 2:219, note "Moloch the King."

PART TWO

Kingdom, Crown, and Prophecy

10

The Rise of the House of David:
The Problem of Legitimacy

David is the legendary king of Israel, the hope of the nation and the object of its dreams for thousands of years.[1] The emblem of the modern State of Israel is the *Magen David*—the "Shield of David." He is the fearless youth who, with a slingshot and a handful of pebbles, won a brilliant victory over the Philistine giant Goliath, whom no Israelite warrior dared to face. David is the beloved of God. His sins are forgiven him, and he has the upper hand in every fight. He and his son Solomon share between them all that is exalted in the human spirit. A man of sensitivity and fierce faith, he is a warrior, a great conqueror, a poet, and the author of numerous psalms. Solomon is the epitome of wisdom and the builder of the Temple. They are credited with authorship of some of the greatest texts ever written. In their days the unified kingdom of Israel reached its peak of greatness, a legendary golden age.

Moreover, David's kingdom was sanctified both in biblical historiography and the people's memory. This was no ordinary realm like those of other nations, where dynasties rose and fell, to be replaced by others. The house of David was promised eternal dominion, and the Messiah who would redeem Israel is to come from its seed. For this reason, the way in which David and Solomon won the throne presents a serious problem as to the legitimacy of their ascent to power.

---

[1] The history of King David and his reign continues to stimulate interest. Recent books on the subject include Baruch Halpern, *David's Secret Demons: Messiah, Murderer, Traitor, King* (Grand Rapids, Mich.: Eerdmans, 2001); Steven L. McKenzie, *King David: A Biography* (New York: Oxford University Press, 2000); Yair Zakovitch, *David: From Shepherd to King* (Hebrew) (Jerusalem: Yad Ben-Tswi, 1995).

The main purpose of the legend of the house of David was to justify the removal of Saul's dynasty and to explain how David took its place. To do so it is necessary to confront the fact that Saul was a legitimate king, anointed at God's command by Samuel, the leading prophet of his time. Moreover, Saul worshiped the God of Israel and never turned to other gods.

As for Solomon, the question is how he became king despite being one of the youngest of David's sons and being the child of a marriage as problematical as that of David and Bathsheba. This question is dealt with in the chapter on "Succession to the Throne." The present chapter deals with the removal of Saul and the ascendancy of the house of David.

The Rise and Fall of Saul

The background to the book of Samuel is the continuous war between Israel and the Philistines, the bitterest and strongest enemy of that period. As the age of judges came to an end, the leadership passed to the seer Samuel, who was both a religious and military leader. As Samuel grew older, the nation demanded of him the appointment of a king. According to the biblical narrative Samuel succeeded in the struggle against the Philistines. The popular demand arose from his nomination of his own sons as judges, who were greedy, took bribes, and perverted judgment (1 Samuel 8:1–3). But the call for a king probably stemmed also from dissatisfaction with the conduct of the war against external enemies. Samuel was sorely hurt by the demand, for it implied his removal from military and political leadership. But God, while consoling him, ordered Samuel to accede to the people. The result was a division of power between a military and political leader and the prophet-priest. This separation between the religious and the secular authorities was one of the most dramatic events in the annals of Israel, and perhaps the most traumatic for the priesthood. It broke the tradition that originated in the time of Moses, when the tribes became a nation during their exodus from Egypt.

Moses was the model of the religious-political leader in whose personality all authority was unified. Moses met God face to face on Mount Sinai and received the Ten Commandments as well as all of the Torah directly from God. But Moses was also a statesman. He negotiated with Pharaoh, led the nation out of Egypt, judged and guided the people of Israel through the desert on their way to the promised land. This tradition continued throughout the period of Joshua and the judges. The national leader needed no prophet or priest as intermediary to obtain God's guidance and instructions.[2] God spoke directly to Joshua and commanded him to cross the River Jordan (Joshua 1:2). Joshua was more than a political-military leader who succeeded Moses—he received the word of God and was empowered to speak to God. Gideon had a dialogue with an angel of the Lord; he even spoke to God (Judges 6–7) and became both judge and ruler of Israel.

The break came in the time of Samuel. The national and military authority was taken from him and transferred to Saul. Henceforth God would not speak directly to the secular leader, but only to the prophet who would relay his words to the king. The direct link ended: God now worked through intermediaries.

Samuel was compelled to anoint a king who would take his place as national-military leader, and, as the story continues, God helped Samuel choose Saul, son of Kish. At first Saul was successful. He defeated the Ammonites and rescued the inhabitants of Jabesh-gilead from Nahash the Ammonite. Then he won a victory over the Philistines at Michmash. At this point a rift opened between Saul and Samuel, beginning with Saul waiting seven days before the battle for Samuel to come and sacrifice to the Lord. When Samuel did not arrive, Saul offered the sacrifice. Precisely at that moment Samuel arrived and condemned Saul for usurping his function. At this stage the prophet already forecasted Saul's replacement.

The rift deepened during the next war against Amalek, a war embarked upon at Samuel's demand in the Lord's name: to strike Amalek mercilessly and destroy it utterly— men, women, children, babies, and livestock (1 Samuel 15:3). In violation of the injunction, Saul spared King Agag of Amalek and part of his herds.

God then told Samuel that he regretted the choice of Saul as king. Samuel pleaded for a reversal of the judgment but to no avail. The following day Samuel presented himself to Saul, rebuked him, and informed him that God had repented having made him king. Saul tried to justify himself, expressed remorse, and begged for forgiveness, but in vain. Samuel told him: "The LORD has torn the kingdom of Israel from you this very day, and has given it to a neighbor of yours, who is better than you" (1 Samuel 15:28). The story ends with Samuel, the aged prophet, venting his anger on the Amalekite king and personally hewing "Agag in pieces." Then Samuel went home, never to see Saul again.

God then sent Samuel to anoint David, the youngest son of Jesse, a man of Bethlehem. Samuel did so in secret, for, as he told the Lord, if Saul heard that

---

[2] There were exceptions. Thus a man of God came to the priest Eli and prophesied the end of his dynasty (1 Samuel 2:27–36). Eli, who preceded Samuel, was a priest, and he and his sons led the Israelites.

he had anointed a rival, he would have him killed. As subterfuge, the prophet went to Bethlehem ostensibly to offer a sacrifice.

In time David came to Saul's court, according to one version after his clash with Goliath.[3] Saul quickly developed an intense dislike for the youth. Two reasons are offered: the first was jealousy, because when David killed Goliath the daughters of Israel sang, "Saul has killed his thousands, and David his ten thousands" (1 Samuel 18:7); the second was that "an evil spirit from God rushed upon Saul" (1 Samuel 18:10), causing him to throw his javelin at David. But the king's daughter, Michal, fell in love with David, and Saul offered her hand in marriage for a bride price of "a hundred foreskins of the Philistines," believing that David would fall into enemy hands. However, the young man upon whom luck always shone, killed two hundred Philistines and won the king's daughter. Saul continued to fear David and sought to kill him. David's wife helped him to evade Saul's assassins, as did Jonathan, the king's son. He escaped to the desert, pursued by Saul. The Bible tells of two chases, both of which failed, but not without David having an opportunity to kill Saul, an opportunity he was too noble to use. Eventually he and his men reached Philistia and were given sanctuary by King Achish of Gath.

Shortly thereafter the Philistines gathered to fight Israel. David and his men joined the Philistine army but were eventually rejected. They returned to Ziklag without taking part in the battle, which was fought at Gilboa. The Israelites were defeated, Saul fell on his sword, and the Philistines killed his three sons. David decreed general mourning for Saul and his sons, and ordered the execution of the Amalekite youth who brought him the news, on the grounds that the boy had confessed to killing Saul, though apparently at the king's wish.

David settled in Hebron and became the king of the tribe Judah. By this act, the kingdom was split in two, since one of Saul's surviving sons, Ishbaal, was crowned king over the remaining tribes. The split resulted in civil war between Judah, led by David, and the other tribes. As David achieved ascendancy, Ishbaal was betrayed and killed by two of his men. The killers brought his head to David, who executed them as he had done the messenger who brought news of Saul's death.

At this point David became king of all Israel and was anointed for the third time: first, secretly by Samuel, then as king of Judah, and now over the tribes. Nevertheless, the house of David had not achieved full legitimacy as the ruling dynasty of all Israel. In David's own lifetime there were two rebellions.

---

[3] For discussion of the conflicting versions of David's arrival, see the earlier chapter "David and Goliath: Trial by Combat," pp. 32–33.

The first, led by his son Absalom, was an internal matter within the dynasty, but Absalom was supported by dissatisfied elements, among them tribal leaders. The second revolt, led by Sheba son of Bichri, of the tribe of Benjamin—Saul's tribe—reflected on David's leadership outside of Judah: "Now a scoundrel named Sheba son of Bichri, a Benjaminite, happened to be there. He sounded the trumpet and cried out, 'We have no portion in David, no share in the son of Jesse! Everyone to your tents, O Israel!'" (2 Samuel 20:1).

Both rebellions were put down by force, but the rift remained below the surface. It would reappear at the end of Solomon's reign, when a new leader emerged—Jeroboam son of Nebat, who split the kingdom and reigned over most of the tribes of Israel. David's dynasty continued to reign but now only over the small kingdom of Judah.

The legitimacy problem comes down to this: By what right did the house of David depose Saul's dynasty? After all, Saul was God's choice, anointed by Samuel, the foremost priest and prophet of his time; he was the first king to unite the tribes of Israel; he won great victories over the Ammonites, the Amalekites, and the Philistines. So if David's legendary leadership was to be based on right and justice rather than naked force, Saul's replacement must be explained.

The justification is fivefold. First, Saul sinned against the Lord, who became disgusted and decided to replace him. Second, David was chosen by God and anointed by the same Samuel who had anointed Saul. Third, the responsibility for Saul's downfall and his death in battle with the Philistines lies directly with God, not David. Fourth, Saul persecuted and chased David through no fault of his, while David made every effort not to reciprocate Saul's persecution and attempts to kill him. Fifth, the kingdom fell to David following Saul's downfall, not as a result of any action of David's.

This version is awkward, and between the lines and even from the lines an alternate version emerges—with an entirely different story. The rise of David began with the rift between Saul and Samuel, arising from the prophet's fierce grudge against the man who had replaced him. Samuel therefore secretly anointed David king, destined to replace Saul. According to 1 Samuel 16, the Lord sent Samuel to the house of Jesse to anoint one of his sons king. Samuel's natural response was: "How can I go? If Saul hears of it, he will kill me" (1 Samuel 16:2). Anointing a rival king was obviously rebellion and treason, for which the punishment by all the rules was death. Samuel therefore adopted the subterfuge of appearing so as to offer sacrifice to the Lord. Then comes a detailed account of Samuel reviewing all of Jesse's sons, until God chose the youngest, a shepherd boy, "who was ruddy, and had beautiful eyes, and was handsome" (1 Samuel 16:12).

Some argue that this story is a later insertion designed as part of the legitimization of David. But this is a double-edged sword. On the one hand, David was God's choice, anointed by the great prophet Samuel. On the other hand, it means that not only Samuel, but David too, flirted with a death sentence for treason. In any event, it tells us about David's ambitions, which apparently took shape at an early stage.

This also conflicts with the official version of the relationship, according to which Saul persecuted an innocent David, motivated by jealousy and depression due to the evil spirit that possessed him. Yet, the text gives rise to another interpretation, that Saul feared David, believing that he sought to usurp the throne. What evidence did Saul have? The Bible does not elucidate, but this does not mean that Saul did not have solid evidence. The Bible presents the version of David and his supporters, in which Saul is portrayed as pursuing David for no good reason. The fact that David contemplated seizing the throne of the legitimate king is set aside, while the evidence that Saul may have had is not mentioned at all.

We can only guess as to the evidence. Had David, after his marriage to Michal, demanded to be named heir to the throne? Had David, once ensconced in Saul's court, begun to organize an independent military force? Was he seeking to divide the kingdom and rule over Judah, as he did after Saul's death? The Bible offers no hint. What does arise is that Saul understood this to be David's objective, as he said to his son Jonathan: "For as long as the son of Jesse lives upon the earth, neither you nor your kingdom shall be established" (1 Samuel 20:31). Apparently Saul was not mistaken, as later developments show. There is a basic contradiction between the description of David being anointed by Samuel in Saul's lifetime and the tale of his being pursued by Saul for no reason. The contradiction cannot be resolved.

David's seizure of power led not only to the loss of the kingdom by Saul's dynasty but also to its physical destruction. The prevailing custom was for the king of the new dynasty to wipe out his predecessor's house so as to avoid endangering his rule. David did so, if in a sophisticated manner, and the extermination was not absolute, as we shall see later.

The risk to the deposed king's dynasty is clearly reflected in the stories, which sound quite improbable, of Saul's pursuit of David. The chases failed. On two separate occasions David had an opportunity to kill his pursuer, yet did not do so. The first time, David and his men were in a cave when Saul entered to relieve himself, unaware that he was not alone. David's men told him that the Lord had delivered his enemy into his hands, but David only cut the skirt off Saul's robe, without being noticed (1 Samuel 24:4). Then David followed the king out of the cave and made a speech teaching Saul a moral lesson.

150

The king was convinced of David's righteousness, burst into tears, thanked his son-in-law for not killing him, and then wished that God would reward him for his goodness (1 Samuel 24:19). But Saul was not finished. He went on to make a remarkable declaration: "Now I know that you shall surely be king, and that the kingdom of Israel shall be established in your hand. Swear to me therefore by the LORD that you will not cut off my descendants after me, and that you will not wipe out my name from my father's house" (1 Samuel 24:20–21). David swore the requested oath, and the two men parted. It is difficult to believe that such a meeting could have taken place. Even if Saul was persuaded that David could have killed him but did not, it is unlikely that the king who up to this point had won all his wars would have accepted the idea that he would be deposed by David and, further, would have begged David not to wipe out his seed and entire household.

On another occasion, Saul and three thousand of his men were pursuing David in the desert. One night David sneaked into their camp and saw Saul asleep, his spear beside his head. Abishai, son of Zeruiah, suggested that David kill Saul, but David explained that the anointed of the Lord was not to be harmed (1 Samuel 26:9). David's position was that it was better that the Lord should strike Saul or that he should die in war. David and Abishai took Saul's spear and water jar as proof that they had held the king in their power. Again Saul was persuaded of David's righteousness and called off the pursuit.

These two highly imaginative stories, with their clear apologetic flavor, were designed to legitimize David's rule. They seek to demonstrate David's nobility, which is all the more dramatic when set against Saul's cruelty, and to show that David bore no responsibility for Saul's death. However, if these stories—or at least one of them—actually happened, they show above all that David had well-developed political instincts and leadership qualities. David wanted to be king, of that there is no doubt. But Saul's reign was well established. To murder him at this stage would have enraged the people and, in any case, would have transferred the throne to Saul's son Jonathan, who would have enjoyed enhanced sympathy.[4]

Another important development followed the two chases in which David slipped through Saul's fingers: he and his men joined the Philistines. This was the worst act of David's life, worse even than the affair of Bathsheba and Uriah. This was treason. The Philistines were, prior to the rise of the great empires alongside the Tigris and Euphrates, Israel's most terrible and greatest enemy, and David's defection to them was unforgivable.

---

[4] According to 1 Samuel 23:17, Jonathan declared that David would rule and that he (Jonathan) would be his viceroy. Even if we accept this version, it is doubtful that David would have relied on it.

Two mitigating circumstances could be offered. First, David was fighting for his life, with no alternative but to flee, though perhaps he could have found sanctuary with another people who did not represent danger to Israel. Second, the flight of a condemned rebel to the camp of an enemy is a well-known phenomenon. Jeroboam, who rebelled against Solomon, found sanctuary with Pharaoh, king of Egypt. In later ages, rebels against the English crown regularly found safe haven in the court of the kings of France (and vice versa!).

Thus David fled to shelter with King Achish of Gath. Like many other stories in the Bible, this one is told twice. The first version appears in 1 Samuel 21:11–16. David pretended to be mad, and Achish retorted, "Do I lack madmen," and drove him away. In this case David was alone, not yet having gathered supporters. But in the second version he had collected followers: "Everyone who was in distress, and everyone who was in debt, and everyone who was discontented" (1 Samuel 22:2). The force gathered around him was not sufficient to confront Saul, so David decided to go to Achish. This time he was received courteously and even given the town of Ziklag, which was under Philistine control close to the border of the tribe of Judah. The friendly reception was not surprising. The Philistines were clearly interested in dividing the Israelite camp, and David's defection served the purpose admirably.

Months later, when the Philistines prepared for war on Israel, David was willing to join, perhaps having little choice. Achish told him to come with his men (1 Samuel 28:1), and David responded, "Very well, then you shall know what your servant can do" (1 Samuel 28:2). The answer was a little vague, and some commentators see it as leaving an opening for later evasion. But then Achish said, "Very well, I will make you my bodyguard for life" (1 Samuel 28:2), which indicates how much faith he had placed in his guest. David and his force joined the Philistine army, but, at the last hour before the battle, they were prevented from taking part, because the other Philistine captains mistrusted David and demanded that Achish withdraw him (1 Samuel 29:3–7). This episode was the low point in David's career.

Thus David returned to Ziklag, where, a few days later, an Amalekite youth fresh from the battlefield on Mount Gilboa reported to him on the defeat of Israel and the death of Saul and Jonathan (2 Samuel 1). The youngster said that he had happened on the scene and saw Saul about to be overtaken by Philistine chariots. Saul begged the lad to kill him, knowing full well what would happen to him in Philistine hands. The boy complied and, as proof, "took the crown that was on his head and the armlet that was on his arm" (2 Samuel 1:10).

The boy's version, therefore, was that he had acceded to Saul's request to kill him, in the knowledge that the king's fate was sealed and he was performing an act of mercy. But the Bible tells us that this was a lie, for Saul had died by falling on his sword. The reason for the boy's deceit was clear: the hostility between Saul and David was no secret. David had rebelled against the crown, and everyone believed, rightly, that David was only waiting for Saul's demise. The boy was therefore expecting a reward for what he had done, but David's response was unexpected. He immediately declared public mourning over the death of Saul and Jonathan and for the defeat of Israel, to which only days earlier he had been prepared to contribute.

The youth was sacrificed on the altar of David's self-interests, after being asked the rhetorical question: "Were you not afraid to lift your hand to destroy the LORD's anointed?" (2 Samuel 1:14). Without waiting for an answer, David ordered his men to execute the boy, who was punished for an act he did not commit.

Some commentators describe this scene as a trial in which David was judging the boy. The difficulty is that the youngster was judged on the basis of his own confession. The rule in Jewish law is that "people may not condemn themselves," so that one may not be sentenced to death solely on the basis of one's own confession. This rule may not have been followed in biblical times, and it has been suggested that in those days it was possible to convict on the basis of confession if there was corroborating evidence.[5] In the case of the Amalekite boy, the fact that he had Saul's crown and bracelet was sufficient to corroborate his confession. It is also possible that the Philistines had given David judicial authority over his own men, and perhaps over all of Ziklag. But the process as described would be called in modern terms a "drumhead trial." According to the boy, he carried out the command of the king of Israel. In these circumstances, was the order plainly unlawful, given that Saul feared falling into the hands of the Philistines, who would enjoy killing him? The result might be explained in terms of the absolute responsibility customary in ancient law, which did not recognize a defense based on lack of fault or mitigating circumstances. But the complete failure even to consider the fact that the boy had acted, by his contention, at Saul's command does call for some explanation.

Moreover, fairness suggests that true justice would have permitted the youth, after he had learned the potentially disastrous results of his lie, to tell what had really happened and to stress that he had not hastened Saul's end. Perhaps the unfortunate boy tried to say as much. There is a hint in David's words: "Your blood be on your head; for your own mouth has testified against

---

[5] For a discussion of this subject, see Aaron Kirschenbaum, *Self-Incrimination in Jewish Law* (New York: Burning Bush, 1970), 26–30.

you, saying, 'I have killed the Lord's anointed' " (2 Samuel 1:16). But this was said after the execution had been carried out, and it was directed at the corpse. Was this a response to the boy's cries before his death, that he had lied in saying that he had killed Saul? In any event it is clear that for a mere lie, though an ugly one, the punishment was excessive. Whatever the case, it is doubtful that David was interested in the truth. The demonstrative gesture of mourning the death of Saul was important to him. Killing the youth was a political execution that served the purpose, and David did not hesitate.

It is difficult to believe the sincerity of David's mourning, given that only days before he had been ready to take part in the war against Saul, and the king's death opened his way to the kingdom of Israel. David did declare mourning, did kill the Amalekite youth, and did lament the deaths of Saul and Jonathan. All this emphasizes David's political sense, his statesmanlike mind and the importance he attached to public relations. The self-control with which he avoided harming Saul during the latter's pursuit of him (if there is truth in the stories) manifests itself in the steps taken after Saul's death. He was aware that Saul, the first king to unite the tribes of Israel, the man who had won a long series of victories over the enemies of his people and who had died a hero's death, would be revered in the nation's imagination. David needed urgently to shed the image of being Saul's enemy, to participate in the national mourning over the defeat, and gradually to take the monarch's place. David knew how to do it; he understood public opinion and how to win it.

What of David's share in Saul's downfall? Saul, who had previously won impressive victories over Israel's enemies, among them the Philistines, sustained a terrible defeat at the foot of Gilboa. First Samuel 28:5–6 narrates that Saul saw the Philistine army and trembled with fear. He inquired of the Lord, but got no response, neither from dreams nor from prophets. In desperation he turned to a medium, who raised the spirit of Samuel, who in turn prophesied Saul's downfall. Nevertheless Saul did not hesitate to prepare for battle, facing the Philistines and death.

What caused the change of fortune and the defeat of Saul, who until that day had won every war? A possible explanation is that the Philistines had changed their tactics and were meeting Saul in a valley where their chariots gave them an advantage. Another possibility is that Saul's strength had been his ability to unite the nation and to mobilize all the necessary force. David's rebellion, which the Bible plays down, had split the nation. David and his men had defected to the Philistines. The tribe of Judah may have leaned toward David and refused to cooperate with Saul. So even though David did not take part on the Philistine side, his rebellion and defection had weakened Saul and contributed to his downfall.

Despite the defeat, the Israelites had not lost their independence or become enslaved by the Philistines. The people had been weakened and had lost territory, but not their national existence. Continued rule by the house of Saul could be expected, and indeed Saul's captain Abner crowned Ishbaal, Saul's surviving son, king of Israel. The book of Samuel refers to the new king by the derogatory name of Ish-bosheth ("man of shame"), but Chronicles uses his proper name. David did not reconcile himself to the continued reign of Saul's dynasty. At first he only succeeded in dividing the kingdom so that he was crowned in Hebron as king of the tribe of Judah. Ishbaal probably tried to regain control of Judah, while David was seeking to become king of all Israel. Hostile relations between the two kingdoms were unavoidable, leading to occasional military clashes: "There was a long war between the house of Saul and the house of David; David grew stronger and stronger, while the house of Saul became weaker and weaker" (2 Samuel 3:1).

Saul's dynasty was in trouble, and Ishbaal's dependence on his general, Abner, grew. But an argument flared up between the two as Ishbaal rebuked Abner and accused him of sleeping with Rizpah, Saul's concubine. Abner resolved to defect to David's camp, and they made an agreement under which Abner was to transfer to David control over all the tribes of Israel. He was also to restore to David his first wife Michal, who had been given to Palti son of Laish. Abner went to David's court but on his way back was murdered by Joab, the captain of David's army, and his brother Abishai. The biblical narrative states that the murder was revenge for Abner's killing of Asahel, brother of Joab and Abishai, in battle. David repudiated the murder, cursed Joab and all his house, and declared general mourning for the death of Abner, as he had done for Saul and Jonathan. But he took no steps against Joab and Abishai, saying that it was not in his power to do so. David, the master of public relations, understood how important it was to appear unstained by unseemly acts on his way to power.

Abner's death caused panic in Saul's camp, and two officers, named Baanah and Rechab, decided to desert to the victor's camp. They murdered Ishbaal, cut off his head, and brought it to David. His reaction was in the already-established pattern. In an angry outburst he recalled what he had done to the boy who reported the death of Saul and accused them of being wicked men who had "killed a righteous man on his bed in his own house" (2 Samuel 4:11). He ordered the immediate execution of the two murderers. His men cut off Baanah and Rechab's hands and feet and hung them over a pool in Hebron so that all should witness David's justice. Thus, Ishbaal, David's enemy with whom he had struggled, was promoted after his death to the rank of "righteous," and his murderers were executed and their bodies displayed for all to see.

The biblical story places this murder in the same line of events as the battle of Gilboa. Saul's house was smitten in actions in which David had no part. Saul and Jonathan were killed by the Philistines. Abner was murdered by Joab and Abishai. Ishbaal was killed by Baanah and Rechab. Each of these deaths brought David closer to his life's ambition: to be king over all Israel. According to the Bible, he was not stained by the blood shed on the way. He even mourned the dead, composed laments in their honor, performed burial ceremonies, and sometimes even wreaked revenge on those he held responsible for their deaths. Nevertheless, it is difficult to shake off the feeling that he had some share in Saul's downfall. Morally, though indirectly, he was responsible for the deaths of Abner and Ishbaal. Their deaths resulted from his splitting the kingdom in two, his takeover of the tribe of Judah, his refusal to recognize the continuity of Saul's dynasty, and his failure to rein in Joab. Moreover, the murder of Ishbaal raises a question whether Baanah and Rechab acted in collusion with David. If not, why did the two men decide to kill their king and flee to David with the severed head of their victim? They must have known that David had executed the youth who claimed that he had killed Saul at Gilboa. These questions are reinforced by the fact that the Bible does not mention any dispute between the two men and Ishbaal, unlike the case with Abner. What, then, could have been the motive for murder except hope of reward from David? In that case, the question arises whether this was an uninformed expectation or a result of some hint or arrangement with David or his men? The biblical story negates this possibility, leaving questions with no answers.[6]

The execution of Ishbaal's killers has parallels in Roman history. Tacitus relates that, after the murder of Emperor Galba and one of his men, quite a few people came forward to claim reward for the murder. The emperor Vitellius ordered them all put to death, not to vindicate the murdered emperor, but to discourage anyone who might contemplate murdering him, lest his successor choose to behave the same way.[7]

Following the double murders of Abner and Ishbaal, David assumed control of all the tribes without difficulty, and the Israelites were once again united, but the rift he had caused never healed. Revolts against David were put down by force, but the ferment continued. The united kingdom continued

---

[6] The question of David's responsibility for these murders is discussed in Halpern, *David's Secret Demons*, 81–84.

[7] Tacitus, *Annals* 1.44. Galba was murdered in 69 C.E., i.e., about one thousand years after David's reign. This is not the only example. It is said that Claudius ordered the execution of Caligula's murderers, despite the latter's monstrous behavior and his own rise to power as a result of the murder.

through the reign of Solomon, but upon his death Jeroboam, of the tribe of Ephraim, raised the standard of rebellion, and the kingdom was again split in two: the kingdom of Judah with its satellites (primarily the tribe of Benjamin); and the kingdom of Israel with Ephraim at its center, joined by all the others. The two kingdoms would never again come together. They maintained their separate existence until Israel was destroyed by Assyria.

Saul's Sins and the Reasons for His Downfall

The Bible seeks to offer order and logic in history and to explain them in terms of divine right. In simple terms it may be said that the Bible's purpose is to demand that Israel keep God's commandments. God, for his part, behaves justly, punishing sinners who break the laws and protecting the righteous who observe them. This approach serves to depict the destiny of the individual, as well as a basis for understanding historical processes. The nation's sins are a source of pain and catastrophe, while repentance leads to conquest of the land, victories over enemies, peace, and prosperity.

The trouble is that in many cases reality does not conform to the simplistic theory. There are many examples of very serious crimes that not only went unpunished but were actually rewarded. On the national level, there were a number of kings who observed the commandments yet suffered disasters, and of evil monarchs under whose rule the nation prospered. The book of Samuel, however, still follows the stick-and-carrot theory in its simple form, and so it was Saul's sins that led to his downfall.

What were those sins? The stories clearly indicate that Saul believed in God and did not worship pagan gods. He seems to have faithfully followed God's commandments, including the driving out of wizards and spirit-mediums. But this did not prevent the search for other sins, the first of which (Samuel 13) was Saul's offering of the sacrifice before the battle of Michmash, after waiting in vain seven days for Samuel to arrive. In response, Samuel prophesied the end of Saul's reign. Saul could not really be blamed, and even in the terms of those days, it is difficult to describe the act as a transgression justifying removal from power.

The offering of sacrifices by the king was certainly not a sin. At best it could be argued that Saul disobeyed Samuel's instruction that the sacrifice should be left to him. It is difficult to regard this clash of authorities and Samuel's pride as just cause for the removal of a king. Moreover, the battle of Michmash actually ended in a resounding victory for Israel. By biblical logic, it is hard to accept that God was angry with Saul's action yet allowed him a major victory.

In his *Antiquities of the Jews,* Flavius Josephus explains, at the end of book six, that Saul's end was caused by two other sins: ignoring the ban of the Amalekites, and the killing and destruction of the priestly city of Nob. Josephus does not list the sacrifice issue as a factor in Saul's downfall, though he does mention it. As for the killing of the priests, based on present-day concepts this was by far Saul's worst act.[8] Yet it is not listed in the Bible among the sins that caused his fall.

His most serious sin, at least in biblical eyes, was the violation of the ban on Amalek. First Samuel 15 relates that Samuel, acting on God's instruction, initiated the war on Amalek as revenge for the way that this nation had behaved hundreds of years earlier, during the exodus from Egypt. He ordered Saul to go to war and to destroy all that was Amalek, meaning he was to exterminate men, women, children, and livestock. Saul won and destroyed everything except King Agag of Amalek, who was taken alive. Saul also destroyed the lesser property but spared the best of the sheep and oxen (1 Samuel 15:9). Samuel appeared, fuming because his injunction had not been obeyed in its entirety. In their dialogue, Saul explained that the people had spared the best of the flocks, that it was done in order to sacrifice them to the Lord, and finally that most of the instruction had been carried out and that King Agag was captive and could still be killed.

Samuel rejected all these arguments out of hand. Regarding sacrifice, he stated: "Has the LORD as great delight in burnt offerings and sacrifices, as in obeying the voice of the LORD?" (1 Samuel 15:22). These fine words, which nowadays serve as an expression of social justice and a demand to prefer honesty over ceremony, were here meant to demand rigorous adherence to the order of total destruction. Samuel repeated his harsh prophecy that God would tear the kingdom of Israel from the house of Saul and give it to a better man.

Not content with speech, Samuel did not stop at words. He carried out the killing of Agag himself, hacking the Amalekite king with a sword. There is no mention of Samuel making an attempt to destroy the sheep and cattle booty, perhaps because destroying the animals would have enraged the people and Samuel, fighting for public opinion, avoided this unpopular act.

The entire episode can be explained by Samuel's extreme zealousness about his authority. It will be remembered that the installation of Saul as king involved separation of the political-military authority from the religious authorities. Samuel was the first religious leader to have the secular authority

---

[8] See the earlier chapter "Saul Kills the Priests of Nob," p. 128.

taken from him, and we have seen that pain and humiliation gave rise to his distaste for Saul. The separation of powers inevitably brings up an issue of the division of authority. In the present case the issue was control over the principle of total destruction, which Samuel considered a divine command. Previously, the supervision had been in the hands of a leader who had both political and religious authority, although God occasionally intervened directly by punishing the Israelites for breaking the ban. This time there was no such intervention, no plague or punishment, not even defeat in war. On the contrary, the Philistines were beaten shortly thereafter in the battle in which David killed Goliath. The defeat in Gilboa took place many years later, and only a very flexible interpretation of the principle of reward and punishment could attribute that disaster to the violation of the ban so many years earlier.

The present question concerns who determined the boundaries of the ban and whether there was room for some easing, namely, by not including the best sheep and cattle, for which there were precedents.[9] Perhaps Saul, who commanded the army and won the victory, believed that such flexibility was within his jurisdiction. In Samuel's eyes this was a religious question, and Saul's behavior was another incursion upon his religious power by the secular authority.

Finally, the Bible does not describe Saul's act as a blow against Samuel's authority but rather as violating God's command. The decision to depose Saul was also made not by Samuel, but by God. The Almighty informed Samuel, who is described as pleading for the reversal of the decision (1 Samuel 15:11). This is the model that the Bible applies to David, for he too was not responsible for Saul's downfall and the destruction of his house. That result was solely the outcome of God's decree.

The Destruction of the House of Saul

During the period of the biblical kings, a change of dynasty was often an occasion for the mass destruction of the outgoing house.[10] This was the case

---

[9] This happened in the conquest of Jericho. See the earlier chapter "To Kill and Take Possession," p. 101.

[10] Following David's reign, there were no changes of dynasty in Judah. David and Solomon reigned over all Israel, and their descendants over Judah, up to the destruction of the first Temple. There were internal killings, but the dynasty remained in power for four centuries, from 1000 B.C.E. to 586, with the sole exception of the six or seven years when Athaliah ruled. One version has it that she was the sister of King Ahab of Israel (2 Kings 8:26), while another states that she was his daughter (2 Kings 8:18). Athaliah married King Jehoram of Judah, who was followed by Ahaziah, son of Jehoram and Athaliah. He was murdered by Jehu while meeting with Joram son of Ahab (2 Kings 9:27), whereupon Athaliah seized power in Judah, destroying the house

when Baasha rose against Nadab, son of King Jeroboam of Israel. Baasha killed Nadab and "all the house of Jeroboam; he left to the house of Jeroboam not one that breathed" (1 Kings 15:29). Baasha was followed by his son, Elah. This time the rebel was Zimri, captain of half the king's chariots. After he killed Elah and became king, "he killed all the house of Baasha; he did not leave him a single male of his kindred or his friends" (1 Kings 16:11). That apparently was Zimri's only achievement. Next came the house of Omri, which won great victories. His son was Ahab, who was killed in battle with the Syrians. Then came his son Joram, who ruled for eleven years until Jehu rebelled, killed him, and seized power. The Bible gives a detailed description of the terrible massacre: Jehu ordered the execution of Ahab's seventy sons; then he turned on all the remaining family members in Jezreel and Samaria and left no vestige of them.

Such occurrences were common and widely known, and they are hinted at in the stories of David and Saul in a special manner. In Saul's pursuit of David, it is said that when the king realized David's righteousness, he begged David to swear that he would not eradicate all his seed and erase his memory, and David complied (1 Samuel 24:20–22). The plea that the author puts in Saul's mouth reveals the implications of the loss of power in those days. This plea, however, detracts from the credibility of the story. The unlikelihood of the king begging in this way is augmented by the fact that Saul knew full well what would befall his family if the fugitive became king. David's oath joins a series of oaths between David and Jonathan. What became of David's oath to Saul is clear from the rest of the story. After Saul and three of his sons fell at the battle of Gilboa, the fortunes of the family declined until David was crowned king of all Israel.

Yet this was not the end of the tribulations of the house of Saul. After three consecutive years of famine David inquired of God and was told that Saul and his house were to blame, because Saul had killed the Gibeonites (2 Samuel 21). There is no account of that killing or indeed of any disagreement between him and them. However, that neither adds nor detracts. The point of the story is not the historical background of Saul and the Gibeonites but the political use made of an old dispute from the days of a king long dead.

Aside from the question of the justice of punishing a whole nation by famine for a sin committed by a king many years before, the episode raises additional doubts. The Bible has a number of catastrophe stories ascribed to

---

of David (2 Kings 11:1). The one survivor was Joash son of Ahaziah (and grandson of Athaliah), who was hidden from her. Six years later, in a revolt against Athaliah, Joash became king. Though it was stated that she had destroyed "all the seed of the kingdom," it is not clear whether she intended to raise another dynasty instead of the house of David, though this would have happened had she succeeded in her mission. It seems that her prime ambition was to establish her own rule, and the Bible provides no clue as to her thinking on the subject.

some sin or transgression where it was necessary to locate the transgressor. The divine interrogatory technique used in such cases was based on binary method: the public was divided into groups, each of which was tested by the casting of lots or appearance before the Urim and Thummim (divining stones) until the offender was found. So it was in the days of Joshua, in order to discover who had violated the ban. A similar process took place after the battle of Michmash, in which Jonathan was found to have broken his father's oath. It seems that this was also the case with Jonah, who was responsible for the storm that endangered the ship on which he was sailing.

But the murder of Saul's remaining family members was not preceded by such a process. This time God was not consulted by the accepted binary process but was asked a general question about the cause of the famine and responded by blaming the house of Saul. The impression is that this was a cynical use of the deity in order to eliminate Saul's dynasty. An interesting aspect is the absence of any priests and prophets from the story. Either David claimed to have spoken directly to God and received an answer, or he acted with the assistance of some priest or prophet but chose not to reveal any names.

It is significant that the justification for killing Saul's family is placed in the injustice that Saul did to the Gibeonites. They play a central role in the apologia designed to purge David of any responsibility for the extermination of the house of Saul. The members of Saul's family are not killed by Israelites, for had they done so at David's command, he would be held responsible, and the Bible seeks to keep him out of the murder. The apologia is based on a number of elements: first, there was no choice, for there was no other way to end the famine; second, the deed was required by God; finally, it was not carried out by David or his men. The victims were handed over to the Gibeonites, who were supposedly acting on their own initiative, and it was they who carried out the execution. The biblical version is a striking example of cynicism: David sought to spare Saul's sons and grandsons and asked the Gibeonites to redeem them with money, so that the killing would be avoided (2 Samuel 21:3). But the Gibeonites refused, saying that they had no interest in Saul's gold or silver. They wanted blood. They demanded seven of Saul's descendants, so that they could hang them before God (2 Samuel 21:6).

In accordance with their demand, David gave the Gibeonites Saul's sons from Rizpah and five sons of Merab.[11] The Gibeonites executed them and displayed them on a mountain, a way of dishonoring the dead. There follows a

---

[11] The Bible speaks of five sons of Michal, Saul's daughter, by Adriel, but all the commentators agree that it was Merab who was Adriel's wife, while Michal was childless. The traditional explanation for the present text is that Michal raised her sister's children.

touching story of Rizpah remaining by the bodies of her sons to prevent the birds from touching them by day and the beasts by night. This convinced David that he had gone too far, and he ordered their burial in the Kish family tomb, alongside Saul and Jonathan. With this positive step, control passed from the Gibeonites back to David, and he was the one to arrange honorable burial for the dead.

The reader is thus supposed to conclude that David was in no way responsible for the murder of the offspring of Saul; in fact, he even tried to redeem them with money, to save their lives. The responsibility lay with the Gibeonites. They were carrying out blood revenge, having an account to settle with the house of Saul. They refused David's generous offer of money for the lives of the victims. And so once again David was free from guilt. It was all in the hands of God or in the hands of others outside of David's control. In every case, David arranged a decent burial and took care of public relations and the illusion of honor to the house of Saul. The story had a happy ending: the sacrifice of Saul's family assuaged the rage of God and the famine ended.

Some side issues remain. One concerns David's oath: the Bible tells us that David spared Mephibosheth (Merib-baal in Chronicles), Saul's grandson, because of an oath sworn to his father Jonathan. But David had sworn oaths not only to Jonathan but also to Saul not to exterminate his family. If so, then the oath was not kept, at least not in good faith, according to our present-day standards. It does not matter if such an oath was in fact made. The editor of the book of Samuel had to be aware of the text in which David swore to Saul and of the need to make the versions consistent. Technically it could be claimed that David had not breached his oath, because he did not kill Saul's family; he only handed them over to the Gibeonites. By present-day conceptions, the argument would be rejected as being too devious and disregarding the reality of the situation. But perhaps in the concept of those days, the fact that the act of killing was not done by David or his men, nor even at his order, would provide a basis for the argument that David's action did not constitute breach of oath.[12]

We should also recall David's demand, after he took the throne of Judah, for the return of his wife, Saul's daughter Michal, who had been given to Palti son of Laish. Abner and Ishbaal conceded, and Michal was returned. Why did David want her back when the emotional link between them had been severed and he had taken other wives? One explanation, deriving from the text, is that he considered her to be "his property," having purchased her with the

---

[12] See the earlier chapter "Stories of Disguise," pp. 55–58, for discussion of evading oaths.

Philistine foreskins. But David may have had another motive, connected to his ambition to eradicate Saul's dynasty. He wanted to prevent Michal from bearing children to Palti son of Laish and preferred to have her in his harem, under his watchful eye. Michal had no children. Perhaps she was barren, but it is also possible that David had no intimate relations with her because he did not want her to bear children.

How might history have looked if Michal had borne David a son, who would have ruled after him? Such a son would have united the two dynasties, reconciled Judah and Israel, and prevented the rift that followed the death of Solomon. The Wars of the Roses, between Lancaster and York, in fifteenth-century England may serve as a good historical analogy. That war lasted through many decades and cost much blood. It stopped with the ascendancy to the throne of Henry VII, who defeated Richard III at the battle of Bosworth Field. On his mother's side, Henry belonged to the House of Lancaster, and he married Elizabeth, the daughter of Edward IV of the House of York. The marriage united the dynastic claims on the crown, and the son, Henry VIII, was father of Queen Elizabeth I. No such process took place in Israelite history. Michal remained childless, alone and abandoned in David's court.

The sole remaining survivor of Saul's family was Mephibosheth, son of Jonathan, who was lame as the result of a childhood injury. The Bible says that David took pity on him because of his oath to Jonathan. The traditional view is that Mephibosheth was disqualified from the succession because of his disability and in any case was incompetent. The fact is that after the battle of Gilboa Mephibosheth was not crowned king of Israel, though he could have been a candidate.[13] In his place, his uncle Ishbaal, son of Saul and Jonathan's brother, was installed as king. Did Mephibosheth have children? Did his infirmity allow him to have a family, and would David have allowed it? The book of Samuel says nothing about it. It does say that, after Absalom's revolt, David abstained from killing Mephibosheth, though had he wanted to do so he could have found a justification (2 Samuel 16–17). First Chronicles 9 states that Jonathan's son was Merib-baal, who in turn fathered Micah, who also had children of his own—so the dynasty did endure through several generations. These details may have been added in order to prove that David kept his oath, but it is equally possible that the dynasty continued through Mephibosheth, who was protected by his infirmity.

There is a further reference to Saul's dynasty in the book of Esther. Mordecai, the Jew, a hero of the book, was son of Jair, himself the son of Shimei,

---

[13] The question was whether the crown would pass to the king's eldest son and through him to his eldest son. See the later chapter "Succession to the Throne" for the proposition that there were no firm rules in this regard.

son of Kish (Esther 2:5). Was this Kish the father of Saul? Ibn Ezra rejects this possibility on the ground that had this been the case the author would have said so and named the most important ancestor. Had there been a king in the ancestral chain, the author would certainly have noted the fact. Since the text does not mention Saul, Mordecai was not a direct descendant. Yet, while the book of Esther does not expressly call Mordecai a Saulite, it connects Haman to Agag, the king of the Amalekites, and thus with a wink and a nod the text hints at the old feud between Israel and Amalek.

The house of Saul certainly never achieved greatness again, but the split between the tribes was not prevented, and the unity of the nation under the rule of the house of David came to an end with the death of Solomon.

In Conclusion

Whoever seeks to attribute Saul's downfall, the loss of his monarchy and the removal of his dynasty by David, to Saul's sins will find that a difficult assignment, and even harder when compared with David's sins. But David's sins were forgiven, while Saul's were not. Some commentators tried to exaggerate the severity of Saul's sins and the damage they caused. The aggadah (legend) suggests that between the moment when Saul could have killed Agag to the moment when Samuel did, Agag managed to beget an offspring, and from this cobra came the asp known as the evil Haman.[14]

But the downfall of Saul can be explained on grounds other than divine punishment. His monarchy was created at a difficult moment for the Israelites, who were facing many enemies, among them the Philistines, who equaled or even surpassed them in military terms. Saul's kingdom involved the separation of the political-military authority from the religious authority wielded by Samuel. The transfer of secular power from Samuel to Saul infuriated Samuel, who did his best to undermine the king's standing. Over time another dangerous rival arose in the person of David, the charismatic leader of Judah. This caused a rift in the nation, which reached its climax in David's defection to the Philistine camp. It can be assumed that, at this stage, Judah did not lean toward cooperation with Saul. The secession of the big and powerful tribe of Judah weakened Saul in difficult times, when he was en route to his defeat at the hands of the Philistines in the battle of Gilboa.

---

[14] Ginzberg, *Legends of the Jews*, 4:68. See also the references in 6:233–34 n. 68, which include a legend about a death blow delivered by Agag's posthumous child to Saul in the battle of Gilboa.

11

Prophecy in Times of Upheavals

✧

This chapter deals with issues that affected prophecy in ancient Israel, particularly the changes in its nature through the biblical period and whether it was linked to the upheavals caused by the rise of great powers that crushed the Israelite kingdoms.

Types of Prophets

The prophets played many and varied roles that changed in the course of time, but generally speaking the categories are as follows:

The Prophet As National Leader

Moses has been revered in Jewish tradition as the greatest prophet of all. He was the national leader in the negotiations with Pharaoh, brought the Israelites out of Egypt, and led them through the desert. He also held face-to-face dialogues with God and accepted the Torah directly from divine hands. Samuel was much the same, in that he led the nation in its struggle with the Philistines. But the era of prophet as national leader came to its end when Samuel was compelled to anoint Saul as king (ca. 1025 B.C.E.). Consequently, the political-military authority was separated from the religious one.

The Court Prophet

In King David's day, Gad and Nathan were court prophets.[1] The king consulted them regularly for divine instructions and often followed their advice.

---

[1] See Uffenheimer, *Ancient Prophecy in Israel*, 155; and the earlier chapter "To Kill and Take Possession," pp. 80–85.

Sometimes the intermediary was Abiathar the priest, who came to David wearing the ephod, the priestly garment that held the Urim and Thummim—the stones by which God responded to questions. This technique was used, for example, when David asked if the townspeople would betray him to Saul if he stayed in Keilah (1 Samuel 23:11–13) and whether to pursue the Amalekites who had raided Ziklag (1 Samuel 30:7–8).

The two prophets are reported to have rebuked David: Nathan after the murder of Uriah, and Gad after the king held a census (2 Samuel 24:11–13). But, as we saw in the chapter "To Kill and Take Possession," their attitude was relatively moderate, and no physical punishment was inflicted on David. The rebuke was behind closed doors, and they never turned to the people or sought an alternative leader.

Presumably, all the kings of Judah and Israel had court prophets. Like the Urim and Thummim, they were means by which the king chose a course that would satisfy the Almighty and guarantee success. In this sense they could be compared with the Greek oracle at Delphi. However, after David and Solomon, the Bible describes most court prophets as false, sometimes because they worshiped alien gods and sometimes because, though they claimed to speak for God, this was not so. Such was the case when King Ahab of Israel and King Jehoshaphat of Judah prepared to fight Syria and liberate Ramoth-gilead. Ahab convened some four hundred prophets, who advised him to go to war and predicted victory (1 Kings 22:6). Only Micaiah, son of Imlah, prophesied that Ahab would die in battle, as indeed happened.[2] For our purpose, it is enough to note that Ahab was well supplied with court prophets to advise him.

In a later period, Jeremiah's prophecies were given in the kingdom of Judah, some two hundred years after the death of Ahab and a century after the kingdom of Israel was destroyed by Assyria (ca. 720 B.C.E.). Jeremiah forecast the destruction of Jerusalem by King Nebuchadnezzar of Babylon. His gloomy predictions displeased the king's courtiers. Here again, we hear of court prophets. Pashhur the son of Immer, "chief officer in the house of the LORD," hearing Jeremiah's prophecy, beat him and had him put in the stocks[3] (Jeremiah 20:2). When Jeremiah was released, he cursed Pashhur and prophesied that the priest would be exiled to Babylon, where he would die for being a false prophet. The false prophets are again mentioned when the forces of Babylon besieged Jerusalem but were forced to lift the siege temporarily to fight the advancing Egyptian armies. Jeremiah was thrown in prison, but King Zedekiah, who remained fearful, summoned him secretly and asked what God had said.

---

[2] See also the earlier chapter "Stories of Disguise," pp. 42–43.

[3] The biblical term can mean either a prison or a form of torture that held the prisoner in a painful posture.

Jeremiah repeated his dire prophecies, asking where were the prophets who had predicted that the king of Babylon would not come (Jeremiah 37:19).

In summary, the Bible speaks of true court prophets during David's reign and remains silent regarding Solomon's court. After Solomon, when the kingdom was split, the kings continued to use prophets whom the Bible considered to be, at least in part, false prophets.

Opposition Prophets Who Overthrow Dynasties and Crown Kings

This category includes Ahijah the Shilonite, Elijah, and Elisha. Samuel may also be included, though at first he was a national leader but, with the rise of Saul, lost his political and military functions. Eventually he fell out with Saul and prophesied the end of his reign, then anointed David, thereby becoming a prophet who overthrew a dynasty.

But it was mostly during the two-kingdoms period that kings were overthrown and replaced. In the tenth century B.C.E. Ahijah the Shilonite incited Jeroboam, son of Nebat, to rebel and divide Solomon's kingdom:

> About that time, when Jeroboam was leaving Jerusalem, the prophet Ahijah the Shilonite found him on the road. Ahijah had clothed himself with a new garment. The two of them were alone in the open country when Ahijah laid hold of the new garment he was wearing and tore it into twelve pieces. He then said to Jeroboam: Take for yourself ten pieces; for thus says the LORD, the God of Israel, "See, I am about to tear the kingdom from the hand of Solomon, and will give you ten tribes. One tribe will remain his,[4] for the sake of my servant David and for the sake of Jerusalem, the city that I have chosen out of all the tribes of Israel." (1 Kings 11:29–32)

This prophecy, made to a potential rebel, was not pure prediction, but incitement. Had Solomon learned of it, Ahijah the Shilonite would probably have been executed. For that reason, it was delivered "alone in the open country," without witnesses. Jeroboam did raise a rebellion, but failed and took flight to Egypt. He tried again after Solomon's death and was successful this time. The kingdom split in two, with Judah on one side, and all the other tribes, led by Ephraim, on the other.

Time passed and Ahijah the Shilonite again prophesied to Jeroboam that his house would fall and his dynasty be exterminated, because he had made golden calves and followed other gods (1 Kings 14:10–11). This time the prophecy was given "privately" to Jeroboam's wife, and the name of the new

---

[4] Ahijah the Shilonite speaks at first about twelve tribes (the twelve strips). Ten would be given to Jeroboam and one to the house of David. Rabbi David Kimchi (Radak) in his interpretation to this verse explains that the twelfth tribe was Benjamin, which joined Judah so that the two were therefore referred to as one.

king was not mentioned. This prophecy was not, therefore, incitement to rebellion. Jeroboam lived out his life in peace. The revolt, when it came, was led by Baasha against Nadab, Jeroboam's son.

The two most important prophets in this category are Elijah and his protégé Elisha, who followed one another in the ninth century (roughly 870–790 B.C.E.).[5] Around these two prophets arose a series of marvelous legends, as rich as the legends of the exodus from Egypt. Elijah won a sacrifice competition, apparently designed to bring rainfall, against no fewer than 450 prophets of Baal. During the contest, the prophets of Baal proved unable to burn their sacrifices by the power of prayer, while Elijah, who had turned to God, could do so. Immediately thereafter, taking on a new mission, he slaughtered all of Baal's prophets. His work on earth ended when God took him to heaven in a chariot of fire.

Elisha's many and varied miracles included dividing the waters of the Jordan in two using Elijah's coat, ending the barrenness of a woman of Shunem, reviving a dead youth, and curing leprosy.

Elijah and Elisha were also busy undermining Ahab's dynasty and making kings. Originally the task was given to Elijah. After slaughtering the prophets of Baal, he fled to the desert, where God instructed him to anoint Hazael king of Syria, Jehu king of Israel, and Elisha as his own successor (1 Kings 19:15–16). All this preceded the incident of Naboth's vineyard, after which Elijah, in blunt terms, prophesied to Ahab his death and the total obliteration of his house. But the Bible states that the fate of Ahab's dynasty was decreed before the Naboth affair and without any connection to it, since Elijah had already been ordered to anoint Jehu, implying that Ahab was to be deposed. Elijah's prophecy to Ahab was delivered in private and therefore could not be construed as incitement to revolt.

Though Elijah was ordered to anoint Jehu, the act was actually left to Elisha. After Ahab was killed in the war with Syria, his son Ahaziah ruled briefly, but died shortly from a severe illness. Next in line was Ahab's second son, Joram (Jehoram), who reigned twelve years, during which Elijah ascended to heaven. Late in this period (ca. 840 B.C.E.), the war between Hazael of Syria and Israel was renewed. Joram was beaten and wounded. This was an appropriate moment for a revolt. Elisha sent a prophet to the Israelite camp in Ramoth-gilead, where—acting on Elisha's instructions—he poured oil on Jehu's head and told him: "Thus says the LORD the God of Israel: I anoint you king over the people of the LORD, over Israel. You shall strike down the house of your master Ahab.

---

[5] Elijah began to prophesy in Ahab's reign, which began ca. 870 B.C.E. and lasted twenty-two years. It is not clear exactly when he started. Elisha died in Joash's reign, which lasted fifteen years from about 800 B.C.E. The date of Elisha's death is unknown.

. . . For the whole house of Ahab shall perish. . . . The dogs shall eat Jezebel in the territory of Jezreel, and no one shall bury her" (2 Kings 9:6–10).

Having said his piece, the prophet fled. This time it was no pure prophecy, but incitement. Had the revolt failed, both he and Elisha would have been executed. But it did not fail—Jehu became king and immediately set about the business of revolution and elimination that accompanied it. He killed Joram, the king of Israel, and took the opportunity to kill King Ahaziah of Judah, who happened to be visiting Joram.[6] Then he went to Jezebel, Ahab's widow and the mother of Joram. That evil and brave queen, knowing what awaited her, painted her face and, looking out the window as Jehu approached, said, "Is it peace, Zimri, murderer of your master?" (2 Kings 9:31). Jehu ordered her thrown out of the window, trampled her with his horses, then celebrated the event with food and drink.

This was only the beginning. Jehu then ordered the elders and notables, who were holding seventy sons of Ahab, to execute them. At first they refused, but after additional warning they slaughtered the seventy and sent their heads in baskets to Jehu. Continuing the massacre, he "killed all who were left of the house of Ahab in Jezreel, all his leaders, close friends, and priests, until he left him no survivor" (2 Kings 10:11). It still was not enough. Jehu caught the brothers of King Ahaziah of Judah (one view considers that it was his sons) and slaughtered them.

Slaughtering people was Jehu's strong suit. When the initial killing was over, Jehu announced that he intended to worship Baal and erect a great altar in his honor. By this device he rallied the pagan god's followers and, having got them all together under one roof, had them killed, smashed their idols, and turned the temple into a latrine.

But the mass slaughter, and the fact that Jehu was obeying the Lord zealously in wiping out the followers of Baal, did not endow him with power or heroism vis-à-vis Israel's enemies. He sustained bitter blows at the hands of Hazael of Syria, who oppressed Israel brutally and reduced the kingdom to a virtual vassal.

Such were the results of the revolt against the house of Ahab, initiated by the prophet Elisha. Particularly puzzling is the story of Elisha's involvement in

---

[6] Archaeological excavations in Tel Dan (in the north of Israel) discovered an inscription in Old Aramaic in which King Hazael of Aram boasted that he, not Jehu, had killed Joram and Ahaziah. To explain the contradiction between the biblical account and the inscription, it has been suggested that Jehu's revolt was either supported by Hazael or at least had his implicit approval. Hence, though Jehu might have committed the murders, Hazael, who regarded Jehu as acting on his behalf, could claim credit for the deed. See Eric H. Cline, *The Battles of Armageddon* (Ann Arbor: University of Michigan Press, 2000), 84–87.

the anointing of Hazael as king of Syria. Evidently, Elisha was not content with his part in deposing the house of Ahab. God's words to Elijah had included an instruction to make Hazael king of Syria. Again it was Elisha's fate to perform the act, and the manner in which he did so was not exactly praiseworthy. He arrived in Damascus when King Ben-hadad of Syria was ill. Sent by the king, Hazael asked Elisha about Ben-hadad's chances of recovery. Elisha advised him to tell Ben-hadad, "You would certainly recover," yet predicted to Hazael the king's imminent death and his own ascendancy. The prophecy was followed by tears, as Elisha explained to Hazael: "I know the evil that you will do to the people of Israel; you will set their fortresses on fire, you will kill their young men with the sword, dash in pieces their little ones, and rip up their pregnant women" (2 Kings 8:12). Hazael understood perfectly what he had to do. He told Ben-hadad that he would live and, the next day, murdered him and took his place. After defeating Israel, he turned his anger on Judah. Joash, of whom it was said that he did right in the eyes of the Lord, was forced to send the temple and palace treasures to Hazael, to persuade him to lift his threat from Jerusalem (2 Kings 12:18).

The crowning of Hazael at Elisha's instigation was an exceptional occurrence. The Bible does not usually speak of the involvement of God and God's prophets in foreign dynasties. The story implies Elisha's greatness and shows that the power he derived from the Lord knew no territorial boundaries. At the same time, the tale shows the dark side of Elisha's behavior in inciting Hazael to murder his king and seize power, when the expected result was the destruction of Israel. Elisha's tears are supposed to justify the deed, as if to show that he acted despite himself because of God's command. Nevertheless, a bitter taste remains, augmented by the fact that God's considerations have ceased to be clear to mere mortals. Elisha made no attempt to remove the dire decree, to avoid playing his role—or to run from it (as did Jonah). The story also attributes more than prophecy to the prophet. Elisha not only spoke of future events but contributed, as he did with Jehu, to the unfolding of the horrors.

The two crownings in which Elisha was involved changed the nature of prophecy and the role of prophets.

Prophets of Moral and Social Opposition

Elisha died around 790 B.C.E. A new generation of prophets, beginning with Amos a few decades later, brought a new style and completely different personalities from those of Elijah, Elisha, and their predecessors. The later prophets, also known as the "prophets of the Book," the foremost being Amos, Isaiah, and Jeremiah, emphasized moral issues.

Some later prophets were in the opposition rather than part of the establishment,[7] but the violent actions of Elijah and Elisha were at an end, as was the involvement in rebellions and removal of dynasties. These prophets also differed from their predecessors in that they did not perform miracles and were not involved in supernatural adventures. Moses had performed an enormous number of miracles, competing with the Egyptian magicians. His brother Aaron's staff, thrown to the ground, changed into a serpent that consumed the Egyptian magicians' reptiles (Exodus 7). The ten plagues that gained Israel its freedom from slavery were inflicted through Moses' agency. He lifted his staff, and the Red Sea parted. He extended a hand over the water, and the sea covered the Egyptian chariots and horsemen (Exodus 14). He threw a tree into bitter water and made it sweet (Exodus 15:25). He brought forth water out of rock (Exodus 17:6). He raised his arms and assured Israel's victory over Amalek (Exodus 15:11–12). And plenty more . . .

Samuel also had some skill in this field. Furious that the people had forced him to appoint a king, he warned them, emphasizing the greatness of God, whom he represented, and the evil they did in asking for a king. It was the harvest season, but Samuel called on God to bring down rain in midsummer (1 Samuel 12:18).

Miracles and magic also protected the prophets Moses, Elijah, and Elisha. They were dangerous men to confront. Korah and his tribe rejected Moses' authority and demanded equal status, claiming that all their members were holy and that Moses had no right to be superior (Numbers 16:3). The response was not long in coming—the earth opened up and swallowed Korah, his tribe, and all their property (Numbers 16:32). Miriam, Moses' sister, and his brother Aaron complained that Moses had taken a Cushite wife, arguing that God also spoke to them. Miriam was immediately struck by leprosy, and only Moses' plea and a week of quarantine outside the camp could remove the punishment (Numbers 12).

Magic protection also extended to Elijah and Elisha. On one occasion, Ahab's son Ahaziah dispatched two captains of fifties, one after the other, to bring Elijah to him. On both occasions bolts of fire from heaven consumed the commander and all his men. For Elisha, it took much less to arouse God's fury. Children who mocked Elisha, calling after him, "Go away, baldhead! Go away, baldhead," were attacked by two bears that ripped apart forty-two of them (2 Kings 2:23–24).

---

[7] Isaiah's prophecies were not directed against the kings of Judah and their policies. He even prophesied, to the benefit of Hezekiah, that Sennacherib would not conquer Jerusalem. He was not in opposition to the regime, but many of his prophecies express disagreement with social injustice. In this respect he was antiestablishment.

But the magic evaporated for the latter-day prophets.[8] Amaziah, the priest of Bethel, drove Amos out of the kingdom of Israel and into Judah. Amos responded with a vigorous curse: "Your wife shall become a prostitute in the city, and your sons and your daughters shall fall by the sword, and your land shall be parceled out by line; you yourself shall die in an unclean land, and Israel shall surely go into exile away from its land." (Amos 7:17). The story breaks off at this point: it is not known what happened to Amos, Amaziah, or his family. Possibly Amaziah relented and Amos emerged unscathed. Clearly, unlike Elijah and Elisha, there was no protective aura around this prophet.

One hundred and fifty years later, in Jeremiah's time, prophets were vulnerable and completely defenseless. Jeremiah 26 tells of a prophet named Uriah, the son of Shemaiah, whose prophecies were similar to those of Jeremiah. He predicted the destruction of the kingdom of Judah and Jerusalem by the Babylonians, for which King Jehoiakim wanted to put him to death. "But when Uriah heard of it, he was afraid and fled and escaped to Egypt. Then King Jehoiakim sent Elnathan son of Achbor and men with him to Egypt, and they took Uriah from Egypt and brought him to King Jehoiakim, who struck him down with the sword and threw his dead body into the burial place of the common people" (Jeremiah 26:21–23).

After the collapse of the Assyrian Empire in 612 B.C.E., Egypt briefly dominated Israel, and Jehoiakim himself was crowned by Pharaoh Neco II. It seems that Jehoiakim was beholden to the Egyptian and cooperated in the planned struggle against Babylon. It is no wonder, then, that the Egyptians were willing to surrender Uriah to Jehoiakim's emissaries. Once again a prophet did not enjoy divine protection.

Jeremiah himself was defenseless. On one occasion he was beaten and imprisoned by Pashhur, a priest and false prophet of the king of Judah (Jeremiah 20:2). Later he was accused of planning to defect to the Babylonians. Again he was beaten and imprisoned in stringent conditions, but luckily King Zedekiah wished to hear him prophesy. Jeremiah was forced to humble himself and plead for his life in pitiful tones: "Now please hear me, my lord king: be good enough to listen to my plea, and do not send me back to the house of the secretary Jonathan to die there" (Jeremiah 37:20). God's protection had thus faded, and one of the greatest prophets was forced to humble himself before a

---

[8] An exception is Jonah, who, at the rise of the kingdom of Assyria, miraculously survived three days in a fish's belly. Jonah's danger did not come from external enemies but from his own flight from God. The book of Jonah differs from the other Latter Prophets. The book of Daniel also has its miracles, when Shadrach, Meshach, and Abednego were saved from the Babylonian fiery furnace. However, this book is not included among the Latter Prophets.

king of flesh and blood. The plea worked, and Zedekiah ordered him taken to the guardhouse and provided with a loaf of bread each day, until the city ran out of bread because of the siege.

The moral prophets were, thus, humans exposed to the dangers that threaten mere mortals. However, the main distinction between them and their predecessors lies in their admonitions against gross exploitation and oppression and in their rebellion against social injustice.

Ritual-Hierarchical and Moral Transgressions

It is customary to distinguish between behavior that is intrinsically wrong or evil *(malum per se)* and that which is improper solely because it is forbidden by law *(malum prohibitum)*. The first category includes transgressions that are immoral, whether or not the law specifically forbids them, such as murder and theft. These acts are evil in themselves. Their wrongness is self-evident and does not depend on the existence of a legal prohibition.[9] The second category consists of actions that are defined as offenses because of contemporary exigencies—for example, nonpayment of tax or noncompliance with traffic regulations. Moral fault can be attributed to such offenses, but it lies in the fact that the act is prohibited by a law.

Moral prohibitions of intrinsically wrong conduct are regarded as eternal. Murder was prohibited as early as Cain and Abel. Conversely, prohibitions that derive only from the law change over time, according to the needs of society. But the distinction is sometimes hard to maintain, as moral principles are also clearly linked to social conceptions that often proved variable. Thus, for example, criminal law has changed its attitude to suicide and homosexual or lesbian relationships because of sweeping changes in society's moral attitudes.

Genesis 2 and 3 illustrate the distinction between an inherently forbidden act and one that is forbidden only because of some command. In Genesis 2 God forbade Adam to eat the fruit of the tree of knowledge of good and evil. Eating that fruit was not forbidden per se—it was a sin solely because God had forbidden it. The obvious assumption is that humans are subservient to God and must obey divine commands no matter what they may be.[10] Yet, in

---

[9] The Greeks imagined a world totally without jurisprudence, even of moral values. Such was the world of the Cyclops, described in Homer's *Odyssey* 9.105–115, where people could do as they wished and the Cyclops could dine to his heart's content on the flesh of his visitors.

[10] The name of God is based on the Hebrew phrase "I AM WHO I AM" (the Lord's words to Moses, Exodus 3:14). The question is whether this means that God's command must be obeyed whatever it may be.

chapter 4 the story of Abel's murder by his brother Cain does not mention any prior prohibition: we are not told that God forbade humans to murder or steal. The murder is sharply condemned, even though God did not explicitly forbid it. Jewish tradition distinguishes between the laws known as the "commandments of the children of Noah" (which include, inter alia, the prohibition of murder and theft), and the laws of the Torah given after the children of Israel left Egypt. The latter apply only to Israelites, and that only after the giving of the Torah. The commandments of the children of Noah, on the other hand, form a basic moral code valid from the creation of the first human, and they apply to everyone, including Gentiles.

Secular legislators can, of course, define offenses that belong to both categories, but they are generally required to explain or justify the prohibitions that they impose on the public. The forbidding of acts that are wrongful in themselves does not usually provoke difficulties—it is enough to fault the action in order to justify the ban. But that does not hold for the second category, where reasoning that justifies the law is required. Secular lawmakers are not free to act arbitrarily. Their prohibitions must be justified by such considerations as necessary public spending, managing road traffic, and so on.

The divine legislator is, at least in theory, exempt from the need to justify laws. Clearly, religious legislation would benefit from explanations that improve the chances of the public being convinced to observe it. But the Bible sets out from the premise that God's commandments do not require any justification. The supreme law is the one requiring the observance of God's laws, instructions, and commands. This is the core of the faith that the Bible tries to promulgate. The greatest evil of all—disobeying God's instruction—is contrasted by the greatest good, which is obedience to God's commands. Abraham is the most righteous of people, as is shown by his willingness to carry out God's command and sacrifice his beloved son. The harder and more painful the command, the seemingly less purposeful or rational, the greater the virtue of the person who obeys without question.

Other examples, discussed earlier in the chapter "A Godly Man Killed by a Lion," include the order not to eat bread or drink water in Bethel and a prophet's request to a colleague, in the name of God, to beat and bruise him. In both cases, the men who disobeyed were killed by lions. The obligation to obey God's command is absolute, regardless of content or the person's ability to understand the purpose.

God's commands and instructions can be divided into two categories. The first deals with instructions that touch on human relations to God, and they include ritual laws (for example, sacrifices), prayer, permissible and forbidden foods, and the like. The second category deals with human relationships.

Broadly speaking, these categories mirror the secular distinction between behavior that is wrong only because it is forbidden by law *(malum prohibitum)* and behavior that is inherently wrong *(malum per se)*. But the congruency between religious and secular law is incomplete. *Malum prohibitum* is designed to serve the needs of the time and is subject to change with altering conditions. But the ritual commandments of religion, such as sacrifices and the prohibition of non-kosher food, are not intended to serve practical purposes,[11] apart from the central aim of obeying God's will and acquiring his grace. These commandments are, at least theoretically, eternal and are not divorced from moral principles, as conceived by the Bible. The worship of alien gods, which the Bible regards as the worst transgression, is not only a violation of ritual prohibition but ingratitude to the benevolent God who brought the Israelites out of slavery in Egypt. More, it was a violation of the covenant between Israel and God—an obvious moral flaw.

The first prophets concentrated on ritual transgression—offenses against God—with little consideration for those against humans. The prophet leaders (particularly Moses and Samuel) also focused on a special type of transgression: questioning the authority and rule of the leader.

The laws of the Torah are replete with instructions about relations between humans. There is a noticeable concern for the poor and weak, widows and orphans. Moses himself, especially at the beginning of his career, comes across as a humanitarian who saw the suffering of the children of Israel and whose main interest was in defending the weak. When he saw two men fighting, he rebuked the aggressor, "Why do you strike your fellow Hebrew?" (Exodus 2:13). After fleeing to Midian, he rescued Jethro's daughters from shepherds who had driven them away from a well and enabled them to water their flocks (Exodus 2:17). Moreover, the deliverance of the children of Israel from Egyptian bondage was not only a nationalistic move but also a humanitarian one. Yet, the stories about the years in the wilderness clearly indicate a focus on transgressions other than those against the weak, the oppressed, and the poor and needy. The worst sin of that period was the making of the golden calf, which the children of Israel demanded of Aaron while Moses was on Mount Sinai. They were sacrificing to it when Moses descended from the mountain. He saw the performance and, in his fury, threw down and smashed the tablets on which God's finger had inscribed the covenant. He had another

---

[11] Some argue that the ritual commandments are based on rational considerations and serve practical purposes; for example, that kosher food is healthier. But this is doubtfully the basis for the dietary laws. Firstly, there is no irrefutable evidence to this effect, and, secondly, if this was the case, there would be room to adapt the dietary laws to new data about different types of food and their effect on health.

outlet for his anger. Summoning the Levites to him, he told them to take their swords and to go "from gate to gate throughout the camp, and each of you kill your brother, your friend, and your neighbor" (Exodus 32:27). No fewer than three thousand of the Israelites were massacred.

Two other stories of sin and punishment—in fact, death by stoning—concerned the blasphemer, who took God's name in vain (Leviticus 24:11), and the man who gathered sticks on the Sabbath (Numbers 15). Both committed ritual transgressions against God, and both were brought before the divine court. In the case of the blasphemer, contemporary belief might have held that his curse could have blighted its subject. And the case of the gatherer of sticks might be explained in terms of the Sabbath instruction being not purely ritual but to ensure the worker's rest, whether or not that was the intent. But if that was the case, the social concern would focus on a prohibition on the employment of others on the Sabbath (mostly slaves or other subservients).

Transgression in the ritual sphere did not pass over Moses' close family. His brother Aaron was involved in the golden calf affair. He came out of it unscathed, but two of his sons, Nadab and Abihu, died, "when they offered unholy fire before the LORD" (Leviticus 10:1–2; Numbers 3:4).

Another kind of offense during the years in the wilderness was undermining Moses' authority or complaining against the Almighty (antihierarchical transgressions). The case of Korah clearly illustrates the fate of those that dared to deny the leader's authority. The case of Miriam, who criticized her brother's choice of wife, was another such example. An additional, very grave example was that of the spies sent by Moses into the promised land. Here the questioning of authority was joined by harm to the people's interests. The spies found a land flowing with milk and honey, but all of them except Joshua son of Nun and Caleb son of Jephunneh were terrified by the inhabitants and the giants among them. Their message struck fear into the hearts of the children of Israel, who complained bitterly against Moses and God for bringing them out of Egypt only to die at the hands of the Canaanites. This heresy brought down a heavy punishment: those "who brought an unfavorable report about the land" died in a plague (Numbers 14:37), and all Israelites of twenty years and older who complained to the Lord died in the wilderness. Only Joshua and Caleb were allowed to lead the desert generation into the promised land.

The transgressions of which Samuel complained were also hierarchical-ritual. Samuel accused Saul of two offenses: at the battle of Michmash, Saul had made sacrifices to God, though it was Samuel's role to do so, and in the war against Amalek, Saul violated the command to destroy Amalek and all his properties. He and the people spared King Agag and the choicest of his herds.

The first offense was damaging to Samuel's status; the second was noncompliance with Samuel's command, given in God's name. Nothing was said about acts that were flawed morally, but Samuel prophesied to Saul that the kingdom would be torn from him and given to another.

Interestingly, in response to Saul's apology, in which he claimed to have spared the herds of Amalek because he wanted to sacrifice them to the Lord, Samuel replied, "Has the LORD as great delight in burnt offerings and sacrifices, as in obeying the voice of the LORD? Surely, to obey is better than sacrifice, and to heed than the fat of rams" (1 Samuel 15:22). Samuel depreciated the sacrifices, though not in order to place moral principle above ritual, but to set obedience above all.

Biblical history is replete with tales of sin and punishment. The typical sin was ritual, mostly the worship of alien gods. King Solomon, who had seven hundred wives and three hundred concubines, was drawn by them to pagan worship and erected altars to Chemosh the god of Moab and Molech the god of Ammon. It is said that his punishment was the breakup of his kingdom in the reign of his son. That legendary king had many skeletons in his closet. He ordered the murder of Joab, David's loyal general who had sought to install Adonijah the son of Haggith on David's throne. He did the same for Adonijah, his elder brother, because the latter wanted to marry Abishag the Shunammite. Solomon built magnificent palaces and lived happily with his thousand women in pomp and luxury previously unknown in Israel. To maintain all this, he imposed heavy taxes on the people, and this was the prime reason for the breakup of the kingdom when his son Rehoboam refused to lighten the burden. Yet, when the split took place, nothing was said about all this. The only reason given was God's anger with Solomon: "Because his heart had turned away from the LORD, the God of Israel, who had appeared to him twice, and had commanded him . . . that he should not follow other gods; but he did not observe what the LORD commanded" (1 Kings 11:9–10).

After Solomon's death, Jeroboam ruled the kingdom of Israel, but he too received a harsh prophecy from Ahijah the Shilonite. The reason again was idolatry (1 Kings 14:9–11).[12] After Jeroboam's death, a revolt broke out against his son Nadab, and the throne passed to Baasha, who was also accused of Jeroboam's sin, both for himself and for leading Israel. Jehu, son of Hanani, delivered him a prophecy akin to Jeroboam's.

The trend continued through the next dynasty, that of the house of Omri, whose most famous member was King Ahab of Israel. His main sin was also

---

[12] On Jeroboam's sins and a discussion of whether he worshiped the God of Israel or other deities, see the next chapter "Jerusalem the Eternal Capital: Assyria's Contribution," pp. 189–91.

ritual: he followed pagan gods. This time, though, the response was immediate. Elijah informed him that there would be no rain or dew upon the land, unless he so ordered (1 Kings 17:1). At their next meeting Elijah accused Ahab of a single sin: "you have forsaken the commandments of the LORD and followed the Baals" (1 Kings 18:18)—which did not prevent Ahab from winning a great victory over Syria and then making a treaty with the defeated King Ben-hadad. But one of God's unnamed prophets would not let him be: once again he was accused of a serious transgression in not having killed Ben-hadad, a failure to obey a divine command (the assumption being, of course, that God's messenger had so commanded Ahab).

There were a few exceptions among the early prophets. Foremost among them is the case of Elijah, who prophesied to Ahab that in the place where dogs licked Naboth's blood, they would lick his (1 Kings 21:19). Conversely, in the murder of Uriah the Hittite, King David's court prophet, Nathan, took a more moderate position despite the severity of the crime. Moreover, in the case of Naboth, the prophet focused on a specific injustice and made no protests about Ahab's treatment of his subjects.

The great change occurred with the later, moral prophets, the first of whom was Amos, a century after the deaths of Ahab and Elijah. In strong words Amos admonished about social injustice, oppression of the poor, and miscarriages of justice. Amos was fierce and forthright: "Thus says the LORD: For three transgressions of Israel, and for four, I will not revoke the punishment; because they sell the righteous for silver, and the needy for a pair of sandals" (Amos 2:6). He addressed the wives of the wealthy: "Hear this word, you cows of Bashan who are on Mount Samaria, who oppress the poor, who crush the needy, who say to their husbands 'Bring something to drink'" (Amos 4:1). He protested against oppression, fraud, bribery, and injustice. He depreciated mere ritual observance, saying in the name of the Lord: "I hate, I despise your festivals, and I take no delight in your solemn assemblies. Even though you offer me your burnt offerings and grain offerings, I will not accept them; and the offerings of well-being of your fatted animals I will not look upon" (Amos 5:21–22). Samuel had also said that God had no interest in sacrifices as such, but there is an immense difference between the two. Amos demanded justice, honesty, and the protection of the poor and needy. Samuel demanded strict obedience and, more concretely, the killing of Agag, who was a prisoner of war.

The struggle for social justice, dramatically expressed, is also reflected in the prophecies of Isaiah and Jeremiah. Isaiah described the moral deterioration of Jerusalem: "How the faithful city has become a whore! She that was full of justice, righteousness lodged in her—but now murderers! . . . Your princes are rebels and companions of thieves. Everyone loves a bribe and runs after gifts. They do not defend the orphan, and the widow's cause does not come before them" (Isaiah 1:21, 23). But the rebuke about alien gods was not forgotten: "Hear, O heavens, and listen, O earth; for the LORD has spoken: I reared children and brought them up, but they have rebelled against me. The ox knows its owner, and the donkey its master's crib; but Israel does not know, my people do not understand" (Isaiah 1:2–3). Isaiah also devalued the importance of ritual, stressing social justice, honesty, and integrity. Strict observance of ritual could not cover up injustice and would not provide shelter for the evildoers: "What to me is the multitude of your sacrifices? says the LORD; I have had enough of burnt offerings of rams and the fat of fed beasts; I do not delight in the blood of bulls, or of lambs, or of goats. . . . Who asked this from your hand? Trample my courts no more; . . . Even though you make many prayers, I will not listen; your hands are full of blood. . . . Remove the evil of your doings from before my eyes; cease to do evil, learn to do good; seek justice, rescue the oppressed, defend the orphan, plead for the widow" (Isaiah 1:11–12, 15–17).

Jeremiah took a similar tack. He rebuked idolatry but aimed his most vitriolic attacks at the oppressors of widows and orphans (Jeremiah 7:6). He also reiterated the idea that atonement for unjust acts cannot be bought with sacrifices (Jeremiah 6:20).

It is said of old Hillel that a stranger asked to be converted and to be taught the whole Torah while standing on one leg. This happened after Rabbi Shammai had turned down a similar plea, but Hillel's answer was: "Do not do unto others that which you would not wish to be done to you—that is the whole Torah; the rest is commentary—go and learn."[13] These words underline the code of the moral prophets. Asked to sum up the Torah in one sentence, Hillel chose the moral rule applying to human relations and did not mention the ritual. Rabbi Hillel had come to the land of Israel from Babylon and began his activity some thirty years before the birth of Jesus, continuing into the first years of the new era—namely, almost six centuries after Jeremiah.

The teachings of Jesus, which Christianity views as the words of the Son of God,[14] were given only a few years after Hillel's death and belong in effect to

---

[13] Babylonian Talmud, *Shabbat* 31a.

[14] In Islam, Jesus is a prophet and emissary of God, though the Qur'an does not concede that he is the Son of God. In the view of Judaism, prophecy ended with the fall of the Persian Empire and its conquest by Alexander the Great, more than three centuries before Jesus. Nevertheless, various prophets did flourish in Jewish society in the Second Temple period, and even close to its destruction, but none became canonized in Jewish tradition.

the same period. They climaxed the transition to moral obligations while detracting from the value of ritual obligations. Speaking for God, he said, "I desire mercy and not sacrifice" (Matthew 12:7) and drew broad conclusions. When his hungry disciples plucked ears of wheat on the Sabbath, the Pharisees said they were violating a prohibition, but Jesus justified their act: "The sabbath was made for humankind, and not humankind for the sabbath; so the Son of Man is lord even of the sabbath" (Mark 2:27–28).[15] He went further on *kashrut* (dietary laws): "Do you not see that whatever goes into a person from outside cannot defile, since it enters, not the heart but the stomach, and goes out into the sewer? . . . For it is from within, from the human heart, that evil intentions come" (Mark 7:18–21). He also exempted his disciples from ritual handwashing, claiming that there was no external source of impurity and therefore all foods were permissible.

When Jesus was asked by a wealthy young man what precepts he should observe to have eternal life, Jesus answered: "You shall not murder; You shall not commit adultery; You shall not steal; You shall not bear false witness; Honor your father and mother; also, You shall love thy neighbor as yourself" (Matthew 19:18–19). The young man asked what else he should do, and Jesus told him to sell his property and give the proceeds to the poor, for "it is easier for a camel to go through the eye of a needle than for someone who is rich to enter the kingdom of God" (Matthew 19:24). All the commandments cited by Jesus belong in the category of interpersonal relations; none involves ritual. The commandment to "love your neighbor," reiterated by Jesus, comes from Leviticus 19:18, but the idea had been amended by Hillel to "Do not do unto others that which you would not wish to be done to you." Jesus had reverted to the original, which differs from the latter as ideal differs from reality.[16]

In Judaism, emphasis on the interpersonal commandments did not imply a rejection of the ritual. But ritual sacrifices ceased with the Roman destruction of the second Temple in 70 C.E., not because Judaism was negating them, but because the Temple had held a monopoly on the cult.[17] Christianity, on the other hand, did not inherit from Judaism the ceremonial ritual of sacrifice. With the spread of Christianity over Europe, hundreds of years after Jesus'

---

[15] This does not necessarily mean that Jesus was willing to disregard the rules of Sabbath observance but that he gave them a liberal interpretation that the picking of grain for personal consumption, not for commercial purpose, was permissible. See Brad H. Young, *Jesus the Jewish Theologian* (Peabody, Mass.: Hendrickson, 1995), 103–8.

[16] For comparisons with other abstract formulations in ancient law, see Reuven Yaron, "Social Problems and Politics in the Ancient Near East," 21, 25–27.

[17] See the next chapter "Jerusalem the Eternal Capital: Assyria's Contribution," pp. 193–95.

death, sacrifice ended on that continent.[18] The reason was ideological, unlike Judaism, where the cause was destruction of the shrine devoted to the ritual.

The creation of the State of Israel brought, for the first time in almost two thousand years, the reintegration of the Jewish religion into a governing establishment. As a result, there was a spate of religious rulings, the implementation of which is enforced by the institutions of government. At the center of these injunctions are ritual laws (between humans and God), such as the dietary laws, the prohibition of the sale of leavened bread at Passover, and Sabbath observance.

The Historical Background of the Moral Prophets

Amos prophesied in the kingdom of Israel during the reign of Jeroboam II, the grandson of Jehu, who had led the successful rebellion against the house of Ahab. Jeroboam ascended the throne in 785 B.C.E. and reigned for forty years. It was said of him that he did evil in the eyes of the Lord and did not "depart" from the sins of Jeroboam I, son of Nebat, who had led Israel into the path of wrongdoing (2 Kings 14:24). Nevertheless, the kingdom grew powerful, extended its rule, and enjoyed economic prosperity during his reign, all of which became possible when the kingdom of Aram/Damascus was broken up by Assyria. But the terrible period in which Israel was suppressed and trampled into the dust by Syria was not forgotten. Indeed, Amos began his prophecies with a declaration: "Thus says the LORD: For three transgressions of Damascus, and for four, I will not revoke the punishment; because they have threshed Gilead with threshing sledges of iron" (Amos 1:3). No doubt, the gloomy days of King Jehu, anointed on the prophet Elisha's instructions to replace the idolaters of the house of Ahab, were also remembered. Ahab and Jezebel, his wife, worshiped Baal, but Ahab was a brave warrior and gifted commander who defeated the Syrians and, eventually, died a hero's death in war against them. His son Jehoram was defeated by Syria, but Israel maintained its independence. Jehu's revolt against Jehoram (Joram) ended in tragedy. The destruction of the dynasty and the terrible massacre that Jehu initiated probably weakened the kingdom of Israel and left it vulnerable to Syrian aggression. A dynasty that followed pagan gods was uprooted and replaced by a king who worshiped the Israelite God and was supported by a prophet. But instead

---

[18] Christianity was declared the official religion of the Roman Empire in the reign of Constantine (in the Western Empire, from 306 C.E.). He gained control over the Eastern Empire and reigned until 337 C.E. The offering of sacrifices was prohibited by his sons, Constatius and Constans.

of improving things, Israel's standing reached its nadir. Paradoxically, prosperity recurred during the reign of Jeroboam II, who had done evil in the Lord's eyes. Perhaps this is the explanation for the inclusion of the Naboth affair in the chronicles of Ahab. The difficult questions posed by the revolt and its results called for other reasons for Elisha's action in initiating the uprising—Ahab's idolatry was insufficient. The Naboth affair was needed to supply moral justification, in addition to the ritual grounds for removal of the house of Ahab.

Isaiah son of Amoz (the First Isaiah) began to prophesy in Jerusalem, in the kingdom of Judah, some thirty years after Amos. His prophecies, beginning around 734 B.C.E., lasted at least until 701. Isaiah predicted the total destruction of the kingdom of Israel, which was crushed by the Assyrian empire in 720 B.C.E. Judah, where Isaiah was active, paid tribute to Assyria and became its vassal. Years after the destruction of Israel, the Philistine coastal cities rebelled against Assyria. The revolt was put down by force in 712, when Assyria conquered Ashdod. The kingdom of Judah did not take part in the revolt and so did not suffer from its failure.

A few years later, with Egypt's encouragement, another revolt broke out. This time, King Hezekiah of Judah decided to join in. Some commentators have argued that Isaiah opposed the revolt,[19] but I doubt this. It was said of Hezekiah that he was righteous: "He trusted in the LORD the God of Israel; so that there was no one like him among all the kings of Judah after him, or among those who were before him. For he held fast to the LORD; he did not depart from following him but kept the commandments that the LORD commanded Moses" (2 Kings 18:5–6). It is unlikely that the Bible would have described him in these terms had he defied Isaiah. Isaiah's position is unclear. On the one hand, he warned against those who relied on Egypt: "Who set out to go down to Egypt without asking for my counsel, to take refuge in the protection of Pharaoh, and to seek shelter in the shadow of Egypt; Therefore the protection of Pharaoh shall become your shame, and the shelter in the shadow of Egypt your humiliation" (Isaiah 30:2–3). On the other hand, he prophesied the destruction of Assyria by the Lord: "Then the Assyrian shall fall by a sword, not of mortals; and a sword, not of humans, shall devour him; he shall flee from the sword, and his young men shall be put to forced labor" (Isaiah 31:8). The prophecy did not materialize. Assyria was destroyed, but only one hundred years later, when Nineveh was conquered by Babylon and the Medes. We might add that Judah fell from the frying pan into the fire following the harsh Babylonian conquest.

---

[19] Hayim Tadmor, in *History of the Jewish People* (Hebrew) (ed. Haim H. Ben-Sasson; 3 vols.; Tel-Aviv: Dvir, 1969), 1:142.

Jeremiah's prophecies, some seventy-five years after Isaiah, expressed a sharp opposition to rebellion against Babylon and illustrate how a prophet can voice disagreement. There is no resemblance between his words and Isaiah's pronouncements.

In any event, Hezekiah's revolt against Assyria ended in terrible tragedy. Sennacherib, king of Assyria, embarked on a punitive expedition, capturing the fortified cities of Judah, among them Lachish. Thousands were killed, and many were exiled. The Assyrian king gave parts of Judah to Philistia. He also planned to conquer Jerusalem, but the city was saved when Hezekiah paid a very heavy tax and returned to vassal status.

Jeremiah began to prophesy in approximately 625 B.C.E. He foresaw Assyria's collapse. Josiah was then king of Judah and was said to be righteous. Josiah renewed the covenant with God, ordered all the idols dedicated to Baal removed from the Temple, and smashed Jeroboam's altar in Bethel, thereby fulfilling the prophecy to that king.[20] According to the Bible, "Before him there was no king like him, who turned to the LORD with all his heart, with all his soul, and with all his might, according to all the law of Moses; nor did any like him arise after him" (2 Kings 23:25).

Hopes for liberation following the collapse of Assyria, and in light of Josiah's righteousness, were dashed. Josiah himself was killed in an encounter with the Egyptians near Megiddo.[21] Judah was again subjugated, first to Egypt, then to the mighty Babylonian Empire. Jeremiah witnessed all these events as well as the rebellion against Babylon, against which he warned. He also witnessed the conquest of Jerusalem by Nebuchadnezzar and the destruction of the first Temple in 586 B.C.E.

Can this historical background offer an explanation to the change that took place in Israelite prophecy from the times of Amos and the sharp transition from ritual to moral pronouncements? There is no clear-cut explanation for the flowering of a new faith or the changed social viewpoint. All that can be said is that the historical processes might account for it. The naive theory of causal linkage between evil doing and punishment that appears quite often in the first prophets collapsed. It had rested on the belief that, if Israel observed

---

[20] See the earlier chapter "A Godly Man Killed by a Lion," p. 112–13.

[21] The circumstances of his death are not altogether clear. For example, 2 Chronicles 35:20–25 describes a battle between the Israelites and the Egyptians in which Josiah was killed, but 2 Kings 23:29 merely states that as Pharaoh Neco went up against the king of Assyria, Josiah moved toward him and was killed by Neco in Megiddo. Thus the version in 2 Kings conforms with the possibility that there was no battle between the Israelites and the Egyptians but that Josiah met Neco, who seized him and had him killed. For a discussion, see Cline, *Battles of Armageddon*, 90–100.

the—mostly ritual-hierarchical—commandments, God would sustain it and award well-being and victory over enemies.

For example, Leviticus 26 demonstrates the belief in a causal connection between the observation of God's commandments and subsequent rewards. It offers a clear promise that

> If you follow my statutes and keep my commandments and observe them faith-fully, I will give you your rains in their season, and the land shall yield its produce, and the trees of the field shall yield their fruit. . . . And I will grant peace in the land, and you shall lie down, and no one shall make you afraid; I will remove dangerous animals from the land, and no sword shall go through your land. You shall give chase to your enemies, and they shall fall before you by the sword. Five of you shall give chase to a hundred, and a hundred of you shall give chase to ten thousand; your enemies shall fall before you by the sword. (Leviticus 26:3–8)

In Jehu's day, the destruction of the house of Ahab, at Elisha's command, the smashing of the altars of Baal, and the killing of his followers did not promise peace, prosperity, or victory over the Syrians. Hezekiah's great virtue in Isaiah's time or Josiah's in Jeremiah's time—a virtue that was mostly ritual—did not save them from the dire fate that history had in store for them. Hezekiah's revolt against Assyria failed, Lachish and other fortified cities were destroyed, and the kingdom remained subjugated by the great empire. He could take comfort in the fact that Jerusalem was not destroyed, but that still could not make up for the catastrophe that befell a righteous king. Josiah's fate was even harsher. He was defeated in battle against the Egyptians and lost his life. Such was the miserable destiny of righteous kings. By contrast, the great sinner, Jeroboam II, won victories, prospered, and succeeded in everything he turned his hand to.

How could such reality, so contrary to traditional faith, be explained? The answer came in an attempt to break the direct link between sin and punishment and between the righteous act and its reward. Such a link exists in legends from the ancient period of the Bible, which often emphasize the immediate connection between action and retribution. The stories of the plagues in Egypt were all founded on the immediate response to Pharaoh's wicked obstinacy. For each refusal to let the Israelites go, one of the ten plagues descended on Egypt. After the exodus from Egypt, Korah's clan challenged Moses' leadership. They were invited to compete against Aaron and Moses' loyal followers in burning incense to the Lord; they lost and were immediately swallowed up in the earth, along with all their property (Numbers 16). Miriam criticized Moses for marrying a Cushite and was immediately struck by leprosy (Numbers 12). During the battle of Jericho, Achan violated a ban. The Israelites were defeated, but the culprit was discovered, and he and his household and flocks were immediately stoned to death. For that response, Israel was at once rewarded with a victory. In Elijah's contest with the prophets of Baal, shortly after his triumph and their slaughter, welcome rain began to fall on the land (1 Kings 18:45).

But the history of the period closer to the writing of the Bible, which was certainly chronicled as it happened, did not fit this simple model. Many of the great kings in the kingdom of Israel worshiped alien gods, yet they enjoyed long and often successful reigns. After their deaths, when their dynasties or their people were visited by tragedy, the Bible interpreted it as punishment for their acts. But retribution many years after the deed and the transgressor's death casts doubts about the connection between crime and punishment. Jeroboam I did evil in the eyes of the Lord, but he reigned for twenty-two years and died peacefully. His dynasty was destroyed only in his son's time, and the Bible relates its destruction to the prophecies of Ahijah the Shilonite. Jeroboam's dynasty was replaced by Baasha, who followed in his predecessor's footsteps. He apparently did not believe in a causal link between Jeroboam's idolatry and his own success in rebelling against the son. Baasha saw himself free to do as he pleased and received his own prophetic admonition from Jehu son of Hanani. But again the "response" came only in his son's reign, and Baasha himself reigned for twenty-four years. Jeroboam II did evil in the eyes of the Lord, but in his time the kingdom of Israel reached the height of its power and prosperity. The punishment came decades after his death.

Jehu, who brutally exterminated the house of Ahab, killed the followers of Baal, and smashed the altars, sustained heavy defeats at the hands of Syria. The reward for his actions, which the Bible depicts in a favorable light, was postponed for later generations: "The LORD said to Jehu, 'Because you have done well in carrying out what I consider right, and in accordance with all that was in my heart have dealt with the house of Ahab, your sons of the fourth generation shall sit on the throne of Israel'" (2 Kings 10:30). Similar logic seeks to explain the bitter fate of the righteous king Josiah, who was killed in battle with the Egyptians: "The LORD did not turn from the fierceness of his great wrath, by which his anger was kindled against Judah, because of all the provocations with which Manasseh had provoked him" (2 Kings 23:26). In other words, Josiah was punished because his grandfather, Manasseh, had worshiped idols and had introduced a statue of Asherah into the Temple. But the sinful king had not been punished. Indeed, his reign, the longest in the history of Judah, lasted fifty-five years. However, 2 Chronicles 33 relates that Manasseh was captured by the Assyrians, who deported him to Babylon. After he repented the Lord returned him to his country, where he dutifully worshiped the God of Israel. The story of his repentance, which does not conform to the text of Kings, was probably designed to offer a solution in the spirit of reward and punishment for the long reign of Manasseh.

In summary, it seems that in the days of the later prophets, and maybe earlier, historical realities caused the collapse of the simplistic model in which observance of the commandments brought abundance and victory over enemies. A new model emerged of a causal link between observance or violation and reality, suggesting that repentance may win a reprieve, thus explaining the fact that David came out of the Bathsheba affair and the murder of Uriah unscathed or that reward and punishment were deferred to future generations. The failure of the virtuous and the success of sinners became dependent on events that occurred many generations earlier. This approach opened unlimited possibilities, for every people has its ups and downs. If peak moments can be attributed to good behavior in an earlier generation, and troughs to long-past transgressions, then anything can be explained. The theory is, however, morally flawed, since it means that one pays for one's ancestors' sins (Jeremiah 31:29–30). In addition, the tremendous flexibility of this theory leaves it devoid of explanatory power. No wonder that Jeremiah protested, "You will be in the right, O LORD, when I lay charges against you; but let me put my case to you. Why does the way of the guilty prosper? Why do all who are treacherous thrive?" (Jeremiah 12:1). This is joined by the cry, "Pour out your wrath on the nations that do not know you . . . for they have devoured Jacob . . . and have laid waste his habitation" (Jeremiah 10:25). The plea is repeated in Psalm 79, which cries out that heathens, who do not believe in God or keep God's commandments, have overcome Israel. The book of Job concludes with the acquiescence that humans cannot understand the ways of God.

To contend with the difficulty, the theory of the end of days was proposed. There is already a hint in Amos: "Alas for you who desire the day of the LORD! Why do you want the day of the LORD? It is darkness, not light" (Amos 5:18). A more detailed belief appears in Isaiah 24–27. For our purpose there is no need to discuss the belief or its motifs. It suffices to note that it is a sophisticated version of the idea of deferred reward and punishment. The simple notion of postponement was based on the assumption that the existing world order would continue, that history assured that reward or punishment would be given in the second or third generation. Apart from the difficulty of seeing the logic of the method, no order or consistency can be found in it. If Josiah was punished for the sins of his grandfather, why were not his son and grandsons rewarded for his righteousness? In the twenty odd years between his death and the destruction of the Temple, his descendants of the house of David suffered a series of catastrophes, culminating when Zedekiah rebelled against Babylon. The Babylonians destroyed Jerusalem and the Temple and slaughtered Zedekiah's sons before his eyes, which they then tore out. He was led in shackles to Babylon.

Later visions of the end of days, which anticipate many themes of still later apocalyptic texts like Daniel, also postponed the divine justice, though in a more sophisticated way. It proposed a novel and unprecedented event that did not have to meet the test of reality. Moreover, the vision suggested a new universal order in which God would control directly and justice would prevail. It is also likely to be a happy time, at least for the righteous, and it even contained the promise of eternal life: "He will swallow up death forever. Then the Lord GOD will wipe away the tears from all faces, and the disgrace of his people he will take away from all the earth" (Isaiah 25:7–8).

The historical developments and the rise of the great powers also heralded a changed view of God's role in Israel's wars. In the early period of the settlement and the wars with the peoples of Canaan, the Philistines, and others, God was believed to support the side of Israel against enemies and to ensure victory—of course, conditional on the Israelites observing their ritual obligations. The rise of the great empires changed this view. Israel could not defeat them and therefore had to avoid conflict. The vision of God directing history remained, but in a different way. The people of Israel could not bring about the fall of the great powers. Isaiah prophesied that the Lord would break Assyria and remove its yoke from Israel, but the Israelites would have no part to play in the process (Isaiah 14:24–25). Jeremiah, in similar terms, prophesied the downfall of Babylon, which had trampled the kingdom of Judah, but God would do so without Israel's participation, using other means. Jeremiah 50–51 are devoted to Babylon's collapse. These chapters are full of celebration and delight, but the following is sufficient to exclude Israel: "For I am going to stir up and bring against Babylon a company of great nations from the land of the north. . . . Their arrows are like the arrows of a skilled warrior who does not return empty-handed. Chaldea shall be plundered; all who plunder her shall be sated, says the LORD" (Jeremiah 50:9–10). God now uses other players.

Finally, we may note the link between hardships suffered by Israel and the transition from ritual to moral admonition. The end-of-days prophecies contended with the failure of the Torah's link between ritual transgression and punishment by altering the idea of *consequences*. Sin did not necessarily incur immediate results; these could wait till the end of days. At a later stage, a solution was found in the image of the next world, in which sinners are punished in hell while the righteous go to heaven.

Another way of dealing with the failure of the original reward-and-punishment thesis was by examining the *cause*. Ritual rules are characterized by their clarity: they are technical, easily testable as to whether they have been

187

observed or not. It enabled an easy examination of the causal link between the ritual act and reward or punishment. This led to a conclusion that the causal-linkage theory did not conform to reality. The later prophets redefined the deed that called for punishment or reward. Alongside ritual demands, which they tended to devalue, they placed moral principles, ideals without technical regulations. These moral principles were binding not only on kings or priests but also on the entire nation. It is doubtful whether they were ever fully implemented in their ideal form. Failure, which was quite naturally widespread, could supply the reason for the tragedies that befell Israel with the rise of the great empires in the region and their invasion of the promised land.

12

Jerusalem the Eternal Capital: Assyria's Contribution

✠

The city of Jerusalem is the eternal capital of the people of Israel, the object of dreams for thousands of years. Its sacred status in the Jewish religion passed to Christianity and Islam, both of which regard it as holy.

Jerusalem fell into Israelite hands fairly late. It was conquered from the Jebusites in David's reign, after all the tribes of Israel had settled in the country. David made it his capital and gave it the first spark of holiness when he transferred the ark from Kiriath-jearim. The next important step came when Solomon built the Temple. But before the city had consolidated its place in the religious and national awareness, a serious crisis threatened its status. After Solomon's death, the kingdom split into two: Judah and Israel. Jerusalem's wings were clipped, and the city—the capital of a big and powerful monarchy during the reigns of the two kings—became the center of the small kingdom of Judah. Israel, to the north, was bigger and stronger, the home of ten tribes of Israel, led by Ephraim. Jeroboam, who had rebelled against the house of David and became the first king of Israel, was crowned in Shechem, which became the capital of the ten tribes until the center moved to Tirzah and eventually to Samaria.

The kingdom of Israel needed its own religious services, and Jeroboam did not care to be dependent on the Temple and priests of Jerusalem. So he chose to consolidate the temples at Bethel and Dan, placing a golden calf in each. He told his people: "You have gone up to Jerusalem long enough. Here are your gods, O Israel, who brought you up out of the land of Egypt" (1 Kings 12:28). The calves recalled the events in the wilderness, when the Israelites demanded of Aaron to make them a god, while Moses was on Mount Sinai—an act for which they were severely punished.

Various hypotheses have centered around the status and role of golden calves and the link between Jeroboam and the desert incident. Some researchers maintain that the calf was considered a seat for God, thereby fulfilling a role similar to the cherubs on the holy ark, whose wings, according to one interpretation, served as God's throne.[1] According to another interpretation the story of the golden calves at Bethel and Dan was a later addition to the Bible, designed to condemn the form of worship in Jeroboam's reign and thereafter.[2] Suffice it to say that the two shrines apparently served, at least some of the time, the God of Israel, and not pagan gods such as Baal.[3] First Kings, which is hardly sympathetic to Jeroboam, does not accuse him in chapter 12 of worshiping Baal or Asherah, though in chapter 14 the prophet Ahijah the Shilonite does accuse him of making images and casting the God of Israel behind his back. In chapter 12, the accusation is that he made an inappropriate image of God for improper worship.

Jehu destroyed the house of Ahab, killed all the priests of Baal, and smashed their altars. The description of his actions and his attitude to God contains internal contradictions: "Thus Jehu wiped out Baal from Israel. But Jehu did not turn aside from the sins of Jeroboam, son of Nebat, which he caused Israel to commit—the golden calves that were in Bethel and Dan" (2 Kings 10:28–29). A similar contradiction appears in the next two verses. God rewarded Jehu for his massacre of the house of Ahab and the priests of Baal, speaking directly to him: "Because you have done well in carrying out what I consider right, and in accordance with all that was in my heart have dealt with the house of Ahab, your sons of the fourth generation shall sit on the throne of Israel" (2 Kings 10:30).[4] Yet the next verse seems to contradict it:

---

[1] Moshe David Cassuto, "Bethel," and Moshe David Cassuto and Richard D. Barnet, "Cherubs" (Hebrew), in *Encyclopaedia Biblica* (Jerusalem: Bialik Institute, 1972–1982); Yehezkel Kaufmann, *History of the Israelite Religion* (Hebrew) (Jerusalem: Bialik Institute; Tel-Aviv: Dvir, 1955–1956), vol. B. 259–62.

[2] For a discussion, see Oded Bustenai, "Introduction to 2 Samuel 11," in *The World of the Bible* (Hebrew) (24 vols.; Tel-Aviv: Davidson-Atai, 1993–1997). The names of Jeroboam's sons were almost identical to the names of two of the sons of Aaron (Moses' brother, who was implicated in the affair of the golden calf after the exodus from Egypt), and all of them met an unfortunate fate. Aaron's sons, Nadab and Abihu, died when they offered "unholy fire before the LORD" (the story is repeated three times in the Pentateuch: Leviticus 10:1–2; Numbers 3:4; 26:61). Jeroboam's sons, Abijah and Nadab, also died prematurely. Abijah fell ill and died in childhood (1 Kings 14), and Nadab succeeded his father on the throne but was murdered two years later in the revolt of Baasha (1 Kings 15:25–28).

[3] Cassuto, "Bethel."

[4] The traditional commentators did not accept the possibility that God had spoken directly to Jehu. Rashi and Radak suggested that the message was given by the prophet Jonah son of Amittai, hero of the book of Jonah.

"But Jehu was not careful to follow the law of the LORD the God of Israel with all his heart; he did not turn from the sins of Jeroboam, which he caused Israel to commit" (2 Kings 10:31).

A possible explanation is that Jehu, and apparently Jeroboam, worshiped the God of Israel, but in the temples of Bethel and Dan, and that the rites may have involved a golden calf and other symbols that distinguished it from the practices of Jerusalem. Jeroboam and Jehu's sins were in following different rites and doing so in places other than Jerusalem. This was apparently a manifestation of the rivalry between the temples of Israel and Judah.

Through most of its history, the kingdom of Israel probably preferred the temples of Bethel and Dan over Jerusalem. It must be remembered that Jerusalem had been part of Israel for only a few decades, through part of the reign of David and all of that of Solomon, while Bethel had a long tradition of holiness, going back many generations. Abraham had erected an altar between Bethel and Ai (Genesis 12:8). Jacob slept in Bethel on his way to Laban's house in Paddan-aram, and it was there that he dreamed of a ladder set up on the earth, the top of it reaching heaven and the angels of God ascending and descending on it—and above it God, who promised the land to him and his seed (Genesis 28:12–13). When Jacob awoke, he cried: "Surely the LORD is in this place—and I did not know it! . . . How awesome is this place! This is none other than the house of God, and this is the gate of heaven" (Genesis 28:16–17). It was a glorious tradition that could rival Jerusalem.

In addition, through most of the period that Israel existed alongside Judah, it was the larger, stronger, and wealthier of the two kingdoms. Occasionally the kingdoms cooperated. In Ahab's time, King Jehoshaphat of Judah joined him in making war on Syria. Ahab was, of course, the leader. At other times, the two fought each other, and Israel was usually victorious. In one case, Amaziah of Judah wanted a contest with Jehoash of Israel, but the latter replied, "A thornbush on Lebanon sent to a cedar on Lebanon, saying, 'Give your daughter to my son for a wife'; but a wild animal of Lebanon passed by and trampled down the thornbush" (2 Kings 14:9). The arrogant response was well founded: "Judah was defeated by Israel. . . . King Jehoash of Israel captured King Amaziah of Judah . . . and broke down the wall of Jerusalem, . . . a distance of four hundred cubits. He seized all the gold and silver, and all the vessels that were found in the house of the LORD and in the treasuries of the king's house, as well as hostages; then he returned to Samaria" (2 Kings 14:12–14).

The Bible illuminates the rivalry between the tribes of Judah and Ephraim in texts that were probably written when the kingdom of Israel existed in all its glory and were so entrenched that the later editors of the Bible, though belonging to Judah, could not remove them. For example, Genesis reports that Reuben lost his primogeniture because he defiled his father's bed by sleeping with Bilhah, Rachel's maidservant. From Jacob's blessing to his sons in Genesis 49, it is clear that Judah won the primacy, for it was said that his brothers would bow down before him (49:8). But Jacob's favorite son was Joseph, the son of his beloved wife Rachel, and Joseph's younger son Ephraim received the best of his grandfather's blessing (Genesis 48:19–20). Moreover, 1 Chronicles 5:1 relates that the birthright was taken from Reuben and given to the sons of Joseph, son of Israel. These texts reflect the great power of the tribe of Ephraim.

We may therefore assume that the Bethel temple was no less splendid and no lower in status than the Temple in Jerusalem, and this would remain true as long as the kingdom of Israel existed. Bethel is only twelve miles north of Jerusalem. In the days of its glory the ten tribes were proud of it and probably preferred it to the Temple in Jerusalem. This period lasted some two hundred years, from 930 B.C.E., the year of Solomon's death, to 720 B.C.E., when the kingdom of Israel was destroyed by the Assyrian Empire—and the entire picture changed.

Some twenty years after the destruction of Israel, King Hezekiah of Judah revolted against Assyria. In 701, Sennacherib of Assyria led his army to put down the revolt. The Assyrian army sowed death and destruction; many fortified cities, among them Lachish, were conquered and razed to the ground. But the prophet Isaiah prophesied that Jerusalem would be saved and that "concerning the king of Assyria: He shall not come into this city, shoot an arrow there, come before it with a shield, or cast up a siege ramp against it" (2 Kings 19:32–33). The chapter goes on to say that an angel of the Lord struck Sennacherib's army, killing 185,000 men, whereupon the king returned to Assyria. While this description, which glorifies the prophet Isaiah and the wonders of the Lord, is historically doubtful, the fact remains that Jerusalem was not destroyed at that time. Hezekiah, according to the text, groveled before the Assyrian king: "I have done wrong; withdraw from me; whatever you impose on me I will bear." Sennacherib demanded of King Hezekiah of Judah three hundred talents of silver and thirty talents of gold (2 Kings 18:14). Hezekiah paid the heavy levy and became again an obedient vassal of the empire. The conflict between Hezekiah's capitulation and the blow struck by the angel of the Lord is difficult to resolve. Both versions appear in the Bible, one after the other, beginning with the levy paid to Assyria. Then, ignoring it, Sennacherib sends his army to besiege Jerusalem, and the next chapter records a plague and a miracle that saved the city. The impression given is that there is no connection between the events. However, reason suggests that the heavy tax paid to the Assyrian king was a decisive factor in saving the city, and whether or not a plague did strike the army, and in what force, remains in doubt.[5] Yet some scholars maintain that the salvation of Jerusalem, attributed to a miracle and a divine protection, in fact strengthened the city's status as holy.[6]

I believe that the main reason for Jerusalem's rise in status was connected to the destruction of the kingdom of Israel. The capture of Samaria, capital of Israel, by Assyria in 720 B.C.E., spelled the end of the kingdom. Many of its inhabitants were exiled, and the city itself descended from the stage of history. Jerusalem's relative status changed accordingly, as the temples of Bethel and Dan had lost their royal patronage and many of their followers who both needed their services and supplied economic support. The shrine of Bethel continued for another century, but it led an impoverished existence compared with its days of glory. Jerusalem was the main Israelite city, and its Temple became the central place of worship of all Israelites.

When Josiah ascended the throne in Jerusalem, around 640 B.C.E. or eighty years after the destruction of the kingdom of Israel, a new and dramatic phase began in the status of the eternal city. Second Kings 22 relates that, in the eighteenth year of Josiah's reign, a book of the Torah was discovered in the Temple and was read to the king. He tore his clothes and renewed the covenant with God. Many scholars believe that the book was Deuteronomy, which was written in part or edited during Josiah's reign. The book lays down the principle of centralized and monopolistic worship: "Then you shall bring everything that I command you to the place that the LORD your God will choose as a dwelling for his name: your burnt offerings and your sacrifices, your tithes and your donations, and all your choice votive gifts that you vow to the LORD. . . . Take care that you do not offer your burnt offerings at any place you happen to see. But only at the place that the LORD will choose in one of your tribes—there you shall offer your burnt offerings and there you shall do everything I command you" (Deuteronomy 12:11, 13–14). Significantly, the text does not name

---

[5] Herodotus, *Histories* 2.141, notes that Sennacherib suffered a defeat at the gates of Egypt (not of Jerusalem), after a miracle in which a horde of field mice gnawed away the Assyrian archers' bowstrings. That was attributed to a dream of Sethos, in which God promised to help in the war against Sennacherib. Herodotus wrote in the fifth century B.C.E., some 250 years after the Assyrian expedition, and he may have drawn on more than one tradition about divine assistance that led to the Assyrian retreat. A number of attempts were made to reconcile Hezekiah's payment and Sennacherib's downfall. One suggests that, after receiving the levy, the Assyrian broke his agreement, besieged Jerusalem, and failed. Another claims that there were two Assyrian forays: in one of which the tax was paid, and in the other they were compelled to retreat (Baruch Kaplinski, *Hezekiah the Fourteenth King of the Davidic Dynasty and His Period* [Hebrew] [Tel-Aviv: Society for Biblical Research, 1990], 278, 297).

[6] Hayim Tadmor, *History of the Jewish People*, 1:145.

Jerusalem, and indeed its name is not mentioned even once in the Penta-teuch.[7] In any event, the principle of centralized ritual contravened the cus-tom of generations. The Bible is full of descriptions of sacrifices to God in a variety of places. However, beginning with Josiah's reign, Jerusalem claimed an exclusive status, and the Temple became the exclusive site for offering sacri-fices. Josiah used force to maintain this policy: he destroyed altars and the Bethel temple; Jeroboam's altar was smashed and then defiled by burning human bones on it. Henceforward, Jerusalem would zealously protect its status and monopoly, and this would gain expression in the Second Temple period.

Josiah destroyed Bethel in 620 B.C.E. Thirty years later, in 586 B.C.E., Jerusa-lem was conquered by the Babylonians, and the Temple was destroyed. Cyrus's famous declaration, permitting the return of the Babylonian exiles and the building of the second Temple, was fifty years later, in 538 B.C.E. Building was completed in 515, and for almost six centuries, until the Romans destroyed the Temple in 70 C.E., Jerusalem's ritual monopoly was virtually absolute.

The battle to maintain the monopoly was not confined to the land of Is-rael. In southern Egypt, in ancient times, there was a city named Yeb (Abu)—called Elephantine by the Greeks—on an island in the Nile. Documents found there reveal that in the fifth century B.C.E. when Egypt was part of the Persian Empire, Yeb was garrisoned by a company of Jewish mercenaries, whose job was to protect Egypt's southern frontier. The Jewish community of Yeb built a temple, but in 410 B.C.E., about a century after the erection of the second Temple in Jerusalem, a dispute between the Jews of Yeb and the priests of Khnum led to the latter razing the Jewish temple. The community asked the authorities for permission to rebuild, which was granted, but subject to the condition that the temple would not be used to offer animal sacrifices. One theory suggests that the restriction originated with the priests in Jerusalem, who objected to such sacrifices outside the Temple in the holy city.[8]

In the second century B.C.E. another Jewish temple was built in Egypt. After Antiochus IV Epiphanes became king of Syria his persecutions led to the Maccabean revolt (167 B.C.E.). Onias, a son of the family of the high priest in

---

[7] Genesis 14:18 mentions Melchizedek, the king of Salem, which has been tradi-tionally taken to mean Jerusalem. For the various explanations why Jerusalem is not mentioned in the Pentateuch, see Yairah Amit, *Hidden Polemic in Biblical Narrative* (Leiden: Brill, 2000), 130–68.

[8] Zeev Ben Haim, "Yeb" (Hebrew), in *Encyclopaedia Biblica*. A legal analysis of documents of the Jewish community of Yeb is to be found in Reuven Yaron, *Introduc-tion to the Law of the Aramaic Papyri* (Oxford: Clarendon, 1961). On the Jewish com-munity in Yeb and the story of its temple, see Joseph Mélèze Modrzejewski, *The Jews of Egypt: From Rameses II to Emperor Hadrian* (Princeton N.J.: Princeton University Press, 1992), 21–44.

Jerusalem, fled to Egypt and obtained permission from King Ptolemy VI Philometor and his wife Queen Cleopatra II to build a temple in Leontopolis. Sacrifices to God were offered in this temple, which functioned for well over two hundred years. Its end came shortly after the destruction of the Jerusalem Temple in 70 C.E. The Romans, fearing that the Onias temple would become a center of anti-Roman agitation, ordered its closure in 73.[9] The Onias temple ranked far below the Jerusalem Temple and left no mark on Jewish tradition. It is referred to in the Mishnah (tractate *Menahoth* 13:10) and the Talmud. But its holiness was denied. It is described as "the house" (not "the temple") of Onias and the Mishnah states that "the priests who ministered in the house of Onias may not minister in the Temple in Jerusalem."

The exclusive status gave the priests and the entire city of Jerusalem considerable prestige coupled with immense economic interest. The offering of sacrifices was a well-paid occupation and gave rise to widespread economic activity that enriched the Temple. A hint of this appears in the New Testament story of Jesus driving the merchants from the Temple and overturning the moneylenders' tables and the seats of the dove traders. Jesus quoted from Isaiah: "For my house shall be called a house of prayer for all peoples" (Isaiah 56:7). He went on: "But you have made it a den of robbers" (Mark 11:17 [alluding to Jeremiah 7:11]).

So entrenched was the monopoly that when the Temple was destroyed the practice of sacrifice stopped with it. "Temple" became a synonym for the Temple in Jerusalem, to such an extent that it is virtually impossible to conceive of Judaism with any other holy sanctuaries.

Let us return to the role that Assyria inadvertently played in establishing the centrality of Jerusalem and its worldwide status. Clearly, while the kingdom of Israel existed alongside Judah, the city could not attain such primacy, and its kings could not prevent the existence of other temples. The special holiness of the Temple, and Jerusalem's status, were guaranteed only after the Assyrian Empire ruthlessly destroyed the kingdom of Israel. This enabled Josiah to smash the temple of Bethel and grant Jerusalem its uniqueness and its eternal place in the memory of the nation.

---

[9] Flavius Josephus, *Jewish Antiquities* 13.3; Flavius Josephus, *Jewish Wars* 7, 10; Modrzejewski, *The Jews in Egypt*, 121–33.

13

Succession to the Throne

When the Israelites asked Samuel to give them a king, the prophet responded with fury, warning the people of a monarch's ways and how he would exploit them (1 Samuel 8:11–17). But Samuel was forced to capitulate to the demand, though it meant the loss of his military and political role. According to the Bible, God himself ordered Samuel to comply, saying, "They have not rejected you, but they have rejected me from being king over them" (1 Samuel 8:7).

Elsewhere the Bible expresses support for the monarchy—for example, in the prophet Nathan's blessing of David: "Your house and your kingdom shall be made sure forever before me; your throne shall be established forever" (2 Samuel 7:16). Moreover, Deuteronomy contains a specific divine injunction: "You may indeed set over you a king whom the LORD your God will choose. One of your own community you may set as king over you; you are not permitted to put a foreigner over you, who is not of your own community" (17:15). There follows a list of rules for the king's behavior, among them a prohibition on keeping too many horses or wives, a command to obey the laws of the Torah, and the avoidance of exalting oneself above the other members of the community (Deuteronomy 17:18–20).

However, nowhere does the Bible spell out the rules of royal succession. God, through the agency of his prophets, would choose the king. But what would happen after the death of the first king? Would God choose another from among the people, or would the monarchy pass from father to son? And if it did pass, what would be the governing rule? Must it pass to the eldest son, or was the king free to choose from among his sons? And if there were no sons, could a daughter inherit the crown? The Bible maintains an absolute silence.

Postbiblical Jewish law sought to regularize all these issues. Maimonides regarded the appointment of a king as a command that the children of Israel were obliged to obey upon their entry into the promised land.[1] He went on to say that a woman was not eligible to reign, because the injunction specified a "king," not a queen.[2] The throne was to pass to the eldest son and, Maimonides said, this was to be true not only of the monarchy but of all the positions in Israel. This shows how much Jewish law was influenced by its environment. Maimonides flourished in the Muslim world, which did not permit women to wear the crown. In his day, the Christian world was much the same—there was considerable opposition to the crowning of women, and exceptions were very few.[3] Queens did rule sometimes, though not in the biblical period, when the only one was Athaliah, daughter of Jezebel. She seized the throne illegally and was finally overthrown and killed.

Maimonides' rules for the succession have no basis in the Bible. His attempt to disqualify queens by referring to the masculine form of *melek* ("king") in the Bible is not convincing. In Hebrew the masculine form in legislation automatically includes the female.

Thus it is obvious that the commandment "You shall not murder," which is worded in the male form, is directed at men and women alike. Maimonides' theory was also inappropriate for the realities of the Hasmonean period, when public offices were often assigned to women. We may notice in passing that the religious establishment of modern Israel quoted Maimonides in its efforts to keep women off the benches of the rabbinical court and out of the religious councils. That position was rejected by the Supreme Court in *Leah Shakdiel v. The Minister of Religious Affairs* in 1988.[4] The judgment, written by Justice Alon, himself an observant Jew, quoted Maimonides and others. The outright rejection of gender discrimination in effect made clear that Maimonides' interpretation, given in a different age and circumstances, had no bearing on the modern world.

---

[1] Maimonides, *The Code of Maimonides (Mishneh Torah): Book 14, The Book of Judges,* part 5: Laws concerning Kings and Wars 1:1.

[2] Ibid, 1:5.

[3] In 1135, the year that Maimonides was born, Henry I of England persuaded his nobles to swear that they would pass the throne to his daughter Mathilda. But her cousin, Stephen, won the civil war and the monarchy. Fifty years later, the great Queen Tamara ascended the throne of Georgia, in the Caucasus, beginning what was to be the golden age of that country and its expanded frontiers. The stories of Mathilda and Tamara are told in Antonia Fraser, *The Warrior Queens: Boadicea's Chariot* (London: Weidenfeld & Nicholson, 1988), which also mentions Queen Urraca of Aragon and Teresa of Portugal from the same period.

[4] 42(2) P.D. 221 (Hebrew).

As for inheritance of the throne, ancient law in the main coalesced out of customs based on mores and behavior patterns and the belief that well-tried solutions surely were appropriate when the same problems again arose. The difficulty was when the issue of monarchy first appeared and there was as yet no precedent to draw on. The question was also unlikely to arise more than once in each generation. The lust for power is among the strongest of human cravings, and one who succeeded in seizing political ascendancy became naturally immune, since there was no system that could punish a man for the way in which he reached absolute power. Apart from personal interests, there was also the public view: society had a vital interest in choosing a successful leader, particularly in times of crisis or conflict with external enemies.

Many ancient societies, therefore, had difficulty in formulating a clear rule of succession, and this was a significant factor in civil wars and much bloodshed. In the absence of a clear law, conflict between contenders was inevitable, and it has been compared by some to Darwin's "survival of the fittest."[5] Destructive conflict over the right to the throne made for brutal extermination of potential rivals. The Bible, like other historical chronicles, is replete with stories of fratricide and the destruction of overthrown dynasties.

To take an instructive parallel, fratricide became part of the tradition of the Ottoman Empire.[6] Bloody struggles for power between the sons of deceased Ottoman rulers were already common in the early stages of the empire. After the death of Bayezid I in Mongol captivity in 1402, war broke out between his four sons, who divided the kingdom between them, until Mehmed I overcame his siblings (Bayezid I had himself murdered his brother upon ascending the throne). To prevent conflicts of this kind, Ottoman rulers made a habit of killing their brothers, and if any fled abroad, they were hounded to death. Mehmed II, who ruled from 1451–1481, passed a law making fratricide mandatory in order to preserve the peace of the kingdom. This law was zealously observed: Mehmed III, when he ascended the throne in 1595, had nineteen brothers executed and, to be on the safe side, ordered seven pregnant women from his father's harem put in sacks and thrown into the sea. After he died in 1603, leaving two young sons behind him, the law was amended. Henceforward, the youngest was not to be killed, for fear for the continuity of the dynasty. The king's brothers were to be kept in a closed compound. The

---

[5] Henry Summer Maine, "Royal Succession and the Salic Law," in *Dissertations on Early Law and Custom* (1886; repr., New York: Arno, 1975), 125, 133.

[6] Fratricide in the course of power struggle occurred in other tribes of Turkish descent, sometimes on a considerable scale; see John F. Richard, *The Mughal Empire* (New Delhi: Cambridge University Press, 2002), 151–64, describing the war of succession in that empire in the seventeenth century.

murders did not stop entirely, but gradually decreased. Eventually the empire adopted an ancient rule by which, on the death of a ruler, the kingdom passed to the oldest man in the family, not necessarily a son.[7]

When the question of the right of succession first arose, theoretical considerations naturally pointed to the analogy of property inheritance. These laws were ancient, mostly based on custom, and certainly antedated the rise of monarchies. But the fundamental issues of the two cases were different, and the experience of many nations indicated that generations were to pass before society formulated its laws of succession—not without bloodshed. The development was slow and gradual, and there were no precedents to supply easy solutions.

Thus, as Islam grew after Muhammad, none of the next four caliphs (Abu Bakr, Omar, Othman, and Ali ibn Abu Talb) rose to power by inheritance. All were chosen by the oligarchy surrounding Muhammad. Three were assassinated, and it was only after the murder of Ali, the fourth caliph, that the primacy consolidated in the hands of the Ummayad dynasty, which did transfer the succession by inheritance.

France was ruled for centuries by the Capet dynasty, which followed the Salic Law, under which only males could inherit the kingdom—and the eldest son of the monarch was first in line. It seemed clear and straightforward. So when Philip IV, "The Fair," died in 1314, the succession seemed to present no difficulty. He left behind him three sons and a daughter, Isabella, who was married to King Edward II of England. But the three sons died one after the other, leaving no male heirs, and Isabella, being a woman, was not qualified. Then her son, Edward III of England, claimed the throne of France. A legal dispute ensued. The daughter of a French king could not succeed her father, but could she pass the right to the throne on to her son? The French said no, but Edward III argued that the answer had to be in the affirmative.[8] In the absence of a judicial tribunal to rule in the matter, the Hundred Years' War broke out between England and France.

The family structure is an important element in the development of the law of succession. There is a fundamental difference between societies based on monogamy and those founded on polygamy. In a stable, monogamous society, the trend was for the crown to pass to the eldest son, as indeed was the case in Christian Europe. There could be rivalry between sons of the same mother, notably when she favored one over the other, as did Rebekah favor

---

[7] Robert Mantran, *Histoire de L'Empire Ottoman* (Paris: Fayard, 1989), 165–67 (Gilles Veinstein); Z. Duckett Ferriman, *Turkey and the Turks* (London: Milles & Boon, 1911), 240–44.

[8] Maine, "Royal Succession and the Salic Law," 139–40.

Jacob over his elder brother, Esau. But intrafamily rivalry is much worse in po-lygamous societies. Quite naturally, every wife of a sovereign would seek the succession for her sons, and the struggle was likely to begin while the king was still alive. And if he had a favorite wife, that relationship might influence the succession, and the tendency would be for the king to nominate his heir while still alive. If this was repeated often enough, it would become customary for the monarch to choose his heir, and this seemed to be the process that devel-oped in the Ottoman Empire.

From the Bible it seems that the Israelites did not formulate a clear law of succession. Biblical law says nothing on the subject, and history itself does not indicate a consistent pattern. The subject first arose in the time of the judges when, following the death of Gideon, his son Abimelech sought to rule. Polyg-amy was established in Israel, particularly among leaders. Gideon had many wives, and Abimelech was the son of a concubine from Shechem. He per-suaded the men of Shechem to crown him king, and, as a first step, perhaps even before he was enthroned, he seized and executed seventy of his brothers. Only his youngest brother, Jotham, hid and survived. Abimelech was appar-ently not Gideon's eldest son, and Gideon himself had refused the kingship. In any event, natural selection did not help Abimelech: three years into his rule, an uprising resulted in his death.

The monarchy became established long after Abimelech, and his conduct supplied neither precedent nor the beginning of a custom. The people had three kings who ruled over all the tribes of Israel: Saul, David, and Solomon. None of them came to power on the basis of an agreed law of succession or in-heritance. The question obviously did not apply to Saul, the first monarch who was selected by a process described in the Bible as divine choice. Nor did David inherit the throne. He rebelled against Saul; at first he acted clandes-tinely, but after Saul's death in the battle of Gilboa he took overt action against Saul's son, Ishbaal. He began by splitting the kingdom and ruling the tribe of Judah from his capital, Hebron. Eventually Ishbaal was murdered and David was crowned king of all the Israelites. The issue of succession arose in the house of David. From the account in 2 Samuel one gains the impression that, at least for a time, the crown was expected to pass to the eldest son. But this was not a dynasty in which peace and quiet reigned supreme. David had both wives and concubines in increasing numbers. He first married Michal, the daughter of Saul, who bore him no children. During his flight from Saul, he married two others: Nabal's widow, Abigail, and Ahinoam the Jezreelite, who bore him his eldest son, Amnon.

Amnon was the natural candidate to succeed his father, though nothing is actually said in the text about this. But perhaps it may be deduced from the story of the rape of his half-sister Tamar.[9] The amazing fact is not that Amnon was capable of such a crime but that David, for all his anger, took no steps against him (2 Samuel 13:21). A possible explanation of this fact, aside from the difficulty of dealing with offenses within the family, was Amnon's special status and that he was the heir apparent.

David's second son was Chileab—called Daniel in Chronicles—the child of Abigail. For some reason he was never considered a potential heir, and he may have died in childhood.[10] The third son was Absalom, born to Maacah the daughter of the king of Geshur. The removal of Amnon would make Absalom the natural candidate. Two years after the rape of Tamar, Absalom ordered his men to kill Amnon, thereby avenging his sister and opening his own path to the throne.

Fratricide as part of the struggle for power, or after its successful conclusion, was a widespread phenomenon. But this time the murder was done at an early stage, while the king still occupied his throne, so that the murderer was vulnerable. Absalom fled to his grandfather's court in Geshur, where he stayed for three years, until David decided to forgive his favorite son. The king's willingness to absolve the murderer might have been influenced by Absalom's newfound status as the eldest and therefore the likely heir apparent. Indeed, soon after his return to court, Absalom began to behave accordingly: "After this Absalom got himself a chariot and horses, and fifty men to run ahead of him" (2 Samuel 15:1). Had matters run their normal course, Absalom would probably have succeeded David, but he was impatient and wanted the kingdom while his father lived. He rebelled, was defeated, and was killed by Joab. But though he had threatened David's life and had caused great bloodshed, the king's mourning for Absalom knew no bounds: "O my son Absalom, my son, my son Absalom! Would I had died instead of you, O Absalom, my son, my son!" (2 Samuel 18:33). David's grief showed not only his great love for his son, but perhaps also the latter's status as heir apparent.

---

[9] See the later chapter "Crimes in the Family: Rape, Murder, and Adultery," pp. 286–88.

[10] See "Chileab" (Hebrew), in *Encyclopaedia Biblica* (Jerusalem: Bialik Institute, 1972–1982); Shalev suggests in *Bible Now* that the name Chileab is indicative of "cross breeding," it not being clear whether Nabal or David was the father (the word *kilab* sounds in Hebrew as consisting of two words, one *kil* and the other *ab*; the sound of *kil* has some similarity to either the Hebrew word "all" or the word "cross breeding"; *ab* sounds like the word "father" in Hebrew). This is a variation on the legend relating to the hasty marriage of David and Abigail after the death of her husband, Nabal. Legend has it that to protect them from scorn, God caused Chileab to look very much like David (meaning he was "all father"); see Ginzberg, *Legends of the Jews*, 4:118 and the references at 5:275 n. 140. Ginzberg also refers to a similar legend referring to the likeness of Isaac and Abraham (Isaac was born when Abraham was one hundred years old).

After Absalom's death, Adonijah son of Haggith, David's fourth son, now seemed to be next in line. Like his brother before him, Adonijah began to put on airs: "Now Adonijah son of Haggith exalted himself, saying, 'I will be king'; he prepared for himself chariots and horsemen, and fifty men to run before him. His father had never at any time displeased him by asking, 'Why have you done thus and so?'" (1 Kings 1:5–6). The disparaging term "exalted" is due, of course, to the narrator's sympathies for his rival, Solomon, though many believed that Adonijah would ascend the throne upon David's death. His father did nothing to stop Adonijah's putting on the trappings of royalty. Joab, David's general, and Abiathar the priest supported Adonijah's claim to be the legitimate heir. Events turned out otherwise.

There was a coup in the house of David. Since the only version to reach us is the one penned by Solomon's supporters, the truth is difficult to establish.[11] The group behind the coup included the prophet Nathan, Zadok the priest, an army officer, Benaiah the son of Jehoiada, David's wife Bathsheba, and perhaps Solomon himself, though the text takes pains not to implicate him. Joab had been with David since his flight into the desert to escape Saul, and Abiathar—who had escaped Saul's massacre of the priests of Nob—had also joined David. Both were probably in their late sixties, while much of the opposing group was much younger. David had married Bathsheba when he was almost fifty. Her age is not known, but she was probably in her twenties, if not younger; by now she was in her late thirties or early forties. Solomon's other supporters were only mentioned after David became king. They were probably also in their forties or early fifties, a generation behind David's veterans. Though Joab was commander in chief of the army, Benaiah's command was stationed in Jerusalem, composed of regular soldiers and convenient for any coup d'état—much like the Praetorian Guard in imperial Rome.

The younger group was perhaps eager to improve their status. Maybe they feared a reversal if Adonijah became king. Bathsheba feared for her own life and for that of her son. The group conceived the brilliant idea of not waiting for David's death, when Adonijah would almost certainly ascend the throne, but to make their coup as a total surprise. Unlike Absalom's failed rebellion, the palace revolution had to be in David's name and with his consent, real or assumed. David was old and suffering the ailments of age: "King David was old and advanced in years; and although they covered him with clothes, he could not get warm" (1 Kings 1:1). His servants brought a young girl named Abishag to lie with him and warm him, though there were no sexual relations

---

[11] For another theory about Solomon's succession, see Halpern, *David's Secret Demons,* 391–406.

between them. It is not clear if the "treatment" worked, nor whether the king actually was in charge. The text goes on to describe how Adonijah threw a great feast, to which he invited all the king's sons, except Solomon, and a host of his supporters, including Joab and Abiathar. While the party was on, the coup was staged with dramatic speed and silence.

No one knows who among the conspirators conceived the idea. The Bible attributes it to the prophet Nathan, but Zadok and Benaiah probably had a part in it. Solomon himself may have been involved, though it is not explicit. Whatever the case, Nathan told Bathsheba:

> Have you not heard that Adonijah son of Haggith has become king and our lord David does not know it? Now therefore come, let me give you advice, so that you may save your own life and the life of your son Solomon. Go in at once to King David, and say to him, "Did you not, my lord the king, swear to your servant, saying: Your son Solomon shall succeed me as king, and he shall sit on my throne? Why then is Adonijah king?" Then while you are still there speaking with the king, I will come in after you and confirm your words. (1 Kings 1:12–14)

The separate appearances of Bathsheba and Nathan were meant to confirm each other's versions without betraying their collusion, at a time when, as the text stresses, the king was "very old."

The plan was carried out. Bathsheba came to the king with two arguments: first, that he had sworn to make Solomon king after him; and second, that Adonijah had crowned himself. The clear impression is that both claims were unfounded. As for an oath to Bathsheba, it does not sit well with David's love for Absalom. It is possible, of course, that the promise was given after Absalom's death, but it is not clear why David would have done that. Moreover, if such a promise had been made, it would not have been a secret, and Joab and Abiathar, loyal as they were to David, would not have followed Adonijah. Bathsheba's second argument is likewise dubious. Adonijah had not anointed himself king. He did adopt the trappings of the heir apparent, but David knew this and did not protest. According to plan, Nathan entered and corroborated Bathsheba's story as though independently. He did not claim that David had promised the throne to Solomon but did say that the revelers were crying, "Long live King Adonijah." Then he asked innocently, "Has this thing been brought about by my lord the king?" (1 Kings 1:27). This coronation, whether it happened or not, aroused David's ire. He immediately summoned Nathan, Zadok, and Benaiah and ordered them to crown Solomon. The order was carried out immediately. Solomon was anointed and led through the city riding on David's mule, escorted by Cherethite and Pelethite guard units, commanded by Benaiah. The revolution was over and successful.

This version of Solomon's crowning was meant to legitimize his succession on the basis of David's order and suited the interests of the new monarch. The question remains whether David in fact gave the order. The only witnesses were the conspirators. Reason suggests that after the palace coup no one else had access to the king and that henceforward they kept him in his "golden cage." According to the description in 1 Kings, David did not summon Adonijah or Joab to verify the charge that the former had anointed himself. David's actions were dictated entirely by the information given him by Solomon's party, under whose influence he was. Since the written story was controlled by Solomon and his supporters, why did they choose to reveal Nathan's stratagem to mislead David and to describe in detail what actually went on in David's room? Why did they not simply state that David had promised to crown Solomon and kept his promise? A possible explanation is that a story containing a few inconvenient elements would appear more plausible.[12] Another explanation might be that Nathan and Bathsheba's tactic, including the deceptive things said to David, did not seem serious when the story was recorded and did not detract from the legal validity of the king's order. Possibly it was seen as a sign of the cleverness of the participants in the cabal. Many of the Bible's stories are based on the assumption that deception does not detract from the validity of legal action and is in fact a permissible stratagem in social conflict.

Solomon ruled alongside David for a few years, though we may assume that he held the reins of power. Nevertheless, he did not feel completely secure. After David's death, Solomon ordered the assassination of Adonijah, solely on the basis of his brother's request, through the good offices of Bathsheba, to marry Abishag the Shunammite. He took the same opportunity to order the murder of Joab, on the grounds that this was David's unwritten testament.

Solomon's seizure of the throne necessarily upset the principle of the succession of the firstborn. The idea did not completely disappear during his reign. He himself responded to Bathsheba's request to give Abishag to Adonijah: "And why do you ask Abishag the Shunammite for Adonijah? Ask for him the kingdom as well! For he is my elder brother" (1 Kings 2:22). This implies Solomon's recognition that Adonijah had a claim to the throne, though clearly he did not regard it as legally binding, and his position presumably affected public belief.

King Solomon was the eldest of Bathsheba's sons. Another son she bore as a result of her interlude with David while married to Uriah the Hittite died in

---

[12] This explanation is the main theme of Stefan Heym, *The King David Report: A Novel* (London: Hodder & Stoughton, 1973).

infancy. First Chronicles 3:5 reveals that Bath-shua (as she was named in that book) bore David four sons, and Solomon is listed last. One theory suggests that this was done to remove him from the Uriah affair and possible claims that he was a bastard.[13] I am not convinced that this fear existed, particularly because the concept of "bastard," as defined in the postbiblical Jewish law, did not apply in David and Solomon's time.[14] Another possible explanation lies in the sympathy that the Bible accords to younger sons (Isaac and Jacob were in that category, as was David himself). This may account for the description of Solomon as Bathsheba's youngest.

After Solomon's death, the throne passed to his firstborn, Rehoboam, son of Naamah the Ammonite, but this was insufficient to firmly establish a law of succession of firstborn sons. Given the polygamy customary in Judah and Israel, friction between the king's wives was to be expected, as each vied for her son's inheritance. Bathsheba's involvement illustrates the point. Hence, if the king was under the influence of one of his wives, the effect on the continuation of the monarchy was obvious. In any event, the principle was to be upset once again during Rehoboam's reign. According to 2 Chronicles 11, he had eighteen wives and sixty mistresses. His favorite wife was Maacah, the daughter of Absalom and a granddaughter of David. This preference extended to her son Abijam (or Abijah), though he was not the eldest. As for the name and identity of the favorite wife, the texts are in conflict. Second Chronicles 13 states that Abijah's mother was Micaiah, daughter of Uriel. The traditional commentary tries to resolve the problem with the explanation that these were two names for the same woman, so that Maacah was Micaiah. For our purposes it suffices to point out the fact that Rehoboam in his lifetime granted to Abijah, the son of his favorite wife, powers and status that would ensure his succession.

This phenomenon of a reigning monarch appointing his successor by granting him special status or authority was found in other nations, for example, in imperial Rome, especially during the period of "the five good emperors" at the end of the first century through the second century C.E. The emperor Nerva adopted Traianus as heir, made him co-regent and so ensured his succession as emperor. Marcus Aurelius granted the title *Augustus* to his son Commodos and made him co-regent and thus established him as the next emperor, though this was an unfortunate choice. However, the ruler was not always willing to do that, for fear of endangering his own position. Absalom's rebellion against his father illustrates this danger. And so the practice of

---

[13] Gershon Galil, "Interpretations of 1 Chronicles," in *The World of the Bible* (Hebrew) (24 vols.; Tel-Aviv: Davidson-Atai, 1993–1997).

[14] See the later chapter "Death of a Bastard," pp. 293–96.

delegating power was not widespread, and perhaps this is why it never became a clear rule that the king could nominate his successor.

Another difficulty in trying to deduce the existence of a legal rule of succession derives from the fact that in many cases the Bible reports that when a certain king died his son reigned after him, without stating how he was chosen and whether he was his firstborn. The eldest did succeed in some cases, but this was not necessarily self-evident. King Jehoshaphat of Judah, grandson of Abijah and great-grandson of Rehoboam, gave his sons gifts that included silver, gold, and fortified cities, "but he gave the kingdom to Jehoram, because he was the firstborn" (2 Chronicles 21:3). Still the transition was not smooth: "When Jehoram had ascended the throne of his father and was established, he put all his brothers to the sword, and also some of the officials of Israel" (2 Chronicles 21:4). It does not say why he killed his brothers. Perhaps some of them were plotting to seize power, or perhaps Jehoram was simply preempting that threat. Certainly, the massacre serves to indicate that the principle of the firstborn succession was not quite consolidated.

The book of Deuteronomy stipulated that there could be a king but said nothing about rules of succession. The book seems to have been written during the reign of Josiah, who died in battle against the Egyptians at Megiddo, some twenty years before the destruction of the first Temple and the end of David's dynasty. Josiah was succeeded by his youngest son, Jehoahaz. Why he was chosen instead of his elder brother is unclear. It is said that: "The people of the land took Jehoahaz son of Josiah, anointed him, and made him king in place of his father" (2 Kings 23:30). He had reigned for three months when the king of Egypt intervened, ruled that Jehoahaz could not be king, and replaced him with Jehoiakim, who was two years older. By the end of the dynasty of David, clear-cut legal rules for succession had still not been established. In the four centuries that the house of David ruled, the only recognized principle was that the king of Judah must be of David's dynasty. There was some preference for the firstborn, but never a legally binding rule, and various considerations intervened to transfer power to another member of the family.

Postscript: The Maccabees

More than four centuries after Nebuchadnezzar destroyed the first Temple, the monarchy was renewed following the Hasmonean revolt against the Syro-Hellenistic regime. The Hasmoneans, who led the uprising that erupted in 167 B.C.E., were not of the house of David, and their rule was relatively short-lived. When they came to power, the nation of Israel still lacked a clear tradition for succession, which was a contributing factor in the tragedies that befell the Hasmonean house and eventually the entire nation.

At first the Hasmoneans did not take the crown for themselves. After the death in battle of Judah Maccabeus in 161 B.C.E., the leadership passed to his brother Jonathan. He was murdered in captivity after an act of betrayal. Then leadership passed to Simon, who was also murdered a few years later. Next in line was Simon's son, Yohanan (John) Hyrcanus, who ruled from 134 to 104 B.C.E. Problems of succession were not long in coming. Yohanan wanted to bequeath the throne to his wife, but it did not work out, as a conflict erupted between the wife and his eldest son, Judas Aristobulus. Judas won and, according to Flavius Josephus, had his mother imprisoned and starved to death.[15] He was the first Hasmonean to call himself king. Flavius Josephus relates that, when Judas ascended the throne, he imprisoned his younger brothers, while bringing his brother Antigonus into government, but then had him murdered for fear that he might seize power.[16] Judas reigned only for a year before succumbing to an illness. His widow, Alexandra Shlomzion, promptly released his brothers from prison and married the eldest of them (apparently according to the law of levirate marriage).[17] The husband, Alexander Yannai (Jannaeus), became king with her help. He was the third son of Hyrcanus, and he would rule for more than a quarter of a century (103–76 B.C.E.). According to Flavius Josephus, Alexander had one of his remaining two brothers killed for the usual reason.[18]

Where Hyrcanus was unsuccessful, his son Alexander Yannai did succeed. He left the kingdom to his wife, Alexandra Shlomzion, whose name is revered in Jewish tradition. Queen Shlomzion was the sister of Shimon ben Shatah, president of the Sanhedrin and leader of the Pharisees. Her reign is remembered for her sympathetic attitude toward the Pharisees.

Passing the crown to the king's wife was a sharp deviation from the customs of the first Temple. The development apparently stemmed from the sociocultural environment of the Hasmonean period. These were Hellenistic

---

[15] Josephus, *Antiquities of the Jews* 13.11.1. But according to Yosef Klausner, this version is imaginary; see *History of the Second Temple* (Hebrew) (5 vols.; 5th ed.; Tel-Aviv: Ahiasaf, 1976), 3:141–42.

[16] Josephus, *Antiquities of the Jews* 13.11.2. Klausner (*History of the Second Temple*) also disputes this.

[17] Some consider that Alexander Yannai did not marry his brother's widow, but another woman of the same name. Klausner (*History of the Second Temple*, 144–45) discusses this contention, rejects it, and concludes that Alexander did indeed marry his brother's widow.

[18] Josephus, *Antiquities of the Jews* 13.12.1. Klausner cast doubts on this too (*History of the Second Temple*, 146).

days, when Alexander the Great's empire was being divided between his heirs. Egypt was under the rule of the Ptolemies; the founder of that dynasty, Ptolemy I, had been a general in Alexander's army. The dynasty did accept women rulers, among them Cleopatra III, who followed her husband in 116 B.C.E., and the famous Cleopatra VII, lover of Julius Caesar and Mark Antony. Conflict between mother and son was also not confined to the Hasmonean house. In that same period when Hyrcanus's widow was fighting Judas Aristobulus for the throne, Cleopatra III was successfully suppressing her son, Ptolemy (IX) Lathyros. There was a power struggle between Cleopatra VII and her brother Ptolemy, who was also her husband. At first he had the upper hand, but the support of Julius Caesar secured Cleopatra the crown.

After the death of Shlomzion, a struggle broke out between Hyrcanus II and his brother Aristobulus II. Meanwhile the Romans were approaching the land of Israel. The intervention of the Roman general Pompey granted the throne to Hyrcanus, but it entailed subservience to Rome, and the royal title was taken away. The internal Hasmonean strife passed on to the next generation, when Aristobulus's sons tried their hand again. This was to result in the elimination of the Hasmonean dynasty and the transfer of power to Antipas, father of the Herodian house. The Hasmoneans and the entire nation paid the price of not having an agreed and mandatory law of royal succession.

PART THREE

Family and Matrimony

14

The Prohibition of Another Man's Wife

❧

Abraham and Sarah went to Egypt to escape famine: "When he was about to enter Egypt, he said to his wife Sarai, 'I know well that you are a woman beautiful in appearance; and when the Egyptians see you, they will say, "This is his wife"; then they will kill me, but they will let you live. Say you are my sister, so that it may go well with me because of you, and that my life may be spared on your account'" (Genesis 12:11–13). He was proved right. Pharaoh took Sarah into his harem, "and for her sake he dealt well with Abram; and he had sheep, oxen, male donkeys, male and female slaves, female donkeys, and camels" (Genesis 12:16). But despite Pharaoh's generosity, God brought down plagues on all his house. Pharaoh realized that Sarah was Abraham's wife. He returned her and drove the couple out.

The story, with minor variations, occurs three times. Abraham and Sarah have a similar experience with King Abimelech of Gerar (Genesis 20), as do Isaac and Rebekah (Genesis 26). In both cases, the husband fears that the ruler will kill him in order to take his wife, but there are subtle differences. Abimelech did not touch Sarah, and he did not actually take Rebekah before he discovered the truth. Neither reservation applied to Pharaoh.

What is the deeper implication of this thrice-repeated tale? First, it reflects the fear felt by the nomadic shepherds when they entered the domains of powerful rulers, that they would lose their wives. Second, it reflects the prohibition on taking another man's wife and its significance both for her husband and the prospective taker.

Apparently, when a couple was married, the ruler was barred by his own law and custom from taking the wife as long as the husband lived. To acquire her, he had to kill the husband,[1] while custom may have required the husband to fight to the death to prevent his wife being taken. The ruler could perhaps take any single woman from shepherds passing through, but a married woman had to be widowed. That was true for David, Bathsheba, and Uriah the Hittite. When Bathsheba reported her pregnancy to David and Uriah refused to go home and sleep with her, the king was left with the single option of killing the husband.

In other cultures, with a different sexual morality, the ruler enjoyed greater freedom in the area of matrimonial relations. A thousand years after David, Augustus, the greatest of Roman emperors, took his beloved Livia Drusilla from Tiberius Nero, when she was pregnant.[2] On another occasion, Augustus took the wife of a close friend and protégé, Maecenas. The affair was scandalous, and Maecenas divorced her, only to remarry her later. Relations between Augustus and Maecenas were, however, unaffected. This was a culture that allowed Maecenas to remain silent, keep his life, and, eventually, restore the family.[3] Fifteen hundred years after Augustus, a Spanish cardinal, Roderigo Borgia, became pope in Rome. He chose the name Alexander VI and was to become famous, not only for his own affairs, but also for those of his son, Cesare Borgia. Cesare and his sister Lucrezia were the children of the Cardinal Borgia and his mistress, Vanozza dei Cattanei, who he made sure was respectably married, a fact tolerated by Renaissance mores.

But in the cultural environment of the patriarchs, and of the society in which King David lived, such behavior was unacceptable.[4] Their stories tell us something about the fate of this draconian law. The head of a shepherd family, knowing that he had no choice but to give his wife to an aggressive ruler, avoided death by denying his marriage.

The firm prohibition on taking another man's wife, prevalent in the societies described in the Bible, is also reflected in the laws of the Torah. Adultery

---

[1] Another possibility is that killing the husband was necessary to prevent future revenge. This seems less convincing, as the relative positions of Pharaoh and Abraham were such that the Egyptian had little to fear.

[2] Suetonius, *Augustus* 62. This was not the only case in the history of Rome. Nero took Poppaea Sabina from Otho, who did not even resent the emperor's action (Zvi Yavetz, *Claudius and Nero: From Systematization to Dilettantism* [Hebrew] [Tel-Aviv: Dvir, 1999], 131).

[3] Zvi Yavetz, *Augustus: The Victory of Moderation* (Hebrew) (Tel-Aviv: Dvir, 1988), 79–81.

[4] Genesis was probably written long after the events it narrates, based on ancient traditions. The question remains how well the narrative reflects customs of earlier days and how much was taken from practices prevalent at the time of writing. It does appear that throughout the biblical period rulers could not demand that a husband divorce his wife.

was considered as depriving the husband of his "property," the wife being the husband's possession. Worse, it undermined the lineage by casting doubt on the children's paternity. The prohibition of adultery is one of the Ten Commandments (Exodus 20:14). According to Rashi, adultery meant sexual relations with the wife of another man. The term could conceivably cover other prohibited sexual acts, but the rule relating to a married woman is specified in Leviticus: "If a man commits adultery with the wife of his neighbor, both the adulterer and the adulteress shall be put to death" (20:10). Numbers 5 contains a long and detailed discussion about a woman suspected of adultery and required to submit to the bitter-water test, which was designed for this purpose.[5] There is a certain similarity between these laws and the Code of Hammurabi, which provided that if a married woman was caught lying with another man, they were to be tied together and thrown in a river (§129). But the Code of Hammurabi is not as harsh as the Torah, for the husband could pardon his wife, in which case the act of mercy also extended to her partner in adultery. The Torah is not as forgiving. However, in ancient times, the legal prosecution of any offense was generally in the hands of the offended party. In practice, therefore, if the husband chose to forgive, the result would be similar to that of the Code of Hammurabi. Nahmanides' commentary on the Judah and Tamar incident (Genesis 38:24) refers to the custom of a much later period "in some of the lands of Spain," in which the adulterous wife was handed over to the husband, who could decide if she was to live or die. Similar phenomena existed in other societies. Early Roman law also prescribed death to the adulteress, with the right to demand the punishment put in the hands of the husband, perhaps after a family consultation. However, the death sentence was rarely imposed in practice. The sanction on the woman was usually more moderate, mostly resulting in divorce and the loss of part or all of the dowry.[6]

The biblical texts include examples of punishment for rape, for example, Simon and Levi's revenge on the people of Shechem for the rape of Dinah, and the murder of Amnon by Absalom because of the rape of Tamar. But they do not mention any cases of execution for consensual adultery. The possibility of imposing the sentence lies, however, in the background of a few stories. Genesis 38 tells the story of Tamar, daughter-in-law of Judah, married to Er, who died childless. The task of continuing the line passed to Onan, Judah's second

---

[5] For a discussion of the bitter-water test in the Torah and the Code of Hammurabi's test for adultery, see the earlier chapter "From the Trial of Adam and Eve to the Judgments of Solomon and Daniel," pp. 18–19.

[6] Yavetz (*Augustus*, 307–8) describes a later law that denied the husband and father's authority to impose a death sentence on the adulteress.

born, who spilled his seed rather than comply, and he too died. Tamar wanted to marry Shelah, the third son, but after the death of two sons, Judah withheld his consent. To perpetuate the lineage, Tamar disguised herself as a harlot, hid her face, and tempted Judah himself to fulfill his sons' duty. She became pregnant, and Judah heard that his widowed daughter-in-law "has played the whore; moreover she is pregnant as a result of whoredom" (Genesis 38:24). He immediately passed sentence and ordered her to be burned. Using his signet and other items he had given her during their intimacy, she was able to prove Judah's paternity.

Judah, as head of the family, was judge and jury for all his kin, and as such he could pronounce sentence on Tamar. But if he sentenced her to death, knowing what he now knew, he would be subject to the same punishment. Moreover, Tamar was a widow, not a married woman. She was subject to the levirate rule (which requires a man to marry his deceased brother's widow, if he died childless) and therefore was not free to marry an outsider. Since she was not a married woman, she could not be guilty of adultery. In the early stage of the confrontation, Judah had not yet distinguished these finer points.[7] Possibly, too, the law at that time, which was not yet the law of the Torah, did prescribe death for a woman in Tamar's situation, who had had intimate relations with a stranger. The issue remains unresolved, and no clear-cut conclusion can be drawn from the Tamar incident.

In most cases, the woman was eventually saved from the penalties of adultery. When Bathsheba told David that she was pregnant by him, he tried to send her husband to her, so that Uriah would appear to be the father. When Uriah refused to cooperate, Bathsheba faced the danger of death, though this was never explicitly stated. David's great distress stemmed from this threat, and it impelled him to have her husband murdered. She survived.[8]

The book of Esther describes a banquet that the queen gave in honor of King Ahasuerus and Haman, at the end of which she complained that the latter was planning to destroy her people. The king, in his anger, went out to the garden, while the panic-stricken Haman pleaded with Esther for his life and "had thrown himself on the couch where Esther was reclining." The king returned and cried, "Will he even assault the queen in my presence, in my own house?" (Esther 7:8). It is seems that Ahasuerus thought that Haman was trying to rape the queen, which would have been a particularly grave offense,

---

[7] The death sentence that he passed on Tamar was problematic for the traditional commentators, who raised questions about his decision. Nahmanides suggested that Judah's status was akin to governor, and accordingly Tamar was condemned for "showing contempt for the kingdom."

[8] See the earlier chapter "To Kill and Take Possession" pp. 75–84.

since she was the king's wife.[9] There was no real reason to suspect either offense, but that did not deter Ahasuerus from sentencing Haman to death. The condemned man was innocent of either deed, but no one lost sleep about it, since he was, after all, the evil Haman.

Another incident of punishment by death for adultery, where once again the woman was rescued, appears in the apocryphal additions to the book of Daniel, when two false witnesses accused a married woman named Susanna. Sentence was passed, but she was reprieved when Daniel discovered that the testimony was false.

The New Testament also mentions a case of the death penalty for adultery. In the Gospel according to John 8 the scribes and the Pharisees brought a woman caught in adultery and told Jesus that the law of Moses ordered the stoning of such women, then asked him what they should do. Jesus replied that the one without sin should first cast a stone at her. None of the persons present dared to do it, and the woman was saved.

It is difficult to draw a definite conclusion from all these stories of different periods (Haman's case belongs to a different culture), yet it appears that the death sentence was prescribed for the act of adultery but was rarely implemented.

According to the Torah, a married woman who had been with another man was forbidden to her husband (this prohibition assumes, of course, that she was not sentenced to death for her adultery). But the Torah goes further: if a man divorced his wife she could, of course, marry another; but if she were divorced from the second husband, the first was not entitled to "take her again to be his wife after she has been defiled" (Deuteronomy 24:4). From this it could be deduced that, if the husband was forbidden to take his divorced wife back after she had been married to another, then a fortiori his wife must have been forbidden to him if she had had intimate relations with another (i.e., committed adultery) while being married to him, and it was incumbent upon him to divorce her.[10]

Postbiblical Jewish law added two strict rules. First, children born from an adulterous union are *mamzerim* ("bastards"), a subject that we will deal with later. Second, the married woman who has committed adultery is forbidden not only to her husband but also to the man with whom she had the prohibited relations. Accordingly, under Jewish law, she may not marry the latter. This restriction is not mentioned in the Torah and is the product of a later era.

---

[9] In England, a queen's adultery would be considered treason. Two of Henry VIII's wives were executed for that offense: Anne Boleyn and Catherine Howard. Their alleged partners were also put to death.

[10] According to Jewish law, this rule does not apply if the woman has been raped.

The Torah only says that "she has defiled herself and has been unfaithful to her husband" (Numbers 5:27). From this it may be deduced that she is forbidden to her husband (assuming, of course, that she is not executed for the offense).[11] But the Mishnah devotes extensive interpretation to the concept "defiled," which recurs throughout Numbers 5, in reference to an adulteress. The Mishnah concludes that this "contamination" affects both the husband and the other man. Accordingly, if she is forbidden to the husband, she must also be forbidden to the other (Mishnah, *Sota* 5:1). This ruling was absorbed into Orthodox Jewish law, where it is upheld to this day.

A possible explanation is that the death penalty, which the Torah imposes on both the wife and her paramour, was rarely carried out or not at all. The husband was required to divorce his wife, so that if she were free to marry her lover, it would mean that she had escaped punishment and the adulterous couple had won a prize. The prospect of the sinners escaping unscathed was unacceptable to the Mishnah sages, so they chose to forbid marriage with the lover.

It is interesting to note that Muslim law takes an opposite tack from the Torah in everything relating to a divorcée's remarriage. While the Torah forbids the husband who divorced his wife to remarry her if she has been with another man, Muslim law decrees the reverse. For a divorce all that is needed is a unilateral declaration by the husband. If he divorces his wife by announcing it once or twice, he can take her back. But if he announces it three times—which can be done consecutively without pause—then he may not take her back, unless she has meanwhile been with another husband and divorced him or has been widowed. There is a way to solve the problem: if the husband wants to take his divorced wife back, a "volunteer" is found to marry her, then divorce her, thereby making her eligible to return to her former husband. Such an arrangement sometimes entails payment to the volunteer. Some Muslim villages in Palestine kept an old man, preferably blind, who was nicknamed the "loaned ram," specially for this purpose: his function was to legitimize divorcées for their first husbands.[12] Muslim law requires that the second marriage be consummated, a mere formal ceremony does not suffice, but this demand is not always met.[13] Inevitably the method invites complications, and

---

[11] The case may be one where there was no proof of adultery but the woman was found guilty by the bitter-water test. Such a finding is not sufficient to justify execution but is enough for her to be considered "defiled."

[12] Shlomo Dov Goitein, *Muslim Law in Israel* (Jerusalem: Mif'al Hashichpul, 1957), 137. In *A Thousand and One Nights,* he is called "facilitator" for making it possible for the couple to remarry.

[13] Asaf A. Fyzee, *Outlines of Muhammadan Law* (4th ed.; New Delhi: Oxford University Press, 1974), 157.

the possibility always exists that the second husband would refuse to divorce the wife. In one of the stories in *A Thousand and One Nights* Aladdin finds himself in Baghdad, being offered the role of "facilitator" for payment. He agrees and a contract is drawn up in which he is to be paid for the service but must pay a heavy fine if he does not divorce the following morning. But the couple like each other. Aladdin refuses the divorce and pays the fine.

It seems that the purpose of Islamic law is to deter hasty divorce (the husband, knowing that the only way to get his wife back is for her to consummate a marriage with another, is expected to be extra careful before divorcing her). But the trick used to circumvent the law foils its purpose, and its effectiveness is in any case doubtful. Jewish law chose the opposite road. Paradoxically, it too may have a deterrent effect: the husband, knowing that he cannot get his wife back if she has been with another, will think twice before divorcing her. However, the basis of the Jewish law is not deterrence but a concept of "contamination." But the reason for the "defilement" is not entirely clear, for there is no prohibition on marrying a divorcée (except for *kohanim*—the descendants of the priesthood) or a widow.

The Bible stories contain no example illustrating the law prohibiting a husband from taking back his wife after she has been with another man. Similarly, there are no stories illustrating the prohibition of marriage between a lover and the woman with whom he committed adultery. Indeed, two of the best-known stories of the Bible—David and Michal, and David and Bathsheba—do not conform to the law. David took back his wife, Michal, despite her marriage in the interval to Palti son of Laish.[14] Then he married Bathsheba despite their adulterous relationship when she was married to Uriah the Hittite. Thus he violated the law in both its aspects. It seems, however, reasonable that neither the rule forbidding a husband from taking back his wife after she has been with another man nor the one that prohibits marriage between an adulterous woman and her lover existed in David's time. It is of course possible to assume that the rules existed and that David disregarded them, but this is unlikely, as even a king must think twice before openly disregarding the rules of marriage and divorce.[15]

---

[14] See the later chapter "The Divorce of Michal," pp. 279–80.

[15] For this reason David decided to murder Uriah secretly after Bathsheba became pregnant; see the earlier chapter "To Kill and Take Possession," pp. 75–84. European kings also faced huge difficulties when the rules on marriage and divorce that obtained in their society stood in their way. See the later chapter "The Divorce of Michal," pp. 275–76.

15

The Status of Women: Monogamy, Polygamy, and Surrogate Motherhood

This chapter examines the status of women as reflected in the story cycles about the patriarchal families in Genesis and in the historical parts of the Bible. It illustrates the decline in their status from their strong position in the patriarchal story cycles to their status in the historical parts. This discussion is preceded by a brief examination of the patriarchal structure of the biblical family, which sheds light on the position of women.

The biblical family took the man's name, the offspring belonged to his family, and inheritance went to the sons. Marriage could take place between relatives; according to Genesis, the union could be incestuous, though this was later prohibited. In marriage between different families, the wife left home to join her husband's family. This was, apparently, the reason why she did not inherit. The denial of her right preserved the family property and prevented its transfer to another tribe or family. Over time an exception was introduced if the deceased had only daughters. Numbers 27:3 records that Zelophehad "died for his own sin; and he had no sons." Moses put the case to God, who ruled that the deceased's daughters be given possession of "an inheritance among their father's brothers and pass the inheritance of their father on to them" (Numbers 27:7). To counter fears that they would marry men from other tribes, it was ordered that Zelophehad's daughters could marry any man they wanted, provided that "only it must be into a clan of their father's tribe that they are married" (Numbers 36:6). There was a happy ending, for they married cousins.[1]

---

[1] Postbiblical Jewish law freed inheriting daughters from this restriction regarding choice of mate. The change has been attributed to the belief that humanity's reward

This patriarchal structure, based on the father's genealogy, stands out in the detailed lineage of Genesis. Human history, in Genesis 5 and thereafter, records generations from Adam down to Noah, always through the father: Adam fathered Seth, who fathered Enosh, and so on. For the most part, the mother is not mentioned, and if her name does occasionally appear, it does not affect the relationship of offspring to father. The same view permeates the entire Bible. Saul was the son of Kish; David was the son of Jesse; Mordecai the Jew, the hero of the book of Esther, was "the son of Jair, the son of Shimei, the son of Kish." Even from an etymological viewpoint, there is a linkage between *zakar* ("male" in Hebrew) and *zeker* ("record" or "memory" in Hebrew): offspring are related to the *zakar*—the male—and thus his memory is preserved for future generations.

To the fundamental importance of the continuity of the patriarchal family the Bible adds the element of the covenant and blessing. The covenant between God and Abraham is a pillar of Jewish faith. It is described in detail in Genesis 15 and repeated in Genesis 17. Abraham divided a heifer, a she-goat, a ram, and a turtledove, and in the night a burning lamp passed between the pieces, thereby sealing the covenant, according to which Abraham was to circumcise every male child of his house. God promised Abraham that his seed would multiply: "To your descendants I give this land, from the river of Egypt to the great river, the river Euphrates" (Genesis 15:18). In a later chapter, God said to Abraham: "I will make your offspring as numerous as the stars of heaven and as the sand that is on the seashore" (Genesis 22:17). God's covenant was therefore with the man, and the divine promise and blessing were given to him and his seed. The woman and her contribution to the creation of later generations were apparently insignificant.

Another phenomenon that emphasizes man's higher standing is that God spoke almost exclusively to men. He had long exchanges with Abraham, Moses, and the prophets but avoided speaking to women. Even in referring to Sarah, Abraham's wife, God did so through her husband, informing Abraham that Sarai was henceforth to be known as Sarah and that she had God's blessing. Yet Genesis, which gives women higher status than any other book in the Bible, contains some important exceptions. In the garden of Eden, when God investigated the eating of the forbidden fruit, at first God addressed Adam, who said that the woman had given him the fruit. Then God turned directly to Eve. Concluding the investigation, God cursed Eve—directly to her face.

---

lies in the world to come. The result was a reduction in importance of the passing of the inheritance to the male offspring of the family (Ephraim Urbach, *The World of Sages* [Hebrew] [Jerusalem: Magnes, 1988], 229).

Rebekah also spoke with the Lord. During her pregnancy, while carrying twins and suffering greatly, she turned to God, who replied: "Two nations are in your womb, and two peoples born of you shall be divided" (Genesis 25:23). Beyond the book of Genesis, there are very few instances of God speaking to women. Miriam, the sister of Moses, was a prophetess—as was Deborah, who led the war against Sisera—but there is no specific mention of any speech between them and God. An interesting exception, in Judges 13, has to do with the birth of Samson. An angel of God made the announcement of the coming birth not to the father but to the mother—whom the Bible does not even bother to name. Another exception is the prophetess Huldah, who ostensibly passed on the words of God (2 Kings 22:15). But these exceptions only serve to prove the rule that God spoke to men, through whom commands were passed on, plans revealed, and laws announced.

A decisive influence on the status of women was the monogamous structure of family, as described in Genesis. Even here there were exceptions (Lamech, for example, had two wives: Adah and Zillah), but throughout the book the "natural" family, which seems correct and appropriate in the eyes of the Lord, is monogamous, with one husband and one wife.

The story of the creation of humans, in Genesis 2, is a monogamous tale. One woman was created alongside Adam.[2] The first couple—Adam and Eve—the parents of all the human race, were monogamous. In Genesis, in the garden of Eden, the woman fulfilled a role no less important than that of the man. Monogamy continues and is even emphasized in the story of the flood. Noah was told to save humankind and the animals. Noah had one wife and was required to bring to the ark "of every living thing, of all flesh, you shall bring two of every kind into the ark, to keep them alive with you; they shall be male and female" (Genesis 6:19). Thus, monogamy also applied to the animal world.

The stories of Genesis would serve much later as foundation for the Catholic dogma that rejects not only polygamy but also divorce. The view of Jesus, given in the New Testament, is based on the story of creation: "From the beginning of creation, 'God made them male and female.' 'For this reason a man shall leave his father and mother and be joined to his wife, and the two shall become one flesh.' . . . Therefore what God has joined together, let no one separate" (Mark 10:6–9).

Jewish tradition names, alongside the three patriarchs (Abraham, Isaac, and Jacob), the four matriarchs (Sarah, Rebekah, Rachel, and Leah). They are

---

[2] The story of the creation of Adam and Eve appears twice. In one version the two were created together (Genesis 1:27). In the other, Adam was created first, then Eve was fashioned from his rib (Genesis 2:21–24). In either version it is a monogamous couple.

mentioned in one breath and with equal status. Abraham's story begins in Genesis 11. Immediately after mentioning his name, which was then Abram, it is said that he took a wife named Sarai (whose name later became Sarah). Sarah was barren, a catastrophic condition in those days. The desire to "raise seed," meaning to produce offspring and create the nation of Israel, is a central biblical motif. Sarah's barrenness was, therefore, not only a personal tragedy but also a national one. Yet there is nowhere a suggestion that Abraham should have divorced Sarah or taken another woman in her stead. They bore their tragedy equally, and God referred to Sarah when finally the Almighty intervened, informing Abraham: "I will bless her, and moreover I will give you a son by her. I will bless her, and she shall give rise to nations; kings of peoples shall come from her" (Genesis 17:16). Later, Sarah played a central role when angels came to visit the couple and to tell them that, by the end of the year, she would bear a son (Genesis 18).

Sarah's high status is clearly seen in the story of Hagar and her son Ishmael. Hagar, the Egyptian maidservant, did not belong to Abraham. She was Sarah's slave and under her command. When Sarah could no longer bear her barrenness, she said to Abraham: " 'You see that the LORD has prevented me from bearing children; go in to my slave-girl; it may be that I shall obtain children by her.' And Abram listened to the voice of Sarai" (Genesis 16:2). Abraham's marital relations were, thus, under Sarah's control. The decision to have a child by Hagar—a role that in our day would be called "surrogate motherhood"—was Sarah's, not Abraham's.

Though Hagar was not Abraham's concubine—for the relationship depended on his wife's wishes—tradition refers to her as such, and Genesis hints that Abraham had at least one concubine, possibly more. After the death of Sarah, Abraham took another wife, Keturah, then gave presents to the sons of his concubines and sent them away from his son Isaac (Genesis 25:6). The text speaks of concubines in the plural, but Rashi holds that there was only one: Hagar, who was Keturah. First Chronicles 1 also describes Keturah as Abraham's concubine. But whether she was his wife or concubine, and whether he then had more concubines, need not concern us. In any event, this was a relationship that came after Sarah's death. The main story concerns Abraham and Sarah. During Sarah's lifetime, Abraham had only one wife, and Hagar was Sarah's maidservant, who served as a surrogate mother.

Sarah's status is also reflected in the story of Hagar's exile, which appears twice. The first version says that when Hagar found that she was pregnant, "she looked with contempt on her mistress" (Genesis 16:4). Hagar was obviously unwilling to accept her surrogate role. Like some present-day surrogate mothers who change their minds, Hagar wanted to be a mother and was apparently seeking a higher status than she currently held. Perhaps she also wanted to be free of Sarah or even take her place. Sarah complained to Abraham: "I gave my slave-girl to your embrace, and when she saw that she had conceived, she looked on me with contempt. May the LORD judge between you and me!" (Genesis 16:5). Sarah was the lady of the house, and Abraham replied that Hagar was her maid and that she was free to do to her whatever she wanted. Sarah dealt harshly with Hagar until she ran away. An angel of God found her and told her to return and to submit to Sarah.

There are some parallels to the stories of Sarah and Hagar in the laws of Hammurabi, which date to the eighteenth century B.C.E., the Bible's presumed chronological setting for the time of the patriarchs.[3] Our special interest here is that Abraham came from a region under Hammurabi's rule. Section 144 of the Code of Hammurabi deals with a man married to a *naditu*—a priestess forbidden to bear children—who gives her husband a slave woman, and the slave bears him children. The section provides that in such a case the man is not permitted to marry a *sugitu,* probably a priestess of a lesser order or a sister of the *naditu.* Section 137 imposes financial sanctions on a man who divorces a *sugitu* who has borne him children, or a *naditu* who has given him children (by means of a slave woman). The section also provides that the children will stay with their mother. These laws show the existence of the practice of surrogate motherhood and also that the birth of a child by a surrogate mother strengthens the status of the wife who provided her and puts restrictions on the husband. The situation such as that of Sarah and Hagar seems to have been well known to the drafters of the laws of Hammurabi. Section 146 deals with a case in which a *naditu* gave her husband a slave women who bore him children and the "slave woman aspires to equal status with her mistress. . . . her mistress will not sell her . . . and she shall reckon her with the slave women." Apparently the surrogate mother was of higher status than an ordinary maidservant but still lower than her mistress. Any attempt to rise above that could lead to demotion.

The friction between Sarah and Hagar reappeared years after the birth of Ishmael, when a miracle happened and Sarah gave birth to Isaac. As the baby grew, Sarah saw Ishmael "mocking" (KJV) the child ("playing" in NJPS and NRSV; NRSV adds "with her son Isaac," following the Septuagint). It is not clear exactly what the elder boy did to the younger—whether the "mockery" was verbal or physical—but Sarah was furious.[4] Rashi and Nahmanides speculated

---

[3] For an overview of the historiographical positions on the early history of Israel, see Niels Peter Lemche, "Israel, History of (Premonarchic Period)," *Anchor Bible Dictionary* (ed. D. N. Freedman; 6 vols.; New York: Doubleday, 1992).

[4] See also Joseph Fleishman, "The Reason for the Expulsion of Ishmael," *Diné Israel: An Annual of Jewish Law Past and Present* 19 (1997–1998): 75.

that the expression "mock" in its biblical Hebrew form could relate to idolatry, murder, and incest.[5] The language of the Bible does allow a certain sexual implication—there may be a hint that Ishmael was making homosexual advances to the child. More extreme commentators suggested that Ishmael was following pagan practices and doing physical harm to Isaac, though there is nothing in the text suggesting this. In any event, Ishmael aroused Sarah's fury, not his mother Hagar, who had apparently learned her lesson when it came to Sarah's dignity.

Sarah had another reason for wishing to get rid of Ishmael: she did not want her son's inheritance to be shared with the other boy, an issue that would have been further complicated by questions of primogeniture and the status of a maidservant's child versus the son of Abraham's wife. Sarah told Abraham bluntly: "Cast out this slave woman with her son; for the son of this slave woman shall not inherit along with my son Isaac" (Genesis 21:10). Such a demand undoubtedly hurt Abraham, for Ishmael was his firstborn, but he capitulated. It would be difficult to find more convincing evidence of Sarah's status and power as the absolute ruler in Abraham's house. The Bible explains Abraham's surrender to Sarah's demand by saying that God told him to heed her.

Sarah had told Abraham to have a child for her with her handmaiden Hagar. Nevertheless, it seems that Sarah did not develop maternal feelings for Ishmael, whom she was supposed to regard as her son. Any feeling that there was vanished when she gave birth to her own child. She was prepared to deprive Ishmael of any rights and certainly felt no affection for him.

The high status of the patriarchs' wives is also apparent in the stories of Isaac and Rebekah. Abraham sent his most important slave, his majordomo, to bring a wife for his son Isaac from the land of his own birth, Mesopotamia. The story of the servant's journey, the description of Rebekah, and their journey back to Isaac fills a long and detailed chapter (24), one of the longest in the Bible. Rebekah is the main character in the chapter, which describes the messenger's meeting with her at the well, where she gave him drink and watered his camels. When he asked for Rebekah on Isaac's behalf, her family replied that she would decide, meaning that Rebekah was independent and in control of her own life. Later she would also devise the deception that caused Isaac to give Jacob the blessing intended for Esau. Then she decided to send Jacob to Mesopotamia to escape Esau's anger and revenge. To do this, she manipulated Isaac by saying that she could not bear Esau's Hittite wives. She caused Isaac to do what she wanted, namely, to instruct Jacob to go to Laban's

---

[5] See Pamela Tamarkin Reis, *Reading the Lines: A Fresh Look at the Hebrew Bible* (Peabody, Mass.: Hendrickson, 2002), 74.

house and to marry one of his daughters. Isaac himself comes across as a pale figure, while Rebekah—Isaac's only wife—is by far the stronger and more interesting personality.

The story of Jacob's marriage diverges from the monogamous pattern of his father and grandfather, but the deviation is not shown as desirable or natural, but rather as the result of Laban's trickery: he compelled Jacob, against his will, to marry both his daughters. Laban's motive is not clear, as he presumably understood that polygamy was hard on the wives. When, years later, Jacob fled from Laban, who pursued and caught up with him and the two made peace and swore loyalty to each other, Laban made Jacob swear an oath not to mistreat his wives or to take others in addition to them (Genesis 31:50). Why then did he cause Jacob's bigamous marriage? Perhaps Leah was ugly or disfigured and therefore unmarriageable or unlikely to fetch a bride price.

Jacob met Rachel, the younger sister, immediately upon his arrival at Paddan-aram. The account of his feeling for her is the only story of eternal love in the Bible. There are tales of fleeting passion, such as that of David for Bathsheba or Amnon for Tamar. There are stories of love like that of Michal for David—a love that faded with the years. But Jacob's love for Rachel is the only one that lasted their lifetimes. It contains all the elements that many centuries later would characterize the ballads of medieval knights. It was the kind of love that Cervantes mocked in *Don Quixote,* as his hero's eye settled on Dulcinea. There would be obstacles on the way to fulfillment, but the lovers were prepared for the struggles that would last years, in order to win each other. The songs of the troubadours and the stories of the knights of the Middle Ages often speak of a man's love for a married woman (for example, Lancelot for King Arthur's Guinevere and Tristan for King Mark's Isolde)—an element that gives the tales their tragic aspect. But the story of Jacob and Rachel is a man married, not by choice, to the sister of the woman he loves. This was not a case of two men—the husband and the lover—in love with the same woman but rather of two women in love with the same man. Given that he was tricked into marrying the sister of his beloved, the Bible strays from the monogamous model to offer a somewhat flawed solution: Jacob could marry Rachel as a second wife, if he gave Laban seven more years of labor.[6] The possibility existed because this was a matter of two women and one man (not two men and one woman) and because monogamy, though well rooted in Genesis, was not a binding legal rule.

---

[6] The language of the Bible permits an interpretation by which Jacob was not required to wait an extra seven years. He received Rachel after one week "on credit" and paid the seven years thereafter (Rashi, *Interpretation of Genesis 29:27*).

The arrangement of the slave surrogate mother recurs with Jacob and his wives.[7] Leah was given Zilpah as a wedding gift from her father, and Rachel was given Bilhah. Apparently the two maids were intended in advance to serve as surrogates in the event that their mistresses could not conceive. Here too the handmaid belonged to the wife, not to the husband, and the decision about intimate relations between Jacob and the maid was in the hands of his wife. Leah bore four sons in succession (Reuben, Simeon, Levi, and Judah). Rachel remained barren, and, as her despair deepened, she decided to have a child by Bilhah, whom she sent to Jacob, saying, "Here is my maid Bilhah; go in to her, that she may bear upon my knees and that I too may have children through her" (Genesis 30:3). The decision was Rachel's. Jacob was only carrying out orders. Bilhah gave him two sons: Dan and Naphtali.

The next stage was up to Leah, who chose to use Zilpah as surrogate mother. Again the decision was hers: "When Leah saw that she had ceased bearing children, she took her maid Zilpah and gave her to Jacob as a wife" (Genesis 30:9). That union produced Gad and Asher, which in Hebrew signifies "luck" and "happiness." Naming the sons was up to the mothers, not the father. Leah chose the names for her own sons and Zilpah's, while Rachel named her sons and Bilhah's. The giving of Zilpah to Jacob was irregular, for Leah had already given birth to four sons. The use of a surrogate in this case was apparently due to the competition between the two sisters.

The narrative includes a tale about mandrakes that Reuben, Leah's eldest, found in a field. Mandrakes are rare plants, thought by some to induce fertility. Reuben brought them home to his mother, and Rachel asked for them. The short negotiation was permeated with jealousy and bitterness: "Rachel said to Leah, 'Please give me some of your son's mandrakes.' But she said to her, 'Is it a small matter that you have taken away my husband? Would you take away my son's mandrakes also?' Rachel said, 'Then he may lie with you tonight for your son's mandrakes'" (Genesis 30:14–15). The transaction between the sisters is interesting, not only because of its content, but mainly because Jacob—who was the heart of the matter—was not consulted. He was an object in Rachel's hands, and she could decide about his intimate relations. That evening, when Jacob returned home from the field, Leah informed him that he was to come to her, "for I have hired you with my son's mandrakes." Leah produced Issachar, apparently without the help of the mandrakes, and then Zebulun and Dinah. The mandrakes did not help Rachel. She remained barren for a long time, until after Leah stopped producing children, then gave birth to her first son, Joseph.

---

[7] See also Eilat Negev, "Surrogate Mothers," in *Readings from Genesis* (Hebrew) (ed. Ruti Ravitsky; Tel-Aviv: Yediot Aharonot, 1999), 266.

Even here there were limits to the surrogate arrangement. After Rachel bore Joseph, Jacob preferred him above all his brothers, thereby adding to the hostility of the others. They would eventually sell the youngster into slavery, and he would be taken to Egypt. Jacob extended his love for Rachel to include her natural sons, Joseph and Benjamin, but he did not treat the sons of her surrogate with the same indulgence.

The status of Rachel and Leah is reflected in the continuing saga, when Jacob seeks to flee from Laban's house and return to his own country. The decision was doubly dangerous: first, Laban might pursue him; second, he could be facing death at the hands of his brother, Esau. Jacob did not decide by himself. He turned to his wives, presented his reasons in detail, and only after they both agreed did he take the plunge. The entire family returned to Canaan.

Upon their return to Canaan, Rachel died giving birth to Benjamin and was buried in Bethlehem. Years later, Jacob and his sons went down to Egypt. When he was about to die, Jacob made his sons swear to bury him in the Machpelah cave that his grandfather, Abraham, had purchased from Ephron the Hittite, adding, "There Abraham and his wife Sarah were buried; there Isaac and his wife Rebekah were buried; and there I buried Leah" (Genesis 49:31). The burial conformed to the monogamous pattern of the patriarchal period: three generations, each represented by one father and a single mother. Why did Jacob choose to bury Leah there, rather than his beloved Rachel? The Bible does not say, but perhaps it symbolizes the fact that after the destruction of Israel by Assyria, Judah became the dominant tribe and Judah was Leah's son.

The children of Israel spent several centuries in Egypt (430 years, according to Exodus 12:40). The Bible hurries through the period from Jacob's death until the Israelites' enslavement by the Egyptians. No detail is given about social processes, factors that shaped the family, or the status of women. But it clearly emerges that by the time of the exodus there was an entirely different society, a changed family structure, and a different status of women.

Exodus relates that Moses, while in the house of Jethro, the priest of Midian, married his host's daughter Zipporah. According to Numbers 12, Miriam spoke against Moses, in the presence of Aaron, because of the Cushite woman whom Moses had married. This may have been a second wife, not even named in the Bible, but according to tradition the Cushite was Zipporah, and Moses only had one wife: the dark-complexioned Cushite-Midianite. Whatever the truth of it, Moses' wife (or wives, if there were two) are marginal to the story. The exodus of the Israelites from Egypt, the hardships of their wandering years, the conflicts en route, and the Torah and its laws that they received fill four books (Exodus, Leviticus, Numbers, and Deuteronomy) and scores of chapters. In all of these Moses is the central figure. His wife Zipporah is mentioned only three times in Exodus, and once more in Numbers, if we assume that the "Cushite" was indeed Zipporah. The only reference of any significance is in Exodus 4:24–26, when she circumcised their son. Her father, Jethro, plays a more important part than she does, since he advises Moses to delegate authority to "officers over thousands, hundreds, fifties and tens" (Exodus 18:21).

After the death of Moses, the leadership passed to Joshua, whose heroics, divine support, and the conquest of the promised land are described in the book named for him. His wife, or perhaps wives, are not mentioned at all. His burial is described in Joshua 24:30 and Judges 2:9, but this is not a Machpelah cave story. The image of the woman as the partner of her husband in leadership of the tribe or family vanished together with Sarah, Rebekah, Rachel, and Leah. The foremost female personality in the book of Joshua is the harlot, Rahab, who helped the Israelites in the conquest of Jericho.

The decline in the status of women is seen also in Judges, the historic sequel of Joshua. The book describes the struggles and wars against the nations living in Canaan, the typical model of which is the people doing evil in the eyes of the Lord, being given into the hands of their enemies, and suffering subjugation until a judge arises to save them with the help of God. The model is characterized by the total absence of the judge's wife or wives. In many cases, as, for example, that of Ehud the son of Gera or Shamgar son of Anath, there is no mention of a wife. The few exceptions give no hint of the woman's deeds or personality. Judges 8 notes that Gideon had seventy sons, for he had many wives. He also had a concubine in Shechem, who bore him Abimelech, but the Bible does not bother to mention any of the women's names.

The description of other judges and their many children tells us something about the scope of polygamy. Judges 12:8–10 tells of the judge Ibzan of Bethlehem. Of all his deeds, the Bible chooses to record only that he had thirty sons and thirty daughters. He married off the daughters outside the family and brought in thirty brides for his sons.[8] Another judge, Abdon the son of Hillel, had forty sons and thirty nephews, riding on seventy donkey foals, apparently a source of pride and an indication of the wealth of the family.

The tragic tale of Jephthah's daughter is typical. Jephthah swore an oath to God that, if he was victorious against the Ammonites, he would sacrifice to God the first person to come out of his house to greet him. Upon his return,

---

[8] According to the commentary of David Altschuler, *Mezudat David* (*Fortress of David*), the text is meant to indicate Ibzan's great achievement in having married off all his children in his lifetime.

his only daughter rushed to meet him. He kept his promise to God, after the daughter encouraged him to do so. What was the daughter's name? Who was her mother? Was she alive, and did she object to the sacrifice? The Bible maintains absolute silence. This approach can be contrasted with that of Greek mythology. While the Bible ignores the mother's existence, in the Greek myth about Agamemnon's sacrifice of his daughter Iphigenia to Artemis, the women (Agamemnon's wife Clytemnestra, who was Iphigenia's mother, and Electra, Iphigeneia's sister) play decisive roles.

There are exceptional references in the book of Judges to women with status or independent personality, among them the judge Deborah—the Bible even names her husband, Lappidoth—and Jael the wife of Heber the Kenite, who killed Sisera. A role is given to Samson's mother, barren until visited by an angel who told her that she would bear a son. Despite the importance of the event, the Bible does not bother to note her name. Samson's female companions were significant, but they were all Philistines and are depicted in a negative light.

The book of Samuel opens with a description of Hannah that is somewhat reminiscent of Rachel. She was the beloved but barren wife of Elkanah, whose other wife bore him children. An extensive description is devoted to Hannah, eventually the mother of Samuel, but this too is an exception intended to illustrate the special circumstances surrounding the prophet's birth. Samuel is, of course, the central character in the book named for him. He did have sons, but again his wife was not named.

When David appears on the stage of history, we do encounter a number of female players, some of whom have significant roles. David had many wives. Second Samuel 3 mentions six (Ahinoam the Jezreelite, Abigail, Maacah the daughter of King Talmai of Geshur, Haggith, Abital, and Eglah), to whom must be added Michal, the daughter of Saul, and Bathsheba. He also had concubines. When Absalom's revolt broke out and David and his men were forced to flee from Jerusalem, he left ten concubines to look after his house (2 Samuel 15:16). When Absalom captured the king's house, acting on the advice of Ahithophel, he lay with David's concubines on the roof, in full sight of all Israel. When David returned home after his victory over Absalom, he placed all the concubines "in a house under guard" and had no further intimate relations with them (2 Samuel 20:3). They were isolated, presumably to prevent them having contact with any other men. This also tells us something about the attitude toward women and the way they could be treated.

A few women did, however, play significant parts in David's life. Michal, the daughter of Saul, married David while he was in her father's house, and she saved him from the king. Abigail was the wife of Nabal, who refused to pay

David protection money. She saved her husband's house from retribution at the hands of David and his men and married David after the death of her husband. Bathsheba was the key figure in the affair of Uriah's murder, which led to her marriage to David and the birth of Solomon. However, all these women were secondary to the king and had a temporary role. The book of Samuel describes a long series of events in the life of David. From time to time, a female figure appears who seems about to play an important role, but when the episode ends, she is again relegated to the sidelines. The women in David's life could be compared with those in James Bond novels: in each book there are several women, one of whom develops a deep link with the hero, but in the next book there is a new woman.

The time of the patriarchs was characterized by a husband and wife appearing together on the stage of history. Each had a significant role and an independent personality. The bond between them continued until death. After their death, they were buried together in the family crypt (except for Rachel). The picture changes when the children of Israel leave Egypt and become a nation. The lowest point for women is probably the reign of King Solomon, when the process of downgrading women and blurring their personalities results in almost total erasure. There is only one episode in the life of Solomon where a legendary female figure appears: the Queen of Sheba, who is a royal personage in her own right. But her role is to enhance and glorify Solomon and to illustrate how superior he is to her. He solves all her riddles, and her amazement reaches a point when "there was no more spirit in her" (1 Kings 10:5). She lavishes compliments on him, praises his wisdom, and describes the happiness of his servants who are privileged to hear his words.

All that can be said of Solomon's wives and concubines is that there were a lot of them. He had seven hundred wives and three hundred concubines, none of whom apparently merited a word from the author of the book of Kings. Add to this omission the fact that the women mentioned in later chapters of the book, some of whom do possess personality and show initiative and independence—Jezebel and her daughter—are depicted in a bad light.[9]

Outside of the historical volumes of the Bible, women do play an independent role in the two books that bear their names: Ruth and Esther. These books have a distinct quality that does not permit their insertion into the historical sequence of the Bible. The story of Ruth is close in nature to the family saga of Genesis. It is a story of a monogamous family in which women play a dominant role, while Esther's story takes place in the Diaspora, in a different social and cultural environment.

---

[9] The exception is the prophetess Huldah.

Postscript: Rabbi Gershom's Ban

Rabbi Gershom lived in what is now Germany, approximately between 960 and 1028 C.E. He served as rabbi of Mayence (now Mainz) and won great admiration and the title "Light of the Diaspora." He is credited with the most important ruling on family law to be found in Jewish law, from the biblical period to this day.

Rabbi Gershom's ban forbids polygamy—a dramatic turning point when compared with Jewish law as reflected in the Torah, the Mishnah, and the Talmud.[10] His ruling marked a drastic improvement in the status of women, and it was joined by a prohibition on divorce without the woman's consent or a good cause. Jewish family law still gives preference to the man, but Rabbi Gershom's ban narrowed the gap significantly. The ban had far-reaching effect, including an influence on the laws of levirate marriage. In effect, it restored the basic form of marriage described in Genesis, which had given the woman a secure status.

Rabbi Gershom's ban offers dramatic proof of the deep influence on Jewish law of the nations among whom the Jewish people lived. Such influences are noticeable throughout Jewish history. Even the adoption of monarchy in the biblical period was copied from the customs of surrounding nations. The ban is one of the most impressive examples of external influences, particularly that of the Christian world. The legal tradition that originated in Roman and Greek times was one of monogamy (even though mistresses were common in both societies). Christianity adopted monogamy and, according to the teachings of Jesus, which were based on the Bible, completely rejected the possibility of divorce. That clearly influenced Rabbi Gershom's ruling. Divorce was not entirely abolished but was drastically limited, and the husband's absolute discretion, without concern for the wife's consent, was ended. The Ashkenazi community thereby adapted its laws to those of its surrounding. Clearly, the two systems would not be absolutely identical, but the gap between them was significantly narrowed.

Rabbi Gershom's ban was not adopted by the Sephardi community, which lived, for the most part, in a Muslim environment, which did allow polygamy and permitted the husband the freedom to divorce his wife without her consent. All that was needed was the man's unilateral declaration.

---

[10] Monogamy was also the rule in the Jewish community located in the Egyptian city Yeb in the fifth century B.C.E., some fifteen hundred years before Rabbi Gershom. Although the law practiced by this community did not prohibit polygamy, marriage contracts commonly included a clause stipulating that the husband was not allowed to marry a second woman. See Yaron, *Introduction to the Law of the Aramaic Papyri*, 60; Modrzejewski, *Jews of Egypt*, 35.

The State of Israel adopted the ban for all communities, including its Muslim citizens, and under its laws polygamy is a criminal offense. It is also a criminal offense for the husband to divorce his wife without her consent and without a court ruling that obligates her to accept the divorce. The extreme difference between the rights of men and women, which had been present in Jewish law, was reduced though not entirely eliminated, and women are still discriminated against. The law provides an exception to the prohibition of bigamy, under which a Jewish man may in certain circumstances take a second wife—for example, if he has justifiable cause for divorce but his wife has vanished or is in hiding and cannot be served the divorce papers. For the exception to apply, it must be upheld by a rabbinical court and approved by the President of the High Rabbinical Court.

However, such a solution is not available to the woman. If she has cause for divorce but her husband refuses to grant it, sanctions can be applied to him, but they often prove ineffective. For example, if the husband is sentenced to prolonged imprisonment or flees the country, there is no way to enable the wife to marry another man. On the other hand, a second marriage of a married man is valid under Jewish law, even if he was forbidden to marry and could be imprisoned for it. Yet if a married woman in that situation lives with another man, any children from that union will be considered bastards, with all that this implies.

Hence, in the thousand years that elapsed since the days of Rabbi Gershom, orthodox Jewish law has been unable to take the additional steps required to secure women's equality in marriage and divorce, and even the State of Israel, though committed to the idea of equality, has so far proved equally incapable of coping with the problem.

16

Infertility, Surrogacy, and Sperm Donation

❧

Barrenness is a central theme in the Bible. Often the mother of a future hero only bore her son following divine intervention. All the matriarchs, except Leah, were barren to begin with, and so were Samson's mother and Hannah, mother of Samuel.

The motif of barrenness is a variation on a more widespread theme that focuses on the image of the hero from birth, indicates the impending threat of death, and emphasizes that he was saved in wondrous fashion or by a miracle. Moses was in mortal danger from birth because of Pharaoh's command to cast all Israelite sons into the river. He was saved by Pharaoh's daughter. A Christian parallel is the birth of Jesus in Bethlehem during the reign of Herod. Wise men came from the East to pay homage to the newborn king of the Jews. When Herod heard of it, he ordered all children under the age of two in Bethlehem and its environs to be put to death. Jesus was saved because an angel appeared in a dream to Joseph, the husband of Mary, warning him to take the mother and child to Egypt.

Stories of this sort run through mythology and folklore. Hercules, the great Greek hero, was the son of the god Zeus and a mortal woman, Alcmene of Thebes. He was persecuted by Zeus's wife Hera, who put two giant serpents into his cradle. The baby, already blessed with exceptional strength, strangled the snakes with his bare hands. In this case, the danger occurred after the hero's birth. In barrenness the danger precedes birth, so that the hero might not be born at all. Sometimes the two combine and occur to the same hero. The tale of Perseus has a prophecy made to King Acrisius of Argos that his daughter would give birth to a son who would kill him. To prevent it, the king locked up his daughter, but Zeus got in and the girl bore a son. When the boy, Perseus, was born, Acrisius had mother and son put in a box and dropped into the sea.[1]

In the Bible, barrenness suggests the divine grace accorded to the personality to be born. God removes the obstacle barring the birth, so that divine grace is stamped on the infant, protects him as he grows, and occasionally endows him with special qualities denied other mortals. In this sense, barrenness has an element similar to that of the many legends about people born from the union of a god or goddess with a mortal. Gilgamesh, hero of the Sumerian epic, is the son of a goddess. Genesis 6 speaks of sons of God who came to human daughters, "who bore children to them. These were the heroes that were of old, warriors of renown" (6:4). The theme is very strong in Greek mythology. Zeus, the greatest of the gods, loved many women, who bore him many sons. According to Christian belief, the mother of Jesus was impregnated by the Holy Spirit.[2] The similarity of the barrenness motif to these legends lies in God's intervention in the conception process and in the infant's special traits. However, in mythology the god plays an active personal role; in the case of barrenness the intervention is of divine grace, which in marvelous fashion removes obstacles affecting humans.

Barrenness is a tragedy in our days, but in ancient times it was far greater. The family, not the individual, was at the center of life. It could exist for many generations and was in fact regarded as promising perpetuity, as opposed to individuals, who could not avoid death. The noted legal historian, Henry Maine, compared the family concept of the ancients to the modern corporation, which can continue in existence indefinitely: "The Family, in fact, was a

---

[1] Perseus was saved and went on to kill the gorgon Medusa, whose gaze turned people to stone. Then he saved Andromeda from a sea monster off the shores of Jaffa, where she had been chained to a rock. He killed the monster and married her, but the oracle came to pass: Perseus took part in a sporting event in which he threw a discus that swerved and killed Acrisius. See Hamilton, *Mythology,* 197–208.

[2] In his book *The New Testament and Rabbinic Judaism* (London: University of London Press, 1956; repr., Peabody, Mass.: Hendrickson, 1988), 5–9, David Daube suggests that there is also a trace of a Jewish legend in which the conception of Moses occurred without a human father. The suffering of the Israelites during their bondage in Egypt is described in Deuteronomy 26:7 as "affliction," "distress," and "oppression." "Distress" refers to Pharaoh's command to cast every son who was born into the river (Exodus 1:22), "oppression" to the tasks imposed upon them. But according to the midrash, "affliction" means "the abstention from sexual intercourse," and reference is made to Exodus 2:25, which says that "God saw the children of Israel and God knew." Daube concludes that the "author of the Midrash took 'to know' in the sexual sense" and that "as natural propagation was impossible, the women—or perhaps only the mother of Moses—conceived from God himself." But with the rise of Christianity, Judaism tended to suppress this type of idea.

233

Corporation; and the [patriarch] was its representative. . . . the family had the distinctive characteristic of a corporation—that it never died."[3]

Moreover, in ancient times there was no social system to care for the individual and no police to protect from crime. A person was therefore entirely dependent on the family. No wonder, then, that the breaking of the family lineage by barrenness was an unimaginable catastrophe. In addition, the institution of adoption, which was accepted in various societies—including modern Israel—is not mentioned in the Bible and was presumably unknown among the Israelites. Adoption was acceptable in ancient Rome, where it played a major role in the succession. Julius Caesar adopted Octavian, later to become Augustus Caesar, who in turn adopted Tiberius, his successor. It is said of Arab society before Muhammad that paternity was not determined biologically but by the rearing of the child in the family—a rule that was changed by Islam.[4] But biblical thought endorses the divine blessing to Abraham and his seed, implying the importance of the biological link between father and offspring, a link that is emphasized throughout the historical volumes of the Bible.

In the Bible barrenness is a feminine condition, often accompanied by descriptions of suffering. Rachel expressed her distress in her cry to Jacob: "Give me children, or I shall die!" (Genesis 30:1). Hannah, on the other hand, wept and prayed to God: "only her lips moved, but her voice was not heard," making Eli the priest think that she was drunk (1 Samuel 1:13). The cause was never attributed to the male, even when he had no children by other women. The outstanding example is that of Samson's parents. Judges 13 tells of a man named Manoah from Zorah, whose "wife was barren, having borne no children" (13:2). It does not seem that he had children from other women—at least none are mentioned—but the barrenness is attributed to his wife. An angel appeared and informed the wife that though she was barren, she would give birth.[5] Only in later periods did Judaism acknowledge the possibility of the male being responsible for infertility.[6]

---

[3] Henry Summers Maine, "The Early History of Testamentary Succession," in *Ancient Law* (10th ed.; 1884; repr., Boston: Beacon, 1963), 178–79.

[4] Goitein, *Muslim Law in Israel*, 126.

[5] Zeev Jabotinsky, in his novel *Samson*, describes the birth of the hero as the product of an interlude with an unknown passerby, obviously assuming that it was the husband who was sterile.

[6] The debate over the subject arose with regard to the question whether the command to procreate applied also to the wife and whether she was entitled to demand divorce on the ground of the husband's infertility. Such a claim, of course, would assume that he is sterile. See Elimelech Westreich, "The Woman's Right to a Child in Jewish Law" (Hebrew), in *Law and History* (ed. Daniel Gutwein and Menachem Mautner; Jerusalem: Zalman Shazar Centre for Jewish Studies, 1999), 103. In the

In the patriarchal period, the problem of infertility was dealt with, at least in well-off families, by the use of a surrogate mother, usually a maid who had been given to the bride at her marriage. Such a procedure took place in the marriage of Jacob to Leah and to Rachel, both of whom were given handmaidens as wedding gifts by their father, Laban. It is not known when Sarah was given Hagar, but it is reasonable to assume that it was at her wedding to Abraham.

Surrogate motherhood naturally raises complex emotional and social problems. Nowadays the couple usually want to receive the baby into their hands, then sever the contact with the surrogate mother as soon as possible. The plan does not always work so smoothly, and there are occasional court actions when the surrogate refuses to part with the child. In the ancient world, conditions were different, and such an arrangement could never have been made. The mistress of the house kept the handmaiden with her, and she would remain after the birth with the child and in the family.

The handmaiden who was a surrogate mother could be freed from slavery and sent on her way, but apparently that would obligate sending the child away with her, as Abraham indeed did with Hagar. The rule probably protected the surrogate mother. Desire to preserve her children ensured that she was not abandoned. Setting her free might leave her destitute, as happened to Hagar when she ran away the first time and was forced to return to Abraham's house in order to survive. The result was that the surrogate mother maintained an emotional link with her son, with potential for friction with the mistress of the house, because of their rivalry over the child and their status in the family.

In the ordinary situation, where the mistress was barren and a surrogate bore children, it was understood that these offspring, credited as they were to the lady of the house, would inherit from their father. But if the mistress of the house later gave birth, or the husband had another wife who did bear children, a certain difficulty would arise. Section 170 of the Code of Hammurabi refers to a situation where a man has children by his wife, in which case the children of his slave woman (possibly a surrogate mother) will inherit together with the others only if the father has declared these children to be his children and has thus included them with his wife's sons. If he has not done so, then the slave's children will not inherit. However, they will not remain slaves to the children of the mistress of the house, for section 171 stipulates that, in such a case, the slave women and her children are to be freed. It is unclear how relevant these rules are to the present instance. The reference in sections 170

---

aggadah (legend) literature as well childlessness was ascribed to both men and women; see Yael Levine-Katz, "Childlessness in Aggadic Literature" (Hebrew), *Te'uda: Marriage and the Family in Halacha and Jewish Thought* (Tel-Aviv University) 13 (1997) 79.

and 171 is to the husband's slave woman, and the situation is different from that in which the mistress's handmaiden fulfills the role of her surrogate.

It can be assumed that in the social environment that the stories of Abraham and Jacob describe, the sons of a surrogate handmaiden would inherit together with the sons of the mistress of the house, without any need for special declarations by the father. This conclusion seems to follow from Sarah's demand of Abraham to drive out Hagar and her son Ishmael, lest he inherit together with Isaac (Genesis 21:10). This act, which must have involved her freedom from slavery, in practice prevented the inclusion of her son in the inheritance but may have included valuable presents, primarily cattle and sheep, which would ease her life (Genesis 25:6).

The institution of surrogacy, as described in the stories relating to the patriarchal period, vanished from the scene in the times of the judges and kings. We have seen that the centuries between the two periods witnessed sweeping changes in the structure of the family and the status of women. The ancient surrogacy took place in conditions of monogamy or near monogamy (in the case of Jacob), in which the wife had her own handmaiden and could control her husband's intimate relations, so that she was in a position to demand that he give her children by way of the handmaiden. These conditions ended as the status of women declined in the polygamous society of the era of judges and kings. In a society where the rulers had several or even a great many wives, the choice from among them was made by the husband. From his viewpoint, there was no need for surrogate mothers, and it is inconceivable that any of his wives could have caused him to maintain intimate relations with her maid for the purpose of procreation.

We have seen that the Bible makes no reference to male sterility, but the phenomenon certainly did exist, and the ancient Israelites were probably aware of it. Today the situation can be addressed with a sperm donation from another man and the technology of artificial insemination. In biblical times there was the option of illicit relations between the wife of a sterile husband and another man. This was clearly forbidden, since it fell in the category of adultery, punishable by death—yet it is reasonable to assume that it did on occasion happen. Jabotinsky's fictional version on the birth of Samson assumes that to be the case.

The David and Bathsheba story implies a similar possibility. Bathsheba apparently had no children by Uriah, whether because of the shortness of the marriage, Uriah's prolonged absences, or the undeniable possibility that he was sterile. Had Uriah complied with David's request that he should go home and sleep with his wife, everything would have been put right. Uriah would have lived, and the newborn son would have been attributed to him, even though David was the biological father.

According to 1 Samuel 2 Eli the priest heard of the deeds of his sons, Hophni and Phinehas, "and how they lay with the women who served at the entrance to the tent of meeting" (2:22). This scene may reflect a sexual permissiveness prevalent in the temples of many ancient nations. In any event, since childless couples did come to the tabernacle to ask God for offspring, these practices may have been a solution to male sterility.

A somewhat indirect approach to male sterility appears in the laws for levirate marriage: "When brothers reside together, and one of them dies and has no son, the wife of the deceased shall not be married outside the family to a stranger. Her husband's brother shall go in to her, taking her in marriage, and performing the duty of a husband's brother to her, and the firstborn whom she bears shall succeed to the name of the deceased brother, so that his name may not be blotted out of Israel" (Deuteronomy 25:5–6). The text goes on to state that, if the brother refuses to carry out his duty, he must undergo a humiliating legal ceremony to release him from the obligation.[7]

The laws of levirate marriage, as written, do not deal specifically with male sterility but rather with absence of children for whatever reason—for example, a short marriage, a marriage at too young an age to conceive, prolonged absences of the husband, and the like. Moreover, according to Jewish law, the obligation of levirate marriage arises also if the deceased has a child who dies before him—clearly not a case of male sterility. But it can be assumed that in many cases the lack of offspring did originate in the husband's sterility. The possibility of male sterility existed at least in the story of Ruth, to which I refer in detail below. Briefly, the family of Elimelech went to live in Moab, where his two sons married Moabite women, Orpah and Ruth, and remained in Moab for ten years (Ruth 1:4). Then both died childless. The probability of male sterility was very high, since at least as far as Ruth was concerned, it is known that she bore a child to Boaz.

There are some parallels between dealing with male infertility by means of levirate marriage and female barrenness by surrogacy. One such parallel is that the child is related to someone other than the biological parent; the other lies in the continued practical link between the child and its biological parent. In the ancient world, the surrogate mother remained in the family, so that the child had in effect two mothers, with all the complications that this could bring. In the modern age, when the man is sterile, focus moves to accepting sperm from a donor. Here too the clear trend is to sever the link between donor and child. The usual technique even preserves the absolute anonymity

---

[7] The possibility of the widow refusing is discussed in the next chapter "Levirate Marriage and Incest," pp. 255–59.

of the donor, thereby preventing any bond with the recipient family. In ancient times none of this was possible. The identity of the levirate husband was of course known, and he remained in the family. The child had two fathers: the dead brother for whom the child was named, and to whom he was related, and the biological father, in whose home the child was raised, and who served as the father in all respects.

While female surrogacy took place only when the barren woman was alive, the male role played by the levirate brother only took place after the death of the husband whose place he was taking. Another distinction between surrogate motherhood and fatherhood has to do with the family property and the issue of inheritance. In biblical times the family structure was patriarchal, and the estate passed to sons. In principle, daughters did not inherit, except when there were no sons, in which case the daughters were expected to marry within the family. In female surrogacy, the son inherited since he was the father's child, assuming that the mother remained with him in the family. In levirate marriage, there arises the question of the deceased inheritance. The general rule was that the estate of a person who died childless would pass to his brothers (if the father was still alive, then the estate would pass to him, and only after his death, to the brothers). But if the levirate condition was fulfilled, and the surviving brother married the widow, the following question arose: Would the estate be divided between all the brothers, or would it all be bequeathed only to the one who married the widow? Or perhaps the heir would be the first son born to the widow after her marriage to the brother, for that son was related to the dead brother. It appears that the latter solution (inheritance by the son) conformed to the levirate institution as determined in Deuteronomy 25. But this question as well as many others remain unresolved.[8] Postbiblical law confronted the issue and changed the order of inheritance, as we shall see later in this chapter. The problem of inheritance added to the complexity of emotional family situations resulting from a brother being required to marry the widow, who may not want him or whom he may not want.

Keeping this in mind, let us look at two Bible stories, those of Tamar and of Ruth. Both illustrate the existence of a practice similar to levirate marriage, but neither is in line with the basic legal text of Deuteronomy. The case of Tamar

---

[8] For example, Deuteronomy does not clarify what would happen if the first child born to the widow were a girl. On the face of it, the condition of preservation of the deceased's name was not being fulfilled. Nevertheless, it is difficult to assume that an additional child would be credited to the deceased, and reason suggests that the girl must be considered the daughter of the dead brother and, as the single offspring, would be subject to the ruling regarding marriage within the family (this rule was actually abolished in postbiblical Jewish law; see n. 1 to the chapter "The Status of Women: Monogamy, Polygamy, and Surrogate Motherhood," p. 218).

has to do with the origin of the tribe of Judah, and it takes place in the time of the patriarchs. Judah, the son of Jacob, had three sons. Tamar was married to the eldest, who died childless. Judah demanded of his second son, Onan, to marry Tamar. Onan went through the motions of taking Tamar but had no intention of producing a child for his brother: "But since Onan knew that the offspring would not be his, he spilled his semen on the ground whenever he went in to his brother's wife, so that he would not give offspring to his brother" (Genesis 38:9). Onan's behavior was evil in the eyes of the Lord, who killed him.

Judah was unwilling to give Tamar to his third son, Shelah, for fear that he should die like his brothers. Tamar shed her widow's garments, dressed like a harlot, covered her face, and waited for Judah by the wayside. Not recognizing his daughter-in-law, he lay with her. She bore him twins, Perez and Zerah, from whom the tribe of Judah descended. The motif of disguise resembles the stories of barrenness discussed above, insofar as the birth of the hero involves an exceptional event. Popular legends provide other examples of disguise in order to give birth to a central figure.

There is a legend that Jesse, father of David, desired his handmaiden. His wife found out and disguised herself as the handmaiden. Taken in by the ruse, Jesse lay with her and thus David was born.[9] The legend of King Arthur is another example of disguise, this time by the man in supernatural fashion. Uther Pendragon lusted after the beautiful Ygraine, wife of Duke Gorlois of Cornwall. The great Merlin transformed Uther into the form of Gorlois, who thereby reached Ygraine's bed. Thus Arthur was born.

Onan's refusal to impregnate Tamar is explained as his unwillingness to donate sperm to his brother. Whether this was due to lack of brotherly affection or other reasons, which may have included hostility to Tamar from fear that she had put the "evil eye" on her husband, is not clear. Onan did not avoid having relations with Tamar, only transferring his seed. In any event, there is no mention of property and inheritance issues, which would play a central role in the story of Ruth. It may be assumed that most of the property was still in Judah's hands, but Onan may have wished to have the family estate eventually divided only between himself and Shelah. Any son supposedly born to the deceased brother, Er, would have meant a division into three parts instead of two, but nothing is said about this.

---

[9] Ginzberg, *Legends of the Jews*, 4:82. The motif of a wife disguising herself as the woman whom her husband desires recurs in a number of stories, including Josephus, *Antiquities of the Jews* 12.4.6; and Marguerite de Navarre, *L'Heptaméron* (1559), story 8. In the latter story the husband who connived with a friend in his attempt to get the maid for both of them is punished by getting not the maid but the wife whom he unwittingly is made to share.

When Onan died, Shelah remained the only candidate for levirate marriage. The belief in the bad luck surrounding Tamar had become almost absolute, and Judah feared to give her to his surviving son. The superstition would eventually take shape in Judaism as the "killer wife" rule, under which a woman who had been married and widowed twice would not be allowed to marry a third. Hence, according to postbiblical Jewish law, there would have been a basis for Judah's refusal. However, Maimonides adopted a relatively moderate position that the circumstances were a mere warning against a third marriage, but he did not support a legal prohibition. Therefore, if such a woman married for the third time, she could not be obligated to divorce.[10]

To overcome her predicament, Tamar dressed as a harlot and seduced Judah, the father of her dead husbands. The biblical law, given hundreds of years after the patriarchs, placed the levirate obligation on the deceased brothers—not on his father or any other relatives. Nevertheless, it seems that Judah accepted Tamar's right to do what she had done: "She is more in the right than I, since I did not give her to my son Shelah" (Genesis 38:26). Perhaps it is possible to deduce from this that the obligation fell on Judah, at least if none of his sons complied. If indeed that was the case, then the story of Tamar indicates that, at least in practice, the levirate law was extended to other close relatives. The Hittite law, enacted in the seventeenth or sixteenth centuries B.C.E., provides in section 193 that the widow shall marry a brother, and if there is no brother, then she shall marry the father of the deceased.

An interesting legal question is to whom Tamar's children should be attributed, since she outlived two husbands, Er and Onan. Tamar gave birth to twins. Perhaps each could have been attributed to a different father. The question, of course, did not arise; Judah was the head of family and the biological father of both. However, if Perez, the elder of the two, was ascribed to Er, then Judah would have been both father and grandfather to the child.

Judah's estate could be inherited by his three sons: Shelah, born to his wife, and Perez and Zerah, the children of Tamar. Her children would inherit both on the grounds of being Judah's sons and by right of their theoretical, deceased, fathers. A certain complication would arise if the eldest son were entitled to receive a larger share of the father's estate than his brothers, as

---

[10] A question of principle is whether the law of levirate marriage takes precedence over the "killer wife" rule or if after the deaths of two brothers, each childless, the levirate process should be discontinued. Maimonides gives precedence to the levirate law, but neither law has any appeal and both should be abolished. The rule regarding "killer woman" is based on superstition, and attempts have been made to circumvent it and occasionally to ignore it. For detailed discussion, see Mordechai A. Friedman, "Tamar, a Symbol of Life: The 'Killer Wife' Superstition in the Bible and Jewish Tradition," *AJS Review: The Journal of the Association for Jewish Studies* 15 (1990): 23.

provided in Deuteronomy 21:17, which grants the firstborn twice as much as the others. The question is thus whether Perez would be entitled to a double share of the firstborn (if he is ascribed to Judah's eldest son, Er). It is conceivable that in the time of the patriarchs there was a rule similar to that laid down in Deuteronomy 21:17 regarding the right of the firstborn, but Genesis makes no mention of it and does not deal with the question of Judah's sons' inheritance.

Tamar obtained Judah's seed by making him think that she was a harlot. This is called "stealing seed," usually in reference to a woman who lies to her partner that she is using a contraceptive, inducing him to have unprotected sex in order to have a child. The Genesis story does not allude to any such fear on Judah's part, which does not alter the fact that seed was deceitfully obtained from him, for had he known the true identity of the woman, he would have avoided intimacy. He would not care if a harlot conceived, as her child would not inherit a share of his estate. The assumption is that heirs had to be living with the father in the same household. It should be remembered that these were shepherds, who might have been moving from place to place. Most of their property was sheep and cattle—not real estate—and sons who did not live with their fathers did not inherit.

The same principle applies to the case of Sarah and Hagar. Sarah demanded that Abraham drive out Hagar and her son Ishmael, to prevent him from sharing the inheritance with Isaac. The legal implication was plain: in this nomadic society of shepherds, expulsion from the family household entailed the loss of inheritance rights.[11]

The story of Ruth describes the origins of the great royal house of David. The story takes place in the time of the judges but is closer in character to that of the patriarchs. A central role is accorded to a woman—rather more like Genesis than the books of Judges or Kings. The story of Ruth is one of a family saga isolated from external political events; there is no mention of kings or judges, wars between nations and tribes, or events concerning the whole tribe. Famine in the land drove a man named Elimelech from Bethlehem to take his wife Naomi, and their sons, Mahlon and Chilion, to live in Moab. The sons married Moabite women, but all three men—father and sons—died in Moab. Naomi decided to return to Bethlehem, and her two daughters-in-law wished

---

[11] Another outstanding example is that of Jephthah, the son of Gilead and a harlot. It is discussed in the earlier chapter "Jephthah Sacrifices His Daughter," p. 134. In the present context, suffice it to say that Jephthah's affair happened centuries after the patriarchs, when the Israelites were settled in their land. Far-reaching changes had taken place, and land ownership had become a central economic asset. Accordingly, inheritance rules might have changed.

to join her. She attempted to dissuade them. Orpah, widow of Chilion, was convinced and stayed behind, while Ruth, widow of Mahlon, went with Naomi. The two women fixed their hopes on Boaz, a kinsman of Naomi's husband, and Ruth began to glean in his wheat fields. She found favor in Boaz's eyes, lay at his feet on the threshing floor, and said to him: "I am Ruth, your servant; spread your cloak over your servant, for you are next-of-kin" (3:9), to which he responded, "Though it is true that I am a near kinsman, there is another kinsman more closely related than I. . . . If he will act as next-of-kin for you, good;[12] let him do it. If he is not willing to act as next-of-kin for you, then, as the LORD lives, I will act as next-of-kin for you" (3:12–13). In the morning, Boaz waited at the city gate for the kinsman and told him that Naomi was selling a parcel of Elimelech's land. He asked the kinsman whether he was willing to redeem the land, received a positive answer, then informed him that it was a "package deal" that included Ruth. The kinsman refused on the grounds that he would be damaging his own inheritance and, in a formal ceremony that took place at the gate, renounced his claim as next-of-kin.

The right of redemption passed to Boaz, who declared to the assembled elders: "Today you are witnesses that I have acquired from the hand of Naomi all that belonged to Elimelech and all that belonged to Chilion and Mahlon. I have also acquired Ruth the Moabite, the wife of Mahlon, to be my wife, to maintain the dead man's name on his inheritance" (Ruth 4:9–10). The marriage of Boaz and Ruth produced Obed, the grandfather of David.

The story of Ruth and Boaz is one of love, though not without links to property. In that, it differs from the story of Tamar, where property is not mentioned at all. When Ruth lay with Boaz at night, she addressed him as a "redeemer." He accepted the term, though he noted that there was another closer kinsman. What was the role of such a "redeemer," and how did he differ from a levirate husband? Leviticus 25 discusses the redemption of land in the case of a destitute man who sells his plot and a relative redeems it. The term "redemption" in this chapter takes on the meaning of "release," as in the case of redeemed prisoners of war returned to their homeland. The redemption of land returned it to the family, one of whose members had previously owned it.

When Ruth addressed Boaz as a "redeemer," it is to be understood that she wished Boaz to redeem her from widowhood and poverty. She spoke of herself as one needing redemption, but Boaz, in responding that there was a nearer redeemer, was thinking not only of her but also (and perhaps mainly) of the land. He made it plain that he would redeem her only if the other kinsman

---

[12] According to one traditional commentary, "good" (Hebrew *tov*) was the name of the next-of-kin.

refused. The implication is that Boaz was unwilling to take her with only the clothes on her back, which no one would have prevented him from doing. His words and his conduct show that he saw a "package deal." This means that there was a possibility that the other kinsman would be willing to take the whole package. Boaz did not intend to take Ruth alone.

This brings us to the most obscure element in the story. Whose lands were they? Who had rights over them? What connection was there between Ruth and the land, and how did they come to be lumped together? The only answers are to be found in the dialogue between the next-of-kin and Boaz, though the exchange raises more questions than answers. The dialogue opens with Boaz telling the kinsman that Naomi was selling land that belonged to their brother Elimelech. This would suggest that the kinsman and Boaz were Elimelech's brothers, of whom the kinsman was the eldest (this means that Boaz was the uncle of Mahlon, Ruth's deceased husband).[13] None of this explains the land that Naomi was selling, and it raises two questions: Had she indeed sold the land to a third party, not of the family? Such a possibility accords with the concept of redemption as it appears in Leviticus, in which the redeemer restores property to the family. The second question is: How was Naomi able to sell land that had belonged to Elimelech, when in the patriarchal society a woman did not inherit, and the heirs of a childless husband would be his brothers (or his parents, if they were alive)?

The mystery thickens. As Boaz continued his dialogue with the kinsman, he informed him that when he bought the land from Naomi and Ruth, he was also agreeing to marry Ruth in order to "maintain the dead man's name on his inheritance" (Ruth 4:5). Earlier it seemed that Naomi had already sold the land (apparently to a stranger), but now it appears that the land was in her hands and had to be bought from her. What, then, was the redemption? Does this mean that the dissolution of the marriage by death severed the widow's link to the husband's family and restored her to her own family? If so, Elimelech's family would need to redeem the land from Naomi, who was now considered part of her father's family. Or was the redemption a purchase to prevent sale of the land to a third party?

Evidently Naomi had certain rights regarding the land, the exact nature of which is not elaborated. Perhaps she was entitled to the return of the dowry that she had brought to the marriage or had other rights under the marriage contract, or maybe she was entitled to maintenance from her late husband's estate and had a lien on Elimelech's property to ensure its payment. Such a

---

[13] According to another traditional commentator, Boaz was Mahlon's cousin. This view is based on 1 Chronicles 2:11, which says that Nahshon fathered Salma, who sired Boaz. The assumption is that Salma was Elimelech's brother.

lien, if it existed, is not mentioned in the text. By way of comparison, section 171 of the Code of Hammurabi determines the right of a widow who was a first-degree wife to the return of her dowry and to continue to live in the house of her late husband.

The difficulty with regard to Ruth's rights to the land is that the plot did not belong to her husband but to her father-in-law. The traditional commentators explain that the mention of Ruth in the verse where Boaz speaks of buying the land from both women was meant to show that such was the bond between Naomi and Ruth that the elder woman would not forgo her rights without securing the future of her daughter-in-law. Another possible assumption is that, upon the death of Elimelech, the lands passed to his sons and that Ruth had rights on Mahlon's share to secure her maintenance.

The link between the demand to marry Ruth and the redemption of land is no less obscure. Biblical law makes no mention of any such linkage. Yet the story alludes to a law that links the widow and the land, though it contains little information as to its content. One possibility is that the redeemer of the land had to marry the widow, even if neither of them wanted to do so. Another possibility seems to conform to the story: the widow (in this case Ruth) had the option of demanding marriage with the redeemer of the land, though she did not have to exercise that option. The purpose would have been to secure her source of livelihood.

It seems, therefore, that Ruth was within her rights but was willing to forgo them. The fact is that when Ruth turned to Boaz to ask for his patronage, she made no mention of the land and was prepared to marry him without it. But Boaz apparently was not willing—to him it was a "package deal" involving both the woman and the land. At least as far as the land was concerned, there was someone who had precedence over him. When Boaz met the kinsman at the gate and asked if he was willing to redeem Elimelech's plot of land, Boaz could have accepted the positive answer that he received. He could have taken Ruth, particularly since he saw that the kinsman did not want her. But Boaz was unwilling to give up the land, so he told the redeemer that it was a package: if he was to take Elimelech's land, he had to take Ruth with it. It was a gamble. Had the kinsman taken Ruth, she would have been lost to Boaz, but he was apparently prepared for that. The gamble succeeded, and Boaz won both the woman and the property, though it is hard to say which he desired more.

Why did the kinsman refuse to take Ruth, a refusal that cost him his right to the land? The reason given, in Ruth 4:6, is fear that he would mar his own inheritance. Rashi interprets the fear as stemming from the fact that she was a Moabite: Deuteronomy 23:3 forbids the coming of an Ammonite or Moabite into the congregation of the Lord, the ban to remain in force through the tenth generation. Rashi explains that the kinsman was mistaken, because Deuteronomy uses the male form of Ammonite and Moabite, so that the law does not apply to females of those nations. Ibn Ezra notes that there is a hint that the kinsman's wife would have rebelled if the redemption included another woman. But there may have been another consideration, similar to the case of Tamar: the fear of the "evil eye." Naomi and Ruth were both of a family in which all the men had died. Was that not evidence of an aura of bad luck and of God's wrath? Perhaps the bad luck was catching, and taking Ruth into the family could harm it.[14]

The book of Ruth poses other problems with the levirate law. The Bible, as well as postbiblical law, limits the obligation of marriage to the widow to brothers of the deceased (Deuteronomy 25:5). When Naomi tried to dissuade her daughters-in-law from joining her on the way back to Bethlehem, she addressed them with a rhetorical question: "Do I still have sons in my womb that they may become your husbands?" (Ruth 1:11), adding that even if she remarried, the two women would have a long wait before any sons would be old enough. This suggests that the levirate institution was known to the author, though the term is not mentioned even once. Yet even these words of Naomi's do not conform to the law as it appears in the Bible and its commentaries. Naomi speaks of the theoretical possibility that a son who might be borne to her from a union with another man would marry the widows. But under Jewish law the levirate duty does not apply to the offspring of such union. Were Naomi to marry another man, his children would not be considered kinsman of Elimelech.[15] From the standpoint of Mahlon and Chilion (the widows' late husbands), these male children would have been half-brothers from their mother's side, and under the patriarchal logic of the Bible the levirate duty applied only to brothers from the same father. Naomi's assumption that her sons from a second union would be under a

---

[14] The aggadah (legend) literature also expresses the idea that Ruth, like Tamar, was a "killer wife." It suggests that after the death of her husband, Mahlon, she married his brother Chilion, who also died; see Friedman, "Tamar, a Symbol of Life," 46–49. There is, of course, no basis for this in the biblical text. I believe that superstition is not necessarily based on an exact pattern. The fact that three men died in Elimelech's family, after Ruth joined it, might have been enough to label her the bearer of bad luck, even if she did not meet the usual criterion of "killer wife" (one whose two husbands had died).

[15] If Naomi married under the levirate provision, the children could be attributed to Elimelech, but she was obviously not referring to that option. Having given birth to children of Elimelech who survived him (Ruth 1:3–4), the law would not apply to her (although the children died without issue), and she would have been barred from marrying any of her late husband's brothers.

levirate duty toward her daughters-in-law from a previous marriages is an obvious deviation from the biblical law,[16] though it might have been based on a different law prevailing at the time.

When the kinsman gave up his right and transferred it to Boaz, a formal ceremony took place, which included the removal of the man's shoe. This in no way resembled the humiliating renunciation process as prescribed in Deuteronomy, between the widow and the brother who refuses to comply with his levirate duty. In the present case, neither of the widows (Naomi or Ruth) participated. The ceremony was simply a formal expression, in place of a written document, confirming that the next-of-kin was forgoing his rights in favor of Boaz.

Though nothing is said about the levirate law, and despite the fact that Boaz was under no obligation to marry Ruth, there are indications of that concept. After Boaz acquired the right to redeem all that belonged to Elimelech, Mahlon, and Chilion, he added that he was taking to wife Ruth the Moabite "to maintain the dead man's name on his inheritance" (Ruth 4:10). Obed, the son born to Boaz and Ruth, is described by Naomi's neighbors as a child born to her (4:17). Here "son" clearly meant grandson, but Obed was certainly not her grandson in the biological sense. Mahlon, Naomi's son, died childless. Ruth, his widow, married Boaz, who was not Naomi's son, and gave birth to Obed. The reference to him as a son of Naomi conforms to Boaz's declaration that he was marrying Ruth to raise the name of the dead, namely, to establish the son's relationship to Mahlon. According to the levirate practice, Obed had two fathers, one biological and the other "attributed," to preserve Mahlon's name. Obed is a central figure in the line that will lead to the throne: his son Jesse will father David, king of Israel. Jewish tradition does not preserve Mahlon's name as one of the ancestors of the dynasty. He is not considered to be David's grandfather, and 1 Chronicles simply notes that Boaz fathered Obed, who fathered Jesse (2:12). Mahlon's name vanishes, and the main purpose of the levirate law, to preserve the name of the deceased, is not fulfilled.

The common denominator of Ruth and Tamar is that both stories deal with levirate obligations, though the term is not mentioned in Ruth. But the levirate rule as it appears in the Bible was not applied in either case, indicating that, though the concept underlying the rule did play some role in the mores

---

[16] Indeed, Maimonides states that brothers from the same mother do not count as brothers in matters of levirate marriage and *halitsah,* since "there is no brotherhood except by the same father." See *The Code of Maimonides (Mishneh Torah): Book 4, The Book of Women* (trans. Isaac Klein; New Haven, Conn.: Yale University Press), part 3: Laws concerning Levirate Marriage and *Halizah* 1:7.

of those days, the practice strayed noticeably from the written word of the law. In the case of Tamar, the brother of the deceased refused to comply with the levirate obligation and impregnate the widow, and in the case of Ruth the nearest kin refused to marry her. This shows up the difficulties inherent in the law and the complications that it could cause. In both cases, a replacement was found for the next-of-kin. For Tamar it was Judah, who unwittingly performed the duty, while for Ruth it was Boaz, who complied enthusiastically. Both cases accepted the notion that the son to be born would be attributed to the deceased husband: in Tamar's case, her first husband Er,[17] and in Ruth's case, Mahlon.

Finally, a word about the inheritance of the son who is supposed to bear the name of the deceased. The underlying logic dictates that the son should inherit the property of the deceased, but that did not happen in the case of Ruth. Boaz declared that he was purchasing from Naomi all the property of Elimelech, Mahlon, and Chilion. He was thereby declaring that the land had become his property—not that of the child to be born who would bear the name of the dead husband.

Postbiblical Jewish law adopted a similar attitude. In contrast to the basic idea of levirate marriage, under which the child of the widow and the brother of the deceased is attributed to the latter, the Jewish law provides that the son is not the heir of the deceased. The inheritance passes to the brother who fulfills the levirate obligation.

Thus, if the deceased had several brothers, the one who marries the widow inherits all the estate (none of it going to other brothers). Like Boaz, the compliant brother wins both woman and property. Of course, the son, while not inheriting from the deceased directly, would be entitled to his share of the estate of his biological father. This solution perhaps sweetens the medicine for the compliant brother who is not in love with the widow, but it does make somewhat meaningless the idea that the child of the new union is continuing the deceased's estate.

---

[17] If it is assumed that Onan, Tamar's second husband, also died childless, then the question arises if the levirate law requires that, should Tamar, the widow of two husbands, bear two children with the third brother, one should be attributed to Er and the other to Onan. This problem, to which the Bible does not refer, is part of the complexity of the levirate law.

17

Levirate Marriage and Incest

Marriage and sexual prohibitions are linked in the postbiblical Jewish law to the severe rule that the child of such an illegal union is a *mamzer* ("bastard"). The prohibitions fall into two categories: first, union with another man's wife; second, relations with kin of defined degree (incest).[1] Historically, the prohibition of another man's wife is much older and appears early in the Bible. Reason suggests that the levirate law could only have come into being in a period when there was no ban on incest or when such prohibitions were of limited scope. Once incest was prohibited, the levirate law became highly problematic. Nevertheless it did survive, though gradually much restricted, but the parts that remain to this day can still cause considerable harm.

Mythologies abound with stories of incestuous unions. Sometimes they are depicted as a breach of a strict prohibition, as for example Oedipus and his mother Jocasta. But other cases are described as natural events. Zeus, the Greek god, was the offspring of Chronus and Rhea, a brother and sister who married each other. Zeus followed in their footsteps and married his sister Hera. In the parallel Egyptian mythology, Isis, who as the most revered goddess compares with Hera, married her brother Osiris. Their brother Seth married another sister, Nephthys.

The union of brother and sister is inevitable in mythologies of the origin of the human race and of the gods that ascribe it to one couple. In Genesis, Adam and Eve are the ancestors of all humankind. Marriage between their

---

[1] There is another category of marriages that are prohibited in Jewish law, which includes, for example, the prohibition of a *kohen* (a man of priestly descent) to marry a divorcée. But such marriage is not in the category of incest, and if celebrated despite the prohibition is valid and the children are not bastards.

sons and daughters was, therefore, inevitable. That same logic appears in the story of the deluge, in the course of which all humanity was destroyed. This time, however, apart from Noah and his wife, all their sons and their wives survived. In the following generation—that of Noah's grandchildren—the marriage of cousins was inevitable. Much the same holds true for the animal world, for Noah had brought them by pairs into the ark.

This description of human history shows why the first prohibitions against incest were vertical—father with daughter, mother with son. This issue was central to the story of Lot and his daughters. Sodom and Gomorrah were destroyed by fire and brimstone that God rained down from heaven. Lot and his daughters fled from Sodom, settled in a cave, and saw that the world around them had become piles of rubble. The daughters got their father drunk with wine and lay with him. The Moabites and Ammonites are supposed to have descended from that union. The story itself does not suggest that Lot's daughters behaved improperly or that they were punished for their action. Hebrew tradition does not disparage their act but rather shows understanding for their motives as the only way to ensure preservation of the human race.[2] Moreover, Ruth the Moabite, grandmother of King David, descended from the union between Lot and his eldest daughter.

Nevertheless, it is arguable that the story contains a hidden element of disapproval of such relations, since the father had to be drunk in order not to notice that he was lying with his daughters. In addition, biblical law provides that "no Ammonite or Moabite shall be admitted to the assembly of the LORD. Even to the tenth generation, none of their descendants shall be admitted to the assembly of the LORD" (Deuteronomy 23:3). But it is not clear whether there is a connection between this prohibition and the origins of the Ammonites and Moabites.

Psychologically, the event could be said to express hidden desires—the justification of the act as lack of choice for the daughters and drunkenness of the father being its cover. Similar psychological interpretation was applied to the story of Oedipus. The subject was supposedly the suppressed desire, fulfilled in the legend either by the parties being unaware that the relationship was between mother and son (Oedipus) or when they had no other choice (Lot's daughters). The same was true for the legendary Queen Semiramis, who seized the throne of Babylon after murdering her husband King Ninus. She fell desperately in love with a man who turned out to be her son, and he caused her death.[3]

---

[2] See also Reuven Yaron, "The Women of Genesis" (Hebrew), in *Essays on Law in Memory of Professor Gualtiero Procaccia* (ed. Aharon Barak et al.; Jerusalem: Sacher Institute, The Hebrew University, 1996), 119, 125–28.

[3] This is the version of Rossini's opera *Semiramis,* which is based on a play by Voltaire. In the version that appears in Giovanni Boccaccio, *Famous Women* (ed. and

The story of Lot's daughters differs from that of Oedipus in that the Bible expresses no criticism and records no punishment. The Oedipus legend reflects fear and disgust about the union between mother and son. The fact that they acted in all innocence is irrelevant. Both were severely punished, and the retribution inflicted on the children from their marriage was truly horrible. The Bible does not contain any story of intimate relations between mother and son. Perhaps this means that the phenomenon was rarer than relations between father and daughter and was prohibited from a very early stage.

A shocking story of father-daughter relations is to be found in the legend about Bethuel, the father of Rebekah.[4] Bethuel is portrayed as a king who exercised the "right of first night," and, at his subjects' demand, the rule was to be applied to his own daughters. In the legend, Rebekah was only three years and one day old when Eliezer came to take her as bride for Isaac. This did not deter Bethuel, who sought to lie with his daughter before her departure. But God intervened and caused his death on that same day, and so Rebekah was saved. The legend has absolutely no foundation in the Bible, but it may hint at an ancient memory of father-daughter relations.

The Code of Hammurabi (§157) provides that if a son lies with his mother, both are to be burned. The punishment for a father lying with his daughter is less severe: he is banished from the city (§154). A severe penalty is imposed on a father who lies with his daughter-in-law. If the infraction takes place after the son has consummated the marriage, the punishment is death by drowning (§155). In such a case the offense actually constitutes the taking of another man's wife. If the son has not yet consummated the marriage, the penalty for the father is only financial: he must pay the son's bride compensation in the amount of thirty shekels of silver and restore to her all that she brought from her father's house. She may marry the man of her choice (§156).

The book of Genesis makes no reference to the extension of the "vertical" prohibition from immediate blood relations (son or daughter) to the partners of either. Reuben, Jacob's eldest son, lay with Bilhah, his father's mistress (Bilhah was Rachel's handmaid and surrogate). The act aroused Jacob's ire: in his blessing to his sons, he described Reuben as defiling his bed. According to tradition, Reuben had thereby lost his birthright as the eldest. But Reuben's act had been performed while his father was alive. If the handmaid was regarded as Jacob's wife, then Reuben had violated the prohibition on the taking of another's wife, a ban that did exist in the patriarchal era. The act could also

---

trans. Virginia Brown; Cambridge, Mass.: Harvard University Press, 2001), ch. 2, Semiramis wittingly took her son as her lover, and he killed her in a fit of rage.

[4] See Ginzberg, *Legends of the Jews*, 5:261–62 n. 294.

be construed as undermining the father's position and attempting to inherit while he still lived.

The broadening of the prohibition from the "vertical" (parents and children, stepchildren and grandchildren) to the "horizontal" (brother and sister or sister-in-law) apparently took place at a later stage. In the book of Genesis there is no sign of such an extension. In fact, Abraham married Sarah, his half-sister by the same father but a different mother. Abraham introduced Sarah as his sister twice—once in Pharaoh's kingdom and again in Abimelech's—and argued that Sarah was indeed the daughter of his father but not of his mother (Genesis 20:12).[5]

The story of Amnon and Tamar also deals with relations between brother and half-sister. Amnon was David's eldest son, by Ahinoam the Jezreelite. He became infatuated with his half-sister Tamar, the daughter of David and Maacah. On the advice of his friend Jonadab, Amnon took to his bed and asked his father to send Tamar to cook for him. David agreed, and Amnon took the opportunity to ask her to lie with him. Tamar refused, begged him to leave her, and proposed that he ask David's permission to marry her: "Now therefore, I beg you, speak to the king; for he will not withhold me from you" (2 Samuel 13:13). It is difficult to learn from these words, which were spoken in distress in an attempt to avoid rape, about the possibility of marriage between a brother and his half-sister, but the sequel indicates that such marriage was indeed possible. Tamar's pleas fell on deaf ears. Amnon overpowered and raped her. After the rape, she begged him to marry her, but his love had turned to hate. "He called the young man who served him and said, 'Put this woman out of my presence, and bolt the door after her'" (2 Samuel 13:17). It thus seems that Tamar believed that her half-brother, Amnon, could marry her, and the only reason preventing it was his brutal behavior, which eventually cost him his life. Two years later, Absalom, Tamar's brother by the same mother, avenged his sister. Additional evidence of the ancient practice of marriage between brother and sister can be found in the etymology of the Hebrew word for "sister" as it appears in Song of Songs: "my sister, my spouse."

Marriages within the immediate family, including between brother and sister, were customary in various periods in the ancient East. Herodotus tells of a Persian, King Cambyses II, who married his sister, Atoosa. He did note, however, that this was not the Persian custom, but Cambyses asked his judges

---

[5] According to Rashi, Sarah was Abraham's niece. He described her as his sister because children were identified with their parents so that a brother's son could be spoken of as "brother" and a brother's daughter as "sister." This interpretation is problematic, especially since Abraham took care to emphasize that Sarah was the daughter of his father but not of his mother.

if he could marry her. The diplomatic response was that they had not found a law permitting a brother to marry his sister but had found one that allowed a king of Persia to do whatever he pleased.[6] Such marriages were very common in the pharaonic dynasties in Egypt, a practice that continued well after the kingdom changed radically. It persisted after the conquest of Egypt by Alexander the Great, in 332 B.C.E. In this context, it suffices to mention Cleopatra, who reigned in the first century B.C.E. and who was famous for her love affairs with Julius Caesar and Mark Antony. She first married her brother, Ptolemy XIII, and when he was killed she married the younger brother, Ptolemy XIV.

The book of Genesis does not mention prohibitions of marriage of a more distant kinship, which, after the giving of the law, would be included in the category of incest. Jacob married two sisters, Leah and Rachel. This would afterwards be prohibited: "And you shall not take a woman as a rival to her sister, . . . while her sister is still alive" (Leviticus 18:18). This prohibition ends with the death of one sister, whereupon the husband may marry the other.

The affair of Tamar and Judah is yet another example of incestuous relations. Biblical law imposes a severe prohibition on relations between a father-in-law and his son's wife (Leviticus 18:15). But since Genesis predates "the giving of the Torah," there are in Jewish tradition no reservations about Tamar's behavior, but rather a positive view. The fact that the tribe of Judah—from which King David sprang—could be credited to her action speaks for itself.

Another marriage that conflicted with the incest prohibition, this time from a later period, was that of Amram and his aunt Jochebed, the union that produced Moses, the greatest leader of Israel of all time, and his brother Aaron. After the exodus from Egypt, Moses brought the Israelites the word of God, including the law forbidding marriage between a man and his aunt as incest (Leviticus 18:12–13).

The incest prohibitions of Leviticus 18–20 can be divided into two groups. One is based on blood kinship and includes mother-son, grandfather-granddaughter (from which derives father-daughter), brother-sister, including of one parent only, and son-aunt. The second group prohibits unions in which there is no blood relationship between the parties but a family relationship exists to another person related by blood or marriage to the prohibited party. This category includes marriage with mother and her daughter, the union of a man with his wife's sister while the wife is alive, relations with a father's wife, though she is not the biological mother, relations between a man and his daughter-in-law, between a man and his sister-in-law (his brother's wife), and between a man and the wife of his father's brother (an aunt by marriage).

---

[6] Herodotus, *Histories* 3.31.

The reasoning behind the permissible and the forbidden is not always clear. For example, marriage of a man with his aunt (Amram and Jochebed) is forbidden, but the marriage of a woman to her uncle is allowed. Indeed, in the Song of Songs, the word "uncle" is used to describe "beloved," and later Jewish law encouraged such unions. Maimonides said that the sages have considered it a blessing "for a man to marry his sister's daughter, and likewise his brother's daughter."[7]

Apparently, the incest prohibitions crystallized at a relatively late stage, and for a long time there were no such rules, or only limited ones. This may be partly due to the fact that the patriarchs were nomadic shepherds. Relations with the settled population required extreme caution, and endogamy—marriage within the family—seemed a natural solution.

These were the conditions in which the law of levirate marriage developed and in which its logic may be understood. Briefly, the law stated that if a man died childless, his brother had to marry the widow, and the first son born to this union would carry the dead brother's name.[8] The law, as it appears in the Torah, is not absolute. The surviving brother can refuse to carry out the duty, in which case there is to be a humiliating ceremony *(halitsah)* that releases him from the obligation. On the other hand, the Torah ignores the possibility of the widow refusing to marry her late husband's brother. This probably reflects the harsh predicament of a widow, left dependent economically on her deceased husband's family. It was assumed that the widow desired a levirate marriage, which would rescue her from distress.

The levirate law is a vestige of the marriage of kin in forbidden degrees (incest) that was customary in the patriarchal period but completely prohibited later on. The law was created when marriage within the family seemed natural and reflected the need to preserve family property and the memory of the family member who died childless. It is also possible that the levirate law reflected the view of the widow as "property" to be passed on by inheritance. In those days when a man died his property was usually divided between his brothers, their right to it being clearly laid down in Numbers 27:9 (according to biblical reasoning, the right should pass to the father, and this is stipulated

---

[7] Maimonides, *The Code of Maimonides (Mishneh Torah): Book 5, The Book of Holiness* (trans. Louis I. Rabinowitz and Phillip Grossman; New Haven, Conn.: Yale University Press), part 1: Laws concerning Forbidden Intercourse 2:14.

[8] A similar idea is to be found in the ancient Indian epos, *The Mahabharata*. It tells that King Vichitravirya died without issue, leaving two wives. The king's mother appealed to the deceased's half-brother on his father's side to impregnate the widows in order to continue the line. He refused, and the task was undertaken by the maternal half-brother. See R. K. Narayan, *The Mahabharata* (New York: Viking, 1978; repr., New Delhi: Vision Books, 1987), 24–27.

in the Talmud, but the father usually died before the son, and so the brothers inherited). If, according to ancient thinking, the widow too could be inherited, this would also account for the levirate-marriage law and the fact that the Torah ignores the possibility of the widow rejecting such a marriage.[9]

Over the ages, far-reaching social changes undermined the basis for this law, though sadly it continues to be practiced to this day, albeit in restricted scope. The levirate law was first weakened by the development of incest laws. This resulted from the widening of the family framework to the dimensions of a tribe and the growing relations with neighboring groups. Awareness also arose of the difficulties caused by marriage between kin that involved friction, jealousy, and rivalry in the family, possibly augmented by accumulating information on the negative genetic influence of such unions.

The primary collision between levirate and the incest laws arose from the prohibition of brother-in-law–sister-in-law marriage and its categorization as incest. If the two laws were to coexist, some compromise had to be reached. This was done by determining that the levirate law was an exception to the incest prohibitions. The prohibition on a man having intimate relations with his brother's wife would generally be in force, except in the case of a widow whose husband died childless, in which case the levirate law, rather than the incest law, would apply. The prohibition of incest continued for all other cases, including a brother's divorcée or the widow of a brother who left children.

Nevertheless, an uneasy feeling remains when a union between a man and his brother's former wife, which is strictly forbidden as incest, becomes in one case a virtue and an obligation. The difficulty is augmented by the fact that the line dividing the levirate obligation and the incest prohibition is sometimes extremely fine. The point can be illustrated by a case discussed in the Mishnah, *Yevamot* 10:3: a woman's husband and only child traveled overseas; some time later she is told that both had died, the son first. The woman marries her brother-in-law (levirate marriage), only to discover that the husband died first. In such a case, Jewish law does not allow for levirate marriage, because at the time of death the husband did have a son (the fact that the son died later would not affect the rule). The result is that the widow's marriage to her husband's brother is incestuous and void. They have to part, and their son is a *mamzer* ("bastard").

---

[9] Frazer (*Folk-Lore in the Old Testament*, 343–49) describes the customs of various tribes in which the widow is passed to one of the deceased's younger brothers. Frazer links the law to the mores of tribes in which the widow, during the mourning, is to remain silent for a set length of time. He also points to the etymological link between the Hebrew word for widow (*almanah*) and silence (*illem*) but agrees that this is a very tenuous proof of the custom among the ancient Hebrews.

The subject attracted considerable debate, with the commentators who sought to replace levirate marriage by *halitsah* ("release"), pointing out that such unions are incestuous. In my view, both laws are flawed, each for different reasons. The incest law is too broad. The prohibition of a brother's wife is understandable when both brothers are alive. When one dies, there is no reason to prevent the other brother from marrying the widow, if both wish it. Such a marriage is permissible within the levirate provisions, but not if the deceased brother had children, whereupon it becomes incest. The parallel situation is the prohibition on marriage to two sisters (Jacob with Leah and Rachel). As we have seen, the Torah forbids this as long as the married sister is alive. If she dies, so does the prohibition. However, when brothers are at issue, the incest prohibition continues after the death of the married brother, unless the levirate provision applies. This was of considerable importance in the case of Henry VIII's marriage to Catherine of Aragon, to which I refer later in the chapter. In the present context, it is difficult to justify the distinction between brother and sister. A sister dies, and the widower is free to marry his sister-in-law. A brother dies, and his widow is not free to marry his brother, except under the levirate provision.

Levirate Law—To the Present

The main flaw in the levirate law is not its potential for collision with the law of incest but the coercion that it applies to the parties forcing a choice between levirate marriage and release *(halitsah)*, and the resulting hardship upon the widow. The law, which is still in force where Jewish law is followed, gives rise to endless difficulties and complications, such as:

(1) If the brother who is under the obligation is already married, it means that unless he chooses *halitsah,* he must take a second wife or divorce the first.

(2) If the brother who is under the obligation is a minor, he cannot perform his duty, nor can he release the widow by *halitsah.* The widow must, therefore, wait until he reaches majority, and until then, under Jewish law, she is not allowed to marry.

(3) There is a possibility that the brother is willing to marry the widow, but she is not interested. In such a case, the brother could refuse to release the widow *(halitsah),* leaving her unable to marry another man. The brother could also demand money for the release, and until it is received the widow is trapped. The demand of such a payment is blackmail, but the history of Jewish law is replete with examples where the widow was left with no choice but to pay.

(4) There is a clear inequality between the brother and the widow. He may be married to another woman and have no interest in another marriage, or he may be a bachelor and want to marry another woman. In such a case, his refusal to release the widow does not prevent his marriage. Jewish law does allow for legal procedure to compel *halitsah,* but the process is long and complex, leaving the widow unable to marry until it is over.

Some limitations upon the levirate-marriage law were imposed rather early. In the language of the Bible, the law took effect if one of the brothers died without a son (Deuteronomy 25:5), but the customary interpretation says either a son or a daughter. Accordingly, the levirate law would not apply if the brother left only a daughter, although he had no sons. The law applies if the deceased had a son who died before him but is inapplicable if the son died after his father, although in both cases the primary purpose of preserving the brother's name is not fulfilled. These mitigations were insufficient to solve the many difficulties of the levirate law.

The confrontation of Jewish law with the issue was long and convoluted and is reflected in a dispute that goes back to the days of the Mishnah. The question was which took precedence: the levirate marriage or the release by way of *halitsah.* The dispute still exists, with the Ashkenazi community opting for *halitsah* above all,[10] while the Sephardi community gives the priority to levirate marriage. The question is of significance in several situations, some of which have been mentioned. For instance, what is the ruling for a widow who refuses levirate marriage? If precedence is given to levirate marriage, the brother is not compelled to grant release if he does not wish to do so, and the widow may face financial sanctions, such as loss of her rights under the marriage contract. If precedence is given to release, then her rights will not be affected if she refuses levirate marriage and demands release.

The ban of Rabbi Gershom against polygamy, which was adopted by the Ashkenazi community, was of particular importance. Rabbi Gershom not only

---

[10] Mordechai A. Friedman, in his article "The Commandment of Pulling Off the Sandal Takes Precedence over the Commandment of Levirate" (Hebrew), *Te'uda: Marriage and the Family in Halacha and Jewish Thought* (Tel-Aviv University) 13 (1997): 35, suggests that the innovation of setting *halitsah* first arose from the growing belief in the afterlife. In biblical times there was no such belief, and the procreation of children was the only way to immortality. Levirate marriage was therefore required for those who died without issue. The concept of reward and punishment in the world to come assured the eternity of the righteous, even if they had no children to preserve their names. This belief weakened the need for the levirate marriage. Urbach (*World of Sages,* 229) holds that it was the belief in the afterworld that led to far-reaching changes in the laws of inheritance. Henceforth a man could write a will in which he disinherited his sons. Similarly, daughters who inherited (in the absence of sons) were freed of the Torah requirement that they marry a man of the family.

prohibited bigamy; he also ruled that a woman could not be divorced against her will. As a result, if the brother facing the levirate obligation was married, the process was impossible, and release remained the only option, so that the brother was compelled to grant *halitsah*. The difficulty remained if the brother was unmarried, but over the years reservations against levirate marriage grew as the concept itself became unacceptable, and rules were needed to compel release. It reached the point where, even if the widow and the brother wanted to marry, efforts were made to dissuade them and even actively to prevent the union. This position reduces the possibility of extortion but does not eliminate it. If the brother refuses to grant *halitsah,* the process of forcing him to do so may be long and complex, and while it is pending the widow may be exposed to his pressure.

The Sephardi community adopted a different approach under which the levirate law was acceptable. Rabbi Gershom's ban did not apply to the Sephardi community, so that levirate marriage could take place even if the brother was married. Still, the accepted view was that in such a case the widow was entitled to refuse, as she could do for another good reason, for example, a large age gap. In such cases, attempts were made to persuade the brother to grant *halitsah*. He was not coerced, so the possibility of extortion remained, since the widow could not marry anyone else without the release from the brother.

In the Sephardi community, levirate marriage enjoyed a clear preference over *halitsah,* and some even held that the process was not only a virtue, but mandatory, as the Bible implied. There were even cases in which the brother divorced his wife in order to marry the widow. According to Goitein, this happened in the Yemenite Jewish community, for fear of divine punishment if the levirate obligation was not fulfilled[11]—it will be remembered that God killed Onan for refusing to impregnate Tamar. Though neither the Sephardi nor the Yemenite communities forbade polygamy, nevertheless the brother might divorce his first wife in order to carry out the obligation, possibly to avoid disputes in his home, or because he felt that he could not support two wives.

There is thus a fundamental difference between the Ashkenazi viewpoint, which rejects the levirate obligation and favors *halitsah,* and that of the Sephardi and other communities, which prefer the first option. It seems that the difference between the communities originated from the Ashkenazi acceptance of Rabbi Gershom's ban. Since the married brother was prohibited from performing levirate marriage, the rabbis chose not to distinguish between him and his bachelor counterpart and decided to prefer *halitsah.*

---

[11] See Jacob Katz, *Halakhah and Kabbalah: Studies in the History of Jewish Religion, Its Various Faces and Social Relevance* (Hebrew) (Jerusalem: Magnes, 1984), 157.

The historian Jacob Katz does not accept this explanation, arguing that when the brother was married both communities accepted this as sufficient cause for the widow to refuse to marry him and that in most cases the obligation was only fulfilled when the brother was free.[12] This argument is not convincing. It is reasonable that the prohibition of polygamy was an important factor in the Ashkenazi position. It meant that coercion processes needed to be applied to the married brother to compel him to release the widow.[13] Conversely, the Sephardi community held back from coercion, even in cases in which they did prefer the *halitsah* solution. Moreover, the ban on polygamy expressed an important fact about the status of women: their position clearly was stronger under monogamy.

The Ashkenazi rejection of levirate marriage and the coerced release of the widow improved her status and reduced her dependence on her brother-in-law. It was reasonable that such a system of laws would develop in a monogamous society, in which the woman's status was better than under polygamy. Rabbi Gershom's ban reflected the great influence of the Christian surrounding on the laws of the Jewish Ashkenazi congregations in their midst. Levirate marriage did not conform to the status of women in Christian society and had not been adopted by canon law.

Israeli legislation has imposed Jewish law on marriage and divorce of Jews taking place in Israel, including the levirate and incest laws as they developed over the centuries. The result is that a man may not marry his brother's divorced wife or widow. Such marriage is considered incestuous. In the case of a widow, this rule applies when the deceased brother left a child.

As for levirate marriage, which represents an exception to the incest law, the Chief Rabbinate adopted the position of the Ashkenazi community, according to which release *(halitsah)* takes precedence over the levirate duty. However, Rabbi Ovadia Yosef, the leading Sephardi authority, has taken the position that this does not apply to the Sephardi community, because of its traditional stance that levirate marriage takes preference over release.

In sum, the position of Jewish widows under Israeli law is as follows:

(1) If the deceased left a child, the widow may not marry his brother. If she does the marriage is void, and the offspring will be considered "bastards" *(mamzerim)*. The widow is, of course, free to marry anybody else.

(2) If the deceased died childless, the marriage of the widow with the deceased brother (levirate marriage) is valid, though the Rabbinate in Israel objects to it. Consequently, the couple may face difficulty in finding a rabbi to conduct the

---

[12] Ibid., 149.
[13] This is the view of Levy Ginzburg, described by ibid., 148–50.

ceremony. However, they may marry abroad or in a private ceremony. The situation for members of the Sephardi community is less clear, but in view of Rabbi Yosef's position, they may be able to find a rabbi to conduct the ceremony in Israel.

In the more common case in which the brother is married or he and the widow do not wish to marry each other, the widow does need *halitsah* before she may marry another. If the brother refuses to release her, legal steps may be taken against him. However, the process is arduous and may take a considerable length of time. In addition, if the parties are of the Sephardi community, Rabbi Yosef's ruling may be followed, and the widow will be required to provide a suitable reason for not accepting levirate marriage. Otherwise the rabbinical court may refrain from pressuring the brother to grant release. In any event, it may be assumed that so long as *halitsah* has not taken place, no orthodox rabbi will agree to perform a marriage ceremony for the widow. She can, of course, marry abroad or in private ceremony or opt to live with a man as his "common law" wife. The prohibition of marriage without *halitsah* is not severe enough to make the union between her and the man of her choice incestuous under Jewish law, and therefore their children will not be bastards.[14]

Postscript: Queen Shlomzion, John the Baptist, and Henry VIII

Judas Aristobulus was the first Hasmonean ruler to proclaim himself king (104 B.C.E.). He did not reign for long and died of a serious illness within a year. His widow Alexandra Shlomzion married his brother, Alexander Yannai (Jannaeus), who with her help won the throne and reigned for more than twenty-five years (103–76 B.C.E.). This was nine hundred years after King David, and it can be assumed that the laws prohibiting incest were well established. The marriage, which would have otherwise been incestuous, became permissible—and even virtuous—under the levirate law, since Judas Aristobulus had died childless. The law had originally envisaged the naming of the first child for the deceased husband, but no hint of that remained. It was a successful marriage, and Shlomzion continued to reign for a few years after Yannai died. But the rivalry between the offspring of this union was to lead to a terrible tragedy.[15]

John the Baptist, who paved the way for Jesus and baptized him in the Jordan, flourished a century later than Shlomzion. This was after the death of Herod I, when the realm had been divided between his heirs. The New Testament recounts that Herod Antipas, the tetrarch of Galilee, married Herodias,

---

[14] See also n. 1, p. 248.
[15] See the postscript to chapter 13, pp. 206–8.

who had previously been the wife of his brother Philip, the tetrarch of Golan. John protested against this incestuous union, telling Antipas in no uncertain terms that Herodias was forbidden to him. The protest would cost John his life in dramatic circumstances that captured the imagination and fed many works of literature and the arts, including a play by Oscar Wilde and an opera by Richard Strauss. At Herod's birthday feast, Salome, Herodias's daughter by her previous marriage, danced for the tetrarch, exciting him so much that he offered her anything up to "half the kingdom." Salome consulted her mother, who suggested that she should demand the head of John the Baptist. Antipas felt bound by his promise: John's head was delivered to her on a platter, which she presented to her mother. The New Testament does not state if Herodias's husband, Philip, was alive when she married Herod Antipas. In principle the marriage could have been levirate if it took place after Philip's death and if he left only a daughter, but no sons. The levirate law would have been interpreted as applying to such a case (as mentioned earlier, although Deuteronomy 25:5 speaks of the case in which the deceased left no son, according to traditional interpretation levirate marriage is excluded even if he left a daughter). The text offers no hint, though it does give the impression that levirate marriage was not appropriate and that the union was incestuous.

The story is told differently by Flavius Josephus. He also says that the marriage was contrary to the incest prohibitions, not because Herodias was married previously to Philip, but because she had previously been married to another brother, also named Herod (after his father). This is the widely accepted version today, and the New Testament story is considered to be in error. Josephus also states that Herodias's former husband, Herod, was still alive when she married Antipas, in which case there is no doubt that the marriage was incestuous. But Josephus does not mention Salome's dance or any of the New Testament descriptions of the circumstances in which John the Baptist met his death. According to Josephus, Antipas had John killed because many were flocking to his teachings, and the tetrarch feared a revolt.[16] This sounds more plausible than the New Testament version, but it is not surprising that the story of a woman accused of incest and using her daughter's erotic dance to take revenge fired the imagination and won a place in literature and art.

The incest prohibitions of the Bible were adopted, with certain changes, by the other monotheistic religions. The provision forbidding marriage with the wife of a brother was to have a special significance in one of the important historical developments in the Christian world.

---

[16] Josephus, *Antiquities of the Jews* 18.5.2; Klausner, *History of the Second Temple,* 4:189–95.

King Henry VIII ruled England for about forty years (1509–1547). He was the second son of Henry VII and father of Queen Elizabeth I. His elder brother Arthur married Catherine of Aragon, the daughter of Ferdinand of Aragon and Isabel of Castille, the reigning monarchs of Spain. Her parents had completed the defeat of the Moors, united Spain under their rule, supported Columbus's voyage in which he discovered the New World in 1492, and, in the same year, expelled the Jews from their country.

Arthur's marriage to the daughter of the most powerful rulers in Europe of those days took place in 1502. He died a few months later, leaving Henry as the heir apparent. He ascended the throne in 1509, when he was eighteen. He wanted to marry Catherine, who was six years older, but this raised a problem that had its origins in biblical law, as adopted by the Roman Catholic Church. The ruling forbade marriage to the wife of a brother, even after his death. Had the Church also adopted the levirate law, there would have been no problem, as Arthur died without offspring. But the law had not been accepted by the church, though it did have some significance, as we shall see. This was an obstacle in the way to Henry's marriage to Catherine, so they applied to the pope for a special dispensation. Catherine claimed that her union with Arthur had never been consummated. There was no practical way to investigate that claim (which Henry himself would confirm at a later date). The pope, who appreciated the powerful interests that favored a marriage between the daughter of the king of Spain and the ruler of England, allowed the marriage of Henry VIII and Catherine of Aragon.

In the course of their marriage, Catherine bore Henry six children, but Mary was the only one to live. Henry, who sorely wanted a son, looked for a way to be free of Catherine so that he could marry his new love, Anne Boleyn. But now he encountered another obstacle in the shape of the Roman Catholic prohibition of divorce. Another law, well established in England and Europe, that stood in his way barred children born out of wedlock from inheriting their father's estate—and a fortiori the throne. Henry had such a son: the duke of Richmond. His status as possible heir had apparently been considered but discounted. According to biblical law, there would of course have been a possibility of divorce, though Rabbi Gershom's ban provided that a woman should not be divorced against her will, except for good reason. In addition, biblical law does not bar children born out of wedlock from inheriting. Henry VIII, however, had to contend with the Church's rejection of divorce and the disqualification of children born out of wedlock.

Henry was a learned man who had written a book in which, ironically, he challenged the anti-Catholic teachings of Martin Luther, the founder of Protestantism in Germany. This book had earned Henry the title "Defender of the

Faith," granted by the pope. But now Henry was trying to break out of a marriage, contending that it was void, being forbidden by a biblical law: as proof, Catherine's children had died—a sign of divine punishment for entering into a prohibited union.

This contention conflicted with the position that Henry had taken when he wanted to marry Catherine. But this did not deter him from claiming that the marriage was incestuous and void and could not even be made good by papal dispensation. The legal argumentation around the issue was long and convoluted. Henry's position was that the prohibition of marriage to the ex-wife of a brother, as provided in Leviticus 18:16, was a ruling from God. The counterargument was based on the provision regarding levirate marriage in Deuteronomy 25:5–6. The legal scholars of the Church, like their Jewish counterparts, debated exhaustively how to accommodate the two injunctions. Henry and his supporters claimed that despite the levirate law, the prohibition of marriage to a brother's widow remained in force, even if he died childless, and that levirate union was possible only by special decree from God (the pope's dispensation being insufficient). But most canon-law scholars adopted a different position. The accepted view was that the divine prohibition of marriage with a brother's widow is subject to an exception in the case of a brother dying without offspring. Even then the church forbade the marriage, but the prohibition was not rooted in divine or natural law. It merely constituted part of the positive law of the church, and as such, the pope was authorized to dispense—that is, to allow—it, as indeed he had done.[17] Thus, most of the bishops held that, since the pope had approved the marriage of Henry and Catherine, it was valid and must remain so. The pope himself was under the influence of the Spanish monarchy and was not willing to rule that the marriage was void or should be dissolved. Henry even tried to persuade Catherine that the union was invalid, but she of course rejected the contention, which would have made their daughter Mary illegitimate.

Henry was not deterred from marrying his beloved Anne Boleyn. In his view, it was not bigamy, because his marriage to Catherine was invalid. But there was need for an appropriate legal authorization. He decided to break off from the Roman Catholic Church and the authority of the pope. He persuaded Parliament to enact a law empowering an English clerical court to decide his case, with no right of appeal to Rome. The court, led by Henry's loyal archbishop, Cranmer, ruled that the marriage to Catherine was void, so that

---

[17] See J. J. Scarisbrick, *Henry VIII* (New Haven, Conn.: Yale University Press, 1997), 163–97.

Henry could marry Anne Boleyn.[18] The implication was that Catherine's daughter Mary was illegitimate and that Catherine herself resumed the status of dowager (Arthur's widow).

The separation of England from the Roman Catholic Church led to the establishment of the Church of England, headed by the king of England. The act shocked the Roman Catholic world and left a deep mark on all Christianity. Henry VIII was not noted for his observance of biblical law. Years before, Anne Boleyn's sister Mary (later to be Mary Carey) had been Henry's mistress. An argument could thus be made that his marriage to Anne was, therefore, incestuous under biblical law.[19] Anne was eventually executed for adultery, which in the case of the queen constituted treason. Two days before the execution, Cranmer's court declared her marriage to Henry annulled, because he had had intimate relations with her sister before their wedding.[20]

Catherine of Aragon died of an illness in 1533. Her rival, Anne Boleyn, was executed in May of the same year, and a few days later Henry married his third wife—Jane Seymour. Out of this union, which was not disputed, was borne the son who would later become Edward VI. Parliament authorized Henry to determine the succession in his will. Meanwhile, Henry softened toward his daughter Mary, after forcing her to sign a document recognizing the supremacy of the king of England over the pope and the annulment of the marriage with her mother. Toward the end of his life, when he was free of pressing legal problems, he wrote in his will that the throne was to pass to Edward and his offspring. In second place in the succession he put Mary, the daughter of Catherine, and in third place Elizabeth, the daughter of Anne Boleyn.[21] After Henry's death, and the early passing of Edward, the throne passed to Mary. She persuaded Parliament to enact a law recognizing her parents' marriage, thereby assuring her own legitimacy. Mary was a devout Roman Catholic, and one of her victims was Archbishop Cranmer, who was burned at the stake. Mary married Philip, shortly to become king of Spain, who was eleven years younger than she. The couple had no children.

---

[18] Ibid., 311–13; Jennifer Loach, *Parliament and the Crown in the Reign of Mary Tudor* (Oxford: Clarendon, 1991), 66–67.

[19] According to postbiblical Jewish law, intimate relations with a woman, outside of marriage, would not exclude the possibility of marrying her sister.

[20] Scarisbrick, *Henry VIII*, 349. The conclusion from this court ruling had to be that Elizabeth, the child of this marriage, was illegitimate. That indeed was the opinion of the Roman Catholic world, which did not recognize Henry's marriage to Anne Boleyn, because it took place while he was married to Catherine, a marriage that the Catholic Church considered valid.

[21] Jasper Ridley, *The Life and Times of Mary Tudor* (London: Weidenfeld & Nicolson, 1973), 78–79.

She was succeeded on the throne by Elizabeth I, the daughter of Henry VIII and Anne Boleyn.

The possibility of marriage between Philip II and Elizabeth I was briefly considered. Such marriage between a widower and the half-sister of his late wife would have been permissible under biblical law, but the idea was dropped for reasons that had nothing to do with levirate or incest laws. England had become largely Protestant, while Spain was the heart of Roman Catholicism. Elizabeth represented the spirit of freedom and English national pride, and she had no interest in being overshadowed by Spanish patronage. Elizabeth never married. Philip II married four times (Mary Tudor, queen of England, was the second) and survived all his wives. In 1588 he sent a vast armada against his former sister-in-law, but it was destroyed by storm and a sea battle. The English victory was to mark the country's rise as a maritime and imperial power.

In 1600, some fifty years after the death of Henry VIII, and in the closing years of his daughter's reign (Elizabeth died in 1603), William Shakespeare published his most famous play, *The Tragedy of Hamlet, Prince of Denmark*. Hamlet's father had been murdered by his brother, who then married the queen—Hamlet's mother—and gained the throne. The marriage was, of course, incestuous, both under canon law and biblical law (the levirate provision could not apply, for the murdered king had not died childless). Indeed Hamlet accuses his mother of incest,[22] but this gloomy affair is overshadowed by the main crime, that of murder followed by inheritance.

Finally, a brief comment on the development of incest laws. During the Middle Ages, the Church extended these laws far beyond those of the Bible. The result was that Jewish law was relatively more liberal, in that it allowed certain kinship marriages that the Church banned—for example, marriage between uncle and niece and between cousins. But there have been significant changes since then. In many Western countries family law is now ordered by secular legislation. The general tendency has been to limit incest prohibitions, in particular those concerning relatives who are not related by blood. For example, England abolished the absolute ban on marriage between a man and the widow (or divorcée) of his brother (the marriage of Henry VIII with Catherine). In Israel, these laws still obtain as far as Jews are concerned, with the result that Israeli incest prohibitions are more severe than those of most Western countries, particularly with regard to relationship from a previous marriage. Conversely, Jewish law does permit marriage of uncle and niece, even where there is a blood link. So this category of marriage is permissible in Israel but forbidden in many other countries.

---

22 Act 3, scene 4.

18

The Wives of the Father and of the King

⚜

The Bible has no story to compare with *Oedipus Rex* and mother-son relations, but it does have examples of sexual relations between a son and his father's wife. The problem is typical of polygamous societies, though it is conceivable in monogamous settings, where the father is divorced or a widower and has remarried. Greek mythology hints about this in the story of Phaedra, wife of the legendary Theseus, who is chiefly famous for killing the Minotaur, to whom the king of Crete offered human sacrifices. Theseus's wife Phaedra fell in love with Hippolytus, his son from a previous marriage, who rejected her. She revenged herself by accusing him of making amorous advances to her. Theseus cursed his son, causing his death, and Phaedra committed suicide.[1] The story of a potential relationship differs from the way it would have been depicted in the Bible: first, because it did not materialize, and second, because the initiative came from the father's wife. In the Bible, it is the son who takes the initiative. Finally, the tragic ending, characteristic of Greek mythology, is utterly unlike the realistic quality of the biblical stories, in which suicides are extremely rare.[2]

---

[1] Hamilton, *Mythology*, 220–23. The story of Phaedra and Hippolytus inspired the tragedy *Hippolytus* by the classical Greek tragedian Euripides and the play *Phaedra* by the seventeenth-century French playwright Jean Racine. Aliza Shenhar, in her article "Brought in a Hebrew unto Us to Mock Us," in *Readings from Genesis* (Hebrew) (ed. Ruti Ravitsky; Tel-Aviv: Yediot Aharonot, 1999), 303, compared that story with that of Joseph and Potiphar's wife (Genesis 39:7–20).

[2] In fact, there are no examples in the Bible of suicide committed because of suffering, remorse, or mental distress. The rare cases of suicide recounted in the Bible are of a different nature. An outstanding example is that of Samson, who chose to die with Philistines rather than endure the torments of captivity. Saul's suicide, by falling on his sword rather than being taken prisoner by the Philistines, had a similar motive.

In a polygamous society, each child has a blood relationship only with his or her birth mother. The relationship with the other wives is merely that of their marriage to the father. Another significant element that affects inter-family relationship is the view of women as property, so that the sons may claim to inherit them as part of their father's estate. Additionally, there are age differences between the father and his wives and between them and the sons. The wealthier and the more powerful the father, the more likely he is to have a large number of wives, with a wide age range between those acquired in early maturity and in old age. The more recent wives could be close in age to the sons or even younger.

The case of King David's wives illustrates this perfectly. In the course of his life David married a good many women. By the standards of those days, he lived to be quite old and infirm: "King David was old and advanced in years; and although they covered him with clothes, he could not get warm" (1 Kings 1:1). The answer provided by his servants was Abishag, a Shunammite virgin who lay with the king to warm him, "but the king did not know her sexually" (1:4). The king was probably in his sixties, while Abishag might have been fourteen to sixteen or younger. David's grown sons were certainly older.

After David's death, his son Adonijah sought to marry Abishag, and the desire cost him his life. The incident illustrates the possibility of powerful passions between the wives or concubines of an aging father and his grown sons. This would naturally give rise to disputes and frictions in the family, and this was the source of the prohibition of relations between a son and the father's wives. Leviticus 18:8 expresses an absolute ban, and postbiblical Jewish law designated the offspring of such a union as bastards. But the rights of sons in a polygamous society must now and then lead to painful challenges to the ban. A distinction must be drawn between such relationships in the father's lifetime and after his death. While the father is alive, the prohibition of the father's women is compounded by the equally stringent laws regarding another man's wife. After the father's death, it would be possible in principle for the widows to remarry, but the ban excludes their union with the late husband's sons.

The Qur'an, written centuries after the Bible, adopted many of the Jewish rules, among them that men are forbidden to marry women who had been married to their fathers; this is defined as "an immoral obscenity."[3] At the same time, it acknowledges that this practice had existed in the past.

The first example in the Bible of relations between a man and a woman who was his father's concubine appears in Genesis 35. After Rachel died giving birth to her second son, Benjamin, "Reuben went and lay with Bilhah his

---

[3] Qur'an, Women 25.

father's concubine; and Israel heard of it" (35:22). Traditional commentators discussed the psychological aspects of the affair: Bilhah was the handmaiden of Jacob's beloved Rachel. She had also served as surrogate mother of Dan and Naphtali. Rashi explained Reuben's relations with Bilhah thus: "Jacob took his bed, which had always been in Rachel's tent . . . and put it in Bilhah's. Reuben came and argued that this was an insult to his mother. He said, 'If my mother's sister was her rival, surely the handmaiden of my mother's sister is my mother's rival.'"

Even after Rachel's death, the despised wife Leah received no more attention from Jacob, who preferred Bilhah. As long as Rachel was alive, Bilhah was under her control, and Jacob's relations with the handmaiden depended on Rachel's consent and took place at her bidding.[4] The Bible does not describe Bilhah's position after her mistress's demise. Perhaps she became Jacob's property, or she may have enjoyed a measure of independence. There is no suggestion that she was punished because of the incident with Reuben.[5] Neither was Reuben himself, at least not at the time. Perhaps this is an indication of Jacob's frailty. The patriarch was already very old, and the time for Reuben to succeed him was near. The old man could no longer restrain his son and could only take revenge in his testament. A last will and testament, as it is understood today, is not mentioned in the laws of the Torah or in the biblical stories. The custom was for the father to give his sons a last blessing, a matter of great importance, and perhaps it was an opportunity to give instructions about the transfer of responsibilities to one of his sons; this would become very significant in the time of the monarchy. Jacob's deathbed blessing to his sons included a rebuke to Reuben, which possibly denied him the primogeniture (Genesis 49:3–4; 1 Chronicles 5:1).[6]

The offense, it must be noted, was of a son lying with his father's concubine while the old man was still alive. The main violation, therefore, was of the prohibition against taking another's wife (Jacob would have been no less angry had the offender been a stranger). Whether or not there was an element of incest in the case is not clear. In other words, we cannot deduce from this episode if Reuben could have inherited Bilhah after his father's death.

Another famous case of relations between a son and his father's women comes up in connection with Absalom's rebellion against David. At first the

---

[4] See the earlier chapter "The Status of Women: Monogamy, Polygamy, and Surrogate Motherhood," p. 225.

[5] Meir Sternberg drew my attention to the fact that "lay with" in a biblical context could mean rape, as might have been the case in the Reuben and Bilhah affair.

[6] Biblical law decreed that the eldest son should receive a double portion of the estate. According to biblical logic, this rule did not apply before the giving of the Torah.

revolt went well: David and his men were forced to flee from Jerusalem, while Absalom seized temporary control of the kingdom. Then Ahithophel advised the rebellious son to lie with his father's concubines, which he did, in public: "So they pitched a tent for Absalom upon the roof; and Absalom went in to his father's concubines in the sight of all Israel" (2 Samuel 16:22). According to Josephus, this was to demonstrate that the rift between father and son was beyond repair.[7] Rashi, writing many centuries later, noted that this was done to allay the fears of Absalom's men that father and son would be reconciled, in which case they would have been punished. But it is more reasonable to assume that the act was a demonstration that the son had succeeded the father and taken his place—which leads to the conclusion that, by law or custom, a son would inherit his father's wives and concubines. In this case, it was an attempt to show that the succession had taken place while the king still lived. The affair also shows that the incest laws of the Torah did not apply.

Absalom's conduct shows that the strict ban in Leviticus of intimate relations between sons and their fathers' women did not apply in David's time. Incest prohibitions were so stringent that even kings could not ignore them, certainly not in the overt and demonstrative manner of Absalom. Greek mythology describes the terrible punishment inflicted on Oedipus, and his whole family, because he unwittingly lay with his mother. The affair of David and Bathsheba leads to the same conclusion. When Bathsheba informed him that she had conceived, David made a desperate attempt to send Uriah home, so that the pregnancy could be attributed to him. When the attempt failed, David—feeling that he had no alternative—gave an order to kill Uriah. The story makes clear that there was a strict prohibition against the taking of another man's wife, and even the king could not ignore it.

Nevertheless, Absalom followed Ahithophel's advice and acted openly and with premeditation. In these circumstances, it is difficult to believe that the act was against law or custom of the day. The conclusion has to be—as stated in the Qur'an—that it was customary for the son to inherit his father's women.

Absalom, like Reuben, sought to succeed while his father was alive. The obvious contravention of the laws of the Torah, done in public, means that those laws were not observed in biblical times. The question remains whether the act violated the prohibition against taking another man's wife (assuming that it included concubines), and if so, how Absalom dared to do this. Perhaps Absalom and his counselor Ahithophel believed that he had won the right to the women as part of the kingdom. Another argument could be that when

---

[7] Josephus, *Antiquities of the Jews* 7.9.5.

David fled the city he lost the bond with the women he had left behind in Jerusalem, and so the new king, Absalom, was entitled to take them for himself, or even give them to another man, as Saul had given David's wife Michal to Palti son of Laish.[8]

The struggle for David's throne broke out while he was alive, probably in the belief that he was too old to rule. One possible heir was Adonijah, the eldest of David's living sons. The other candidate was Solomon, Bathsheba's son. Solomon and his followers won the contest, and he was anointed king. After David's death, Adonijah asked Bathsheba to obtain Solomon's consent to let him marry Abishag the Shunammite. Bathsheba agreed and went to Solomon:

> Then she said, "I have one small request to make of you; do not refuse me." And the king said to her, "Make your request, my mother; for I will not refuse you." She said, "Let Abishag the Shunammite be given to your brother Adonijah as his wife." King Solomon answered his mother, "And why do you ask Abishag the Shunammite for Adonijah? Ask for him the kingdom as well! For he is my elder brother." . . . Then King Solomon swore by the LORD, "So may God do to me, and more also, for Adonijah has devised this scheme at the risk of his life! Now therefore as the LORD lives, . . . today Adonijah shall be put to death." So King Solomon sent Benaiah son of Jehoiada; he struck him down, and he died. (1 Kings 2:20–25)

Solomon promised his mother to accede to any request but broke his promise when he heard what she was asking. What can we learn about the status of the king's women? First, Adonijah apparently had to ask Solomon for Abishag. Whether Abishag was consulted, or whether she was even interested, is not known. This already tells us something about the status of David's women. Second, the fact that it was up to Solomon suggests that he owned Abishag, and we may assume that having inherited the kingdom, he also inherited David's concubines, and perhaps even his wives—except, of course, his mother, who as the dowager queen had special status. Since Abishag belonged to Solomon, he could give her to others. The text does not say if Solomon had any interest in her or had intimate relations with her. This event took place when Solomon was young. He had already married Naamah the Ammonite, who had given him a son, Rehoboam, who would rule after him. The many wives for which Solomon was famous were still in the future.

The fact that Adonijah made his request for Abishag through Bathsheba suggests that he was well aware of its delicacy. Where did he feel that the problem lay? The simplest and most convenient answer is that he chose the indirect route because his relations with Solomon were uneasy, since they had been

---

[8] See the next chapter "The Divorce of Michal," pp. 275–80.

269

rivals for the crown. He might have thought that Solomon would see the request as a personal insult. It is hard to believe that Adonijah imagined Solomon would interpret the move as the beginnings of a revolt against him. Solomon's response deviated from any expectations and give the impression that he was using the opportunity to get rid of a potential rival. Indeed, immediately after the killing of Adonijah, and almost in the same breath, Solomon proceeded to remove his half-brother's supporters. He told Abiathar the priest that he deserved to die but would only be exiled to Anathoth, perhaps because he feared harming a priest. But he ordered the execution of Joab, the loyal commander of his father's armies. Solomon was obviously hostile to Joab because of his earlier support for Adonijah, but being clever and following in the ways of his father, he sought a better pretext. There was no evidence that Joab had anything to do with Adonijah's request to marry Abishag, so Solomon declared that the murder of the general had been decreed in David's will. In fact, there is no evidence that such a document existed or that such a request was made orally, and it appears that at the end of his life the old king was helpless and under the control of Solomon and his supporters.

Adonijah's wish to marry Abishag did not involve an aspect of incest. The fact that she had been David's concubine was not an impediment. It was not mentioned when he talked to Bathsheba. Nor did Solomon cite that aspect either. From what Solomon did say, Adonijah's request was viewed as a threat to his throne. That incest was not an issue can perhaps be explained by the text that David "had not known her." But the absence of any reference to it indicates that the incest law did not concern any of the parties involved in the affair, which would make it comparable with Absalom's conduct with David's concubines.

The idea that a new king inherits his predecessor's wives receives some support from Herodotus, who relates that, after the death of the Persian king Cambyses, the throne was taken by someone impersonating his brother, who took for himself two of his predecessor's wives: Phaedima and Atossa. According to Herodotus, Phaedima was the one to reveal the impersonation, a revelation that eventually led to Darius's revolt. Darius followed the same course, taking Phaedima and Atossa, among others. So these two women were inherited twice and married to three successive rulers.[9]

David's history contains a hint that he inherited Saul's wives. This is supported by the words of the prophet Nathan, who, after telling David the parable of the poor man's ewe lamb, preached him a moral sermon. Noting God's benevolence to the king, he quoted the Lord: "I gave you your master's house,

---

[9] Herodotus, *Histories* 3.68, 88.

and your master's wives into your bosom" (2 Samuel 12:8). This led commentators to speculate that David had acquired Rizpah, Saul's concubine. Rabbi David Kimchi (Radàk), a traditional commentator, suggested that David's wife Eglah had been Saul's wife, though others argue that this was in fact an affectionate nickname of Michal, Saul's daughter.

Rizpah's name had appeared earlier. When, after Saul's death, the kingdom was divided between Judah, ruled by David from Hebron, and Israel, ruled by Saul's son Ish-bosheth, the latter kingdom was dominated by Saul's general, Abner the son of Ner. Second Samuel 3 records that Ish-bosheth reprimanded Abner for lying with Rizpah, Saul's concubine. Abner was furious enough to defect to David's camp, thereby bringing closer the demise of Ish-bosheth's regime. The question arises in what way Abner's behavior harmed Ish-bosheth. Perhaps, like Solomon, Ish-bosheth interpreted it to mean that Abner was claiming to be Saul's heir and would use the act to seize the throne. This seems unlikely. It was Abner who put Ish-bosheth on the throne after Saul's death (2 Samuel 2:8–9). If he had wished, then as commander of the armies, he could have taken Ish-bosheth's place on the throne, rather than use his position to have an affair with Rizpah.

Another explanation is that Ish-bosheth regarded her as his property and held that no one had the right to take her without his permission. Radak, among others, suggests that Abner's act offended the honor of Saul and the monarchy, as Rizpah was by law a king's widow and therefore prohibited to a commoner. According to this theory, the king's widow was akin to material property, such as his scepter. Any use of the king's property was an attack on his honor. Maimonides stated in *Hilkhot Melakhim* 2:1–2: "Much honor is accorded the king . . . None may ride his horse, none may sit on his throne, touch his scepter . . . or any other of his accoutrements. And when he dies, they are all burnt. And no one may use his slaves and maidservants except another king. Accordingly, Abishag was permitted to Solomon and forbidden to Adonijah. But the wife of a king may never be given to another; not even the king will take the widow or divorcée of another king."

We may note that this was not the rule in Christian Europe. For example, Catherine Parr, Henry VIII's sixth wife, married him when she was thirty-one, having already been twice widowed. She survived Henry and soon after his death married her fourth husband, Thomas Seymour.[10]

Maimonides' opinion may be supported by David's attitude to the concubines with whom Absalom had lain. When David returned to Jerusalem, he

---

[10] Karen Lindsey, *Divorced, Beheaded, Survived: A Feminist Reinterpretation of the Wives of Henry VIII* (Reading, Mass.: Addison-Wesley, 1995), 181–203.

had the ten women sequestered until the day they died (2 Samuel 20:3). The rule, as Maimonides described it, did not oblige David to forgo relations with these women, but under Jewish law a married woman who has been with another man is forbidden to her husband, whether king or commoner. It is doubtful that this rule obtained in David's day. It certainly did not apply to his relations with Michal, whom he took back from Palti the son of Laish. According to postbiblical Jewish law, the prohibition does not apply to rape, and it could be argued that David's concubines had had no choice but to succumb to Absalom.

Nothing is said in the Bible about the identity of those concubines and whether some may have been, in fact, wives of the king. When David and his men fled from Jerusalem, they had to move fast to reach safety. It is unclear if they took the wives with them; they probably left them in Jerusalem. Did Bathsheba join David? Nothing is said on the subject, but her son Solomon was still a child, and it may be assumed that she stayed in the city. According to 1 Chronicles 3:5, Bath-shua (as she is named there) had three other children, who were probably all born before Absalom's revolt. It is therefore unlikely that she joined that dangerous flight. Did she fall into Absalom's hands, and was she treated like the concubines? If so, there was good reason to say nothing about it. Tradition links the incident to Nathan's prophecy to David after the murder of Uriah: "Thus says the LORD: I will raise up trouble against you from within your own house; and I will take your wives before your eyes, and give them to your neighbor, and he shall lie with your wives in the sight of this very sun. For you did it secretly; but I will do this thing before all Israel, and before the sun" (2 Samuel 12:11–12).

The prophecy speaks of David's wives, not his concubines, but it throws no light on what actually happened. The Bible says that the concubines were put "in a house under guard." But Bathsheba was at liberty to move around the palace and even to enter David's room, as she did prior to the coup that put Solomon on the throne.

To return to the concubines: Did Solomon inherit them, and did they really remain in confinement until they died? We may assume that some of them were young enough to survive David for many years. Nor does the text reveal if the harsh treatment of the concubines had its source in any special laws that related to the king's women (as some traditional commentators assume), or whether the reason was that they had been raped or taken in violation of a law against relations with another's man wife, a rule that the king would certainly have applied to his women. Rape, whether of a married or single woman, was a defilement, and a defiled woman was not to be touched. Jacob's daughter Dinah, who was raped by Shechem the son of Hamor, was

272

"defiled" though she herself was clearly innocent. David's daughter Tamar became unmarriageable because she had been raped by Amnon. The fact that she was an innocent victim was irrelevant: she had been defiled, and suffered the consequences. The impure state attaches to the victim regardless of his or her behavior. We have seen in the chapters "Saul Kills the Priests of Nob" and "A Godly Man Killed by a Lion" how ancient law linked impurity with strict responsibility and collective responsibility. In light of those concepts David may not have had a choice.

We shall never know if Solomon granted a pardon to those concubines who were still alive or took them for himself (on the assumption that time had eventually erased impurity).

19

The Divorce of Michal

꙲

After David came to Saul's court, the king offered him his eldest daughter, Merab, in marriage (1 Samuel 18:17). The previous chapter (17:25) relates that Saul had promised his daughter to the man who would kill Goliath, but chapter 18 makes no mention of that promise and of David's right to marry the king's daughter by virtue of his victory over Goliath. Instead, the chapter suggests that Saul's offer was made because of his fear of David and his desire to eliminate him. Saul therefore made the offer conditional upon David fighting the Philistines in the hope that he would be killed in battle. David refused the offer politely: "Who am I and who are my kinsfolk, my father's family in Israel, that I should be son-in-law to the king?" (1 Samuel 18:18). So Saul gave Merab to Adriel the Meholathite.

This was not the end of it. Saul had another daughter: "Now Saul's daughter Michal loved David. Saul was told, and the thing pleased him. Saul thought, 'Let me give her to him that she may be a snare for him and that the hand of the Philistines may be against him'" (1 Samuel 18:20–21). New negotiations began between Saul and David, the former using his servants as mediators. At first David repeated his refusal, saying, "I am a poor man, and of no repute"—a hint, perhaps, that David either could not afford or did not wish to pay the bride price. The servants returned to Saul with David's answer, and the king took the hint and sent them back with the statement: "The king desires no marriage present except a hundred foreskins of the Philistines, that he may be avenged on the king's enemies" (1 Samuel 18:25). The proposal was accepted. David preferred to kill Philistines rather than pay dowry, while Saul hoped he would be killed in battle.

The story of Jacob and Rachel also describes a preference for the younger of two daughters but stresses that Jacob loved her, and he asked for her hand

(Genesis 29:18). The biblical text does not say that David loved Michal but that the offer originated with Saul and that considerable persuasion was needed until David agreed. Equally clearly, David was not forced into the marriage. His standing enabled him to refuse Merab, though he was willing to marry Michal. The text indicates that he saw advantage in marrying into the king's family, rather than any love for his bride-to-be.

Shortly thereafter, Saul suspected that David was rebelling against him. He threw his spear at David, but missed. David fled home, and Saul sent men to bring him back. Michal, knowing what awaited her husband, preferred her love for David over loyalty to her father. She warned David and helped him to escape:

> So Michal let David down through the window; he fled away and escaped. Michal took an idol and laid it on the bed; she put a net of goats' hair on its head, and covered it with the clothes. When Saul sent messengers to take David, she said, "He is sick." Then Saul sent the messengers to see David for themselves. He said, "Bring him up to me in the bed, that I may kill him." When the messengers came in, the idol was in the bed, with the covering of goats' hair on its head. (1 Samuel 19:12–16)

David owed Michal his life, but later developments show that gratitude was not his strongest side. He fled to the desert and gathered a band: "Everyone who was in distress, and everyone who was in debt, and everyone who was discontented" (1 Samuel 22:2). He and his men lived by the sword and on protection money they collected. David did not renounce family life—during this period he married two women (Nabal's widow, Abigail, and Ahinoam the Jezreelite)—while his first wife remained abandoned in her father's home. Did Michal want to join David but was prevented by Saul, or did she prefer the comforts of the king's house to the hard life of the desert? This is not known. In any event, David's marriage to the two women he picked en route are mentioned in 1 Samuel 25:42–43, after which, "Saul had given his daughter Michal, David's wife, to Palti son of Laish" (25:44).

How could Saul do that? Under later Jewish law, Michal was a deserted wife. Physical contact with her husband was severed, but the legal bond remained. The only way to free Michal was for David to give her a *get* (divorce), which evidently he did not do. The prohibition on taking another man's wife was very strict, and it is hard to believe that even a king could ignore it.

European history illustrates just how hard it was even for a king to ignore the laws of marriage and divorce and how extreme the measures that were sometimes taken to close the gap between royal desire and customary law. When Henry VIII of England wanted to be free of his first wife, Catherine of Aragon, he had to wage a prolonged legal battle. Only after his break with the

Roman Catholic Church and creation of the Church of England was he able to marry Anne Boleyn.

The French crown also experienced complications arising from the laws of marriage and separation. Philip IV (1285–1314) had three sons: Louis, Philip, and Charles. The sons' three wives were involved in an adultery scandal. Marguerite de Bourgogne, queen of Navarre and wife of Louis, and Blanche de Bourgogne, Charles's wife, took themselves two lovers: Gauthier and Philip Aunay. Jeanne de Bourgogne, Philip's wife, assisted in the fun and provided cover but apparently did not play an active part. When the affair came to light, the Aunay brothers were horribly tortured and sentenced to death. The wives were treated more leniently: they were sentenced to imprisonment. The complications were not long in coming. Philip IV died, and his eldest son Louis came to the throne, but Marguerite, his wife, was in prison. She had borne a daughter before the affair was discovered, but Louis X did not have any sons, and, of course, he wanted to continue the dynasty. Not long after he ascended the throne, Marguerite was murdered in her prison at Chateau Gaillard. Then Louis could marry again. After his death, his brother took his place as Philip V. He forgave his wife, Jeanne, who had only been convicted as an accessory, not as a traitor to her husband. After Philip's death, the third brother became Charles IV. He promptly obtained a dispensation from the pope, married another woman, and Blanche was sent to a convent.[1]

These examples are taken from a different period, culture, and a set of laws based on monogamy and a ban on divorce. It was, of course, a radically different culture from that of the Israelites in the time of Saul and David. But they share the common denominator that even kings could not ignore prohibitions in the sphere of marriage and divorce. That was clear in the David and Bathsheba affair. The restrictions occasionally led to extreme responses, including murder, but these were carried out in secret.

This brings us back to the question: How could Saul marry off his daughter to Palti son of Laish, an act that must have been public? The traditional commentary sought to dispose of it by the usual method: assuming that the law was indeed that of the Torah but was wrongly or mistakenly applied. It suggested that Saul assumed David and Michal's marriage was based on mistake and therefore invalid. What was the mistake? The reference was to a legal rule that developed in the postbiblical Jewish law known as "reliance." The rule deals with a conditional promise, made when the promisor is convinced that the condition will not be fulfilled. In that case, the promise is invalid,

---

[1] The affair is described in the historical novel by Maurice Druon, *Les Rois Maudits* (Paris: Le Livre de Poche, 1971).

since the promisor did not really intend to obligate himself or herself. The marriage of David and Michal took place after Saul had made the condition that David kill two hundred Philistines and bring their foreskins as proof of their deaths (1 Samuel 18:27; one hundred in 2 Samuel 3:14). David killed them and won Michal. The "reliance" argument was based on Saul not believing that David could fulfill the condition; therefore his promise to David was not binding.[2]

This is a very weak argument. First, there was no reason to assume that David was bound to fail. Second, the argument should have been made before the marriage; once the marriage took place, it was inconceivable that its validity would be questioned on such grounds. Finally, the "reliance" rule reflects a postbiblical development in Jewish law that required great sophistication. There is no hint at this rule in the Bible, and there is no reason to believe that Saul knew it or claimed to act accordingly.

So there must be another explanation for Michal's marriage to Palti son of Laish. It seems that in Saul's day Israel followed a law under which a marriage ended if the husband abandoned his home, deserted to the enemy, or rebelled against the kingdom, so that the wife was free to marry another.[3] This was not the rule of divorce prescribed in the Torah and recognized by Jewish law, under which the husband has to give the wife a divorce *(get)* in order to release her. Until this is done the marriage remains in force. But the story of Michal's marriage shows that the law in Saul's time was different and that the union between Michal and David was broken when David fled and was considered a rebel.

Support for the existence of such a law is found in the Code of Hammurabi. The Code imposed the death penalty for adultery, but prescribed special rules when the husband was taken captive or had fled from the city. In the case of the captive husband, if his wife was left without sustenance, she was allowed to form a union with another man and even bear him children. If afterwards the husband returned from captivity, he got back his wife (§§134–135). The rule for a deserter differed in two respects. First, his wife could form a union with another man even if she had sufficient means, and second, if the deserter returned he did not get his wife back (§136). Clearly, in all these cases, the wife was not guilty of adultery and suffered no punishment.[4]

---

[2] David Altschuler, *Mezudat David (Fortress of David)*, commentary to 1 Samuel 25:44, mentions that there is disagreement on this issue.

[3] For discussion of whether a similar explanation can be offered for Absalom's relations with David's concubines after the king's flight from Jerusalem, see the previous chapter "The Wives of the Father and of the King," pp. 268–69.

[4] Driver and Miles, *Babylonian Laws*, 1.205–90, who also discuss the relevant Assyrian law.

Similar provisions that make no mention of destitution are to be found in the Laws of Eshnunna.[5] Sections 29–30 provide that if a man is captured or kidnapped during a raid and his wife marries another, the wife shall be returned to him when he comes home. But if he repudiates his city and his master and flees and his wife marries another, then he will not get her back when he returns.

These laws reflect two ideas. First, if a husband stays away for a long time and no one knows when he will return, the marriage bond is broken, or at least suspended (in the Code of Hammurabi, the rule applies to a prisoner of war only if the wife is destitute). The second is concerned with the rivalry between the husbands. The idea that a woman could have two husbands was unthinkable in those days, and so the question was which husband prevailed. The answer depended on the circumstances that led to the first husband's absence: if he deserted, the second marriage was binding; but if he was taken captive, the first marriage had precedence, and the second marriage was dissolved.

The difference between these laws and the Torah is clear. The Torah recognizes the possibility of ending a marriage, but only by a document *(get)* given by the husband. If this is not done, and the husband is alive, the bond of marriage continues, the woman is forbidden to any other man, and her subsequent marriage is invalid. The Torah does not accept the idea that a marriage is terminated or suspended because the husband has been kidnapped, has deserted, or is a prisoner of war. But Michal's marriage to Palti son of Laish indicates the existence of another law, closer in nature to the Code of Hammurabi and the Laws of Eshnunna.

Another example of divorce and remarriage of this kind appears in the cycle of Samson stories. Judges 14 relates that Samson married a Philistine woman. According to postbiblical Jewish law, marriage between a Jew and a Gentile is void, but in those days it was permissible and valid. At the wedding banquet Samson posed the Philistines a riddle about the honey and the bees in the corpse of a lion that he had killed. They solved the riddle by extorting the answer from Samson's wife.[6] Angered by his wife, he left her and returned to his father's house.[7] This was interpreted by her father as divorce, and she was

---

[5] The Laws of Eshnunna were enacted some twenty years before the Code of Hammurabi. See, generally, Reuven Yaron, *The Laws of Eshnunna* (2d ed.; Jerusalem: Magnes, 1988).

[6] See the earlier chapter "Samson Loses a Bet," p. 70.

[7] After Samson married a Philistine wife, the couple lived in her father's house. Robert Graves sought to deduce from this that Samson, whose name suggests a connection with the sun god, came from a matriarchal tradition, in which men left their birth families and joined those of their wives (*White Goddess,* 344). Graves was referring to the affair of Samson and Delilah, in which the woman remained among her

married to a Philistine, described as a friend of Samson. There is no mention of any divorce ceremony. Samson's departure was evidently understood to mean that his wife was free to marry again. But Samson soon regretted his action and wanted to return to his wife. When he found out what had happened, he took his revenge on the Philistines by his own special methods. However, his wife and her family were presumably acting according to what was customary and acceptable, not only among them but also among the Israelites.

The next step in the relationship of David and Michal was also inconsistent with Torah law. David was crowned king of Judah in Hebron, and Saul's son Ish-bosheth was ruler over the other tribes. There was conflict between the two kingdoms, but, luckily for David, a dispute broke out between Ish-bosheth and his general, Abner, who decided to join David. In their negotiations David strongly demanded the return of Michal (2 Samuel 3:13). He made a similar demand to Ish-bosheth, who conceded. Michal was taken from Palti and delivered to David. There is no mention of a divorce between Michal and Palti. The detailed description in 2 Samuel 3:15–16 simply says that Michal was taken, while Palti followed her weeping until they reached Bahurim, where Abner ordered him to go home.

From the standpoint of Jewish law, there was indeed no need for a divorce procedure, for the marriage between Michal and Palti was clearly null and void. Michal was married to David and had never been divorced. A second marriage of a wife to another man has no validity.[8]

But in the concepts of those days the marriage of Michal and Palti was valid. The lack of a divorce ceremony between them when Michal was returned to David again raises the question about the law that considers a marriage bond to be broken or suspended where the husband has fled, deserted, or been taken captive. As we have seen, this law is likely to determine

---

own people. But Samson did not marry Delilah—the text says only that he loved her. However, the statement may be applied to his marriage to his first Philistine love. For the view that there is not enough material in the Bible to indicate a matriarchal source and that the regime reflected in the Bible as a whole was patriarchal, see Jacob Liver, "Family" (Hebrew), in *Encyclopaedia Biblica* (Jerusalem: Bialik Institute, 1972–1982).

[8] The Mishnah (*Yevamot* 10) deals with the case of a wife whose husband had gone away and who was told that he was dead, married again, and then the first husband turned up. The Mishnah rules that "she shall remove herself from him and him, and must have a divorce from both" (10:1). She must separate from her first husband because of the rule that a married woman who has been to another man is forbidden to her husband. The application of this rule in the present context is problematic, as is the requirement of divorce from the second husband (the marriage to him is void anyway). See Samma Y. Friedman, "The Case of the Woman with Two Husbands in Talmudic and Ancient Near Eastern Law" (Hebrew) *Shenaton Ha-Mishpat Ha-Ivri: Annual of the Institute for Research in Jewish Law* 2 (1975): 360.

the circumstances in which the wife returns (or is returned) to her first husband. Presumably her return would be without a ceremony of divorce from the second husband. The very fact of the wife leaving her second home to return to the first husband is sufficient to break the second bond and renew the first.

This does not end the difficulties in Jewish law posed by the David and Michal affair. Another Torah law prohibits a divorced man from taking his wife back after she has married another. This reasoning also forbids a man from living with his wife if she has committed adultery. Clearly, the return of Michal would violate this later law.[9]

The traditional commentators resolved this difficulty with an artificial tale that has no basis in the Bible. According to that tale, quoted in Rashi's commentary, Palti never consummated the marriage with Michal, and throughout their marriage a sword separated them in bed (Rashi on 2 Samuel 3:16). How, then, can Palti's deep sorrow be explained? According to Rashi, he was mourning the loss of his virtuous act, the abstinence he had imposed on himself to avoid sexual relations with Michal. I think it more reasonable to assume that the law of the Torah did not obtain in those days and that prevailing law permitted a man to take back his wife, even if she had been for some time with another man.

The relationship between David and Michal did not fare well. After she was brought to David's house, she mocked him for leaping and dancing before the holy ark. He responded angrily and arrogantly that the Lord had chosen him to rule in place of her father and all his house (2 Samuel 6:21). Michal never had any children, whereas her sister Merab had five children, who were apparently raised by Michal, but David, in his campaign against Saul's dynasty, handed them to the Gibeonites, who hanged them.[10]

Why, then, did David want Michal back? There was no great love, as subsequent events showed. Perhaps he had never loved her at all. Shortly after he left her he took a number of women. Second Samuel 3 lists no less than six wives (before Michal's return). One commentator suggests that the renewed link with Michal would strengthen David's rule, for it would portray him as the successor to the house of Saul.[11] I doubt this explanation, since it seems

---

[9] The events could be interpreted on the assumption that Saul gave Michal to Palti against her will, and then she could be regarded as having been raped (in which case she is not forbidden to her husband by postbiblical Jewish law). I doubt that the bond between Michal and Palti was against her will, when she knew that David was marrying other women. Nor does it fit with Palti's great sorrow when she was taken from him.

[10] See the earlier chapter "The Rise of the House of David: The Problem of Legitimacy," pp. 160–62.

[11] Jacob Liver, "Michal" (Hebrew), in *Encyclopaedia Biblica* (Jerusalem: Bialik Institute, 1972–1982).

that David had no desire to be seen as continuing Saul's regime. The legitimacy of his dynasty rested on God's rejection of Saul and choice of David as king, a point that David made forcefully to Michal.

An explanation close to the spirit of the Code of Hammurabi is that David's demand to return Michal was meant to demonstrate the injustice of Saul's giving her to another. David rejected the charge that he was fomenting rebellion and claimed that he was being persecuted for no reason. Therefore, his legal standing should not have been that of a deserter according to the Code of Hammurabi (and perhaps a similar law practiced in Israel at that time), whose wife could leave him for another man. He was demanding Michal as his property, paid for with two hundred Philistine foreskins, and his rights could not be rejected in Saul's period.

There was another consideration. David sought to exterminate—cautiously, but without qualms—the whole of the house of Saul, whose descendants were likely to endanger his monarchy. The taking of Michal from Palti ensured that she would not bear him children who could threaten David's dynasty. Did David have intimate relations with Michal after she was returned? The Bible does not tell us.

Had Michal borne David a child, and had that child inherited the kingdom, it would have been a satisfactory ending to the conflict between the two dynasties and a way of reuniting the tribes of Israel. But it is possible that David did not want that. He wanted to show that he and his offspring ruled by divine will, and not by virtue of any connection with Saul's family. He already had sons—his eldest Amnon, Chileab, and Absalom—so it is doubtful that he needed or desired to renew relations with Michal. His interest may well have been to neutralize the house of Saul.

The assumption that David did not have intimate relations with Michal is to some extent supported by his attitude toward his concubines, with whom Absalom would lie in public during his rebellion. When David returned to Jerusalem after the suppression of the revolt, he had these women shut away. Michal's case was different. Absalom took the concubines before the eyes of the nation, while David was king. It was not only a stinging personal insult but also a humiliation of the throne. Michal, on the other hand, was given to Palti before David was crowned. There is no suggestion in the texts that he had Michal shut away like the concubines. But he clearly viewed Saul's action as an insult and a violation of his rights. The fact that he did not imprison Michal does not signify much. She was the daughter of a king, and David was careful not to dishonor Saul's house publicly. His treatment of the concubines may suggest that he had Michal brought back but then avoided intimacy. In that case he was observing the biblical rule under which the wife who has been with another man is forbidden to her husband. But this rule did not exist in David's day, and there is no reason to assume that he had it in mind. In fact, under Jewish law David was obligated to divorce Michal and not merely to abstain from having relations with her. It may well be that David did not want Michal to have children, for she was of the house of Saul, which he was trying to eradicate. Also, Michal's love for David may have turned to hate after she learned the fate of her father and brothers and grasped how David had seized power.

Michal's story ends with the statement that she had no children (2 Samuel 6:23). Rashi interpreted it to mean that she had no more children but that David had already had a child from her. He based this argument on 2 Samuel 3:5, which lists David's wives and children in Hebron. The text mentions Ithream, the son of Eglah, and Rashi contends that Eglah was Michal.[12] But this is pure legend and has no basis in the text.

Michal's story is told very laconically in a text in which the men hold center stage and the women are secondary players. But she is the most tragic in this narrative, far more than her father, who died a hero's death in battle against the Philistines. As a very young woman, she loved David and saved his life, only to find out later how her father's house had been destroyed, how David had seized his place, and how he had killed the children of her sister and her half-brothers. David took her by pressure and threats from her loving husband, behaved arrogantly to her, preferred other women over her, and all that was left to her was to eat the bread of charity in his court and to remember her days as the daughter of a king in a family that was cruelly exterminated.

---

[12] Rashi derived this interpretation from Babylonian Talmud, *Sanhedrin* 21a.

20

Crimes in the Family:
Rape, Murder, and Adultery

✠

The first murder described in the Bible was fratricide. Cain was jealous of Abel because God had accepted his offering, while for that of Cain he "had no regard."

> Cain rose up against his brother Abel, and killed him. Then the LORD said to Cain, "Where is your brother Abel?" He said, "I do not know; am I my brother's keeper?" And the LORD said, "What have you done? Listen; your brother's blood is crying out to me from the ground! And now you are cursed from the ground. . . . When you till the ground, it will no longer yield to you its strength; you will be a fugitive and a wanderer on the earth." (Genesis 4:8–12)

As we have seen, this is one of the rare cases in the Bible in which God conducts the legal proceedings personally.[1] The reason is obvious: in the ancient world it was the role of the family to protect its sons and daughters; blood vengeance, or private justice, was the rule. In a world without a central authority to preserve the peace and defend people from each other, blood vengeance was a means of defense and deterrence. In other words, it fulfilled the functions that are nowadays performed by the police and the courts of law. Anyone who wanted to harm another knew that to do so was to risk one's own life, and perhaps the lives of family members, and that punishment would probably ensue.[2]

---

[1] See the earlier chapter "From the Trial of Adam and Eve to the Judgments of Solomon and Daniel," pp. 9–10.

[2] Posner, *Law and Literature*, 49–57.

TO KILL AND TAKE POSSESSION

But when the crime was within the family, the system of private revenge became very problematic,[3] as it is in our times, though to a somewhat lesser extent. The basic issue has not changed: members of a family in which one of their number has been harmed by another often hesitate to call the police, aware that it cannot help the hurt party, while the offender will be punished, causing the family more damage. Modern legal systems try to deal with the problem, not always successfully. Ancient law, with the system of blood vengeance, was in a much worse plight. Cain's father could hardly be expected to avenge his murdered son's blood by killing the other son. Perhaps that was why Cain's trial took place before God, who pronounced sentence.

In this story God has a similar role to that of the Erinnyes, or Furies, in Greek mythology, the spirits whose task it was to chase and punish transgressors who murdered a family member. Imposing the duty on a superhuman force was understandable, given the limitations of the family when it came to blood vengeance in this situation. The fear of the Furies largely deterred murder inside the families of Greek mythology. For example, King Acrisius of Argos was told that his daughter would give birth to a son who would kill his grandfather. Fearing to kill his daughter because of the Furies, Acrisius had her locked away. When the stratagem failed and she bore the god Zeus a son, Perseus, Acrisius again feared to kill the boy. Instead, he had mother and son sealed in a casket and thrown in the sea. That way, he hoped, the boy would die without arousing the Furies.[4]

Cain's trial is unique because, despite the wrath of God, he was not sentenced to death, but only to wander the earth,[5] until he finally settled "in the land of Nod, east of Eden." In his exchange with God, Cain expressed the fear that anyone who found him would kill him. Taking this into consideration, God promised to avenge anyone who harmed Cain. Then God "put a mark on Cain, so that no one who came upon him would kill him" (Genesis 4:15). Cain's fear apparently reflected the situation of a wanderer, lacking a family's protection in a world full of dangers. The traditional commentators, responding to the question regarding whom there was to fear when according to Genesis, there were no other humans, explained that Cain was afraid of the animals.

---

[3] Ibid.

[4] Hamilton, *Mythology*, 197–99.

[5] For punishment by exile, see Haim Hirshberg, "Blood Vengeance" (Hebrew), in *Encyclopaedia Biblica* (Jerusalem: Bialik Institute, 1972–1982). The Mishnah also speaks of the accidental killer's "exile" to the city of refuge (*Makkot* 2:1, 4). But the possibility of exile is only open to the one who kills unwittingly, not to the intentional killer.

A later parallel to Cain's exile was in Absalom's flight after he murdered his brother Amnon. The outstanding difference between the cases is that Absalom, at least in the concepts of the day, was justified, whereas Cain was not.

Greek mythology provides an extreme example of revenge and "intra-family" murder in the stories of the house of Atreus.[6] The chain of events begins with Tantalus, the son of Zeus, who killed his son and offered the boy's flesh to the gods. He was punished for the crime, and a curse hung over his descendants. Tantalus's grandchildren were Atreus and Thyestes. Atreus was furious because his wife had betrayed him with his brother, and he took a terrible revenge. He killed both of Thyestes's sons and fed their flesh to their father. Atreus's two sons, Agamemnon and Menelaus, won a kingdom and are celebrated as heroes of the Trojan War. Agamemnon led the Greeks to war, but his fleet could not sail for lack of wind, so he sacrificed his daughter Iphigenia to the goddess Artemis to get the winds he needed.[7] In his absence, his wife Clytemnestra took Aegisthus as lover. When Agamemnon returned from the war, he was murdered by his wife, with her lover's assistance. The pair used the opportunity to murder Cassandra, the daughter of the king of Troy, who had been Agamemnon's lover. Agamemnon's murder was revenge for the sacrifice of Iphigenia, but this did not end the chain of murders. Orestes, Agamemnon's son, encouraged by his sister Electra, avenged his father's death by murdering his mother. He was pursued by the Erinnyes but was eventually brought for trial in Athens and acquitted.

Richard Posner emphasizes that the motive of revenge underlies blood vengeance and points out that it is associated with an uncompromising form of strict liability: it ignores the circumstances of the crime, the question whether the act was deliberate or a mistake or the result of necessity, and any other grounds for mitigation. It also makes the victim's family the judge in its own cause. Revenge calls for response, which leads to counterresponse, a process that can carry on a conflict from generation to generation. In Orestes' trial, which ended in acquittal, Posner sees a transition from absolute liability, enforced by revenge, to legal liability based on guilt.[8]

A comparison between the misadventures of the house of Atreus and the Bible stories shows that though the latter do not lack cruelty, there are no parallel tales of children's flesh fed to their parents. There are the Bible stories of blood vengeance, but these do not usually go on for generations. Conflicts continuing for generations occur in struggles between nations, chiefly Israel

---

[6] Posner, *Law and Literature*, 60–66; Hamilton, *Mythology*, 199–209.

[7] In another version Iphigenia was saved and a gazelle was sacrificed instead, while she became a priestess in the temple of the goddess.

[8] Posner, *Law and Literature*, 64–65.

and Amalek.[9] But there are almost no such prolongations of personal revenge.[10] Posner also maintains that every act of revenge, even if justified, must result in counterrevenge. The fact that Clytemnestra had some "justification" for avenging the death of her daughter did not obviate the need to wreak revenge on her for what she did. The laws of the Torah, which accepted blood vengeance, did not adopt this position. It holds that if the avenger acted correctly, he was exempt from punishment.

But the problem of the victim's family sitting in judgment remains and is reflected in the Bible, and at a certain stage of social development a judicial ruling was required in order for the blood vengeance to be implemented. The court would pass a death sentence on the murderer, and the avenger's role was limited to carrying out the sentence. This is already reflected in the laws of the Torah,[11] but the biblical stories themselves suggest that the avenger acted on his own initiative with no need for a judicial ruling. That was the case when Joab and Abishai killed Abner to avenge the killing of their brother Asahel, and so it was when Absalom killed his half-brother Amnon to avenge the rape of his sister Tamar.

The fact that David took many wives did not conduce to a peaceful household, and the royal court became the scene of rape and murder. David's eldest son Amnon raped his half-sister Tamar.[12] The Torah law does not impose the death penalty for rape of a virgin or an unmarried woman. The sanction was financial, and the rapist had to marry the woman, with no possibility of divorce during his lifetime (Deuteronomy 22:28–29). The reasoning, apparently, was that the rape had defiled the woman and damaged her chance of marrying another, perhaps for good. This solution might therefore be acceptable to the victim's family. It is not at all clear whether this family could take stern measures against the offender, as did Simeon and Levi after the rape of their sister Dinah. Possibly such a sanction could be imposed if the rapist refused to marry his victim or if she refused to marry him (with the risk that this implied for her future chances). Tamar's life was apparently ruined, and there is no reference to her marrying.

In the ancient world, it was Tamar's family who had to protect her. Had the act been committed by someone other than the king's son, it can be assumed that retribution would not have been long in coming. But the perpetrator was

---

[9] "I will utterly blot out the remembrance of Amalek from under heaven. . . . The LORD will have war with Amalek from generation to generation" (Exodus 17:14, 16).

[10] The murder of Saul's sons, delivered by David to the Gibeonites, is an exception. They were killed as an act of vengeance for Saul's actions (2 Samuel 21).

[11] Numbers 35 distinguishes between the deliberate murderer, whose sentence is death, and the accidental killer, who is entitled to flee to a city of sanctuary: "Then the congregation shall judge between the slayer and the avenger of blood" (35:24). The text obviously suggests a judicial process.

[12] See the earlier chapter "Levirate Marriage and Incest," p. 251.

Amnon, the victim's own brother. The decision was, therefore, up to the king, primarily as head of the family rather than king of Israel, though his position would have made it easier to inflict punishment had he wished it. David took no steps against Amnon, nor did he demand that he marry Tamar. All the Bible says is that David "became very angry" (2 Samuel 13:21).

David's reasoning is unknown. He must have decided to forgive Amnon, perhaps because he was the eldest and the heir to the throne. Nor did David demand that Amnon marry Tamar, perhaps because he disapproved of brother-half-sister marriages or thought that such a union following a rape would damage the monarchy. The Bible, with its usual brevity, does not explain David's silence. The fact remains that David had to choose between Tamar and Amnon, and he preferred Amnon. Yet David did not correctly assess the anger caused by a criminal going free and even expecting the throne as his reward.

The one who decided to avenge the crime was Absalom. Two years after the rape, Tamar's full brother ordered his men to kill Amnon. The killing served another purpose in that it removed Amnon from the line of succession, but the Bible takes no note of that consideration and mentions only revenge for the rape. There is no doubt about Absalom's affection for his sister. Indeed, after the event she went to live in Absalom's house, and he named his beautiful daughter Tamar after her.

After the killing of Amnon, David probably meant to punish Absalom, who fled to the court of his grandfather, the king of Geshur, where he stayed three years. By then Joab realized that David was ready to forgive Absalom, so he asked a woman of Tekoa to dress as a widow and to tell the king:

> Alas, I am a widow; my husband is dead. Your servant had two sons, and they fought with one another in the field; there was no one to part them, and one struck the other and killed him. Now the whole family has risen against your servant. They say, "Give up the man who struck his brother, so that we may kill him for the life of his brother whom he murdered, even if we destroy the heir as well." Thus they would quench my one remaining ember, and leave to my husband neither name nor remnant on the face of the earth. (2 Samuel 14:5–7)

David took pity on the woman and promised to protect her son. But he realized soon that the widow's appeal was a stratagem devised by Joab to draw attention to his own situation and the likelihood that he would lose both the murdered and the murderer sons. He pardoned Absalom and allowed him to return. But then for two years David refused to see him. Absalom ordered his men to set fire to a field belonging to Joab. The two met, and Absalom complained about his exclusion by David: " 'Why have I come from Geshur? It would be better for me to be there still.' Now let me go into the king's presence; if there is guilt in me, let him kill me!" (2 Samuel 14:32).

Absalom's view is worth noting. The murder of Amnon had not been blood vengeance, but rather the avenging of a rape and of the rapist's refusal to marry his victim. It was similar to blood revenge, if not according to the law of the Torah, at least under the customs of those days. Absalom's challenge, "if there is guilt in me, let him kill me," implies that he was pleading innocence, on the grounds that the killing of Amnon was justified and a recognized form of vengeance for the harm to his sister's honor.[13]

The chain of events does show that punishment for the killing of Amnon was up to David, not as the king, but as the father of the victim's family. It was also in his power to forgive Absalom. The solution was a three-year period of exile, followed by two years of refusal to see him. David's exclusion of Absalom was painful and may have enhanced the son's fear of losing his claim to the throne later on. Absalom's sense of the injustice done to him by his father may have contributed to his decision to rebel. David himself clearly did not appreciate the effect of the sanction that he imposed or its future consequences. In a way, it was a moderate punishment, but Absalom thought that there was no reason for any penalty. He believed that since David did not react to the criminal rape committed by Amnon, he should not have reacted to the justified killing of the rapist. The difference in David's reactions may have stemmed from different views on rape and murder, but it is much more likely that it stemmed from Amnon's status as the firstborn, a far higher position than that of Tamar, the king's daughter—yet another indication of the status of women in David's time.

The Amnon, Tamar, and Absalom affair, together with the parable of the woman of Tekoa, tell us a good deal about the problems of applying the law within the family. The text makes very clear the existence of a custom of blood revenge. The fact that retribution was in the hands of the victim's family—whether the decision to punish or only to implement the punishment—allowed the family to forgive (this would usually be against compensation).[14] The advantage of this private arrangement lay in its ability to prevent uncontrolled violence; its disadvantage lay in the ability of the offender to get away

---

[13] See also the commentary of R. David Kimchi (Radak) to 2 Samuel 14:32.

[14] The question whether the blood avenger could forgive the murderer was debated in postbiblical Jewish law. According to one view he was obliged to carry out the death sentence, while another view considered that he was free to spare the murderer. Maimonides concluded that "If the blood avenger is unwilling or unable to kill him . . . the court must put the murderer to death by sword" (*The Code of Maimonides [Mishneh Torah]: Book 11, The Law of Torts* [trans. Hyman Klein; New Haven, Conn.: Yale University Press, 1954], part 5: Laws concerning Murder and the Preservation of Life 1:2). In any event it was held that the blood avenger was not entitled to accept payment in exchange for sparing the murderer (Maimonides, ibid. 1:4). The realities of the biblical time were probably different, and we may assume that the victim's family could come to terms with the killer and his family.

unpunished. Another question has to do with which family member was authorized to forgive or come to terms with the offender. Reason suggests that it should be the head of the family, but problems could arise if some of the members did not accept his authority to decide. In the case of Amnon and Tamar, David appears to have forgiven Amnon, but Absalom was clearly unwilling to accept the pardon.

The woman from Tekoa told David a parable to convince him to pardon Absalom. It resembles the parable of the poor man's ewe lamb, in that the king was being asked to resolve a fictitious dispute. He gave his verdict, then discovered that he was the subject of the parable. The prophet Nathan put it simply: "You are the man!" The woman from Tekoa was more subtle, but in both cases David fell for the trick.

The woman's parable raises some questions. She said she was a widow, with two sons who had been fighting. One killed the other, and she was being required to deliver the killer to be executed by the blood avenger. Her appearance as a widow was designed to arouse David's compassion, and since there was no suggestion of other offspring apart from the two brothers, the husband's name was destined to perish. The killer was her only remaining son, so the avenger would have to be another member of the family (possibly the dead husband's brother). Was he also the family member authorized to decide if the offender should be executed, pardoned, or given a lesser sentence than death? Were any legal proceedings taken, and what was their outcome? From her testimony, there appears to have been no judicial decision ordering the execution of the killer, and it may be safely assumed that there was no need for such a decision, for otherwise she would have obviously referred to it.

Another question raised by the fabricated story relates to the potential interest that the avenger might have in the outcome, either because of his relation with the murderer or in terms of the law of inheritance. Clearly, after the death of her remaining son, her husband had no progeny. From her story it appeared that the two sons were childless, for otherwise the father's name would not have perished with their deaths. According to the Torah, the inheritance would have passed to the brother of the deceased. It was, therefore, possible that the avenger had an interest in getting the estate or part of it. If so, it underlies the difficulties raised by this internal family struggle. The "judge" and "executioner" are not devoid of personal interest. In many such cases, he might wish to defend the transgressor, while in others he would want him out of the way. This was the case with Amnon and Tamar, where Absalom's desire for revenge was augmented by his interest to remove Amnon from the line to the throne.

The last question relates to David's authority to intervene in the affairs of the woman from Tekoa. The Torah does not suggest that the king had powers of pardon. Other Bible stories are no more forthcoming on the subject. Was David trying to seize that authority? The system of blood revenge left the matter of punishment up to the bereaved family, and this necessarily included the right of pardon, as it was always possible not to carry out the blood revenge. Therefore, David may have intended to use his status to influence or to threaten the avenger, one way or the other. Since the conflict was intrafamilial, intervention was probably easier. If it had been between two families, he might have refused to intervene.

Adultery is another internal family matter, in that it is the wife transgressing against her husband.[15] But the internal aspect is doubled if the wife's partner in adultery is a member of the husband's family, in which case the offense is often compounded by incest. That was the case when Reuben lay with Bilhah, Jacob's concubine, for which his father took revenge in his last will and testament. The same kind of question arises with regard to Absalom, who lay with his father's concubines. In any event, Absalom was slain by Joab in the battle that ended his revolt. Obviously there was no further issue of punishment for the affair of the concubines.

According to the Torah, the punishment for adultery was death for the adulterous wife and her partner, and again the mechanism of punishment was presumably in the hands of the husband. The Code of Hammurabi authorized the husband to pardon his wife. No such option is mentioned in the Torah law or in the biblical stories. However, reason suggests that in practice that option did exist. Retribution being up to the husband, he was free not to insist on it, and as we have seen the death penalty for this transgression gradually disappeared to be replaced by other arrangements (sometimes divorce, accompanied by economic sanctions, and sometimes internal family sanctions against the wife).[16]

The Bible describes another intrafamily crime in Jacob's family, which also passed almost unpunished: Jacob's sons sold their brother Joseph into slavery, after which he was taken to Egypt. The families of Jacob and David have much in common, although the two men were diametrically opposed in character. David was a warrior, skilled in war, experienced in defying authority and spilling blood, and driven by powerful, sometimes uncontrolled, passions. Jacob, on the other hand, was a plain man dwelling in tents who shied away from violence. The common denominator between the two was their failure as fathers and educators and the consequent loss of control over their sons, with

---

[15] According to the Torah, a husband's relations with another woman was not considered an offense. Adultery only applied to a married woman.

[16] See the earlier chapter "The Prohibition of Another Man's Wife," pp. 213–15.

recurring episodes of internal family crime. Absalom lay with his father's concubines, and Reuben lay with Jacob's handmaiden.

The daughters of both families were raped. In both cases, the fathers preferred restraint, while the brothers chose violent revenge, despite their father's disapproval. The response to Dinah's rape was sharp and painful. Jacob's sons persuaded the men of Shechem that they would agree to let the rapist marry their sister Dinah, provided that all the male inhabitants of the town of Shechem were circumcised. Three days later, while the townsmen were still in pain, Simeon and Levi came and killed all the males, including Shechem son of Hamor (the rapist) and his father. They also freed Dinah, who had been imprisoned in Shechem's house.[17] The difference in the response in the cases of Dinah and Tamar lies, of course, in the latter being inside the family. In such a case punishment would have been applied only to the offender. The avenger was unlikely to harm other, innocent, family members, if only because that would weaken his own family. In the rape of Dinah, the offender belonged to another people, allowing for the contemporary ideas of collective punishment. Jacob himself repudiated the act and rebuked Simeon and Levi. Having always feared violence, he pointed to the danger that the other inhabitants of the land would retaliate against him and his family. His displeasure found additional expression in his will (Genesis 49), where he again rebuked the two avengers and as punishment decreed that their descendants would be scattered among the other tribes of Israel.

In David's family, Absalom murdered his brother Amnon in revenge for the rape of Tamar. The parallel in Jacob's family was the planned murder of Joseph by his brothers, a plan exchanged for his sale to slave traders. Jacob, like David, failed miserably in bringing up his sons. He loved Joseph more than any of the others, because he was the child of his old age (Genesis 37:3), and because the boy was the son of his beloved Rachel. He did not try to disguise his partiality for Joseph, for whom he made "a coat of many colors" (KJV) that was apparently not only valuable but also a source of envy to his brothers. Jacob's insensitivity was exacerbated by the imperviousness of Joseph, whose behavior left much to be desired. Working as a shepherd with his brothers, he "brought a bad report of them to their father" (Genesis 37:2). He also told everyone about his dreams, in which he was to rule over his brothers and parents. Some time later, Jacob sent Joseph out to join his brothers. They saw him coming and decided to kill him, but the eldest, Reuben, talked them into throwing him into a pit. Meanwhile, an Ishmaelite caravan approached, and

---

[17] Arguably the killing was necessary to free Dinah. For discussion, see Sternberg, *Poetics of Biblical Narrative*, 445–75.

now it was Judah who convinced the others (Reuben was not present) to sell Joseph. The caravan continued on its way to Egypt, where Joseph was sold into slavery. The brothers dipped Joseph's coat in the blood of a goat and convinced Jacob that his beloved son had been eaten by a beast. The affair, which began on the verge of murder, continued in the stealing of a human being and his sale as a slave and ended in the deception perpetrated on Jacob. As in many intrafamily crimes, there was no retribution. The crime was concealed from the father for many years. But even had he known, Jacob was helpless, having neither the strength nor the willpower to punish his sons.

Years later, when Joseph had attained greatness in Egypt, the land of Canaan was struck by famine. Jacob's sons went to Egypt to buy food and in so doing found themselves face to face with Joseph. He recognized them, but they did not recognize him. Joseph tormented them, he imprisoned them for a few days, then demanded that they bring him their youngest brother Benjamin, leaving Simeon as a hostage. The harassment continued when they returned with Benjamin, but in the end Joseph revealed his identity, forgave them, and the entire family settled in Egypt. Thus he revenged himself by tormenting his brothers with uncertainty about their possible fate. But it was a mild punishment compared with the gravity of their crime. This is understandable given that the punishment was in the hands of a family member who had been the victim, yet still loved his family. Perhaps the fact of his rise to greatness in Egypt, thanks to his brothers' crime, had contributed to his moderation. The passing years also contributed, and perhaps a mature Joseph understood that his youthful behavior had not been perfect. Finally, it is noteworthy that when the whole affair became known to Jacob, he did not punish his sons in the one way still open to him, namely, by means of his deathbed blessing, in which he foretold their future. He did not forget to rebuke Reuben for lying with Bilhah, and he reprimanded Simeon and Levi for their cruelty. But the terrible crime of selling Joseph into slavery and the deception practiced on himself were not mentioned.

21

Death of a Bastard

❦

"A bastard shall not enter into the congregation of the LORD; even to his tenth generation shall he not enter into the congregation of the LORD" (Deuteronomy 23:2 KJV). The word *mamzer* (bastard) appears once more in the Bible, in Zechariah, who prophesied in the Second Temple period, about 500 B.C.E.: "And a bastard shall dwell in Ashdod, and I will cut off the pride of the Philistines" (Zechariah 9:6 KJV). Here the meaning of the term is not clear. Rabbi David Kimchi (Radak) noted that some commentators believe it to be a reference to the son of a foreign nation, while other traditionalists hold that Zechariah was speaking of a son of an incestuous union (according to the postbiblical Jewish law).

Deuteronomy, which lays down harsh rules for bastards, does define the category, or the real meaning of the term, and biblical stories give no example of a person labeled *mamzer*. It is widely believed that Deuteronomy was largely written in the reign of Josiah, in the late seventh century B.C.E., shortly before the destruction of the first Temple, so it is possible that the law concerning bastards was not known in the time of the judges or kings, which ended in 586 B.C.E.

One affair that clearly raises the issue of bastardy is that of David and Bathsheba, but before discussing it, let us look briefly at the content of the law as formed in the postbiblical time. Jewish law does not recognize the concept of illegitimacy in the sense of a child born out of wedlock. All children, born in or out of wedlock, are entitled to full rights, including that of inheritance. In that sense, Jewish law is most liberal, certainly by comparison with the law that obtained until fairly recently in Christian European countries that were influenced by canon law.

But postbiblical Jewish law did establish severe rules regarding bastards, defined as children born to a Jewish couple whose marriage is void. The law distinguishes between a forbidden marriage and union that is both forbidden and void. Examples of forbidden marriage are between a *kohen* (a man of priestly descent) and a divorcée, and between a widow who needs a levirate release *(halitsah)*[1] with someone other than her deceased husband's brother. Such marriages, though forbidden, are valid once they have taken place, and the children are not bastards. Indeed, the children would not be deemed bastards, even if the parents were not legally married.

But a child born to Jewish parents whose marriage is both forbidden and void is a bastard. This category includes children born from an incestuous union (for example, brother-sister or father-daughter) and the offspring of the adulterous relations between a married Jewish woman and a Jewish man other than her husband. Paradoxically, the bastardy law—at least according to prevailing opinion—does not apply to adultery where the relationship is between a married woman and a non-Jew. The reason for this strange exception is that in order for the bastardy law to apply, both parents should be marriageable according to Jewish law (though their marriage to each other is void), and this would not be the case if one of them was not a Jew. By the same logic, the bastardy law does not apply to a Jewish woman married to a non-Jew who has an adulterous relationship (irrespective of whether the partner is Jewish or not, so long as the union is not incestuous). Since the marriage of a Jewish woman and a non-Jew is void under Jewish law, it is not subject to the rules applicable to a married woman.

The result of bastardy is truly dreadful. As we have seen in Deuteronomy, the bastard may not enter the congregation of the Lord up to the tenth generation. It means that he or she may not marry anyone except another bastard or a proselyte.[2] The case of a woman whose husband has abandoned her without giving her a divorce *(get)* is especially hard. If he has vanished, or if it is not known if he is dead or alive, she may not marry, and any children born of her relationship with any other man are likely to be classified as bastards.

---

[1] See the earlier chapter "Levirate Marriage and Incest," pp. 253, 255–59.

[2] A bastard was also allowed to marry a freed female slave, an option that no longer exists. Paradoxically, this was the one way of "purifying" one's descendants. It is the rule in Jewish law that a Gentile who converts to Judaism joins the people of Israel free from any inherited taint. Orthodox Judaism considers the son of a bastard by a Gentile woman to be a Gentile, but if he converts he would be a kosher Jew, free from that taint of bastardy. While Jewish law forbids relations between a Jew and a Gentile woman, a bastard was allowed to have children by a Gentile female slave. As such, they were slaves, too, but their master could free them, and being converted they would be considered Jews. In this way the bastard could free his children from the taint of bastardy.

The biblical narratives make no mention of bastardy, but one child about whom the question could have been raised was the first son of David and Bathsheba, the fruit of their liaison while Bathsheba was married to Uriah. When it transpired that Bathsheba was pregnant and clearly not with Uriah's child, David ordered his murder[3] and then married Bathsheba.[4] Hence, the first child of David and Bathsheba was conceived while she was married to Uriah, yet the Bible does not describe the child as a bastard, a term that, it will be remembered, does not appear anywhere in the historical narratives. However, in light of the developments in postbiblical Jewish law, he would have been defined as bastard. Another cloudy issue is Uriah the Hittite's[5] status and whether he joined at some point the tribe of Judah and the Jewish people. His name indicates that he came from one of the seven nations whom Israel was commanded to destroy and whom Israelites were forbidden to marry. According to one view, Uriah was from the Jebusite nation that had ruled Jerusalem before David's conquest of the city.[6] Mixed marriages were common in the biblical period (they were only forbidden in Ezra's period, in approximately 450 B.C.E.), including with Hittites. Clearly, mixed marriages were considered valid until Jewish law moved with Ezra to prohibit them. Thus, regardless of Uriah's status, his marriage to Bathsheba was valid. Perhaps he was regarded as a Jew because he served in David's army, was listed among David's thirty-seven heroes (2 Samuel 23:39), married a Jewess, and bound his future to that of David's kingdom. In those days there were no formal ceremonies or requirements for conversion to Judaism. Therefore, if we assume that Uriah was considered a Jew, or that his marriage was valid, and if the provisions of later postbiblical Jewish law relating to bastardy are taken into account, then it may be concluded that Bathsheba's first child by David was a bastard. Conversely, it could be argued that the idea of *mamzer* was unknown in David's time, and that is why the text makes no mention of it.

Seeking to solve the problem of David and Bathsheba's affair, the traditionalists used the legend that each of David's warriors, before going to war, wrote a conditional divorce *(get)* for his wife, so that if he died in battle she

---

[3] See "To Kill and Take Possession," pp. 75–84.

[4] Under the postbiblical Jewish law, a lover is prohibited from marrying his partner in adultery, so that David was prohibited from marrying Bathsheba. See the earlier chapter "The Prohibition of Another Man's Wife," pp. 215–16.

[5] The description "Hittite" in this context does not refer to the ethnic group that lived in Anatolia, the famous Hittites, but to a smaller indigenous group called more properly the "Hethites."

[6] "Uria" (Hebrew), in *Encyclopaedia Biblica* (Jerusalem: Bialik Institute, 1972–1982).

was retroactively divorced from the day that he left to go to the war.[7] Because Uriah the Hittite died in battle, Bathsheba was considered a divorcée and therefore was not "another man's wife." Thus by murdering Uriah, the murderer—King David—had cleared himself of the sin of adultery. This interpretation has another advantage in that it resolves the problem of the prohibition of a marriage between adulterous couples (if Bathsheba was retroactively divorced, there was no adultery). The same may be said of bastardy: if she was not married at the time of conception, then the child was not a bastard. It is difficult to admire such an interpretation, even in the guise of a legend, that rewards murder. In any event, the problem of bastardy was resolved differently. Using the parable of the poor man's ewe lamb, Nathan prophesied to David that the child would die. After it happened, David and Bathsheba had another child, Solomon, of whom it was said that God loved him, and the prophet Nathan named him Jedidiah ("friend of God").

It is interesting to compare the circumstances of the birth of David and Bathsheba's first son with the birth of Arthur, Britain's legendary king. Arthur's father, Uther Pendragon, invited the nobles of his kingdom, with their wives, to his court. Among the visitors was Gorlois, duke of Cornwall, and his wife Ygraine. Uther lusted after the beautiful Ygraine, but she rejected his overtures and told her husband. Gorlois and his wife fled to Cornwall. Uther summoned Gorlois back to the royal court, but the duke refused. Uther besieged Gorlois's two castles; Gorlois was in one of them, Ygraine was in the other. The king asked Merlin's aid, and the magician transformed him into the likeness of Gorlois. In this disguise, he entered Ygraine's castle. The result of their interlude was the birth of Arthur. A few hours earlier, Gorlois had sallied forth from his fortress and was killed by Uther's men. Thus, according to Sir Thomas Malory's 1485 C.E. account of the legend, in *Le morte d'Arthur*, Ygraine was widowed three hours before she lay with the man she believed to be her husband. Uther married the widow.[8]

There are clear parallels between the two stories, but also significant differences. One has to do with the moral code that applied in each case. The Bible expresses strong disapproval at David's act, whereas the Arthurian legends give no indication of any reservations about the events leading up to the birth of Arthur. The overriding impression is of a kind of divine intervention, leaving no room for any complaint. Another aspect was the timing of the woman's first intimate relations with the man responsible for the husband's

---

[7] Rashi, in his commentary on 2 Samuel 11:15, based on Babylonian Talmud, *Shabbat* 56a. See also Ginzberg, *Legends of the Jews*, 4:103.

[8] Thomas Malory, *Le morte d'Arthur* (ed. and abridged Norma L. Goodrich; New York: Washington Square, 1953).

death. Morally, the question may be asked if it made any difference that the act was committed hours after the victim's death, as opposed to hours before. But from a legal viewpoint, there is a world of difference between the two incidents. In the past, intimate relations with a woman while her husband lived was an offense punishable by death, though in the case of David and Bathsheba that offense was overshadowed by the more serious crime of the murder of the husband. In the case of Uther and Ygraine, their relations took place after the death of Ygraine's husband, so that was not adultery. This difference between the two stories leads to another sharp distinction concerning the status of the son born of the problematic union. If the intimate relations took place before the husband's death, the son would be considered a bastard, but if the event took place afterwards, even a few seconds later, there would be no question of bastardy under Jewish law. Under canon law the child would be legitimate if the parents subsequently got married as Uther and Ygraine did. The Arthurian legend takes care to stress that the boy was conceived a few hours after Gorlois's death. David and Bathsheba's first son was conceived while Uriah the Hittite was still alive.

According to Jewish law, a woman who commits adultery, if she survives the threat of death as the penalty for her offense, is forbidden to her husband, and he must divorce her. As we have seen in the chapter on "The Prohibition of Another's Wife," the law was expanded to forbid her also to her partner in adultery. Accordingly, after the divorce she may not marry her lover, though she may marry someone else.

On the face of it, David's marriage to Bathsheba was prohibited according to postbiblical Jewish law. The difficulty can be overcome if the legendary solution noted earlier is accepted, namely, the existence of a signed instrument of retroactive divorce in case of the husband's death in battle. Such an instrument would have rendered Bathsheba a divorcée from the outbreak of war against the Ammonites, and so her adventure with David would not have been adulterous. This explanation is too contrived to be taken seriously. It is more reasonable to assume that the law prohibiting a married woman from marrying her partner in adultery did not exist in David's day, but only much later. Yet even if their marriage was forbidden, that did not make their offspring bastards. The marriage was forbidden, but that was not invalid, and so the children were exempt from the harsh rule of bastardy. Solomon's status was different from that of the first son, who died young of an illness. The first boy who resulted from adultery, while his mother was married to Uriah, has to be considered a *mamzer* (bastard). Solomon, like King Arthur, was conceived after his mother's first husband had died. He was, therefore, legitimate.

22

The Expulsion of the Foreign Women:
Ezra's Legal Revolution

❧

Nebuchadnezzar's armies conquered Jerusalem and destroyed the Temple in 586 B.C.E. Zedekiah, the last king of David's dynasty, was punished severely for his rebellion against Babylon. His sons were slain before his eyes, and then—after witnessing the horrible sight—his eyes were put out. Bound in fetters of brass, he was led to Babylon (2 Kings 25:7). This was the end of the dynasty. Despite God's promise, it would never rise again.

The Babylonian Empire fell and was replaced by the Persian Empire. Some fifty years after the destruction of the Temple, the Persian king Cyrus proclaimed that the exiles could return home and rebuild the Temple. Construction of the second Temple was completed in 515 B.C.E., seventy years after the destruction of the first. The situation of the Jews in Israel was grim, though they were reinforced from time to time by more returnees from Babylon. In 458 B.C.E., the scribe Ezra led a convoy of immigrants. Ezra had held a position in the Persian court, and the king had provided him with silver and gold and with a royal writ permitting him to appoint judges.

Upon his arrival Ezra was shocked to find the prevalence of mixed marriages: " 'For they have taken some of their daughters as wives for themselves and for their sons. Thus the holy seed has mixed itself with the peoples of the lands, and in this faithlessness the officials and leaders have led the way.' When I heard this, I tore my garment and my mantle, and pulled hair from my head and beard, and sat appalled" (Ezra 9:2–3).

To deal with the situation, Ezra called a mass gathering in Jerusalem, warning that anyone who failed to come would be banned and excluded from the congregation (Ezra 10:8). The meeting convened in bitter cold and rain, while Ezra extracted from his shivering audience a general decision: "Separate yourselves from the peoples of the land and from the foreign wives" (Ezra 10:11). The ruling was enforced with a heavy hand. The Jews who were married to foreign women drove them and their sons out. Ezra himself is sanctified in Jewish tradition, and it was said of him: "Ezra was deserving to receive the Torah for Israel, had not Moses preceded him."[1]

The stories of the patriarchs in Genesis reveal an interesting phenomenon: their wives, known as the four matriarchs, were all of the same families as their husbands. Abraham married Sarah, who was his half-sister, and came with her from the Ur of the Chaldeans to Canaan. Years later, Abraham sent his majordomo to his family in Mesopotamia to bring back a bride for his son Isaac. He made his servant swear that he would not take a woman "from the daughters of the Canaanites, among whom I live, but will go to my country and to my kindred" (Genesis 24:3–4).

The servant went to Mesopotamia and brought from there Rebekah, the daughter of Abraham's nephew, Bethuel, and she was married to Isaac. When Jacob's turn came, Rebekah demanded sharply of Isaac that their son should not marry a local woman, but rather someone of the family: "I am weary of my life because of the Hittite women. If Jacob marries one of the Hittite women such as these, one of the women of the land, what good will my life be to me?" (Genesis 27:46). By this means Rebekah also got Jacob safely away from his brother Esau, who was threatening to kill him for stealing his father's blessing. Isaac accepted Rebekah's demand and ordered Jacob not to take a wife from the daughters of Canaan but to go to Paddan-aram to get a wife from among Laban's daughters, Rebekah's nieces. Jacob went and ended up marrying two of them, Rachel and Leah.

The line from Abraham to the sons of Jacob, who fathered the tribes of Israel, ran through women who were of the family, to differentiate them from the sons of alien women. Abraham had another son, his eldest Ishmael, born to the Egyptian Hagar, who played no role in the ancestry of Israel. Isaac also had Esau, who married Hittite women, to the annoyance of Isaac and Rebekah (Genesis 26:35). The nation of Israel descended from Jacob, who preserved the purity of the family line. The picture is not complete, for some of Jacob's sons were the offspring of Rachel and Leah's handmaids, who it must be assumed were not members of the family by birth. But, as surrogates, their sons were attributed to their mistresses, thus keeping the line within the family.

Having dealt with the lofty status of the matriarchs elsewhere, let me note here that the emphasis on family purity of the matriarchs was unusual. It is

---

[1] Babylonian Talmud, *Sanhedrin* 21b.

difficult to know what caused it, and whether the stress on the importance of the woman and family purity were added in Ezra's time or at a later date, when his position was adopted. The stories of the patriarchs are not supported by any other sources. All that can be said is that the stories relating to later periods indicate a decline in the status of women and a rise in mixed marriage. The family line, by the patriarchal system, was determined by the man, and the origin of the woman did not affect its purity.

In practice, the formula of marriage within the family frame had ceased to exist by the end of the patriarchal period as described in Genesis. Jacob's son Judah married a Canaanite woman. Joseph, who achieved greatness in Egypt, married Asenath the daughter of Potiphera, priest of On, who bore him two sons—Ephraim and Manasseh, the forefathers of two tribes of Israel. Four centuries later, approaching the exodus from Egypt, mixed marriage was widespread. Moses married Zipporah, a daughter of Jethro, a priest of Midian. Samson married a Philistine. David married Maacah, the daughter of the king of Geshur; she bore him Absalom and Tamar. Solomon had hundreds of wives, many of them strangers—including a daughter of an Egyptian pharaoh—Moabites, Ammonites, and others (1 Kings 11:1). Solomon was succeeded by his son, Rehoboam, whose mother was Naamah the Ammonite.

Two books of the Bible bear the names of women, both of whom were in mixed marriages: Ruth the Moabite was first married to a Judean named Mahlon and, after his death, to Boaz. She gave birth to Obed, the father of Jesse and grandfather of King David. David's origin, therefore, can be traced back to a mixed marriage. The second woman to have a book named for her was Esther, and she married a king of Persia, a marriage that brought relief and salvation to her fellow Jews.

All these marriages were considered legitimate and binding in every aspect. There are, however, certain prohibitions on mixed marriage among the laws of the Torah. Exodus 34:15–16 contains a warning against making a covenant with the people of Canaan and against marrying their daughters. The main prohibition is in Deuteronomy 7, which opens with God's promise to bring the Israelites to the promised land, which they would inherit from seven nations: the Hittites, Girgashites, Amorites, Canaanites, Perizzites, Hivites, and Jebusites. Israel was instructed to destroy them, with a special proviso forbidding marriage with them: "Do not intermarry with them, giving your daughters to their sons or taking their daughters for your sons" (7:3). All the commentators agree that this prohibition of mixed marriages is limited to the seven nations.[2] Another prohibition was added in Deuteronomy 23:3: "No

---

[2] Cohn, "Studies in the Book of Ezra," 1:57.

Ammonite or Moabite shall be admitted to the assembly of the LORD. Even to the tenth generation." This prohibition does not relate directly to marriage. However, if they may not come into the congregation of the Lord, then they certainly were not desirable marriage partners for Israelites. In any event, there is no general prohibition of mixed marriages in the Torah.

When were the specific marriage prohibitions added to the Torah? Clearly the restrictions were not practiced throughout the biblical period until Ezra. Uriah the Hittite, whose name alludes to his origins in one of the seven nations that Israel was supposed to destroy, was not prevented from marrying Bathsheba. Ruth the Moabite, the great-grandmother of King David, belonged to another forbidden nation. Solomon married Naamah the Ammonite—another banned people—and she bore Rehoboam, who reigned after him.

So the biblical stories reveal a centuries-long tradition of mixed marriages. That Ezra found mixed marriage when he came to the promised land should not have been a surprise. What, then, prompted his ruthless and dramatic change of direction? To my mind, the explanation lies in the total loss of Israel's political independence. Throughout the long period from the beginnings of the settlement in the land and until the destruction of the first Temple in Zedekiah's reign, the tribes of Israel enjoyed independence or, at least, autonomy in their internal affairs when they were under foreign rule. This ended with the failure of a rebellion against Nebuchadnezzar. The Temple was razed, Jerusalem went up in flames, and much of the nation was exiled to Babylon. The situation became even worse after the assassination of Gedaliah son of Ahikam, the Babylon-appointed governor of the remaining Jewish population in the country.

After these events, David's dynasty would never return to power. The idea of Jewish monarchy was over, to be revived four centuries later by the Hasmoneans, and that only for a brief interlude. Cyrus allowed the Babylonian exiles to return and rebuild the Temple, thereby granting them religious autonomy, but neither he nor any of his successors agreed to the renewal of the monarchy or to political independence. The country was directly governed by the Persians. Ezra's position was not based on any internal Israelite authority but rather on the power granted to him by the Persians. Thereafter, Jewish existence centered on religious life, and the question arose as to how Jewish identity was to be preserved after political authority had been lost.

In its days of independence Uriah the Hittite could join the nation of Israel by enlisting in David's army and showing loyalty to the political entity headed by the king. Ruth the Moabite could join the Israelite people by staying with Naomi, the mother of her first husband, declaring, "Where you go, I will go; where you lodge, I will lodge; your people shall be my people, and your

301

God my God. Where you die, I will die—there will I be buried" (Ruth 1:16–17). The declaration sounded more like personal loyalty than conversion, but it sufficed.

In Ezra's time, the picture changed completely. A person settling in Bethlehem or Jerusalem did not become a subject of an Israelite government or sovereignty. The sovereign was the Persian Empire and its king. The people were not centered in the land of Israel; many were dispersed in foreign lands as a result of Babylon's deportation policies and fears of war. An important Jewish center arose in Babylon itself, and for a long period its intellectual and economic power exceeded that of the community in the land of Israel. This center existed within the political frame of an alien nation. At the same time the Assyrian and Babylonian rulers had settled a large foreign population in Israel, and some of them lived in constant friction with the Jews. The question confronting Ezra and the community leadership was how to maintain the Jewish identity and the distinctness of the nation without independence, amid mixed population both inside Israel and in exile. In addition, there was the memory of the ten tribes that constituted the kingdom of Israel. When that kingdom was destroyed by the Assyrian Empire and its population was exiled, the tribes were lost forever, absorbed into other nations. Ezra and the leadership that worked with him were seeking a religious answer to the problem of the existence of the Jewish people. The preservation of the Jewish religion would secure the future of the nation that had lost its sovereignty and control over its homeland.

Driving out the foreign women was the first ruthless step required by the process.[3] These women, brought up in alien religions, were likely to divert their husbands and children from Judaism. Further steps were required to achieve the objective, and thus began in Ezra's days the legal revolution that dealt with such issues as the validity of mixed marriages, the status of their offspring, and how to define those who belonged to the Jewish camp. This was the question of Jewish identity now known as "Who is a Jew?" The answers, which began to be given in Ezra's time, led to a drastic change in the laws of personal status to such an extent that they bore little resemblance to the laws of the earlier biblical period.

A central tenet was that mixed marriages were void and were deemed nonexistent. According to the postbiblical Jewish law, a Jew married to a non-Jewish

---

[3] It is interesting to note that during the period of Ezra there was a thriving Jewish community in Egypt, on an island in the Nile, in the city of Yeb (Abu), called Elephantine by the Greeks. Documents found there reveal that mixed marriage was allowed and that the offspring could be integrated in the Jewish community. See Modrzejewski, *Jews of Egypt,* 35.

woman did not need to divorce her, because they were not considered married. This was, of course, a drastic deviation from the ancient law, which did not doubt the validity of such marriages.

The new laws also determined that a child's "Jewish identity" was based on the mother's. Previously, in a patriarchal society, the children belonged to the family of the father, and the genealogies did not even mention the name of the mother. Nobody would have doubted David's Jewishness because his great-grandmother, Ruth the Moabite, was not Jewish.[4] Likewise, no one would have contended that David's son Absalom, who would have succeeded him but for his revolt, was not Jewish because his mother was the daughter of the king of Geshur. Absalom was David's son and was brought up in his court. That was sufficient, as it was for Solomon's son Rehoboam, whose mother was an Ammonite.

The legal revolution did not change the patriarchal structure of the family and society, and the rule that linked the child's identity to the mother's was an important exception. In fact it was a powerful deterrent to the practice of mixed marriage. A Jew who married a Gentile woman risked not only the nonrecognition of the union but also the rejection of his children from the community.

Other rules applied to the entry into Judaism. The Bible itself does not refer to any process of conversion—that was ensured by the people's sovereignty and independence in their land. All that Ruth the Moabite had to do to join the tribe of Judah was to wish it, to come to Bethlehem with Naomi, and to comply with the obligations of a daughter of the tribe. But after the loss of independence and in the conditions prevailing in Ezra's time and afterwards, that could not suffice. And so, after the biblical period, processes of conversion were devised.

Postscript: The Case of Major Benjamin Shalit

Almost 2,500 years after Ezra convened his public meeting in Jerusalem, the Supreme Court of Israel, in the same city, ruled on a petition submitted by Benjamin Shalit, in his own name and that of his children. Shalit was born in Haifa. In 1958, while studying in Scotland, he married a Scots woman whose father came from a Zionist family and whose mother was French "of a family

---

[4] In fact, even according to the postbiblical Jewish law, this was of no importance. The question was whether David's mother, the wife of Jesse, was Jewish. In all probability she was, though her identity is unknown to us. In the patriarchal fashion, the author saw no need to mention her name.

known to have no religious affiliation."[5] Upon completing his studies, Shalit returned to Israel with his wife and enlisted in the Israel Defense Forces. Two children were born to them in Israel, and the question arose regarding their registration. In accordance with the provisions of the Registration of Population Ordinance of 1949,[6] the Ministry of the Interior registered both "religion" and "nationality." There was no dispute about Shalit's boys not being of the Jewish religion. The question was whether to accept their demand to be registered as Jews by nationality. The Ministry adopted the position that religion and nationality of Jews cannot be separated and that both followed those of their mother, who in this case was not Jewish nor had she been converted according to Jewish law.

The decision was rendered by a panel of nine justices, the largest panel to sit on a case up to that day—in fact, the largest possible in 1968, when the case came up. In those days there were ten justices on the Supreme Court, and the panel had to be of an uneven number. Paradoxically, the question debated was of no practical importance. The registration of a person as being of one nationality or another neither granted rights nor imposed any obligations. Another paradox was that the term "Jew" appears in various pieces of legislation, but its meaning may change according to the context. Thus, for example, in the law governing the rabbinical courts, which have jurisdiction over marriages and divorces of Jews in Israel, the meaning of the term "Jew" is according to the halakah: the codex of Jewish orthodox religious law. The reason is obvious: these courts are orthodox religious institutions, and it is clear that they apply the rules of the halakah. But this is not necessarily the case where the term is used in legislation that is to be applied by secular bodies.

The registration of someone as a Jew in the Population Registry is not binding on the rabbinical courts, for whom Shalit's children were not Jewish. But the absence of practical significance did not detract from the emotional and symbolic significance of the issue. This was the reason why the Supreme Court was sitting, for the first time in its history, in maximum complement of nine justices. Justice Silberg, who was in the minority, opened his opinion as follows: "The question before us is of greater value and importance than anything brought before this court since its inception and till the present day. . . . The debate and its ideological components will necessitate profound soul searching about our identity as a people, our being as a nation, and our political-Zionist role in the revival of this land."

---

[5] The facts are described in the decision of Justice Y. Sussman, 23(2) P.D. 477, 504 (Hebrew).

[6] This ordinance has since been replaced by the Registration of Population Law, 1965.

The decision, given in January 1970, was by a five to four majority. The majority justices held that the Registrar must record under the item "nationality" whatever the citizen tells him, as long as it is told in good faith and is not patently false. Accordingly, the children of a Jewish father and a non-Jewish mother, who grow up in Israel and are loyal to the State, can be registered under nationality as "Jews," even though the halakhah does not recognize them as such.

The decision set off a public and political storm. Shortly thereafter, the Population Registration Law and the Law of Return were amended. The amendment was based on a compromise: the law adopted the halakic definition of "Jew" and defined a Jew as "a person who was born of a Jewish mother or has become converted to Judaism and who is not a member of another religion." The halakic position was thus accepted, though it remained unclear what constitutes conversion and whether it is necessarily orthodox or can be otherwise.[7] The result was that the Shalit's next child could not be registered as of "Jewish" nationality.[8]

However, the other part of the amendment reflected a liberal approach that is clearly not in line with that adopted in the times of Ezra. It provided that the rights of a Jew under the Law of Return and under the Law of Nationality as well as the rights of a Jewish immigrant to Israel *(oleh)* under any other enactment, "are vested in a child and grandchild of a Jew, the spouse of a Jew, the spouse of a child of a Jew and the spouse of a grandchild of a Jew, except for a person who was Jewish and converted of his own volition."[9]

---

[7] The issue of conversion continues to haunt Israeli society and politics. The Orthodox position is that the only way that a Gentile may join the Jewish people is by Orthodox conversion, which requires the convert to become an Orthodox Jew. However, the Conservative and the Reform movements have their own conversion procedures. Again the issue arose in the context of the Registration of Population legislation, and again an expanded panel of the Supreme Court, this time consisting of eleven justices, was convened to decide the case of *Naamat: A Movement of Working and Volunteer Women v. The Minister of Interior.* The decision of the ten to one majority, rendered in February 2002, was delivered by President A. Barak and Justice M. Cheshin. It followed the Shalit decision and held that the Registrar is bound to register a convert as Jew irrespective of whether the conversion was Orthodox, Conservative, or Reform and regardless whether it was done in Israel or abroad. The Israeli Parliament (Knesset) is now considering the deletion of the section of "Nationality" from the identity card. But other problems loom on the horizon, in particular, whether a Reform or Conservative conversion entitles the convert to the rights of a Jew under the Law of Return and whether the State of Israel must accept that private organizations in Israel and abroad—Orthodox, Conservative, or Reform—are free to confer, at their own discretion and procedure, extensive rights (including a right to citizenship) under Israeli law.

[8] *Shalit v. Minister of Interior* 26(1) P.D. 334.

[9] Law of Return (amendment no. 2), 1970.

Mixed couples are, therefore, entitled to immigrate to Israel and integrate into Israeli society, as are their children and grandchildren.

The position taken by Ezra at the mass meeting that he held in Jerusalem 2,500 years ago was rejected in the Shalit decision and in the amendment to the Law of Return. The resolution adopted at that meeting, under pressure from Ezra, revolutionized family law as it obtained until then. It was caused by Israel's loss of political independence and stemmed from the desire to preserve national identity in the new conditions. The creation of a sovereign State of Israel produced its own revolution and reverted to the situation prior to Ezra, when Israel was in control of its own land. Major Shalit's wife was able to join the nation of Israel, as was Ruth the Moabite, by marrying one of its members. In Ezra's time, the process involved much torment and certainly was not concluded in a day. The process of establishing an Israeli national identity, and the shaking off of long-lasting laws, is similarly not free from disputes and crises.

Conclusion

꽃

This book examines the world outlook of ancient Israelite society as reflected in the rich biblical literature that describes individuals and families as well as historical and political events in the governance and monarchy. In addition to this literature the Bible contains a large body of laws, said to have been given to the Israelites after the exodus from Egypt and before they entered the promised land.

A close study of the biblical narrative reveals an obvious discrepancy between it and the system of laws laid down in the Pentateuch. This book's chapters offer various illustrations of this discrepancy. For example, there are many stories describing acts of deception that were effective and successful, though explicitly forbidden by the pentateuchal laws. Some attempts at reconciling the described events with the laws can be discerned,[1] and in certain matters the laws might have reflected the prevailing customs in the described period, yet on many major issues there is an undeniable gulf between the laws and the biblical stories. This is the case in regard to laws concerning marriage and divorce as well as other aspects of family law and the structure of governance of the kingdom. For example, it would seem that there was a convention

---

[1] The story of Naboth's trial shows that his conviction was based on the evidence of two false witnesses. The two-witnesses requirement appears in Deuteronomy 17:6, and the emphasis on the need for two witnesses in this case gave rise to a speculation that the story of Naboth's trial is an interpolation. See n. 30 on p. 99. Another example is King David's reaction to the ewe-lamb parable told to him by the prophet Nathan. David was outraged and declared that the rich man deserved death and should pay the lamb fourfold. The payment of four times the value of the lamb is in line with Exodus 22:2. There is, however, no death penalty in the Pentateuch for stealing. But §22 of the Code of Hammurabi imposes such penalty for robbery.

permitting a married woman to marry another man, if her husband had betrayed the kingdom or migrated elsewhere. Thus Michal, David's first wife, married Palti son of Laish, though she had not been divorced from David, and Samson's Philistine wife was given to another man when Samson abandoned her. Yet the pentateuchal laws explicitly prohibit such second marriages.

On the state level, the story about Naboth's vineyard indicates that the king was empowered to seize the property of criminals, at least in the case of certain offenses, though the Pentateuch allows no such authority. Likewise, the crowning of Saul as Israel's first king was carried out not as stipulated by the Pentateuch, but in accordance with the customs of nearby nations. And the sacrifice of Jephthah's daughter, which clearly violated the pentateuchal law, indicates the existence of human sacrifice, based on the belief that it could avert a dreadful threat to the individual or the community.

Needless to say, the stories and historical descriptions that cover many centuries reflect a variety of social and moral attitudes. Some are close to the ones prevailing in the modern world and the values we aspire to, while others express viewpoints that are no longer acceptable. For example, the stories about the patriarchs and the book of Ruth depict a largely monogamous family life in which the woman held a central and fairly strong position, whereas the historical descriptions of the courts of judges and kings indicate widespread polygamy and a much lower status of women.

The prophetic stories likewise reflect more than one trend. Some of the prophets laid stress on cultic matters, concentrated on political affairs, and were even involved in them, while the later prophets laid the emphasis on morality and social justice.

As Hebrew culture developed after the fall of the second Temple, it dealt with the problems raised by the biblical stories in a variety of ways. One was that of the midrash and aggadah, which interpreted the biblical stories, generally by introducing other elements to narrow the gap between them and the moral outlook reflected in the pentateuchal laws. Another way was to openly decry some of the events described in the biblical stories and to lay the stress on the study and understanding of the laws. Consequently, religious Hebrew culture concentrated on the pentateuchal laws, the Mishnah and Talmud, demoting the biblical narratives to secondary position and assigning them chiefly to the midrash and aggadah.

The rise of the secular-Zionist movement restored the emphasis on the narrative and historical portions of the Bible, viewing them as depicting the reality of the people of Israel in their independent, self-governing kingdom. Yet clearly a modern state could hardly be run on the basis of the ideas and principles reflected in the biblical stories. The State of Israel, therefore, looked to the Western world and to modern social-political currents in forming its own regime and never sought to restore the monarchy or in any way emulate the political system of the First Temple period. In this sense the Zionist movement and the State acted much as the ancient Israelites had done—namely, it adapted the customs and governance of other contemporary societies.

One topic retains its vitality: the profound admiration for the late, great prophets, who never held official or political positions, enjoyed no divine protection of their persons, and were sometimes subjected to pressure, threats, and even risk of life. These prophets preached social justice and moral principles in human relations, and their texts have lost none of their force. As such, they remain relevant to this day and are explicitly referred to in Israel's Declaration of Independence.

Index of Names and Subjects

with" meaning, 267n.5; punishment
for, 213–14, 214n.7, 215n.10; of Tamar,
129, 273, 286–88

Rashi: on aging prophet and the man of
God, 115; on conditional divorce, 84,
84n.11, 296n.7; on consanguinity of
Abraham and Sarah, 251n.5; on definition of adultery, 213; on Elhanan, 33;
on God speaking directly to Jehu,
190n.4; on her kinsman's refusal of
Ruth, 244–45; on inciters, 123; on
Ishmael's mocking of Isaac, 222; on
Jacob and Laban, 64, 224n.6; on
Keturah as Hagar, 221; on Michal's
"children," 282; on Moabite exclusion,
3, 3n.4, 5; on Rebekah, 49; on Reuben
and Bilhah, 267

Rebekah: Isaac and, 48–49, 52–53, 64,
211, 223–24, 299; legend about father
of, 250; speaking with God, 49, 220

Rechab, 155–56

redemption, 139–40, 179

Registration of Population Law (1965),
304n.5

Registration of Population Ordinance
(1949), 304

Rehoboam, 177, 205, 269, 300, 301,303

Reis, Pamela Tamarkin, 223n.5

"reliance" rule, 276–77

remarriage, 215–17, 294

responsibility: absolute obedience and,
11–12, 65, 125–26, 130, 162, 257; absolute responsibility, 62–63, 115–20, 122,
125–27, 128–33, 132n.8, 153, 291;
aging prophet and man of God,
115–16, 119–20; collective, 12, 128–33,
160–61, 291; contagiousness in,
113–14, 128, 128n.1; false witnesses
and, 23–29, 92–98; instigators and,
86–89, 121–25

retroactive divorce, 84, 84n.11, 295–97

Return, law of, 305

Reuben, 192, 250, 266–67, 290–92

revenge, 92, 116, 212n.1, 284–92

reward and punishment belief, 183–88.
See also punishment

rice-swallowing ordeal, 22, 22n.12, 30

Richard, John F., 198n.6

riddles, 71, 71n.3, 72–73, 278–79

Ridley, Jasper, 263n.21

Riggs v. Palmer, 109

"right of first night," 250

ritual impurity, 114, 128n.1, 129–30,
174–76, 179–80, 216–17, 272–73

Rizpah, 155, 161–62, 271

Robinson, Paul H., 91n.21

Rofé, Alexander, 99n.30, 119n.6

Rossini, Gioacchino, 249n.3

royal succession, 4, 146–47, 153–54,
196–208

Roytman v. Bank Mizrahi, 29n.21

Rumpelstiltskin, 72n.4

Ruth, 3, 229, 237, 241–47, 249, 300–301

Saadia Gaon, 118

sacrifice: animal substitutions, 140; approved, 139; atonement and, 179; destruction dedicated to God, 10–11,
99–101, 130–31, 139; forbidden,
138–39, 181n.18; forfeiture, 10–11,
99–101, 130–31, 139; human, 125–26,
135–41, 136nn.5–6, 308; Samuel on,
158; Saul on, 158; termination of
practice of, 180–81

Safrai, Shmuel, 140n.12

Salic Law, 199

Salome, 260

Samson, 65, 72–73, 220, 265n.2, 278–79,
278n.7

Samson (Jabotinsky), 234n.5, 236

Samuel: Agag of Amalek killed by, 147,
158; as king maker, 4, 14, 99, 147, 149,
171, 196; transfer of secular power
from, 99, 101, 146–47, 158–59, 164

sanctuary, 92, 117, 119, 284n.5, 286n.11

Sarah: Abraham and, 11, 221, 251n.5,
299; Hagar and, 221–23, 235–36, 241

Satan, 121, 141

Saul: David and, 32–33, 64, 148–53,
274–75; disguise of, 44–45; downfall
of, 149–53, 154–56, 157–59, 159–65,
164n.14; Michal and, 277, 280–81;
seven sons of, 131, 160–63, 280,
286n.10; suicide of, 148, 152–53, 156,
265n.2; transfer of secular power to,
101, 146–47, 158–59, 164; women of,
271

Scarisbrick, J. J., 262n.17, 263n.20

scheming witness, 23–29, 92–98

Scott, Austin W., Jr., 96n.26

Sejanus, 104

Seneca, 105

Sennacherib, 192, 193n.5

Sephardi community, 230, 256–58

Index of Ancient Sources

7   171
12:40   226
14   171
15:11–12   171
15:25   171
17:6   171
17:14   286n.9
17:16   129, 286n.9
18:21   227
20:4–5   4
20:10   213
20:12   34
20:14   213
21:15   102
22:1   82, 93
22:2   307n.1
32:27   176
34:7   132
34:15–16   300

Leviticus
10:1–2   176, 190n.2
11:23–25   128
15:19   129
15:26–27   129
18–20   252
18:8   266
18:12–13   252
18:15   252
18:18   252
19:16   90
19:18   180
19:33   62
20:10   76
24:11   126, 176
25   242
25:13–17   62
26:3–8   184
27:28–29   139

Numbers
3:4   176, 190n.2
5   18–19, 213
5:27   216
12   171, 184, 226
14:37   176
15   126, 176
16   184
16:3   171
16:32   130, 171
21   100, 139
23:9   3

26:61   190n.2
27:3   218
27:7   218
27:9   253
30   139
35   117, 286n.11
35:24   92
35:27   117
36:6   218

Deuteronomy
2–3   101
4:40   34
6:18–19   34
7   100, 131
7:3   300
12:11   193
12:13–14   193
12:31   138
13:15–16   100
13:16   131
17   99
17:6   28, 307n.1
17:7   94
17:15   4, 196
17:18–20   196
19   117
19:18–19   28
19:19   94
19:21   94
21:17   52, 241
22:24   117
22:26–27   117
22:28–29   286
23:2   129, 293
23:3   3, 5, 130, 244, 249, 300
24:4   215
24:16   132
25   238
25:5   245, 256
25:5–6   237, 262
26:7   233n.2

Joshua
1:2   147
6   101
7   10–11
7:1   12
9:4–7   46
9:18–19   47
24:30   227

Judges
2:9   227
4:18   65
6–7   147
8   227
10–11   134
11:36   136
12:8–10   227
13:2   234
14   278
14:8–9   70
14:12–14   70
14:15   70
14:18   70
14:19   70
15:16   69–70
16:30   65

Ruth
1:3–4   245n.15
1:4   237
1:11   245
1:16–17   302
3:9   242
3:12–13   242
4:5   243
4:6   3n.4, 244
4:9–10   242
4:10   246
4:17   246

1 Samuel
1:13   234
2:22   237
2:27–36   147n.2
8   99
8:1–3   146
8:5   4
8:7   196
8:11–17   196
10:20–23   14
12:18   171
13   157
14:27   13
14:37   13
14:43   13
14:43–44   118
15:3   147
15:9   158
15:11   159
15:22   158, 177
15:28   147

9:26   99
9:27   159n.10
9:31   169
10:11   169
10:28–29   190
10:30   185, 190
10:31   191
11:1   160n.10
12:18   170
12:21–22   132
14:5   132
14:9   191
14:12–14   191
14:24   181
16:3   140
18:5–6   182
18:14   192
19:32–33   192
22   193
22:15   220
23   113
23:2–3   5
23:10   140
23:18   114
23:25   183
23:26   185
23:29   183n.21
23:30   206
25:7   298
25:25–26   90n.18

1 Chronicles
2:11   243n.13
2:12   246
3:5   205, 272
5:1   192, 267
20:5   33

2 Chronicles
11   205
13   205
21:3   206
21:4   206
28:3   140
33   185
35:20–25   183n.21

Ezra
6:11   102
9:2–3   298
10:8   298
10:11   299

Esther
2:5   164
7:8   214
8:1   102

Psalms
79   186

Isaiah
1:2–3   179
1:11–12   179
1:15–17   179
1:21   179
1:23   179
14:24–25   187
24–27   186
25:7–8   187
30:2–3   182
31:8   182
56:7   195

Jeremiah
6:20   179
7:6   179
7:11   195
7:31   140
10:25   186
12:1   186
19:5   140n.12
20:2   166, 172
22:3   89
26:21–23   172
31:28–29   133n.9
31:29–30   186
32:35   140n.12
37:19   167
37:20   172
41:43   90n.18
50:9–10   187

Ezekiel
18:2   133
18:20   133
23:39   140n.12

Amos
1:3   181
2:6   178
4:1   178
5:18   186
5:21–22   178
7:17   172

8:4–6   74
8:8   74

Jonah
1:7   14

Zechariah
9:6   293

NEW TESTAMENT

Matthew
12:7   180
19:18–19   180
19:24   180
27:15–25   78n.4

Mark
2:27–28   180
7:18–21   180
10:6–9   220
11:17   195
15:6–15   78n.4

Luke
23:17–25   78n.4

John
18:39–40   78n.4

ANCIENT NEAR EASTERN TEXTS

Code of Hammurabi
§22   307n.1
§26   93
§129   20, 213
§131   20
§132   20
§134–135   277
§136   277
§137   222
§144   222
§146   222
§154   250
§155   250
§156   250
§157   250
§170   235
§171   235–36, 244
§229–230   83